THE BOMB

A Life

THE BOMB
A Life

Gerard J. DeGroot

Harvard University Press
Cambridge, Massachusetts

First published in Great Britain in 2004 by Jonathan Cape
Random House, 20 Vauxhall Bridge Road, London SW1V 2SA

First Harvard University Press paperback edition, 2006

Publication of this book has been supported through the generous
provisions of the Maurice and Lula Bradley Smith Memorial Fund.

Library of Congress Cataloging-in-Publication Data

DeGroot, Gerard J., 1955–
The bomb : a life / Gerard J. DeGroot.
p. cm.
Includes bibliographical references and index.
ISBN-13: 978-0-674-01724-5 (cloth)
ISBN-10: 0-674-01724-2 (cloth)
ISBN-13: 978-0-674-02235-5 (pbk.)
ISBN-10: 0-674-02235-1 (pbk.)
1. Nuclear weapons—History. I. Title

U264.D43 2005
623.4'5119'09—dc22   2004057657

To Dr Steve Greene,
one-time neighbour of Klaus Fuchs,
but, more importantly,
someone who reminds me,
every day,
through my daughter Natalie,
that scientists have also brought immense good.

Contents

Preface

Nothing that man has made is bigger than the Bomb. 'If your mountain is not in the right place, drop us a postcard,' Edward Teller, the father of the H-Bomb, once quipped.[1] To the nuclear wizards, the Bomb was not just a weapon, it was a tool for re-shaping the earth. Though the opportunities to move mountains proved few, a restructuring of the world did take place.

Many atomic physicists hoped that the Bomb would be big enough to destroy war itself. The idea seems naïve. The atomic age has not, after all, been very peaceful. But the striking fact of the Cold War is that it remained cold. Though tens of thousands of nuclear weapons were made, after Nagasaki, none were used in anger. We cling to the hope that the bigness of the Bomb continues to be a deterrent against its use.

The sheer size of the Bomb is what makes the topic so attractive. It killed hundreds of thousands of people in a matter of seconds, condemned others to a lingering death and made vast tracts of land unfit for life. It has dominated the minds of those condemned to live in the atomic age, exerting its influence not just on politics, but also throughout popular culture.

Impressive books have been written on the Manhattan Project, the H-bomb, the Cuban Missile Crisis, nuclear deterrence and the disarmament negotiations. The detail of those books runs deeper than has been possible here. But detail was not my primary aim; I wanted to present the entire life of the Bomb in one volume in order to provide a sense of its size and a feeling for its ubiquity. All the main characters are here – Oppenheimer, Teller, Kurchatov, Sakharov, Truman, Stalin, Churchill, Kennedy, Khrushchev, Reagan and Gorbachev. But I've also included minor characters whose lives were affected by the Bomb: the anonymous technicians of the Manhattan Project, the cancer-ridden 'downwinders' in Utah, the genetically damaged communities of Chelyabinsk, the campers of Greenham Common, the displaced peoples of Bikini. Like a great Hollywood epic, this book has a cast of thousands.

The bigness of the Bomb is both a blessing and a curse. I could have written a much bigger book, but I quickly exhausted the tolerance of a generous editor. I am tormented by what I have left out, not just because some areas deserve deeper discussion, but also because so many more good stories remain to be told. In deciding what went in and what got cut I made a strategic decision which I hope will make sense to the reader. It is my sincere feeling that the really big decisions about the Bomb were all made by around the time of the Cuban Missile Crisis. The revolt against the Bomb had evaporated, the H-Bomb was made, tests went underground and the superpowers accepted the doctrine of mutually assured destruction. The period after 1962 was characterized by the rapid progression down a road called proliferation which had been paved long before. The world (or at least most of it) had stopped worrying and had learned to love the Bomb.

This thesis (if we can call it that) explains why I've devoted a great deal more attention to the debates of the 1950s than to those of the 1970s and 1980s. In the 1950s hugely important decisions were made about the shape of the atomic age. Two decades later, that shape had set fast and debate took on a repetitive character; rather like dancers who persist in dancing only the Charleston, but in ever more frenzied a manner. To me, the endless talk over SALT and START seems insignificant compared to the really important decisions made from 1940 to 1962. I know that some diplomatic historians will howl in protest, but I don't consider the arms reduction talks all that important in the lifetime of the Bomb. The puny efforts to bring proliferation under control were always dwarfed by the MAD giant of deterrence. Once the atomic powers decided that the best protection against a Bomb was another Bomb, any talk of arms reduction was rendered irrevocably futile. Real disarmament had to await removal of the animosities which had originally inspired proliferation.

The bigness of the Bomb also explains my treatment of the various anti-nuclear campaigns. I'm struck by how solid was the faith in the Bomb as an instrument of security, not just among politicians, but also among ordinary people. For this reason, the peace movements often seem feeble and sometimes self-indulgent. I admire their devotion but stand in awe at their stubborn denial of futility. The Bomb is a horrible weapon, a manifestation of the worst aspects of human nature. But it cannot be un-invented, and unilateral disarmament by a few countries will not necessarily make the world a safer place.

Real control over the Bomb will come when something bigger takes its place. H. G. Wells thought that the solution would come in the form of world government. Many atomic physicists clung to that hope as a solution to the torment of responsibility. A clutch of religious lunatics have promised that faith in their particular Messiah will provide an effective nuclear shield. Ronald Reagan thought the answer might lie in an assortment of satellites and powerful rays, an idea revived by George W. Bush. But whether the answer lies in politics, science or faith, the only thing that seems certain is that the solution to the Bomb's bigness seems far distant.

A big book on a big subject means a lot of people to thank. The Carnegie Trust, the Arts and Humanities Research Board and the University of St Andrews were generous in giving money to fund my research and the time to carry it out. My colleagues at the university provided a supportive environment in which to work. Staff at various libraries in the US and Britain directed me toward resources I could not have found on my own. The people at the Nevada Test Site were generous not just towards me, but towards every visitor who seeks out those huge holes in the desert. Dr Lisa Ford carried out a massive amount of research on the internet where some of the more fascinating, quirky and obscure aspects of the Bomb's life lurked. Dr Andrew Crumey and Professor Martin Sherwin read the manuscript and found errors which might otherwise have caused me huge embarrassment. On the back of one page I found Andrew's scribblings, including symbols I'd never seen. The result of these calculations was a suggestion that I should change the word 'million' to 'billion' – which is why it's good to consult experts. (The errors that remain are, I admit, my fault.) Dr Mitchell Stewart checked my description of the medical effects of radiation. For manifold small favours I must also thank Anna Blamey, Colonel Frederic Borch, Lt. Colonel (retd) Janet Borch, Professor Peter Hennessy, Sir John Keegan, Professor Steven Shapin,

Professor Hew Strachan, Dr Stephen Tyre, and Elizabeth Trueland. My doctor, John Bell – the model GP – informed me that the pain in the back of my head which I had convinced myself was a great big brain tumour was in fact 'laptop syndrome'. (The pain went away when I finished the manuscript.) My editor at Jonathan Cape, Tristan Jones, showed an immense amount of enthusiasm for this topic and huge faith in me. Finally, thanks to Ellah Allfrey, the editing process passed incredibly smoothly. In the past, it seemed that the test of a job well done was if I hated my copy editor at the end. Ellah proved the exception: I still like her.

My friends in St Andrews made a good impression of real interest when I discussed my research with them. Every author needs good friends. But the lion's share of gratitude goes to my family – Sharon, Natalie and Joshua – who had to live with the Bomb for the years I spent writing about it. Natalie, having heard Daddy talk so often about 'the Bomb', grew convinced that there was just one. If only that were true.

Gerard J. DeGroot
St Andrews, Scotland
July 2003

Abbreviations

AAUW	American Association of University Women
ABM	Anti-Ballistic Missile
ADC	Air Defense Command
AEC	Atomic Energy Commission
ARP	Air Raid Precautions
BHER	Basic High Explosive Research
BNFL	British Nuclear Fuels Limited
CEA	*Commissariat à l'Energie Atomique*, French Atomic Energy Commission
CND	Campaign for Nuclear Disarmament
CPD	Committee on the Present Danger
CTBT	Comprehensive Test Ban Treaty
DOE	Department of Energy
DSM	Development of substitute materials, codename for the Manhattan Project
END	European Nuclear Disarmament
EURT	East Ural Radioactive Trace
FAS	Federation of Atomic Scientists (later changed to the Federation of American Scientists)
FCDA	Federal Civil Defense Administration
GAC	General Advisory Committee (US)
GEN 75	British Cabinet committee on nuclear policy
IAEA	International Atomic Energy Agency
ICBM	Intercontinental Ballistic Missile
IEER	Institute for Energy and Environmental Research
INF	Intermediate Nuclear Forces
JCS	Joint Chiefs of Staff
LIPAN	Alias for the Kurchatov Institute, also known as 'Laboratory Number Two'
MAD	Mutually Assured Destruction
MARV	Manoeuvrable Re-entry Vehicle
Minatom	Ministry of Atomic Energy (Russian)
MIRV	Multiple Independently targeted Re-entry Vehicle
MRV	Multiple Re-entry Vehicle

NDRC	National Defense Research Council
NKVD	People's Commissariat for Internal Affairs (Soviet secret police)
NPT	Nuclear Non-Proliferation Treaty
NSC	National Security Council
NTS	Nevada Test Site
OISM	The Oregon Institute of Science and Medicine
OSRD	Office of Scientific Research and Development
SAC	Strategic Air Command
SALT	Strategic Arms Limitation Talks
SANE	The National Committee for a Sane Nuclear Policy
SBS	Strategic Bombing Survey
SDI	Strategic Defense Initiative
SED	Special Engineering Detachment (US Army)
SIOP	Single Integrated Operating Plan
SLBM	Submarine Launched Ballistic Missile
START	Strategic Arms Reduction Talks
TAC	Tactical Air Command

Illustrations

1. DOG test, 1 November 1951 (*from* 100 Suns *by Michael Light, Jonathan Cape © 2003*)
2. Alpha-1 Racetrack at Oak Ridge (*Oak Ridge National Laboratory*)
3. Oak Ridge (*Manhattan Project Heritage Preservation Association*)
4. Enrico Fermi and Robert Oppenheimer (*© Popperfoto*)
5. Robert Oppenheimer and General Leslie Groves (*© Popperfoto*)
6. Hiroshima (*© Bettmann/Corbis*)
7. The *Enola Gay* (*United States Office of War Information*)
8. Hiroshima victim (*United States Army Corps of Engineers*)
9. First Soviet atomic reactor (*Dr Raisa Kuznetsova*)
10. Igor Kurchatov and Yuli Khariton (*Dr Raisa Kuznetsova*)
11. Fat Man (*Los Alamos Photographic Laboratory, Courtesy of the Harry S. Truman Library*)
12. Yuli Khariton and the first Soviet atomic bomb (*Dr A. Iu. Semenov*)
13. *The Beginning of the End* (*© MGM*)
14. Doom Town mannequins (*Las Vegas News Bureau*)
15. Bomb Shelters Inc. (*Courtesy of The CONELRAD Collection*)
16. Miss Atomic Bomb (*Las Vegas News Bureau*)
17. Doom Town test sequence (*Courtesy of the National Nuclear Security Administration Nevada Test Site Office*)
18. TRUCKEE test, 9 June 1962 (*from 100 Suns by Michael Light, Jonathan Cape © 2003*)
19. Andrei Sakharov and Igor Kurchatov (*Dr Raisa Kuznetsova*)
20. Mikhail Gorbachev and Ronald Reagan (*© Nick Didlick*)
21. Aldermaston March, 1958 (*Courtesy of CND*)
22. Greenham Common (*Photograph by Janine Wiedel*)
23. Edward Teller and the Tsar Bomba (*Courtesy of the estate of Dr Edward Teller*)

Every effort has been made to trace and contact copyright holders. The publishers will be pleased to correct any mistakes or ommissions in future editions.

There is no evil in the atom; only in men's souls.

Adlai Stevenson
18 September 1952

CHAPTER 1

Killing is Easy

On 20 June 1917, a row of tiny coffins was arranged in precise order in front of the altar at All Saints' Church, Poplar, London. Eighteen children were laid to rest that day, eighteen children killed a week earlier in their classroom at Upper North Street School. Most were five years old when they died. Death had come with great efficiency from the air. On 13 June, a German Gotha bomber dropped a single 110-pound bomb on the school. It crashed through the roof, penetrated two floors, and then exploded among the children. Fifteen were killed immediately, three would die of their wounds, another twenty-seven were horribly maimed.

> Who would think that vault benign
> God's last area free from vice,
> Initiates the aerial mine,
> With babes below as sacrifice.[1]

The funeral service was conducted by the Bishop of London, Arthur Winnington-Ingram, whose bellicose sermons had earlier persuaded thousands of young men to join the Army. After the service, the coffins were placed in seven hearses and driven to East London Cemetery, through streets lined with 100,000 mourners, most of them bewildered by this new type of war.

The Germans didn't intend to hit a school, but they did intend to kill people. That was the point of bombing. Total war had brought the civilian into the firing line. The raid of 13 June 1917, which killed a total of 162 people, appears tiny by today's standards, but back then it seemed that the devil had unleashed his wrath on earth. In time, technology would enable man to multiply the effects of the Poplar raid many times over.

Twenty-eight years later, a single American B-29 dropped a single atom bomb on Hiroshima. The bomb hit a hospital. The Americans didn't intend to hit a hospital, but they did intend to kill people. They succeeded beyond man's wildest imagination. The death toll eventually surpassed 150,000 and is still rising. 'How easy it is to kill people when you turn your mind to it,' one atomic scientist subsequently remarked.[2]

A second atomic 'device' followed quickly, levelling Nagasaki. A third was ready for delivery when President Harry Truman intervened to stop the carnage. He didn't like the idea of killing 'all those kids'.[3]

Before the Bomb there were simply bombs, lower-case. The word itself is ancient. It means, simply, a canister in which an explosive or noxious substance is placed. That canister was thrown, shot, dropped, or simply deposited for the purpose of causing mayhem. Prior to the advent of gunpowder, bombs were not explosive, they were merely annoying. A container filled with some vile substance was hurled at the enemy, who would promptly hurl one back. In fact, the concept predates the word. It is easy to imagine that prehistoric man probably took the bladder from an animal, filled it with shit and threw it at his adversary. Bombs are as old as hatred itself. But only since 1945 have we spoken of *the* Bomb.

On 1 November 1911, Lieutenant Giulio Gavotti, a pilot attached to an Italian army artillery unit fighting the Turks in Libya, pointed his Taube monoplane in the direction of the Turkish camp at Ain Zara. He was an experienced reconnaissance pilot, but on this particular day, overcome by ambition, he wanted to do something more than merely observe. Unbeknownst to his superior officers, he took with him on his flight a leather pouch containing four grenades, each weighing about two kilos. When he reached the Turkish camp, Gavotti took a detonator from his pocket, methodically screwed it into a grenade, and tossed the grenade over the side, repeating this process four times. No Turks were injured in this first instance of aerial bombardment, but they were mighty angry.

Gavotti officiated at the wedding of air transport and bombs. The marriage has been enormously successful. At the time, however, this first bombing raid was widely condemned as a gross defilement of the gentlemanly art of war. But, while critics scorned the development, soldiers and scientists looked for ways to make it work.

Less than three years later, during the Great War, bombs were at first delivered by airships. The war was not yet three weeks old when a Zeppelin hit Antwerp, killing six people. Raids quickly intensified, with the British enduring the worst of this airborne menace. On the night of 13 October 1915, five Zeppelins struck London, killing seventy-one people. But the airships, such a large target, were easy prey to ground-based fire and fighter aircraft. In mid-1917 the Germans deployed a new method of delivery, the Gotha.

The British War Minister, Lord Derby, argued that the Gotha raids, while tragic, were militarily insignificant since no soldiers had been killed.

This was not mere bluster. The argument had some logic in the Great War, when battlefields were still paramount. Since the Germans did not have a bomber force sufficiently large to destroy British military power or civilian morale, the bombs were simply canisters of spite. But Derby's logic now seems as old fashioned as the Gothas themselves.

The Gotha raids presaged a new type of war. In the 13 June raid, 10,000 pounds of bombs were dropped. Elementary arithmetic suggested that around 60 pounds of explosive was required to kill one person. If bombers carried a payload of 2,000 pounds (such an aircraft was operational by the end of the war), then each bomber could kill thirty-three people on each raid. A raid of 500 bombers would mean 16,500 deaths. Repeat that every night and a half a million would die after one month of war.

This type of logic inspired General Giulio Douhet to predict a new type of warfare dominated by air power. 'To have command of the air means to be in a position to wield offensive power so great that it defies human imagination,' he wrote in 1925.

> No longer can areas exist in which life can be lived in safety and tranquillity . . . the battlefield will be limited only by the boundaries of the nations at war, and all of their citizens will become combatants, since all of them will be exposed to the aerial offensives of the enemy. There will be no distinction any longer between soldiers and civilians.[4]

Douhet's logic became strategic gospel. The bomber, experts surmised, could not be stopped. Thus, when the British prepared for air attack in the late 1930s, they did not construct defences, they made coffins. Lime was stockpiled to aid decomposition of bodies in mass graves.

It followed (as Douhet predicted) that the nation with the largest air force held insurmountable power. The only defence was attack. 'You have to kill more women and children more quickly than the enemy if you want to save yourselves,' Stanley Baldwin warned the House of Commons in 1932.[5] But defence of this sort was conceivable only if parity in strength could be maintained. For lesser powers, war itself seemed unthinkable, since a conflict which implied total destruction was absurd. Some saw hope in this scenario. The bomber might actually abolish war. But the doom merchants (and they were in the majority) saw instead endless destruction and millions dead.

Douhet was wrong. The Second World War would prove that bombers did not always get through, that bombs seldom hit their targets and that people could be protected. But, while he overestimated the catastrophic potential of air power, Douhet's theories did provide a neat prelude to the atomic age. War was not changed by the bomber, it was changed by the

Bomb. The power Douhet envisaged was demonstrated not at Guernica, Rotterdam or Dresden but at Hiroshima.

It did not take atomic bombs to make war terrible. So claimed J. Robert Oppenheimer, the acknowledged father of the Bomb. Though the remark was made in search of moral consolation, it was true. The inclination to kill is a historical constant. As has been demonstrated from Troy to Gettysburg, Agincourt to the Somme, the prospect of blood and death has never proved a deterrent to war. What has changed is man's capacity to kill – the efficiency of slaughter. Developments in weaponry have made killing easier. The distance between attacker and victim has increased, as has the number of people that can be killed with a single weapon. The development of aerial bombing mirrored this developmental process. The atom bomb brought it to a horrifying terminus.

Running parallel to Douhet's strategic argument was a moral debate about bombing, spoken in undertones. War was supposed to pit soldier against soldier; civilized war did not involve civilians. They might be killed accidentally, but they were not to be killed for the purpose of winning the war. Various international conferences had attempted to codify this moral imperative into law. Article XXV of the 1907 Hague Convention had stated that 'The attack or bombardment, by whatever means, of towns, villages, dwellings, or buildings which are undefended is prohibited.' But that law was written before aerial bombing was possible. The Convention of 1923 attempted to bring law up to date with technology. It prohibited 'Aerial bombardment for the purpose of terrorizing the civilian population, of destroying or damaging private property not of military character, or of injuring non-combatants'. Bombing cities was not, however, ruled out absolutely. The Convention decided that aerial bombing 'is legitimate only when directed at a military objective', which was defined as 'military forces; military works; military establishments or depots; [munitions] factories . . . lines of communication or transportation'.[6] In other words, the loopholes were big enough to fly a bomber through.

War had evolved into a contest not between armies but between peoples. It was the supreme test of a nation. Success required not just a good navy or army, but also an efficient system of organizing the productive capacities of the civilian population. Leaders spoke of 'total war', and gave definition to the home front. Once the home front was defined, it became a target. It did not take a brilliant strategist to realize that an enemy might be defeated by starving his people – or by killing workers in their beds.

But that meant a lot of bombing. As time passed, defences against the bomber were refined, thus reducing its efficiency. The kill-rate of the Gothas would never again be duplicated with conventional bombs. To achieve the purpose Douhet envisaged, a nation would have to mobilize more aeroplanes or make more powerful bombs. But more blast meant greater weight. Until 1945, a bomb with an explosive force equivalent to one ton of TNT weighed slightly more than one ton. The limiting factor in any bombing campaign was the cargo capacity of the bomber.

The limitations of conventional explosives had long intrigued those who explored the atom. Frederick Soddy, a precocious physicist who worked at the Cavendish Laboratory in Cambridge, remarked in 1904 that if the energy contained within the atom 'could be tapped and controlled what an agent it could be in shaping the world's destiny! The man who put his hand on the lever by which a parsimonious nature regulates so jealously the output of this store of energy would possess a weapon by which he could destroy the earth if he chose.'[7] Within the realm of theoretical physics, the idea was hardly revolutionary. It had, in fact, been a talking point ever since Marie Curie's discovery of radium in 1898. That discovery had started physicists thinking seriously about the atom as a source of energy.

Optimists saw hope in the kind of power Soddy envisaged. They assumed that man would never push his aggression to the point of total destruction. It required but a short leap of reason to conclude that an atom bomb might actually mean the death of bombing and perhaps the end of war. (The same thoughts had sustained Alfred Nobel after his invention of dynamite.)

Rendering war explosively unthinkable appealed to H. G. Wells. In *The World Set Free*, published in 1914, he described a world war taking place in 1956 in which the great cities are destroyed by atomic bombs. After the war, man finally learns a lesson and turns away from war. Nuclear energy is subsequently directed to peaceful purposes, causing 'a change in human conditions that I can only compare to the discovery of fire, that first discovery that lifted man above the brute'. With no war, and with endless supplies of power,

> That perpetual struggle for existence, that perpetual struggle to live on the bare surplus of Nature's energies will cease to be the lot of Man. Man will step from the pinnacle of this civilization to the beginning of the next. . . .
> I see the desert continents transformed, the poles no longer wildernesses of ice, the whole world once more Eden. I see the power of man reach out among the stars.[8]

Wells took his idea from Soddy who, in truth, had doubts about atomic power. 'The fact that we exist', Soddy wrote, 'is proof that [the release of atomic energy] did not occur; that it has not occurred is the best possible assurance that it never will. We may trust Nature to guard her secret.' Even Einstein, whose theory of relativity provided a formula for calculating the energy lurking within the atom, doubted whether that energy could be released. 'The line of thought is amusing and fascinating', he once remarked, 'but I wonder if the dear Lord laughs about it and has led me around by the nose.'[9]

Though Nature was a stubborn sentry, that did not stop scientists from trying to break into her fortress. While they were fully aware of the massively destructive powers that would be released if the atom was invaded, that did not inhibit their quest. As J. Robert Oppenheimer once remarked, a scientific discovery depends not on whether it is useful but whether it is possible. Scientists, like pith-helmeted adventurers pushing into the dark reaches of the world, went resolutely forward, oblivious to the possible consequences of their exploration. The British physicist Francis Aston argued that it was futile to attempt to hold back progress:

> There are those about us who say that research should be stopped by law, alleging that man's destructive powers are already large enough. So, no doubt, the more elderly and ape-like of our prehistoric ancestors objected to the innovation of cooked food and pointed out the grave dangers attending the newly discovered agency, fire.[10]

It was probably true that no law could prevent scientists from experimenting with atomic power, no more than law can prevent biologists from cloning sheep or, eventually, humans. But Aston's sophistry camouflaged uncomfortable realities. A campfire and an atomic bomb are different in nature, not just in degree.

In *The World Set Free*, Wells speculated that, in prehistoric times, after the immediate problems of survival were solved, some men turned to science in an attempt to understand their world. The ordinary uncurious folk

> laughed at these eccentric beings, or found them annoying and ill-treated them, or [were] seized with fear and made saints and sorcerers and warlocks of them . . . but for the greater part heeded them not at all. Yet they were of the blood of him who had first dreamt of attacking the mammoth; every one of them was of his blood and descent; and the thing they sought, all unwittingly, was the snare that will some day catch the sun.[11]

The exploration of the atom was initially motivated by scientific curiosity. Until the 1930s the atom seemed innocent. Physicists were aware that it might yield huge reserves of energy, but that is not what drove them forward. They understood the atom's power but were not enslaved to it.

The potential to kill with great efficiency is, however, attractive to soldiers and statesmen. In the 1930s, politics penetrated the cloistered laboratories and gave frightening purpose to the physicists' naïve quest to catch the sun.

CHAPTER 2

Neutrons and Nations

Ernest Rutherford was a giant star in the atomic firmament. A New Zealander by birth, he won a scholarship in 1894 to study at the Cavendish Laboratory, Cambridge, under Professor Joseph Thomson. Four years later, he was awarded a chair at McGill University, in Montreal, where Soddy and the German Otto Hahn joined him for brief periods. In 1907, he returned to England to become Langworthy Professor of Physics at Manchester. Rutherford, perhaps more than any other physicist, embodied the cosmopolitan nature of science. Every physicist played close attention to the discoveries emanating from his laboratory; every one dreamt of joining his team. At least a dozen future Nobel Prize winners worked closely with him early in their careers. Before the Great War, the Vienna Radium Institute loaned him 250 milligrams of precious radium simply because he was an important scientist. Rutherford kept the stuff for five years and then, honest man that he was, offered to return it. The fact that Britain and Austria had, during the intervening period, fought a horrible war, was immaterial.

Rutherford's greatest contribution to physics came in 1910 when he postulated the existence of the atom's nucleus. He proposed that virtually the entire mass of the atom was concentrated in a tiny core which carried a positive charge. For the next nine years, he conducted further experiments to explore the structure of the atom, in particular by using cathode rays to bombard atoms of various elements. From this work came the idea that each element could be assigned an atomic number which would in turn define the properties of that element.

In 1919, Rutherford was continuing his exploration of the atom. He took a small glass tube and filled it with radon gas which emitted alpha particles. This he sealed inside a brass box fitted at one end with a scintillation screen. The box was then filled with hydrogen, and the number of scintillations measured. When he replaced the hydrogen with dry air, Rutherford found that the scintillations doubled when, by logic, they should have decreased. In other words, extra hydrogen atoms were produced, literally out of thin air. Rutherford concluded that the nitrogen in the air, when hit with alpha particles, had been transformed. He explained, all too calmly: 'it is difficult to avoid the conclusion that the long-range atoms arising from collision of [alpha] particles with nitrogen are not nitrogen atoms but probably atoms of hydrogen. . . . If this be the case we must conclude that the nitrogen atom is disintegrated.'

The newspapers said it better: 'RUTHERFORD SPLITS THE ATOM!'[1]

Strictly speaking, it was not a split but a transmutation – an ancient word loved by alchemists who once sought to turn base metals into gold. Unlike them, Rutherford was interested in the process, not the product. There was no value in the hydrogen produced. But, in transmuting a nitrogen atom, he came closer to releasing the massive energy it held.

A few years later, Aston, a better publicist than Rutherford, explained the implications of transmutation. If it were possible to transmute hydrogen into helium, he proposed, around one per cent of the mass would be annihilated in the process. The amount of energy released could be calculated by applying Einstein's relativity formula, $E = mc^2$, or *energy equals mass times the speed of light squared*. Since the speed of light is 186,000 miles per second, *any* mass times c^2 means a lot of energy. If, Aston surmised, the hydrogen in a glass of water was changed into helium, the energy liberated would drive the *Queen Mary* across the Atlantic at full speed – and back.

Or, in a more concentrated form, that sort of energy would make an immensely powerful bomb.

Rutherford's breakthrough caused a massive tremor to pass through the world of physics, but the real world felt hardly a bump. 'Physicists are a narrow caste,' the Russian Iakov Frenkel once remarked. 'The members . . . are well known to one another in all parts of the globe, but at the same time completely unknown even to their closest compatriots.'[2] Separation from the real world was possible in part because of the esoteric nature of scientific research. Scientists were widely respected but not widely understood. Theirs was a mysterious, magical world in which an incomprehensible language was spoken. The nineteenth century had been one of enormous industrial progress, but few people understood that the great engineers had exploited the discoveries scientists had made.

For most people, scientists seemed more like magicians than sorcerers; few feared that a Pandora's Box might be opened. Take, for instance, the reception given to X-rays when first demonstrated to the general public at the end of the nineteenth century. Though their medical importance was recognized, it was their novelty value, demonstrated at amusement parks and county fairs, that appealed.

> The town's ablaze
> With the new phase

of X-rays ways.
I'm full of daze
Shock and amaze;
For nowadays,
I hear they'll gaze
Through cloak and gown – and even stays
These naughty, naughty Roentgen rays.[3]

Marie Curie's discovery of radium in 1898 was widely celebrated not because of the scientific progress it demonstrated, but because the element itself seemed magical. Its luminous quality was automatically assumed to be beneficial, since light is synonymous with life. This inspired a flood of imaginative applications, mostly connected with the patent medicine industry. Dr W. J. Morton sold an elixir called Liquid Sunshine, which supposedly cured diseased organs. Radium was also widely used to bring on menopause. The fashion industry brought out luminous dresses, gamblers played on glowing roulette wheels and farmers fed their crops with luminous fertilizer. The discovery of radium deposits in the Erzgebirge mountains proved a boon to the nearby spa towns of Carlsbad and Marienbad, which could now add radioactivity to their menu of treatments.

The isolation enjoyed by physicists was, however, more imaginary than real. During the Great War, scientists were asked to find solutions to the stalemate that tyrannized armies. Hahn, who would later work on the German atom bomb project, was assigned to poison gas research. When he objected that gas was prohibited by the Hague Convention, his superior, the chemist Fritz Haber, replied 'that the French had already started it . . . Besides, it was a way of saving countless lives, if it meant that the war could be brought to an end sooner.'[4] Technology could shorten war and save lives. Research was essential in order to stay ahead of the enemy. As Haber argued, the scientist should serve the world in peacetime but his country in time of war.

The alchemists had once worried that their research might be exploited by politicians. 'Deny the powerful and their warriors entry to your workshops,' they warned. 'For such people misuse the holy mysteries in the service of power.'[5] By 1919 the laboratory had become a tool of the state, though scientists still pretended otherwise. The Great War had demonstrated that a nation's power emanated in part from its lab-coated warriors. Greater relevance meant greater responsibility. Though scientists could not completely ignore the consequences of their work, many willingly donned blinkers.

After the war, huge grants were given to universities in the hope that they would produce the next generation of lethal weaponry. State support meant that science, and physics in particular, became a much more secure career. In the United States, there were around 2,500 practising physicists in 1932, three times as many as in 1918. That said, nuclear physics remained a highly esoteric sub-discipline. Most people remained blissfully ignorant of the powers locked inside the atom. Nuclear physicists ranked equal with medieval historians as scholars least likely to change the world. 'At the beginning of the 30s everyone considered nuclear physics to be a subject having absolutely no relation to practice or technology,' the Russian Igor Tamm recalled. In 1936 he confidently remarked that 'the idea that the use of nuclear energy is a question for [the next] five or ten years is really naïve'.[6]

In his perfect world, the scientist serves only his discipline and knows no nation. Discovery works best if thought is unfettered. Political issues, or consequences, are unimportant. While soldiers and politicians increasingly looked to the laboratories to provide more efficient instruments of death, the scientists themselves desperately defended the sanctity of their ivory tower. They maintained a community of their own which had no national boundaries and lived according to its own system of law and morality. For those who had to endure the repressive regimes of Central Europe, the liberal laboratory provided attractive refuge. The Hungarian Edward Teller felt that science 'offered a possibility of escaping this doomed society'.[7] For Einstein, 'science . . . was an international fellowship and a culture that could be packed up and taken with one anywhere in the world'.[8]

The new generation of nuclear physicists were brash, brilliant and young. Great discoveries were made by mere students, and anyone over thirty was automatically assumed to be past his best.

> Age is of course a fever chill
> That every physicist must fear.
> He's better dead than living still,
> When once he's past his thirtieth year.[9]

It was perhaps dangerous for men so detached from real life, and so young, to meddle with atoms. But the nuclear physicists considered themselves theoreticians, not engineers. They were not building a bomb, they were merely musing on the structure of the atom. Liberating the energy of the atom harmonized nicely with the liberal environment in which they worked. To most of them, their research seemed as harmless as that of a mathematician who searches for ever higher prime numbers. Rutherford, the first man to 'split' the atom, went to his grave in 1937 believing that those who spoke of exploiting nuclear energy were 'talking moonshine'.[10]

For the physicist, the atom was a world waiting to be explored. The unknown provided great incentive, and endless excitement. 'If anybody says he can think about quantum problems without getting giddy', Neils Bohr once commented, 'that only shows he has not understood the first thing about them.'[11] For some, physics was akin to religion. 'The only way I can tell that a new idea is really important', James Franck remarked, 'is the feeling of terror that seizes me.'[12] When students described their research to Isidor Rabi, he would customarily reply: 'Does it bring you near to God?'[13]

The great scientists like Bohr and Rutherford attracted disciples who hung on their every word and whose job it was to spread and interpret the gospel. They willingly endured a monastic life. 'We worked around the clock, and other interests, apart from science, did not exist for us,' Isaak Kikoin recalled. 'Even girls did not often manage to separate us from our studies.' His colleagues at the Physicotechnical Institute in Petrograd endured enormous hardships simply to be part of an elite research team. When Anatoli Aleksandrov went to the Institute in 1930, he had to share a freezing cold room with eight other colleagues and kept a blanket over his head to keep the rats from gnawing his ears while he slept.[14]

Victor Weisskopf, who researched with the great physicists of the twentieth century, felt that his was the golden age of the science. 'We touched the nerve of the universe. It was a great revolution that allowed us for the first time in history to get at the root of the matter – why are leaves green, why are metals hard, why are the mountains so high and not higher.'[15] Eventually, as a result of their discoveries, those same physicists would be forced to ask themselves why men craved destruction.

Before the Great War, advanced atomic research was concentrated in three institutions: Cambridge, Copenhagen and Göttingen. The three labs worked in symbiosis: discoveries made in Cambridge were explained in Copenhagen and questioned in Göttingen. Scientists behaved like ants: each took a small fragment to a breach in the anthill, only to find that it was then taken away and used elsewhere by another ant.

Universities in the US were mired in 'old fashioned physics', paying little attention to the mysteries of the atom. Until the mid-1920s, Americans who wanted to probe its secrets had to cross the Atlantic. But then, at the University of California, a new centre of excellence emerged, distinct from the European triangle. At Berkeley, Ernest Lawrence began toying with the idea of generating high energies in a particle accelerator. Lawrence was like one of the particles in his machine: from his first days as a research student, his career accelerated rapidly, producing huge amounts of creative energy.

Realizing that a linear accelerator, in order to generate the energy desired, would have to be miles long, Lawrence opted for a spiral, which he christened a cyclotron. At the centre of the device a hot filament acted upon hydrogen gas to produce protons which were directed into a magnetic field. The protons were pushed and pulled around the spiral by two alternately charged electrodes. After about 100 revolutions, the particles were concentrated into a beam and focused at a target. On 2 January 1931 Lawrence produced protons with energies of 80,000 electron volts, with an initial investment of less than 1,000 volts through the electrodes. The first cyclotron, made with sealing wax, wire and other materials from around the lab, could not have cost more than $25.

Thirteen months later, readings topped a million volts. By April, Lawrence was boasting that protons at up to 25,000,000 volts could be produced. But a machine of this order would require a magnet weighing eighty tons. Physics was growing like Jack's beanstalk. In 1919, Rutherford had observed the first transmutations in a small brass box. Thirteen years later, Lawrence's laboratory resembled a factory.

Big meant expensive. Before 1914, the Cavendish lived well on an equipment budget of less than £550 per year. Lawrence's magnets alone cost much more than that. It was not long before even the most benevolent private donors were overwhelmed. Funding had increasingly to come from the state, causing an inevitable change in the relationship between academia and government. Politicians sought assurances about the utility of the research.

Lawrence's cyclotron seemed to provide the energy which might be necessary to invade the nucleus of an atom, but the problem lay with the ammunition itself – the proton. Because it carried a positive charge, it was easily deflected by the positively charged nucleus. The uncharged neutron seemed a more promising bullet, but it existed only in theory. Necessity being the mother of invention, the English physicist James Chadwick discovered the neutron in early February 1932, a defining moment in physics and indeed the world. The discovery inspired celebration, but also foreboding. The French physicist Paul Langevin thought the tiny particle bigger than Adolf Hitler. 'If it gets into the wrong hands, [the neutron] can do the world a good deal more damage than that fool who will sooner or later go to the dogs. It is something which – unlike him – we shall never be able to get rid of.'[16]

The neutron, which pointed the way to nuclear power, meant that physics had intruded into politics. Much more obvious at the time was the way politics was intruding into physics. In the liberal world of Science, genius was supposed to be the only passport. Yet outside the laboratory, the world grew ever more parochial. In Central Europe, strident nationalism embodied an enfeebling contradiction. The Jew, long assumed to belong to no nation, was reviled. Yet a disproportionate number of eminent scientists were Jewish. Consequently, out of racial spite, Germany and Italy deprived themselves of the very people essential to national strength. Even before Hitler's rise, Einstein suffered the taunts of nationalistic German students. Self-styled 'national researchers' openly campaigned against 'Jew science' and dismissed his theory of relativity as 'Jewish world-bluff'. 'Turn around,' Einstein told his wife when they left their home in 1932, bound for Princeton. 'You will never see it again.'[17]

On 7 April 1933 the Hitler government promulgated the Law for the Restoration of the Professional Civil Service. All civil servants of non-Aryan descent were required to give up their jobs. Around 1,600 scholars in universities and state-run laboratories were directly affected, including one quarter of the physicists. Eleven physicists who had won or would eventually win Nobel Prizes lost their positions. Thus ended the golden age of Göttingen. Some brilliant scientists remained, but the laboratory's back – not to mention its spirit – was broken. 'Is it really true, Professor, that your Institute suffered so much from the departure of the Jews and their friends?' a Göttingen scientist was asked by a government minister in 1933. 'Suffered?' he replied. 'No, it didn't suffer . . . It just doesn't exist anymore.'[18]

Thanks to the cosmopolitan nature of the scientific community, plenty of people outside Germany were ready to help the displaced Jews. Committees were formed to find them new labs. At first, the British proved most welcoming, but then the economic slump bit into university budgets. The United States eventually took up the mantle, particularly when the prospect of war increased the value of émigré scientists. Around 100 physicists sought a new life in America between 1933 and 1941.

The USSR was equally wasteful of genius. According to Stalinist orthodoxy, splitting the atom was the ultimate bourgeois act. This dogmatism ensured that most refugee scientists escaping from Central Europe went west rather than east, even though many were more sympathetic to socialism than to American capitalism. Had Stalin been a bit more welcoming, some very good minds would have joined Russian labs. Those who did go to the USSR were allowed to work in relative peace until 1937, whereupon a vicious purge of the scientific community began. The price of genius was often torture and imprisonment.

In 1934, the German physicist Ida Noddack made an important hypothesis. Had she been taken seriously, it is entirely likely that Hitler would have had a Bomb before 1940. Instead, her friend Otto Hahn advised her to shut up since her idea was so preposterous it could only cause embarrassment. At that time, ridicule could ruin a female physicist.

An atom, when split, releases particles and energy. Scientists surmised that if the particles were to bombard surrounding atoms, the process might repeat itself exponentially – a chain reaction. This might produce a sustainable energy source, or a massive explosion. In October 1933, Leo Szilard, who had only recently fled from Hungary, mused that a chain reaction might be made to occur if an element could be found which released two neutrons when bombarded by one. He suspected that uranium might prove a promising candidate.

A few months later, the Italian physicist Enrico Fermi bombarded the elements in the periodic table with neutrons. When he got to fluorine, the Geiger counter ticked – for the first time ever, radioactivity had been generated artificially. That was monumental enough, but what followed was literally beyond comprehension. When Fermi bombarded uranium, the heaviest of the heavy metals, it gave rise to new elements. Fermi concluded that these must be the artificial transuranic elements – heavier than uranium.

Enter Ida Noddack. She decided that Fermi had created isotopes of known elements *lighter* than uranium. He had, quite simply, shattered uranium into pieces. On a much larger scale, this is what happens inside an atom bomb. Ignoring Hahn's advice, Noddack published her findings, but few physicists paid heed. Thus, the atomic age was delayed. A male scientist might have been more assertive about such a discovery and more likely to encounter a sympathetic ear from colleagues. We can be thankful that even the most open-minded scientists back then were occasionally misogynistic.

The idea that neutrons might prove effective in splitting atoms was simply too subtle for the physics community. Raised on Lawrence's highly charged, fast moving particles, most physicists assumed that, if a uranium atom were indeed to be split, it could only happen violently. 'It was as though one were to suggest to troops which had been vainly shelling an underground shelter with guns of the heaviest caliber for a long time that they should start trying their luck with ping-pong balls,' writes physicist Robert Jungk.[19] Neutrons achieved their work not through force but stealth. Their intrusion caused an imbalance within the atom, inspiring it to seek a new stability in the form of two different atoms. In other words, neutrons were subversives, not soldiers.

Not until late 1938 did Hahn and Fritz Strassmann figure out that Fermi's mysterious element was in fact barium, roughly half the atomic weight of uranium. This proved that a split of some sort had indeed occurred. After Hahn sent his findings to the journal *Naturwissenschaften*, 'the whole thing . . . seemed so improbable . . . that I wished I could get the document back out of the mail box'.[20] The article was rushed into print on 22 December, a calculated act of subversion. Paul Rosbaud, the editor, was a British undercover agent who wanted to alert scientists outside

Germany and feared that, if he delayed, the Nazis would embargo publication.

Hahn also sent his findings to his one-time colleague Lise Meitner, a German Jew suffering a lonely exile in Stockholm. While he had correctly identified that barium had been produced, he had not explained how. Meitner received Hahn's manuscript while her nephew Otto Frisch was visiting. Though he wanted a genuine holiday, she wanted to talk physics. On long walks through the snowy countryside, they brainstormed about barium.

They eventually decided that the uranium atom must be unstable, crowded with neutrons and protons. To explain the phenomenon, they resorted to metaphor:

> A nucleus was not like a brittle solid that can be cleaved or broken . . . a nucleus was much more like a liquid drop. . . . the uranium atom might indeed resemble a very wobbly, unstable drop, ready to divide itself at the slightest provocation, such as the impact of a single neutron.[21]

The invading neutron encourages the uranium atom to wobble and tear itself apart, causing two smaller nuclei to form, perhaps of barium or krypton. The American biologist James Arnold decided that the process resembled the way cells divide – a phenomenon called fission. The name stuck.

Frisch and Meitner had also discovered why no element heavier than uranium exists naturally. Stated very simply, the force holding a uranium atom together just cancels out the force pulling it apart. That is why the introduction of a single neutron causes so much turmoil. A problem that had puzzled physicists for five years was suddenly solved. The importance of this solution lay not in the krypton or barium produced, but rather in the energy released. The combined weights of the two smaller nuclei was one-fifth of the mass of a proton less than the weight of the original uranium atom. That mass was converted to energy, which Frisch and Meitner calculated to be 200 million electron volts (MeV), a huge amount to come from a single atom. The most potent chemical reaction might release five electron volts per atom. Frisch calculated that the energy from a single atom was enough to make a grain of sand visibly jump.[22]

The energy contained within a small lump of uranium can be understood if it is appreciated that each gram contains 2.5×10^{21} atoms. If we multiply that figure by 200 million, what results is a vast amount of energy.* In other words, tiny matter yielded huge power. 'I wrote home to my

---

*Admittedly, not every atom would undergo fission. But even an inefficient rate of fission would yield a huge amount of energy.

mother', Frisch recalled, 'that I felt like someone who has caught an elephant by the tail.'[23]

Atomic fission was discovered while Hitler pursued political fusion in Central Europe. It is interesting to speculate what might have transpired had Noddack's interpretation received wide exposure. How might Hitler and Mussolini have reacted to a development which was a major step in the construction of an atom bomb? Emilio Segré, who had taken part in Fermi's 1934 experiments, later remarked: 'God, for His own inscrutable reasons, made everyone blind at that time to the phenomenon of nuclear fission.'[24] Well, not *everyone* – Noddack saw precisely what had happened.

Fission worried Szilard. 'All the things which H. G. Wells predicted appeared suddenly real to me,' he wrote. Since the energy release was higher than anyone had imagined, this might lead 'unfortunately . . . to atomic bombs'. Within the physics community, that possibility had an effect like wiggling a stick in an ant heap. Out in Berkeley, Luis Alvarez told his colleague Robert Oppenheimer about what Frisch and Meitner had discovered. 'He said, "That's impossible" and gave a lot of theoretical reasons why fission couldn't really happen.' Then, 'in less than fifteen minutes Robert had decided that this was indeed a real effect and . . . that some neutrons would probably boil off in the reaction, and that you could make bombs and generate power . . . It was amazing to see how rapidly his mind worked.'[25] Within about a week, a drawing of a bomb appeared on Oppenheimer's blackboard.

While Fermi was bombarding atoms, the Italian Army was blasting Abyssinia. For Fermi, the contradictions of this coincidence were more striking than the parallels. His lab, indeed his entire discipline, was cosmopolitan and liberal. In contrast, Mussolini's army was stridently reactionary and xenophobic. The more aggressive Italian politics became, the more alienated Fermi felt. Anti-Semitic persecution troubled him deeply because his wife Laura was Jewish. Emigration nevertheless posed severe practical problems. Then, in 1938, he was awarded the Nobel Prize for his research on the radioactive properties of elements. The prize, and the trip to Stockholm it implied, offered an opportunity to escape. Since limits were imposed on how much cash an individual could take out of the country, he invested in 'the refugee's trousseau' – a fur for his wife, expensive watches, and jewellery. On 2 January 1939, he arrived in the United States. The loss to Italy was huge, the gain to the US immense.

Now working at Columbia, Fermi began calculating the energy that might be released if a large quantity of uranium was fissioned. He concluded that a lump no bigger than a tennis ball would produce a blast equivalent to around 15,000 tons of TNT. Gazing out of his office window at the grey expanse of Manhattan, he cupped his hands together, faced the city, and said to a colleague, 'A little ball like that and it would all disappear.'[26]

Not any uranium would do. If U-238, the most common isotope, was easily capable of fission, the world would have exploded long ago. The nucleus of U-238 contains 92 protons and 146 neutrons. It can be induced to undergo fission if bombarded by high energy ('fast') neutrons, but it is sufficiently stable to absorb low energy neutrons. It is hugely difficult to make U-238 explode.

U-235, however, is much less stable. It will undergo fission if bombarded with low energy (or 'slow') neutrons. Unfortunately (or, fortunately) a kilo of natural uranium contains just seven grams of U-235. In order to build a bomb, natural uranium has to be enriched about 100 times – the proportion of U-235 has to rise from 0.7 per cent to about 70 per cent. That is immensely difficult. In 1939, processes to enrich uranium dealt with tiny amounts. Yet to build a bomb required a critical mass of about 15 kilos.* No process existed for enrichment on that scale.

Szilard understood immediately that knowledge of fission would become a precious commodity zealously hoarded by the major powers. That knowledge, in the wrong hands, could mean the end of civilization. The only answer was secrecy. Throughout 1938, he warned colleagues that the free exchange of ideas was no longer politically sensible. He urged them to cease publication of their findings and to take out patents on their work. But, within the scientific community, secrecy was abhorrent; it undermined the fundamental principles under which scientists worked. Since Szilard's colleagues did not share his political awareness, they did not feel his fear.

For Szilard, the bomb was not simply an intellectual curiosity. Though susceptible to the Siren of discovery, he was also keenly aware of the tempestuous waters into which physicists were sailing. In early March 1939, he discovered that when one neutron entered a uranium nucleus the resultant split caused at least two neutrons to be emitted. In other words, a chain reaction was no longer a remote possibility. 'That night there was very little doubt in my mind that the world was headed for grief.'[27]

The fate of the world rested on two or three errant neutrons. Szilard decided that the time had come to warn the government about recent discoveries. It so happened that Fermi was going to Washington on 16 March to deliver a lecture. Approaches were made, but politicians reacted with polite indifference. Fermi was handed down the line to Admiral

* A critical mass is the amount of uranium necessary to undergo a self-sustaining chain reaction. If a certain amount of fissile material is suddenly brought together into one piece it will automatically explode. Two pieces of enriched uranium each weighing 7.5 kilos, if kept apart, will not explode. But if they are brought together at speed, they will destroy a city.

Stanford Hooper, technical assistant to the Chief of Naval Operations. He gave Hooper a letter of introduction from George Pegram, chairman of the physics department at Columbia:

> Experiments . . . reveal that conditions may be found under which the chemical element uranium may be able to liberate its large excess of atomic energy, and that this might mean the possibility that uranium might be used as an explosive that would liberate a million times as much energy per pound as any known explosive.* My own feeling is that the probabilities are against this, but my colleagues and I think that the bare possibility should not be disregarded.[28]

A 20 kiloton force does not befit the conditional tense. All those 'mights' and 'mays' convinced Hooper that no action was necessary. After Fermi gave a completely incomprehensible explanation of fission, the Navy thanked him for his time and promised to get in touch.

One month later, in the 22 April issue of *Nature*, Irène† and Frédéric Joliot-Curie announced to the world the secret Szilard was trying to protect. Szilard was furious at the pig-headedness of the Joliot-Curies, who seemed concerned only for the enhancement of their own reputations. Though the Germans would undoubtedly have made a similar discovery quite soon, it seemed insane to show them the way. Just one week after the article was published, the German government decided to commandeer all stocks of uranium and to secure additional supplies from mines in recently conquered Czechoslovakia.

Germany's proactive response was due primarily to her scientists' persuasiveness. At the end of April, Hamburg physicist Paul Harteck wrote to his government:

> We take the liberty of calling to your attention the newest development in nuclear physics, which, in our opinion, will probably make it possible to produce an explosive many orders of magnitude more powerful than the conventional one. . . . That country which first makes use of it has an unsurpassable advantage over the others.[29]

The contrast with the Pegram letter could not be more striking. The first leg of the race to build a Bomb had been won convincingly by Germany.

---

* Pegram was being rather conservative. Other calculations suggested that a uranium explosion would be a billion, or even a trillion, times as efficient as any conventional explosive.
† Irène Joliot-Curie was the daughter of Pierre and Marie Curie.

In early 1939, Joseph Rotblat joined Chadwick's lab in Liverpool, leaving his wife behind in Poland. Rotblat was troubled by the fact that his work on fission pointed inevitably toward a Bomb. 'Should I be looking at this?' he wondered. Eventually, he convinced himself that 'the only way to stop the Germans from using it against us would be if we, too, had the bomb and threatened to retaliate'. That logic provided cold comfort. On a trip to Poland during the summer of 1939, he discussed his misgivings with friends but still found peace of mind elusive. He left Poland assuming that his wife would join him shortly, but his was one of the last trains to leave. When blitzkrieg struck, 'the whole power of the Nazi regime became clear. I decided the immediate danger was so great that one had to put aside one's moral scruples.'[30] The burden of guilt was lifted, but Rotblat never again saw his wife.

Like Rotblat, Szilard advocated a crash programme to build the bomb not because the United States needed it but because Germany could not be allowed to gain possession first. In other words, for them, the bomb was a deterrent, not a weapon. 'It will bring disaster upon the world if the Germans are ready before we are,' Szilard once wrote. 'It may bring disaster upon the world even if we anticipate them and win the war, but lose the peace that will follow.'[31] The nuclear arms race began long before the Bomb was a practical possibility.

The physicists were not megalomaniacs. They hoped to discover that the bomb could not be built. But they also imagined that a weapon of ultimate power might render war itself obsolete, as Wells had predicted in *The World Set Free*. Szilard's friend Eugene Wigner explained:

> We realised that, should atomic weapons be developed, no two nations would be able to live in peace with each other unless their military forces were controlled by a higher authority. We expected that these controls, if they were effective enough to abolish atomic warfare, would be effective enough to abolish also all other forms of war. This hope was almost as strong a spur to our endeavors as was our fear of becoming the victims of the enemy's atomic bombings.

Carl von Weizsäcker, hard at work on the German bomb that Szilard and Wigner so feared, expressed a similar sentiment. 'We were faced with a very simple logic,' he remarked. 'Wars waged with atom bombs . . . do not seem reconcilable with the survival of the participating nations. . . . If that is so, then the participating nations and ultimately mankind itself can only survive if war . . . is abolished.'[32]

The threat of a German bomb was frighteningly real. In the summer of 1939, the German Army, alerted to the potential of nuclear power by Harteck and others, encouraged leading physicists to speed up their research. On 26 September, nine prominent nuclear physicists met to form the Uranium Verein (Uranium Society). The task of building a bomb was analysed and the workload divided. When the group gathered again about a month later, among the new recruits were Werner Heisenberg and von Weizsäcker.

Like their colleagues in America, German physicists were troubled by conflicts between duty and morality. Unlike them, they understood that they were making an aggressive weapon of ferocious power, not simply a deterrent. Hitler cast a long shadow over the laboratory. Most physicists were German patriots, but with varying degrees of enthusiasm toward the Führer. Those who had misgivings about the bomb feared what Hitler might do with it. Hahn, for instance, was so frightened by the prospect of a Nazi bomb that he vowed to kill himself rather than live in such a world.

Heisenberg's position was the most complicated. He later justified his acceptance of the directorship of the Nazi project by arguing that

> Under a dictatorship active resistance can only be practised by those who pretend to collaborate. . . . Anyone speaking out openly against the system thereby indubitably deprives himself of any chance of active resistance. . . . he will naturally finish up a few days later in a concentration camp. Even if he is put to death his martyrdom will in practice never be known, since it will be forbidden to mention his name.[33]

It is difficult to escape the impression that Heisenberg was, quite simply, a worm, adept at wrapping opportunism in a cloak of morality. If indeed he only pretended to collaborate, he did so with great enthusiasm.

Murmurs about German intentions reached Szilard through the gossip network that still linked laboratories. He feared that Hitler might seize additional reserves of uranium, thus depriving the United States. Since the major untapped source in Europe was Belgium, which stockpiled ore from the Congo, Szilard decided that urgent steps had to be taken to protect these stores. Aware that Einstein was friendly with Queen Elizabeth of Belgium, Szilard and Wigner decided to start their own chain reaction. On a hot summer day the two Hungarians trundled into a car and set off in search of the god of physics, then on holiday in Peconic Bay, on Long Island. First they could not find Peconic and then they could not find Einstein. With their quest to save the world nearing collapse, a small boy came to their rescue and escorted them to the great man's house. Einstein, who had devised the formula for calculating the energy that lay within the atom, had surprisingly not seriously considered the possibility of a chain reaction in uranium. But, once explained to him, he was 'very quick to see the implications and perfectly willing to do anything that needed to be done'.[34] Eventually it was decided that, instead of a direct appeal to the Belgian government, they should approach the international financier Alexander Sachs, a close confidant of President Roosevelt.

Sachs immediately agreed to cooperate. He suggested that a letter signed by Einstein outlining the situation should be given to the President. The letter, dated 2 August 1939, warned:

> Some recent work by E. Fermi and L. Szilard . . . leads me to expect that the element uranium may be turned into a new and important source of energy in the immediate future. Certain aspects of the situation seem to call for watchfulness and, if necessary, quick action on the part of your administration. I believe therefore that it is my duty to bring to your attention . . . that extremely powerful bombs of a new type may . . . be constructed.[35]

Subsequent mythology has cast Einstein as the great visionary (or villain) who kick-started the American bomb, but the driving force was actually Szilard. 'We really only needed Einstein to provide Szilard with a halo,' Sachs later confessed. '[Einstein's] entire role was really limited to that.' Somewhat ashamed by his involvement, Einstein later claimed 'They brought me a finished letter and I signed it.' He agreed to help only because he feared a Nazi bomb. 'If I had known that the Germans would not succeed in constructing the atom bomb, I would never have lifted a finger.'[36]

Sachs did not deliver the 'urgent' letter to Roosevelt until 11 October 1939, ten weeks after Einstein signed it. The President was initially unimpressed, remarking that government intervention seemed unnecessary. Sachs nevertheless managed to secure a second appointment for the following day. He spent a sleepless night planning how best to alert the President. On seeing Roosevelt the next morning, he began:

> All I want to do is tell you a story. During the Napoleonic wars a young American inventor came to the French Emperor and offered to build him a fleet of steamships with the help of which Napoleon could, in spite of the uncertain weather, land in England. Ships without sails? This seemed to the great Corsican so impossible that he sent Fulton away. In the opinion of the English historian Lord Acton, this is an example of how England was saved by the shortsightedness of an adversary. Had Napoleon shown more imagination and humility at the time, the history of the nineteenth century would have taken a very different course.

The penny dropped. Roosevelt told a servant to bring a bottle of Napoleon brandy. Two glasses were filled. Still silent, he raised his glass, drank to his friend, and then settled back to listen carefully to what Sachs recom mended. Sachs summarized the problem in laymen's terms, while mentioning the potential peaceful uses of nuclear power. Toward the end of his presentation, he quoted something Aston wrote in 1936: 'Personally I think there is no doubt that sub-atomic energy is available all around us, and that one day man will release and control its almost infinite power. We cannot prevent him from doing so and can only hope that he will not use it exclusively in blowing up his next door neighbour.' Roosevelt then interjected: 'Alex, what you are after is to see that the Nazis don't blow us up?' 'Precisely'.

Roosevelt called in his attaché, General 'Pa' Watson. Pointing to Einstein's letter, he barked: 'Pa, this requires action!'[37]

What followed was hardly action. The director of the Bureau of Standards, Lyman Briggs, was ordered to set up a committee 'to thoroughly investigate the possibilities . . . regarding the element of uranium'.[38] The Bureau, established in 1901, was a national laboratory charged with developing practical applications for scientific research. Briggs, a veteran of forty-three colourless years in government, knew only one direction – 'caution' – and one speed – 'slow'. The job required a beaver. Briggs was a sloth.

Briggs brought in Army Lt. Colonel Keith Adamson and Navy Commander Gilbert Hoover, both ordnance experts and professional sceptics. The first meeting of the self-styled Advisory Committee on Uranium met on 21 October. The Hungarian triumvirate of Teller, Szilard and Wigner presented their case. They described a bomb equivalent to 20,000 tons of TNT, which Szilard rather foolishly suggested might prove too heavy to transport by aeroplane. Adamson oozed contempt. 'At Aberdeen',* he remarked, 'we're offering a $10,000 reward to anyone who can use a death ray to kill the goat we have tethered to a post. That goat is still perfectly healthy.'[39] Neither he nor Hoover could get their minds around a 20 kiloton blast, which seemed like crazy science fiction.

'How much money do you want?' Hoover asked. Surprised by the blunt request, they struggled to name a figure. Without consulting his colleagues, Teller blurted out that he'd like $6,000 to buy carbon. The figure bore no relation to their actual carbon needs, nor to any other development costs. Adamson and Hoover, accustomed to measuring the importance of a project by its cost, grew ever more dismissive. The former launched into a well-prepared speech:

> He told us that it was naïve to believe that we could make a significant contribution to defense by creating a new weapon. He said that if a new weapon is created, it usually takes two wars before one can know whether

---

* Aberdeen was a US Army artillery proving ground.

the weapon is any good or not. Then he explained rather laboriously that it is in the end not weapons which win wars, but the morale of the troops.

Wigner lost his patience. If wars were won by the morale of troops, he interjected, why then did the Army need such a large weapons budget? Adamson, more annoyed at the request itself than at its amount, replied: 'All right, all right, you'll get your money.'[40] 'After the meeting', Teller recalled, 'Szilard nearly murdered me for the modesty of my request; and Wigner, in his gentler way, seemed ready to assist him.'[41]

While American doubt threatened to smother the project, British labs brought it closer to reality. In February 1940, Frisch and his friend Rudolph Peierls reported on their research into a chain reaction in U-235. They calculated that the reaction would develop to an order of eighty generations before the bomb blew itself apart. Such an explosion might reach a temperature equivalent to the interior of the sun. 'Both Frisch and I were staggered,' Peierls recounted.[42]

They then pondered the size of the critical mass. 'To my amazement [the answer] was very much smaller than I had expected,' Frisch wrote. 'It was not a matter of tons, but something like a pound or two.'* Rather optimistically, they predicted that the process they had used to separate U-235 from U-238 could be expanded to factory proportions, so as to produce 'a pound of reasonably pure uranium-235 in a modest time, measured in weeks'. The findings frightened them. 'We stared at each other and realized that an atomic bomb might after all be possible.' Their calculations indicated that five kilos of U-235 would produce a blast equivalent to several thousand tons of TNT and would release radiation equal to one hundred tons of radium. This would be 'fatal to living beings even a long time after the explosion'. Four further conclusions went beyond pure science:

1. The [bomb] would be practically irresistible. . . . no material or structure . . . . could be expected to resist the force of the explosion.
2. Owing to the spreading of radioactive substances with the wind, the bomb could probably not be used without killing large numbers of civilians, and this may make it unsuitable as a weapon for use by this country.
3. It is quite conceivable that Germany is, in fact, developing this weapon . . .
4. If . . . Germany is, or will be, in the possession of this weapon . . . [the] most effective reply would be a counter-threat with a similar weapon.[43]

---

* This was, in fact, an underestimate. Predictions as to the exact size of the critical mass would vary widely during this period, but the important point was that physicists were surmising that the size would have to be sufficiently small to allow the possibility of a bomb.

Frisch sensed a point of no return. He felt himself pulled forward by curiosity, but even more so by fear. The end product would be 'a weapon of unparalleled violence, a weapon of mass destruction such as the world had never seen'. But for precisely that reason, it had to be built. 'We were at war, and . . . very probably some German scientists had had the same idea and were working on it.'[44]

The Frisch-Peierls memorandum was sent to Henry Tizard's Committee on the Scientific Survey of Air Defence. Tizard, like Briggs, had doubts. 'I still . . . think that [the] probability of anything of real military significance is very low,' he told the War Cabinet. The British, like the Americans, answered uncertainty by forming committees. In April 1940, a group headed by G. P. Thomson, professor of physics at Imperial College, looked into the progress of American nuclear research. The Thomson Committee advised that 'If anything likely to be of war value emerges [the Americans] will certainly give us a hint of it in good time . . . it is much better that they should be pressing on with this than that our people should be wasting their time on what is . . . probably a wild goose chase'.[45]

Meanwhile the American bomb, only recently conceived, was in grave danger of being aborted. Another layer of bureaucracy was added when Dr Vannevar Bush formed the National Defense Research Council (NDRC). He thought the bomb might work, but doubted that the engineering problems could be solved quickly enough to affect the war. In May 1941, he moved upstairs to the Office of Scientific Research and Development (OSRD) and installed James Conant at the NDRC. An unashamed sceptic, Conant had little patience for the physicists. '[Their] fancies left me cold . . . until Nazi Germany was defeated all our energies should be concentrated on one immediate objective.'[46]

While the Americans and the British efficiently formed committees, the Germans designed a nuclear reactor. Research had suggested that, if a suitable mixture of U-235 and U-238 could be diluted with the right amount of moderating atoms, the neutrons released in the fission of U-235 might sustain a controlled chain reaction, producing energy and a third isotope, uranium-239. This would then quickly decay, becoming element 94, with an atomic weight of 239. The energy could be converted into usable electricity, while the new element, it was thought, would provide a fissionable core for a bomb.*

As it turns out, naturally occurring uranium, with 99.3 per cent U-238 and 0.7 per cent U-235, is a suitable mixture for this sort of reaction, with the diluting material being either pure graphite or heavy water.†

---

* Element 94, which had yet to be isolated, would eventually be called plutonium.
† Heavy water is chemically the same as regular (light) water, but with the two hydrogen atoms replaced with deuterium atoms. Deuterium, an isotope of hydrogen, has one extra neutron. It is the extra neutron that makes heavy water 'heavy' by about 10 per cent.

While the process was understood theoretically in 1941, the problem lay in making it happen. After a year of theoretical discussions, by September 1941 Heisenberg had a rough idea of how to construct a reactor. 'We saw the open road ahead of us, leading to the atomic bomb.'[47]

Building a successful reactor (or 'pile') required finding a 'moderator' in which the uranium could be encased in order to slow down the neutrons. Fermi had surmised that super-pure graphite seemed the best bet, but agreed not to publish these findings. In contrast, the German Walter Bothe initially concluded that graphite held no promise as a neutron moderator. Thus, by keeping quiet about his findings, Fermi inadvertently caused the Germans to favour heavy water as a moderator.

Since heavy water, in contrast to graphite, was scarce, this rendered the German project considerably more vulnerable. Heavy water had hitherto been used in small quantities in the laboratory, but the Germans now wanted enough to fill a bathtub. They approached the Norsk Hydro plant at Vemork to buy up all the available stocks (about 50 gallons) and to place orders for an additional thirty gallons per month. The Norwegians, used to selling only three gallons a month, grew suspicious. When the Germans refused to explain their need, the Norwegians declined to sell it. Alert French agents then went to Norway to buy up all available stocks. Norwegian obstruction could, however, only go so far. The heavy water problem disappeared when the Germans invaded Norway.

A bigger obstacle to German success was the uneven commitment of her scientists. Some wanted to build a bomb, others were intrigued by the scientific quest but did not want Germany to have a bomb, others merely pretended to cooperate. Occasionally, individuals essential to the programme were scooped up by the military. Overseeing it all was Heisenberg, who played a clever game of self-protection. His first concern was to survive, his second to protect his reputation. 'At present we can see no practicable method of producing an atom bomb during the war with the resources available,' he replied when questioned about progress. 'But the subject, nevertheless, must be fully investigated in order to make sure that the Americans will not be able to develop atom bombs either.'[48] This reasoning was designed to allow him the freedom to work during the war and to escape censure after it.

Back in Britain, Frisch and Peierls came to the conclusion that their optimism about extracting U-235 in large proportion was perhaps un-warranted. 'It was like getting a doctor who had after great labour made a minute quantity of a new drug and then saying to him: "Now we want enough to pave the streets."'[49] Element 94 seemed a better solution. Just prior to Christmas 1940, Fermi concluded that it might undergo slow fission. On the other side of the continent, in Berkeley, the brilliant young chemist Glenn Seaborg managed by March 1941 to isolate a millionth of a gram of element 94. He named it plutonium, after the planet discovered twelve years earlier. Pluto was the Greek god of the underworld – the god of the dead.

Political commitment was still lacking. The American military was too preoccupied with the prospect of fighting a real war to spend much effort promoting an imaginary weapon. Politicians were reluctant to release funds for a project that might in the end prove a pipe dream. Engineers, drafted in far earlier than would have been the case in any other experimental project, had difficulty putting their minds to construction problems based on theories which had not yet been proved. 'We often felt as though we were swimming in syrup,' Wigner recalled. Szilard found the inertia irritating. 'I had assumed that once we had demonstrated that in the fission of uranium neutrons are emitted, there would be no difficulty getting people interested; but I was wrong.'[50] Einstein was persuaded to write a second letter to the President warning of the 'intensification of German interest in uranium'.[51] But this had little effect.

Then, quite unexpectedly, Thomson's group, codenamed the MAUD committee, categorically stated in early July 1941 that building a bomb was possible and that it was 'likely to lead to decisive results in the war'. It recommended that the work be given highest priority and that cooperation with the Americans be increased. The committee admitted that isotope separation remained 'a matter of great difficulty' and that the entire project would be hugely expensive. But, 'in spite of this very large expenditure we consider that the destructive effect, both material and moral, is so great that every effort should be made to produce bombs of this kind'. Even if the war ended before the weapon could be used, 'the effort would not be wasted . . . since no nation would care to risk being caught without a weapon of such decisive possibilities'.[52]

The MAUD report caught the imagination of Churchill's scientific adviser Lord Cherwell who distilled it into a two-page memo for the Prime Minister. Cherwell recommended that construction of an isotope separation plant should begin immediately. He was not, in other words, inclined to leave things to the Americans. 'Whoever possesses such a plant should be able to dictate terms to the rest of the world,' he argued. 'However much I may trust my neighbour and depend on him, I am very much averse to putting myself completely at his mercy.'[53] Churchill, always intrigued by new weapons, agreed.

The British, though deeply embroiled in a difficult war, had decided that there was no reason to delay atomic research. The Americans, though not yet at war, were using the conflict as an excuse for caution. On receiving the MAUD Report, Briggs locked it in a safe without showing it to his

Uranium Committee colleagues. When Samuel Allison, a new member of the committee, eventually discovered it, he was astonished to find that bombs were even an issue. He thought the committee had been considering a new power source for submarines.

The dam of doubt gradually eroded. On 3 October the MAUD report landed on Conant's desk. After reading it, he and Bush decided that a major push was necessary. Bush took the matter to Roosevelt who immediately launched a full-scale development effort. Without consulting Congress, he approved the most expensive weapons programme in the history of the United States. The decision was significant in two ways. First, and most obvious, the US had decided to join the nuclear arms race. Secondly, and more subtly, Roosevelt's decision caused a power shift within the project. The politicians had taken over. The physicists, once the prime movers, were now merely government employees expected to obey orders.

Roosevelt's decision also changed the nature of the Bomb. Up to this point, the scientists thought in terms of a deterrent – the only way to stop a nuclear-armed Germany. Soldiers and politicians, on the other hand, imagined a weapon. Secretary of War Henry Stimson later insisted that it was always Roosevelt's intention to use the Bomb when it became available. 'At no time, from 1941 to 1945, did I ever hear it suggested by the President . . . that atomic energy should not be used in this war . . . on no other ground could the war-time expenditure of so much time and money be justified.'[54] Churchill echoed this assessment: 'the decision whether or not to use the atomic bomb . . . was never even an issue. There was unanimous, automatic, unquestioned agreement.'[55]

Just prior to Roosevelt's decision to embark on a Bomb, Heisenberg and von Weizsäcker visited Neils Bohr in Copenhagen. The outbreak of war had placed Bohr in a quandary. Ever since the Nazi invasion of Denmark in April, he had to face the possibility that his Institute might eventually be used to aid Hitler. The logical response was to leave, but he did not want to abandon junior colleagues who did not enjoy that option. Though he decided to stay put, he still managed to maintain links with colleagues in Britain and America. German scientists also used Bohr as a go-between to get messages out.

This might have been Heisenberg's aim when he approached Bohr at the end of September 1941. According to his wife Elisabeth, Heisenberg 'wanted to signal to Bohr that Germany neither would nor could build a bomb. . . . Secretly he even hoped that his message could prevent the use of an atomic bomb on Germany one day. He was constantly tortured by this idea. . . . This vague hope was probably the strongest motivation for his trip.'[56] If Heisenberg indeed wanted to reassure Bohr (and, through him, others) that there was no threat of a German bomb, he failed. Bohr assumed that the Germans had made great progress toward a bomb. 'Although I tried subsequently to correct this false impression', Heisenberg told Robert Jungk after the war, 'I probably did not succeed in winning Bohr's complete trust, especially as I only dared to speak guardedly . . . I was very unhappy with the result of this conversation.'

Heisenberg later told Jungk that the talk with Bohr 'probably started with my question as to whether or not it was right for physicists to devote them-selves in wartime to the uranium problem – as there was the possibility that progress in this sphere could lead to grave consequences in the technique of war'.[57] It is difficult to believe that Heisenberg travelled all the way to Copenhagen simply to discuss matters of conscience. Bohr certainly had a very different recollection of the meeting and reacted angrily when Heisenberg's claims were printed in Jungk's *Brighter than a Thousand Suns*. He drafted (but did not send) a letter to Heisenberg, pointing out that

> I remember every word of our conversations . . . you and Weizsäcker expressed your definite conviction that Germany would win and that it was therefore quite foolish for us to maintain the hope of a different outcome of the war and to be reticent as regards all German offers of cooperation. I also remember quite clearly . . . the firm impression that, under your leadership, everything was being done in Germany to develop atomic weapons.[58]

Over the following years Bohr periodically returned to this subject in drafts of letters to Heisenberg which were never actually sent. At one point, he referred to Heisenberg's prediction that 'the war, if it lasted long enough, would be decided with atomic weapons'.[59]

Buried within Bohr's papers are recollections of a remark by Weizsäcker to the effect that it was 'fortunate . . . that Heisenberg's work would mean so much for the war since it would mean that, after the expected great victory, the Nazis would adopt a more understanding attitude towards German scientific efforts'.[60] This comment is crucial to understanding Heisenberg's motives. Like so many patriotic Germans, he did not want to lose the war, but nor did he relish the prospect of a victorious Hitler. While on a visit to Holland during the war, he told a Dutch scientist that 'Democracy cannot develop sufficient energy to rule Europe. There are, therefore, only two alternatives: Germany and Russia. . . . a Europe under German leadership would be a lesser evil.'[61] He hoped, rather optimisti-cally, that reason would reassert itself after victory and Hitler would be deposed.

Heisenberg also had high hopes for physics. He and his colleagues had already suffered the psychotic wrath of Nazism. In 1937, the SS attacked him for pursuing 'Jewish physics', for being a 'white Jew' and for being 'representative of the Einsteinian "spirit"'. A frightening Gestapo investigation followed. Though Heisenberg was eventually exonerated, it undoubtedly left him bruised. Over the following years, he tried hard to rehabilitate himself and his discipline. In real terms this meant bending to Nazi will. Every privilege the state subsequently granted him was interpreted as evidence of his rehabilitation.

The atom bomb fits into this recovery. If the practitioners of 'Jewish physics' could provide the nation with new weapons to win the war, or new sources of energy, their place in society would be secure. Heisenberg put it rather succinctly: 'The official slogan of the government was: "We must make use of physics for warfare". We turned it around for our slogan: "We must make use of warfare for physics".'[62]

Bearing in mind what Bohr recalled, one guesses that Heisenberg was in fact trying to signal that the German atomic project had every chance of success. Beyond that, he seems to have wanted to reassure Bohr that the inevitable German victory would not be disastrous for Europe. He had to believe this, since he had already invested so much moral energy into Germany's success. But Heisenberg was also aware that scientists in the United States might soon draw level in the race to build a bomb. What he feared most was an American bomb used against Germany. He perhaps hoped that Bohr might prove helpful in preventing such a catastrophe. In other words, his wife's interpretation of the visit was probably half right and half wrong: Heisenberg wanted to enlist Bohr's help in preventing a nuclear attack, but he also wanted to signal to Bohr that Germany *could* build a bomb.

Heisenberg's fears were justified. American inertia had given way to frenzied activity. In the autumn of 1941, the Nobel Prize winner Arthur H. Compton, with help from Oppenheimer, looked further into the issue of the critical mass. He estimated that it would be no higher than 100 kilos, and perhaps much less. If this mass were to be assembled quickly, 'a fission bomb of superlatively destructive power' would result.[63] Two subcritical lumps of U-235 would have to be brought together at bullet-like speed. If the pieces came together too slowly, pre-detonation would result – the bomb would blow itself apart before the big bang materialized. Since this seemed a simple problem of ballistics, scientists were reasonably confident about building the bomb.

In January 1942 Compton gathered together prominent scientists to coordinate research. He set a tight schedule which called for a workable bomb within three years. During these meetings Oppenheimer shone like a star. 'Under Oppenheimer, something really got done, and at astonishing speed,' Compton later remarked.[64] During the summer, Oppenheimer gathered around him at Berkeley a group of 'luminaries' to brainstorm bomb design. By late August they had calculated that the bomb might be 150 times more powerful than originally anticipated. This gave the whole project greater justification. But the size of the critical mass remained problematic, as did the matter of isotope separation. Further calculations suggested that 30 kilos of U-235 would be necessary for each bomb. Logic suggested that at least two bombs would be needed – one to test and one to drop on the enemy. An isotope previously measured in micrograms would have to be produced in quantities a billion times as large.

While the Americans were surging ahead, the Germans ran out of steam. Theoretical research had progressed significantly, but no cohesive project to build a bomb materialized. Various ventures were sponsored by the War Office, the Ministry of Education and, bizarrely, the Post Office. An opportunity to establish some cohesion and purpose occurred on 4 June 1942, when senior physicists met government and military officials, including Albert Speer, the Minister of Supply. Heisenberg spoke openly about the possibility of building a bomb capable of destroying an entire city. Two days later, he told Speer that 'Definite proof has been obtained that the technical utilisation of atomic energy in a uranium pile was possible. Moreover, it was to be expected on theoretical grounds that an explosive for atomic bombs could be produced in such a pile.' Speer was impressed, but unable to act on Heisenberg's report. Hitler had only recently proclaimed a new policy to the effect that no new weapons project could be embarked upon unless results were guaranteed within six months. The edict was inspired by his assumption that the war was going well. Since scientists predicted that it would be three or four years before anything useful would result from fission research, Speer ordered the bomb project scaled down. He was also disappointed when Heisenberg failed to reassure him that an atomic explosion could not ignite the atmosphere. As Speer recalled, 'Hitler was plainly not delighted with the possibility that the earth under his rule might be transformed into a glowing star.'[65] The worm Heisenberg had been gifted a convenient escape. 'I was pleased to be spared the responsibility of making a decision,' he later claimed. 'The Führer's orders in force at the time ruled out altogether the enormous effort necessary to make an atomic bomb.'[66] Heisenberg later claimed that he had 'falsified the mathematics in order to avoid the development of the atom bomb by German scientists'.[67] For the rest of his life he was tormented by a need to prove that he had taken a moral stand against the Bomb, and an equally consuming need to prove that he could have built one.

Reports on Heisenberg's progress had periodically been passed to British intelligence. These were analysed by Klaus Fuchs, a physicist working with Frisch and Peierls at Birmingham. Fuchs concluded that 'research in Hitler's Germany had reached a dead-end'.* According to the official history of British intelligence, by early 1943 the British government began 'to feel increasingly reassured in relation to Germany's nuclear research programme'.[68] But by this stage the allied juggernaut had reached full speed. It could not be stopped.

On 6 August 1945, a group of captured German physicists listened to a BBC report of the bombing of Hiroshima. There followed a heated discussion. Many excuses for Germany's failure were offered, some preposterous, others candidly honest. Heisenberg maintained that 'We wouldn't have had the moral courage to recommend to the government in the spring of 1942 that they should employ 120,000 men just for building the thing.'[69] There was some truth to this assessment. But, in reality, this was not a matter of moral courage, since no amount of determination on the part of her scientists could have overcome the fact that Germany did not possess the resources to succeed. As the American success would eventually demonstrate, there was no room for half measures. Knowing theoretically how a bomb might be constructed was not enough. Beyond theory, a massive engineering effort was required. The need for large quantities of U-235 or plutonium meant that processes developed in perfect conditions within the laboratory had to be expanded to industrial proportions. That implied resources which Germany simply did not have.

Though British intelligence indicated that German research had stalled, pessimism remained prudent. 'There are still plenty of competent scientists in Germany,' Conant warned. 'They may be ahead of us by as much as a year.'[70] To doubt the German lead seemed dangerously complacent. 'We were told day in and day out that it was our duty to catch the Germans,' one scientist recalled.[71] Another watched in horror as 'Wigner wrote on the blackboard that it would take the Germans two months to build a reactor, three months to take the plutonium out, two months to make a bomb [so that] by Christmas of 1944 they would have the bomb. That scared us shitless, I guess you would say.'[72]

In fact, by the end of 1942, the deadly race had only one runner.

---

* Fuchs, who had by this stage already decided to spy for the Soviet Union, gave a similar conclusion to his Russian contact.

CHAPTER 3

Born in Manhattan

In the race to build the bomb, scientists trampled over their moral doubts and muddied the noble traditions of their profession. 'Physics', wrote Victor Weisskopf, 'our beloved science, was pushed into the most cruel part of reality and we had to live it through.'[1] The liberal ethic guiding scientists conflicted with the pragmatic authoritarianism by which states conduct war. It chafed them – especially those who had escaped repressive regimes – to work in secrecy, not to mention to watch the noble goal of discovery superseded by the coarse practical purpose of building a weapon. But, when chased by a madman, who worries about ruining their shoes?

Once the atomic race was entered, all the stops were removed. The US decided to pursue a number of different courses toward the bomb simultaneously, fully realizing that some (or all) might prove futile. That did not matter. 'If one discards one or two or three of the methods now, one may be betting on the slower horse unconsciously,' Conant warned. He fully realized that 'to embark on this Napoleonic approach to the problem would require the commitment of perhaps $500,000,000 and quite a mess of machinery'.[2] In fact it cost much more than that. And the mess was huge.

A Military Policy Committee was formed to oversee the research. It consisted of three members of the armed forces: General W. D. Styer, Admiral W. R. Purnell and General Leslie Groves, and two civilians: Bush and Conant. On 13 August 1942, the project was given two codenames. The first was 'DSM', for the 'development of substitute materials'. Worried that the term might arouse curiosity, Groves proposed an innocuous title which had nothing at all to do with the goal in view. He suggested calling it the Manhattan Engineer District. Before long, it became the Manhattan Project.

Command was given to Groves, who had previously been deputy chief of construction for the US Army, a job which included supervising the building of the Pentagon. With a budget exceeding $600 million per year, he was no stranger to big projects. But he expected, as a reward for his work on the Pentagon, a field assignment in Europe. Instead, he was told to go and build a Bomb. To sugar the pill he was immediately promoted to Brigadier General. Styer, either out of ignorance or pretence, told Groves that 'The basic research and development are done. You just have to take the rough designs, put them into final shape, build some plants and organize an operating force and your job will be finished and the war will be over.'[3]

The job at first consisted only of construction and supervision of the facilities involved in the production of the bomb. This was a large enough task, but Groves's remit gradually expanded when it became apparent that research could not realistically be left outside the fold. Eventually, it seemed sensible to absorb intelligence and security also. Ever the empire builder, Groves ultimately looked beyond the war, specifically to ensure that 'the postwar position of the United States in the field of atomic energy [should] not be unfavourable'.[4] Thus, he thought not only of building bombs for this war, but of mass producing them after it.

Groves immediately went looking for uranium, and found 1,250 tonnes sitting on Staten Island docks. It belonged to Union Minière and had been moved to the US after the Belgian government had been warned about Nazi intentions. The Belgians had repeatedly informed the American government of its availability, but had received no response. As if to signal a new approach, Groves immediately purchased all of it.

Elsewhere, it soon became clear that Styer's optimism was entirely unwarranted – basic research and development were far from complete. 'The whole endeavor was founded on possibilities rather than probabilities,' Groves later remarked.[5] While ordinary projects proceed systematically from research, to development, to production, this was like a torrent of water rushing down a mountain in completely chaotic fashion. Against his better instincts, Groves eventually learned (as one scientist put it) that 'There is no objection to a wrong decision with quick results. If there is a choice between two methods, one of which is good and the other looks promising, then build both.'[6]

Having familiarized himself with the basic physics involved in an atom bomb, Groves embarked on a whirlwind tour of the laboratories involved in the isotope separation problem. He stopped first at a Westinghouse lab in Pittsburgh, where a centrifugal process was being developed. Unimpressed with the research and with the commitment displayed, he shut the operation down and promptly moved on to Columbia University, where gaseous diffusion was being developed. Commonly used in chemistry and physics, the method's applicability to the enrichment of uranium had yet to be proven. It relied on the assumption that slightly smaller U-235 atoms would pass through a fine porous barrier faster than U-238. Thus, if ordinary uranium was processed, the first quantities to pass through would have a higher concentration of U-235. By continually repeating the process, the concentration would increase. But, since uranium is a solid, not a gas, at normal temperatures, it had to be converted into

...ride, a powerful corrosive capable of dissolving any ...pipe or diffusion barrier. Even if this problem could be ...ined to be seen whether a process suited to the enrichment ...micrograms in a laboratory could be used to produce kilograms in a factory. Despite these concerns, Groves was sufficiently impressed by the facility to give it a green light.

He then proceeded to Chicago where Fermi, Szilard and Wigner were building their atomic pile (reactor) in the squash courts under the University football stadium. Their prominence had acted as a magnet for other brilliant young scientists – a staff of over 1,200 had gathered. Construction of a pile would have two useful purposes. First, it would allow physicists to investigate practically (not just theoretically) a controlled fission reaction. Secondly, it would produce plutonium, which seemed a promising bomb core.

At Berkeley, the next stage of his tour, Groves met Lawrence, who boasted that his cyclotron would solve the isotope separation problem. His latest model, the Calutron, had a huge magnet 20 feet tall. Lawrence explained to Groves how atoms of uranium hexafluoride would be accelerated through the central circular chamber at thousands of miles per second. When they passed through the magnetic field, the two isotopes would behave differently, forming two different streams, which would then be diverted into two containers. The idea seemed entirely logical. 'How long does this thing have to run to get real separation?' Groves asked.

L Well, it takes a long time to make a vacuum in the machine itself. It'll take fourteen to twenty-four hours to get a vacuum that's sufficient.
G But how long do you run it?
L It's never been run for more than ten or fifteen minutes.
G What about separation? How much do you get in these baskets?
L Well, actually, we don't get any sizeable separation at all. I mean not yet. This is still all experimental, you see . . .[7]

The uncertainty was doubly worrying since, even before Groves arrived, approval had been given for construction of a huge calutron at Clinton, Tennessee. Work had begun even though the process itself guaranteed nothing.

Groves was plagued by massive imponderables. Early in the project, he was annoyed to find that scientists could not tell him how much uranium 235 or plutonium would be needed to make a bomb. He wanted an answer correct to within 25 per cent, but got one which the physicists readily admitted might be out by a factor of 10.* 'My position could well be

---

* That was in fact an underestimate, since calculations regarding the critical mass had so far varied by a factor of one hundred.

compared to that of a caterer who is told he must be prepared to serve anywhere between ten and a thousand guests,' he later commented.[8]

Friction inevitably developed between Groves and the scientists. Huge egos were easily bruised. Groves deeply resented the intellectual snobbery of the scientists, while they resented being managed by a boorish layman who did not completely understand the processes being developed. At one of his first meetings, Groves reacted like a cornered beast:

> There is one last thing I want to emphasise. You may know that I don't have a Ph.D. . . . But let me tell you that I have ten years of formal education after I entered college. *Ten* years in which I just studied. I didn't have to make a living or give time for teaching. I just studied. That would be about equivalent to two Ph.D.s wouldn't it?

At his first meeting with his immediate staff – all military personnel – Groves warned, not entirely in jest: 'Your job won't be easy. At great expense we have gathered together the largest collection of crackpots ever seen.'[9] Contempt flowed in two directions. The pragmatism and order of the military was abhorrent to the scientists; while their aimless theorizing seemed dangerously self-indulgent to Groves.

The scientists probably had a higher opinion of Groves than he ever appreciated. If they despised him it was because he was unpleasant, not because he was a buffoon. Teller thought that 'between 1943 and 1945 General Groves could have won almost any unpopularity contest'.[10] Even within the Army, he was widely admired, but not widely liked. 'I hated his guts and so did everybody else,' Colonel Kenneth Nichols, a fellow engineer, remarked.

> He's the biggest sonovabitch I've ever met in my life, but also one of the most capable individuals. He had an ego second to none, he had tireless energy . . . He had absolute confidence in his decisions and he was absolutely ruthless in how he approached a problem to get it done. But that was the beauty of working for him – that you never had to worry about the decisions being made or what it meant. In fact, I've often thought that if I were to have to do my part over again, I would select Groves as boss.[11]

Within the government, his value was fully recognized. Stimson ordered Groves not to travel by aeroplane since he was indispensable. Groves queried this on the grounds that both Stimson and General George Marshall *were* allowed to fly. 'You can't be replaced, and we can,' Stimson replied. 'Who would take your place if you were killed?' Groves replied: 'That would be your problem, not mine, but I agree that you might have a problem.'[12]

Groves justified the project on three grounds. First was the threat that the Germans were building a Bomb; 'there was no evidence to indicat. that they were not striving to do so; therefore we had to assume that they were'. Second was the fact that the only defence against a nuclear weapon 'was the fear of counter-employment' – better known as deterrence. These two justifications were unanimously accepted by the scientists. The third was not. Groves thought a Bomb 'would shorten the war and thus save tens of thousands of American casualties'.[13] In other words, Groves had no doubt that the Bomb was a weapon destined to be used.

After the disappointing tour of the various separation labs, Groves was considerably heartened by his first meeting with Oppenheimer. 'He's a genius. A real genius,' he decided. 'While Lawrence is very bright he's not a genius, just a good hard worker. . . . Oppenheimer knows about everything. He can talk to you about anything you bring up.'[14] Groves had some misgivings about Opppenheimer's suitability as an organizer, but decided to follow his instincts. Oppenheimer's subsequent appointment as director caused considerable surprise and trepidation within the scientific community. 'Some of Robert's closest friends were skeptical,' Luis Alvarez recalled. '"He couldn't run a hamburger stand", I heard one of them say.' Rabi felt that Oppenheimer 'was absolutely the most unlikely choice for a laboratory director imaginable. He was a very impractical sort of fellow . . . he didn't know anything about equipment.'[15]

Oppenheimer's murky connections with communists are by now well known, though not well understood. They proved more of a problem after the war when self-proclaimed patriots found Reds in every bed. During the war, Oppenheimer's physics was much more important than his politics, at least to Groves. On 20 July 1943, he wrote, very simply, to those vetting the scientist: 'it is desired that clearance be issued for the employment of Julius Robert Oppenheimer without delay, irrespective of the information which you have concerning Mr Oppenheimer. He is absolutely essential to the project.'[16] Since Groves was hardly a soft touch on matters of security, this suggests that his judgement of Oppenheimer was not merely pragmatic, but instead based on real trust. He certainly maintained that trust long after the war, when loyalty to Oppenheimer was unnecessary and sometimes dangerous.

Groves could not, however, protect Oppenheimer completely. Lt. Colonel Boris Pash, an Army G-2 security officer, carried out an exhaustive investigation, motivated by preconceived assumptions that Oppenheimer was untrustworthy. Agents bugged his phone, wired his office, opened his mail and tailed him everywhere. They found nothing of substance, but Pash refused to relax his grip. He subjected Oppenheimer to long interrogations, though he never succeeded in getting him to incriminate himself. Despite the lack of hard evidence, Pash stubbornly concluded that

The matter of Oppenheimer's first loyalty to science might have been true, but it could have been levelled at almost anyone on the Manhattan Project. What Pash did not understand was that the scientist who felt this way would not automatically sell his soul for a Soviet cyclotron. Most physicists loved their discipline but also loved their country. Perhaps the most interesting aspect of this sorry tale was that, while enormous attention was directed at Oppenheimer, the genuine spies on the project went undetected.

Oppenheimer was a great synthesizer, a man who could grasp ideas and visualize in a practical sense how they might be applied. That perhaps was his greatest strength and explains why he proved perfect for the job. As Teller realized, the job of director was as much about people as about physics: 'Oppie knew in detail what was going on in every part of the laboratory. He was incredibly quick and perceptive in analyzing human as well as technical problems. . . . He knew how to analyze, cajole, humor, soothe feelings – how to lead powerfully without seeming to do so. He was an exemplar of dedication, a hero who never lost his humanness.'[18] Weisskopf recalled how 'he was present in the laboratory or in the seminar room when a new effect was measured, when a new idea was conceived. It was not that he contributed so many ideas or suggestions . . . his main influence came from his continuous and intense presence, which produced a sense of direct participation in all of us.'[19]

One observer remarked, 'The power of his personality is stronger because of the fragility of his person. When he speaks he seems to grow, since the largeness of his mind so affirms itself that the smallness of his body is forgotten.'[20] He was often recalled in mystical terms:

it was the head that was the most striking: the halo of wispy black curly hair, the fine, sharp nose, and especially the eyes, surprisingly blue, having a strange depth and intensity, and yet expressive of a candor that was altogether disarming. He looked like a young Einstein, and at the same time like an over-grown choir-boy. There was something both subtly wise and terribly innocent about his face. It was an extraordinarily sensitive face, which seemed capable of registering and conveying every shade of emotion. . . . I associated it with the faces of apostles. . . . A kind of light shone from it, which illuminated the scene around him.[21]

Others noted how he seemed intimately involved in everyone's life. 'Each Sunday he would ride his beautiful chestnut horse from the cavalry stable at the east side of the town to the mountain trails on the west side of town greeting each of the people he passed with a wave of his pork-pie hat and a friendly remark,' a Group Leader recalled. 'He knew everyone who lived in Los Alamos, from the top scientists to the children of the Spanish-American janitors – they were all Oppenheimer's family.'[22]

Not everyone warmed to the man. Some found his legendary charm a sham, something selectively applied for pragmatic purposes. He cultivated an image of a highly cultured and deeply sensitive man, which Emilio Segré found ostentatious and at times ridiculous. 'Perhaps I did not sufficiently conceal my lack of supine admiration for Oppenheimer,' he remarked. 'I found him unfriendly . . . for a good part of my career, except when he wanted me to join his team at Los Alamos.'[23] Seth Neddermeyer, who witnessed at first hand how Oppenheimer dealt with failure, found him a rude and insensitive snob. 'He could cut you cold and humiliate you right down to the ground.'[24]

He was politically naïve, ironically so, given the excessive attention paid to his politics. Though a deep thinker, Oppenheimer was often guided by gut emotions. The plight of Jews and his hatred of Nazis awakened in him a 'smouldering fury', which fired his work. By 1942, 'he'd become very patriotic and his ideals had changed', a colleague recalled. 'He was convinced that the war . . . was a mass effort to overthrow the Nazis and upset Fascism and he talked of a people's army and a people's war.'[25]

And perhaps a people's Bomb.

For Groves, secrecy was paramount. He wanted scientists to be restricted from speaking to each other and kept ignorant of progress outside their own lab. Only a select few would be familiar with the entire project; most would not even know what they were making. But all this worked against the basic principles of scientific enquiry. Oppenheimer did not entirely agree with Groves, but he understood the secrecy problem better than his colleagues. As a solution, he eventually suggested 'a central laboratory . . . where people could talk freely to each other, where theoretical ideas and experimental findings could affect each other, where the waste and frustration and error of the many compartmentalized experimental studies could be eliminated'.[26] In other words, Oppenheimer wanted to establish one super laboratory in which he could recreate the old fashioned community of science, as far as was possible within wartime restrictions. The community itself would be open, but secrecy would be maintained by isolating it from the rest of the world. Groves eventually agreed with this solution.

The facility had to be isolated, not just for security reasons, but also because experiments might lead to disaster, either in the form of an explosion or a massive release of radiation. Fortunately, when it comes to remote spots, Americans are spoiled for choice. Los Alamos in New Mexico was chosen because it satisfied the basic requirements, but also because Oppenheimer had a sentimental connection to the area dating back to his boyhood. 'My two great loves are physics and New Mexico,' he used to tell friends. 'It's a pity they can't be combined.'[27] During the war, fusion occurred.

The Los Alamos Ranch School seemed perfect for the relatively small establishment originally envisaged. It had fallen on hard times, so the headmaster welcomed the compulsory purchase order and cheque for $440,000. Oppenheimer first estimated that facilities would be needed for thirty scientists and their families. But he had little awareness of the mundane necessities of such a community. Who would make sure that typewriters had ribbons and the blackboards chalk, or that the toilets were clean?

To: Mr B. E. Brazier
From: Priscilla Duffield
Date: 18 October 1943
Mr Oppenheimer would like a nail to hang his hat on.

To: J. G. Ryan
From: B. E. Brazier
Date: 18 October 1943
While you sent a very nice coat and hat rack this morning, he would still like a nail for his hat. Please put one up in his office.[28]

Thirty scientists could build a paper bomb, but a real bomb required engineers, technicians, clerks, secretaries, purchasing agents, janitors, scullery workers and people to pound in nails. While it was difficult to anticipate these needs, it was impossible to ignore them. Every new complexity meant new recruits. Within a year the establishment grew to 3,500 and a year later stood at over 6,000. The physicist Richard Feynman likened it to 'those moving pictures where you see a piece of equipment go *bruuuuup, bruuuuup, bruuuuup*. Every time I'd look up the thing was getting bigger.'[29]

An isolated community in New Mexico had limited attraction. The temperature ranged from –15°F in winter to the high 90s in summer. It was also very dry, with just $18^{1}/_{2}$ inches of rainfall per year. Scientists accustomed to working out problems while sipping espresso at sidewalk cafés in Rome, Copenhagen or Budapest found the desert seclusion difficult. Oppenheimer tried to make it sound attractive:

We know you will want to have as clear a picture as possible, before coming to Los Alamos, of the many aspects of life here . . . It is set in the pines at 7,300 feet in very fine country. . . . The country is a mixture of mountain country such as you have met in other parts of the Rockies, and the adobe-housed, picturesque, southwest desert that you have seen in Western Movies.[30]

Aware of the sacrifice which coming to Los Alamos entailed, Oppenheimer made sure that personal needs were not neglected. 'We will arrange to have a café where married people can eat out,' he announced. 'This will probably be able to handle about twenty people at a time and will be a little fancy, and may be by appointment only.' A recreation officer would organize 'libraries, pack trips, movies and so on'.[31]

Most recruits were paid their university salary. Those not in an academic position were paid according to their qualifications: a Bachelor of Science earned $200 a month, with those possessing a Ph.D. plus five years' additional experience earning up to $400. Oppenheimer was paid $10,000 per year, which he felt exorbitant – 'I think that neither the University nor I would want to regard work done for the Government of the United States in time of war as the occasion for any essential increase in income.' His efforts to get his salary reduced proved fruitless.[32]

Most recruits were young, the average age being twenty-seven. Many gave up secure jobs in order to join this venture into the unknown. They were drawn to Los Alamos partly out of patriotism, but mainly by the lure of cutting edge research. 'No matter what you do with the rest of your life', Glenn Seaborg told recruits, 'nothing will be as important to the future of the world as your work on this Project right now.'[33] Not all were, strictly speaking, essential to the project. 'Oppie had recruited not only the chemists, physicists and engineers that the project required but also a painter, a philosopher and a few other unlikely characters,' Frisch recalled. 'He felt that a civilised community would be incomplete without them.'[34] But it was by no means a natural community; as one resident remarked, there were 'no invalids, no in-laws, no unemployed, no idle rich and no poor'.[35]

Richard Feynman, then a young researcher at Princeton, recalls being lured by Bob Wilson to join one of the separation projects.

> He told me about it and he said, 'There's a meeting . . .'
> I said I didn't want to do it.
> He said, 'All right, there's a meeting at three o'clock. I'll see you there.'
> I said '. . . but I'm not going to do it.'

Feynman went back to his work 'for about three minutes'. He began to pace the floor.

The Germans had Hitler and the possibility of developing an atomic bomb was obvious, and the possibility that they would develop it before we did was very much of a fright. So I decided to go to the meeting at three o'clock . . . By four o'clock I already had a desk . . . and I had paper, and I was working as hard as I could and as fast as I could.[36]

Oppenheimer cleverly decided to entice a few big names, on the assumption that a flood of eager disciples would inevitably follow. Szilard, Teller, Fermi, Seaborg, Hans Bethe and a few others formed the critical mass. 'Almost everyone realized that this was a great undertaking,' Oppenheimer later reflected.

Almost everyone knew that if it was completed successfully and rapidly enough, it might determine the outcome of the war. Almost everyone knew that it was an unparalleled opportunity to bring to bear the basic knowledge and art of science for the benefit of his country. Almost everyone knew that this job, if it were achieved, would be a part of history. This sense of excitement, of devotion and of patriotism in the end prevailed.[37]

The Manhattan Project was a cross section of those who hated Hitler. In addition to many Eastern Europeans, a small British contingent joined the team after Churchill and Roosevelt signed the Quebec Agreement in August 1943. Churchill recognized that the British did not have the industrial capacity to build a bomb during the war, even if they did possess the expertise to do so. He traded what British scientists knew, or what they could contribute, for an agreement that the technology would be shared after the war. Eventually nineteen British scientists went to Los Alamos and thirty-five joined Lawrence at Berkeley.

Cramming so many huge egos into one tiny community might have been dangerous. But the war encouraged cooperation and tolerance. 'Here at Los Alamos', one scientist remarked, 'I found a spirit of Athens, of Plato, of an ideal republic.'[38] There were no class distinctions and little of the status hierarchy typical of most academic communities. 'When one considers that we lived, day after day, year after year, closely packed together', the wife of one scientist remarked, 'one can't help but marvel that we enjoyed each other so much.'[39] Teller called it 'a big happy family'. 'It was one of the few times in my life when I felt truly alive,' one physicist confessed.[40] Fermi, however, found the enthusiasm unsettling. The physics was fascinating and the company stimulating, but the purpose so distasteful. 'I believe your people actually *want* to make a bomb,' he once chided Oppenheimer.[41]

Los Alamos underwent its own chain reaction: the population doubled, then doubled again. Staff could bring families to Los Alamos only if they were married; those who were single had to say goodbye to sweethearts for the duration of the war. Since men dominated the sciences, this meant that there was a shortage of single women. Female secretaries and clerks stepped into the breach, but not sufficiently to satisfy the desires of the male population. Some women found this a problem, others an opportunity. Wilson, a member of the Town Council, recalled how one female dormitory doubled as a brothel:

> MPs . . . recommended that we close the dorm and dismiss the occupants. A tearful group of young ladies appeared before us and argued to the contrary. Supporting them, a determined group of bachelors argued even more persuasively against closing the dorm. . . . By the time we got that matter straightened out – and we did decide to continue it – I was a considerably more learned physicist than I had intended to be a few years earlier when going into physics was not all that different from taking the cloth.[42]

In the lab the scientists focused on fission, at home on fusion. Nearly 1,000 babies were born between 1943 and 1949, including 200 during the war. Needless to say, a considerable number were born out of wedlock. The population explosion worried Groves; instead of cooing cherubs, he saw demands for more food, more hospital beds and, eventually, more schools and teachers. At one point he ordered the commanding officer of the Los Alamos installation to do something about the babies, but never explained exactly what he had in mind.

Inexorable expansion meant that the cacophony of construction never ceased. While Groves was prepared to spend whatever was necessary on projects essential to the bomb, he resisted wasting money on creature comforts. Minimum standards provoked maximum annoyance. But the most irritating problem was the fragile supply of water during blisteringly hot summers. Staff were advised to share baths and to save water used for rinsing vegetables for washing floors. At the height of the crisis a directive, widely attributed to Groves, announced 'Residents will not use showers except in case of emergency.'[43]

'The only thing typical about the men of science at Los Alamos', one team member remarked, 'was that they were atypical . . . Living among them would not have been such fun had many of them not been a little peculiar.'[44] In the isolated community, eccentricities flourished like rare plants in a hothouse. Teller, for instance, played the piano to clear his head of confusing ideas, a remedy which annoyed neighbours since he mainly did it at night. When a colleague fell ill, friends searched medical books in the library for a diagnosis, instead of consulting on-site doctors. As eminent scientists, they assumed that medicine was a cinch. Oppenheimer had continually to remind colleagues that the official language was English.

They often lapsed into native tongues when deep in discussion of a problem, which made it difficult to maintain a low profile.

The town was a cross between army camp and mountain resort. A radio station was established, along with baseball, softball and basketball teams. By mid-1944, a makeshift golf course had been carved out of the desert. Scientists took to wearing cowboy clothes and got hooked on square dancing. Dances grew so popular that they spilled out of the largest halls. Even Fermi eventually joined in, though in a typically scientific way. He observed the dances, worked out the formula, and then managed to dance competently on his first try. But his partner complained that he 'danced with his brains instead of his feet'.[45] Fermi's fishing technique also annoyed purists. He insisted on using worms rather than the more sporting dry flies, on the grounds that, if the poor fish was going to die, it deserved a last meal.

Scientists were not allowed to tell anyone about the nature of their project nor indeed where they worked. Their address was simply 'United States Army, Post Office Box 1663'. Pseudonyms, or simply numbers, were substituted for real names on identity papers. Letters were censored and phone calls strictly monitored.

> The . . . phone calls were a nuisance. You'd tell Papa, or Uncle Joe, that you went on a picnic last Saturday. He'd ask you where you went and the monitor would cut into the connection to caution your answer. Frequently, you never were able to get your connection again.[46]

Outside the facility, scientists were not supposed to address each other by titles like 'Professor' or 'Doctor', so as to avoid arousing suspicion about the number of academics living in the area. Bodyguards followed the most prominent scientists, partially to protect them but also to keep them from betraying secrets. But, as Feynman discovered:

> There would be big holes in the outside fence that a man could walk through standing up. I used to enjoy going out through the gate and coming through the fence hole, and going out through the gate again, and in through the fence hole until the poor sergeant at the gate would gradually realize that this guy has come out of the place four times without going in once.[47]

Of the thousands of specialists who worked on the Manhattan Project, fewer than a dozen enjoyed an unfettered overview. The vast majority had to make do with rumour and intuition. Research and production processes were carefully compartmentalized, with each unit having little idea what was going on elsewhere. Groves later explained:

My rule was simple and not capable of misinterpretation – each man should know everything he needed to know to do his job and nothing else. Adherence to this rule not only provided an adequate measure of security, but it greatly improved over-all efficiency by making our people stick to their knitting. And it made it quite clear to all concerned that the project existed to produce a specific end product – not to enable individuals to satisfy their curiosity and to increase their scientific knowledge.[48]

Senior scientists often simply ignored the restrictions. 'Those kind of rules could not be obeyed [so] we used common sense,' Szilard admitted. 'Hardly a week passed that somebody did not come to my office at Chicago from somewhere, wanting to convey a piece of information to which I was not entitled. They usually did not ask me to conceal the fact that I came into possession of this information. All they asked was that I conceal from the Army the fact that they . . . had given it to me.'[49]

Locals understandably wondered about the steady flow of new people and the incessant construction. At various times, rumours circulated that poison gas, spaceships, whiskey and even submarines were being developed. Some swore it was a home for dissident Republicans, or a hostel for pregnant servicewomen. Oppenheimer sent colleagues to the La Fonda Bar in Santa Fe to spread rumours about an electric rocket since confusion served his purposes well. Dissimulation was directed not exclusively at the enemy. Groves was determined that 'nothing [should] . . . attract Congressional attention to our hi-jinks'.[50]

Midway through the project, nature reminded the scientists of the danger of their work. A pet cat took sick with a suppurating jaw. One of the Army vets diagnosed bone necrosis caused by radiation poisoning. The cat was transformed from pet to specimen as vets and doctors, unfamiliar with the disease, charted its decline. The poor animal declined according to a now familiar process: its hair fell out, its tongue swelled and ulcers appeared. When scientific curiosity waned, the animal was destroyed.

At the University of Chicago, Fermi's team spent the autumn of 1942 building an atomic pile in the squash courts underneath Stagg Field. The pile was originally planned for a purpose-built facility on the outskirts of the city, but a strike by construction workers forced the team to improvise. To carry out such work in the middle of an urban area involved huge risks, and difficult decisions. There was no real danger of the pile exploding like an atomic bomb but a massive release of radiation was possible. Arthur Compton, who assumed overall responsibility for the project, decided not to tell the university president, Robert Maynard Hutchins, exactly what was going on beneath his football stadium, on the grounds that people should not be told what they cannot understand. 'The only answer he could have given would have been – no. And this answer would have been wrong.'[51]

In December 1942, after months of painstaking research, Fermi and his team completed the first bona fide atomic reactor. The pile consisted of over 771,000 pounds of graphite, 80,590 pounds of uranium oxide and 12,400 pounds of uranium metal arranged in a carefully constructed matrix. The structure took about a month to build and cost about $1 million. A rod coated with cadmium, a neutron absorbing material, acted as a makeshift switch. In order to protect his team and avoid an uncontrolled reaction, the rod was 'connected on a piece of cotton clothesline over a pulley [with] two lead weights to make it "fail-safe" and return to its zero position when released'.[52] When the rod was withdrawn on 2 December 1942, the reaction began. A witness recalled:

> At first you could hear the sound of the neutron counter, clickety-clack, clickety-clack. Then the clicks came more and more rapidly and, after a while they began to merge into a roar; the counter couldn't follow anymore. That was the moment to switch to the chart recorder. But when the switch was made, everyone watched in sudden silence the mounting deflection of the recorder's pen. It was an awesome silence. Everyone realized the significance of that switch; we were in the high intensity regime and the counters were unable to cope with the situation anymore. . . . Suddenly Fermi raised his hand. 'The pile has gone critical', he announced.

The neutron intensity was doubling every two minutes, which meant that it would have reached a million kilowatts in 90 minutes. Fermi kept the process going for around four and a half anxiety-filled minutes, long enough for his colleagues to begin wondering what would become of them. 'It was as though we had discovered fire!' one of the technicians recalled.[53]

A bottle of Chianti was uncorked to celebrate Fermi's success. He reacted with customary aplomb. 'The event was not spectacular,' he later wrote, 'no fuses burned, no lights flashed. But to us it meant that the release of atomic energy on a large scale would be only a matter of time.'[54] Nuclear power had become reality; building a bomb was now simply a matter of engineering. Szilard, standing beside Fermi when the pile was shut down, felt torn between celebration and regret. 'I shook hands with Fermi and . . . said I thought this day would go down as a black day in the history of mankind.'[55] Compton, on the other hand, felt cause for celebration. 'The Italian navigator has just landed in the new world,' he said when he phoned Conant. 'The natives are friendly.'[56]

Less than two weeks later, Groves was ready with a plan for a large reactor. The great problem was where to put it, given the danger of meltdown. The site had to be well removed from centres of population, but also had to have a ready supply of electricity and water. These criteria seemed to contradict each other, but, on the Columbia River in south-eastern Washington, such a combination existed. Electricity could be tapped from the massive Grand Coulee and Bonneville dams and water was virtually limitless. The area, because of its inhospitable climate of freezing winters, scorching summers and low rainfall, was sparsely popu-lated, but for a few turkey farms and orchards.

At the end of January, 1943, Groves purchased nearly 500,000 acres near Pasco at a cost of $5.1 million. The area quickly underwent a massive and mysterious expansion as 45,000 miserable souls gathered to construct the Hanford Engineering Works. The contract went to the DuPont Corporation, despite the directors' initial reluctance to take on work which seemed so unpromising. They relented only after Groves appealed to their patriotism. The contract stipulated that DuPont would withdraw from the work at the end of the war, would be unable to benefit from any patents associated with it, and would be paid only its costs plus a $1 profit.*

Hanford was rock bottom on the list of coveted wartime jobs. Since employment was plentiful in 1943, only the desperate were drawn to Pasco. Toughness was a prerequisite. Advice given to new recruits listed a padlock as the most important item to bring. The favourite after hours entertain-ment was drinking, followed closely by brawling. Builders were instructed to put hinged windows on the saloons, the better for tossing teargas canis-ters in when rowdiness raged out of control. The only perk was that wartime meat rationing did not apply. As with all other Manhattan Project facili-ties, the shopping list of construction materials suited a colony of giants: tons of steel, enough concrete to fill a canyon and mountains of aggre-gate, sand and bricks. Between March 1943 and August 1945, contrac-tors built 554 buildings (not including residential accommodation); 64 underground high-level waste storage tanks, 386 miles of roads, 158 miles of railway, 50 miles of electricity lines and untold miles of fencing.[57]

The combined population of Benton and Franklin Counties jumped from 19,000 to 70,000 in a year. Subsidiary businesses sprang up to cater to the needs of the workers, with the effect that retail sales increased six-fold between 1942 and the end of the war.[58] Though the vast majority of workers were men, 4,000 women were recruited. The gender imbalance and the raucous environment proved a challenge for them. Buena Maris, Dean of Women at Oregon State College, was hired to 'promote stability . . . by providing a happy, safe, and constructive atmosphere in which women could work'. Housemothers were assigned to each of the women's

---

* In the end, government auditors paid the corporation just 66 cents since they had over-estimated the time necessary to complete the job and finished ahead of schedule.

barracks, and a library, Red Cross chapter and bingo nights were organized. A daily bus took women to shops in Pasco, though what they were supposed to buy there was not exactly clear. 'Girl of the week' competitions and beauty contests were designed to bolster morale, though the latter appealed more to the men than the women. On one occasion, the supervisor of Women's Activities complained that gravel roads on the site were destroying the heels of women's shoes, a huge problem given the wartime shortage of footwear. The next day, trucks began spreading asphalt.[59]

Out in eastern Tennessee, in a broad valley cut by the Clinch River and overlooked by the foothills of the Appalachian Mountains, a town grew from nothing. The area had so far been unaffected by war – not just this war, but every war of the previous century. Farmers worked small plots of land that had been in the family for generations. Outsiders found it quaint, but residents harvested little romance from rocky soil. This was the only life they knew, at least until compulsory purchase orders arrived from the 'guvment'. The bomb moved in, and 3,000 hillbillies moved out.

Isolation suited secrecy. But anyone approaching the town by accident inevitably wondered why a smooth four-lane highway led to nowhere. Roads were constructed not for getting people in, but for getting them out – quickly. Groves understood that, at any moment, evacuation might prove necessary. The town itself, and the facilities, were typical wartime construction, homage to minimum standards. Boxy houses moved resolutely toward the horizon, accompanied loyally by miles of barbed wire. Occasionally, despite the frenetic pace of construction, managers were forced to improvise in order to satisfy workers' needs. A huge striped circus tent was turned into a workers' cafeteria.

The project was officially named the Clinton Engineering Works, but it is better known as Oak Ridge – the name given to the nearby housing estate completed in the summer of 1943. Oak Ridge consumed one quarter of the entire Manhattan Project budget, and brought disappointment in similarly massive proportion.

At Oak Ridge, Lawrence's dreams were projected in cinemascope. His latest calutron, when allowed to run for a month, had produced 100 micrograms of partially separated U-235. Oppenheimer wanted 100 kilograms – in other words, demand exceeded supply by a factor of one billion. The ever-buoyant Lawrence remained unfazed, even though his colleagues grew a tad worried. He envisaged magnification of all aspects of his Berkeley machine, so as to produce 100 grams of U-235 per day and a 30-kilo bomb core in 300 days. But, since the Berkeley cyclotron was already pretty prodigious, Oak Ridge had to be huge. Eventually, 268 buildings were constructed to house the Y-12 electromagnetic complex – accelerators, associated machinery, supply stores, offices, etc. It employed 22,000 workers at the peak of wartime production. The total population swelled to 100,000 within eighteen months.

Oak Ridge is testimony to the ingenuity and determination of wartime America. The plant was constructed from scratch in less than a year. The vacuum system of the cyclotron involved perfection tolerances of an order never before encountered in a major construction project. The magnets weighed between three and ten thousand tons and used as much power as a large city. They were so strong that workers could feel their pull through the nails of their shoes, or the pins in their hair. They also caused unforeseen strains on the plumbing system when 14-ton water tanks moved as much as three inches.

Electromagnets require miles and miles of copper wire, yet copper was not exactly plentiful. The US did, however, have lots of silver sitting in government vaults. Representatives from the Manhattan District approached the Treasury and announced that they needed between five and ten tons. That drew a snooty reply: 'silver is never measured in tons; our unit is the Troy ounce'. Eventually they asked for, and got, 395 million troy ounces, or about 13,500 tons. The wiring in the magnets alone was valued at $300 million.*

After the behemoth lumbered to life, its daily yield was still measured in mere grams. Lawrence, ever the optimist, argued for further expansion, promising that production would increase exponentially. He claimed that by doubling the facility 500 grams of 85 per cent pure U-235 could be produced every day. Groves remained suspicious, but found he could not afford to quibble over Lawrence's arithmetic. Since the facility as it stood could not possibly satisfy the demand for U-235, the only option was to expand.

A new set of mysterious glitches then developed. Engineers investigating a malfunctioning machine worked for days before discovering that a mouse had invaded a mechanism thought to be impenetrable. On another occasion, an entire building had to be shut down when a suicidal bird managed to short the power supply. Workers stood idle while engineers sweated. Eventually all of the forty-eight huge magnets had to be sent back to the manufacturer and rebuilt. Bored workers were entertained with music, slide shows, movies and games.

Adjacent to the electromagnetic plant, a massive gaseous diffusion facility – called K-25 – rose from the earth. Entirely new technologies and substances had to be developed in order to make it work. Research led to the development of a new sealing material which, after the war, was applied to frying pans and marketed as Teflon. Thousands of diffusion tanks were

---

* At the end of the war the silver was returned to the Treasury. According to Groves only 0.35 per cent was not recovered, but that's still 47.25 tons of silver.

constructed, some as large as 1,000 gallons. The entire facility was four storeys high, a half-mile long and 1,000 feet wide, or around forty-five acres of floor space. The huge plant, which employed 12,000 workers at its peak, had to be kept as spotlessly clean as a small laboratory, since dirt and grease could quickly foul the process. Construction proceeded even though the problem of a barrier material had not been solved. A massive investment went to a process that delivered little – proof perhaps that Groves was looking beyond the war.

Oppenheimer and Groves hoped that one separation method would eventually deliver the desired yield. They built different plants because they had no idea which would perform best. In early 1944, however, it dawned on them that the various processes might be used to complement each other. Partially enriched uranium from one plant could be further purified elsewhere. As a result of this realization, Oppenheimer looked again at thermal diffusion, a process developed independently, and on a small scale, by Philip Abelson of the Naval Research Laboratory in Philadelphia. Oppenheimer had originally rejected it because it did not promise the purity he needed. But he now thought it might be used in combination with the calutrons at Oak Ridge, particularly given the difficulties encountered with gaseous diffusion. Groves immediately commissioned a thermal diffusion plant, which was built in just ninety days.

In 1939 Bohr had warned that pulling a sufficient amount of U-235 out of uranium ore was impossible unless a country was willing to turn itself into a huge factory. Teller remembered this warning when Bohr visited late in the war. 'I was prepared to say, "You see . . .", Teller recalled. 'But before I could open my mouth, he said, "You see, I told you it couldn't be done without turning the whole country into a factory. You have done just that."'[60] The Manhattan Project, including all the separation facilities, was built by the United States at a cost of around $2 billion, an industrial conglomerate equal in size to the entire American auto industry.

When he took on the project, Oppenheimer thought that a bomb would be available within a year of the Los Alamos facility being established. He, like other eminent physicists, thought that the most important scientific discoveries had been made and all that remained was an engineering job – complex, but manageable. In fact, each solution gave birth to new difficulties.

The most obvious problem was to construct a device capable of making a chain reaction occur. This was, Groves felt, like trying 'to build an automobile full of watch machinery, with the precision that was required of watchmaking, and the knowledge that the failure of a single part would mean complete failure of the whole project'. A number of ideas were discussed, but the most promising seemed to be a gun which fired a sub-critical mass of U-235 into another sub-critical mass at sufficiently high speed to cause both to go super-critical. The gun could not, however, be so large and unwieldy that it was incapable of being delivered by aeroplane.

Another design relied on the principle of implosion. In very simple terms, a quantity of fissionable materials would be squeezed to a point of criticality. Since the compression would have to be of incredibly high pressure and speed, the logical solution seemed to be to use explosives. But conventional explosives were too clumsy; they would blow the sub-critical mass apart rather than squeeze it rapidly and uniformly. Neddermeyer thought that explosive charges might be shaped to act like 'lenses' to focus compression. That solution, however, seemed so implausible that it was not at first given much hope. Neddermeyer suffered considerable derision for doggedly supporting it.

Both bomb types were pursued simultaneously, in the hope that one would work. The gun bomb implied a shape about 17 feet long and just 2 feet in diameter – a very large cigar. It was originally nicknamed 'Thin Man' – in homage to Roosevelt, but, when the barrel was shortened, it became 'Little Boy', in reference to no one. An implosion bomb, on the other hand, would take the form of a large egg – around 5 feet in diameter and slightly over 9 feet long. It became 'Fat Man' – after Churchill. The names were originally conceived to allow those assigned the task of finding and adapting bombers to discuss their work without divulging secrets.

In November 1943, Wilson's team made a hugely important discovery. They found that the neutrons in U-235 were nearly all emitted in the first thousand millionth of a second, quite fast enough to ensure that, if the gun method were used, a suitably intense fission reaction would take place before the gun blew itself apart. This suggested that Little Boy would be successful, as long as the raw materials to make it could be collected in time.

Further research then revealed that the gun design would not work with plutonium since the sub-critical pieces could not be brought together fast enough to prevent premature explosion. By July 1944, Oppenheimer faced a classic dilemma: producing plutonium was relatively easy, but getting it to explode was difficult. Getting U-235 to explode was simple, but producing it was hard. Oppenheimer told Conant that, over the coming year, his team would probably be able to produce only one gun-type bomb, given the difficulty in collecting U-235. A single weapon, assuming it worked, might prove a strategic liability since, once used, it could not be followed with a second strike. One bomb alone might simply stiffen enemy resistance, or, worse, provoke a counter-strike.

Pessimists still assumed that Germany was racing forward with its own bomb. This assumption was reinforced in early 1944, when allied agents learned that a shipment of heavy water was leaving Norway, bound for Germany. The best option for stopping the shipment seemed to be to sink the rail ferry carrying it across Lake Tinnsjö. The Norwegian agent Knut Haukelid, working on instructions from London, managed to get aboard the ferry, thanks in part to a friendly crewman who assumed he was a fugitive from the Gestapo. Haukelid and his team set explosives and then escaped, fully aware that they had condemned their kind-hearted crewman to death. The ferry and its cargo sank like a rock in the middle of the lake, killing twenty-six passengers and crew.

Meanwhile, the plutonium problem inspired renewed enthusiasm for implosion. Oppenheimer was forced to overcome his disdain for Neddermeyer, with whom relations had soured. By August, however, Neddermeyer was no further forward in achieving a symmetrical shockwave and Oppenheimer again lost patience. Implosion was causing so much aggravation that he briefly considered resigning. Despite considerable reluctance, George Kistiakowsky eventually agreed to take over the project even though it meant entering the vipers' nest of colleagues loyal to Neddermeyer.

Implosion was not simply a problem of transferring key personnel. Making a new type of bomb involved wholly new engineering processes, which meant an additional 600 staff had to be brought to Los Alamos. Fortunately, the Army had recently established a Special Engineering Detachment – the draft intake was combed of those with special skills, who were then assigned to weapons projects. Most had been to college; some even had Ph.D.s. Oppenheimer immediately requested a consignment of this new intake. Men who thought they were headed for Europe or the Pacific theatre ended up in Los Alamos instead. Not all welcomed the reprieve. Since the new personnel were soldiers first, Groves treated them as such, cramming them into draughty barracks and forcing them to do mindless drill in addition to their exhausting work in the lab.*

One of the SEDs working for Kistiakowsky was David Greenglass. Unlike the civilian members of the project, those in the Army could not bring their spouses. Greenglass missed his wife Ruth terribly and so was delighted when his generous brother-in-law Julius Rosenberg gave Ruth $150 to travel to Albuquerque for their second wedding anniversary. On the fourth day of their time together, while walking along the banks of the Rio Grande, Ruth mentioned that Julius had friends in the Soviet Union who wanted information from David about what was going on at Los Alamos. David, though a former member of the Young Communist League, was initially appalled, but then came the usual arguments about the Soviet

---

* By May 1945, just over half of the laboratory workforce of 2,200 were SEDs.

Union being an ally and that sharing secrets would all contribute to defeating Hitler. Feeling somewhat indebted to Julius, David relented and, over the following months, fed him information about implosion. Julius was so delighted that he arranged for Ruth to move to a flat in Albuquerque permanently. The massive security network at Los Alamos seems never to have harboured suspicions about Greenglass.

In the autumn of 1944, Los Alamos was a decidedly gloomy place. Success, which might have proved an antidote to exhaustion, was in short supply. Despite extra help, implosion proved elusive. The problem of symmetry defied solution – unless the plutonium core was squeezed uniformly, it would squirt toward the point of weakest force, rather like toothpaste from a tube. Meanwhile, the news from Oak Ridge was consistently dismal.

Conant, after visiting Los Alamos in October 1944, reported to Bush that the gun method seemed as reliable as it could be without testing. He thought that such a bomb would yield around ten kilotons. Implosion provided no such certainty; Conant thought that it might at best yield around one kiloton. A short time later, further disappointments caused the predicted yield to be lowered to 500 tons.

Meanwhile, Kistiakowsky continued testing, in the process consuming a ton of high quality explosives every day. At last, on 14 December, impressive symmetry was achieved. This progress coincided with good news from Hanford, though, as always, three steps forward were followed by two steps back. On 26 September 1944, B-pile, the world's first bona fide atomic reactor, went active. Engineers celebrated, some with whiskey, others with shouts and hugs. But after a few hours, the pile mysteriously died. Panic followed. More time was wasted, but problems pointed the way toward new discoveries. D-pile went critical on 17 December and a repaired B-pile followed eleven days later. By the end of the year, Groves confidently announced that he would have enough plutonium to make eighteen bombs in the second half of 1945.

After a difficult autumn, winter seemed like spring. Implosion tests began to yield better results. Meanwhile, Luis Alvarez developed circuits to enable detonators to fire with millionths of a second accuracy – an essential prerequisite to symmetrical implosion. Though it was still dangerous to assume that all the research at Los Alamos would come together in perfect harmony, Oppenheimer felt confident enough to tell Groves that Fat Man could be tested in early July. Estimates of yield began to rise. Even the separation processes finally delivered good news. On 6 January, Conant calculated that the calutrons would be able to produce enough U-235 for one gun bomb in 6.8 months, which meant that Little Boy would be ready by 1 July.

The relentless progress coincided with a monumental development outside Los Alamos. Alsos, the intelligence unit formed by Groves to collect evidence on Hitler's nuclear project, followed allied armies through France and Germany. The mission, headed by Oppenheimer's old nemesis Pash, included the physicist Samuel Goudsmit. Various leads pointed them to Strasbourg, liberated in mid-November. There they found evidence to suggest that Germany had neither an atom bomb nor indeed a comprehensive programme to build one. Documents found in Strasbourg did, however, indicate that the Auergesellschaft works in Oranienburg, about fifteen miles north of Berlin, was engaged in processing uranium and thorium. Since the plant was in the Russian zone, Alsos agents could not seize it. Groves therefore arranged for it to be destroyed by air attack. On 15 March, 612 Flying Fortresses of the 8th Air Force dropped 1,506 tonnes of high explosive and 178 tonnes of incendiary bombs on the plant, completely obliterating it.[61]

Groves still wanted to know precisely how far the Germans had progressed and what, in particular, had become of their uranium stocks. On 22 April the missing uranium was located near Stassfurt. Groves told Marshall: 'The capture of this material, which was the bulk of uranium supplies available in Europe, would seem to remove definitely any possibility of the Germans making any use of an atomic bomb in this war.'[62] Still not satisfied, however, Groves demanded the capture of the German atom scientists, to prevent them falling into the hands of the Soviets. Pash and Goudsmit headed for the Black Forest town of Haigerloch, where Heisenberg, Weizsäcker, Hahn and von Laue were rumoured to be. There they found a rather crude atomic pile, but no scientists. Pash then raced to Hechingen where most of the scientists were cornered, though Heisenberg and Hahn eluded capture for a few more days.

A year earlier, in March 1944, Stimson had been approached by a Democratic Senator worried about apparent discrepancies in the War Department budget. Hiding an expenditure of $2 billion from prying Congressmen had not been easy. Stimson and Marshall had informed a few senior congressional leaders, who had somehow managed to bury the Manhattan Project costs within the general war budget. Even members of the relevant appropriations committees had been kept in the dark. Most congressmen played ball, but this particular Senator, in charge of a special investigating committee, demanded to know where the money had gone. Stimson found him 'a nuisance and pretty untrustworthy . . . He talks smoothly but acts meanly.'[63] Marshall leaned on him, persuading him not to investigate.

The Senator's name was Harry Truman. Later in the year he was selected

as Roosevelt's running mate. On 12 April 1945, the day Alsos agents discovered that Germany did not have an atom bomb, Roosevelt suffered a
cerebral haemorrhage and died. Truman immediately took over the
Presidency and only then learned where all the money had gone. Ironically,
it was Stimson who first briefed him about 'a new explosive of almost
unbelievable destructive power'. Welcoming the news, Truman concluded
that 'the bomb might well put us in a position to dictate our own terms
by the end of the war'.[64]

CHAPTER 4

It's a Boy!

Scientists at Los Alamos developed a lexicon to go with their work. Building the bomb was equated with pregnancy, the test with giving birth. A successful test would be a boy, a dud a girl. The team desperately wanted, but also dreaded, a son.

The scientists were so certain that Little Boy would work that they made no plans to test it. But, since implosion remained a massive uncertainty, Fat Man had to be tested. As with every other problem, this turned out to be more complicated than originally anticipated. It was not simply a case of taking the device to some desolate spot and detonating it. Every eventuality, no matter how remote, had to be anticipated, including that the bomb might be a great deal more powerful than expected. Psychiatrists were put on alert in case mass panic erupted in New Mexico.

The search for a test site extended as far away as Texas and Colorado, but eventually the team decided to stick to New Mexico. As they explored the plains looking for an appropriate spot to start the atomic age, their progress was monitored by Indian scouts high in the hills who communicated by smoke signal.

The site chosen for delivery of the child was high altitude desert in southern New Mexico, terrain that looked blasted even before it was bombed. The original Spanish settlers seem to have had an inkling of the fate awaiting the land. They called it Jornada del Muerto, or 'journey of death'. The area was owned by the state, which leased tracts to sheep and cattle ranchers. A section had been claimed by the federal government in 1942 and made into the Alamogordo Bombing Range. But a bigger bomb needed a bigger site, so some ranchers had to be evicted. A few agreed, but others proved as stubborn as the unforgiving environment in which they lived. They vacated their homes, but left their cattle behind as symbols of defiance. Soldiers were then sent in to teach the ranchers a lesson in patriotism. The cattle were the first martyrs of the atomic age.

Oppenheimer felt that a momentous event deserved a momentous title. He christened the site Trinity, for reasons which remain unclear. The most likely explanation is that he was influenced by the fourteenth of John Donne's *Holy Sonnets*, which begins: 'Batter my heart, three person'd God'.

But he might also have been recalling philosophical discussions with Bohr, particularly the way the Bomb might mirror the trinity of life, death and resurrection. It would cause terrible suffering, but it would also end the war. It might end war itself.

The facilities required for a test were, predictably, underestimated. Initial plans called for barracks for 160 men, yet 425 were present when test day arrived. Well water on site was heavily laced with alkali – which caused skin rashes – and gypsum – a highly effective laxative. Most water was, therefore, brought in by truck. A fearsome collection of poisonous snakes, scorpions and spiders spread alarm among those entrusted with testing the most ferocious weapon yet devised. But the area had its benefits: isolation allowed the unit at Trinity to win the prize for the lowest VD rate in the Army.

The cost probably exceeded $5 million. Contractors built about forty miles of roads, a network of heavily fortified observation bunkers and a steel tower at ground zero on which Fat Man would rest. The strangest bit of construction was Jumbo, a gigantic steel container shaped like a thermos flask. According to the original plans, Fat Man was to be placed inside this container so that, if the test failed, the plutonium could be recovered. Thus, the container had to be able to withstand the initial detonation of the TNT lenses. Jumbo had walls fifteen inches thick, weighed 214 tonnes and was the heaviest single object ever moved by rail. After it was unloaded from the train, a sixty-five wheel trailer, pulled by nine tractors, hauled it along a specially built road to ground zero. Not long after it was in place, Oppenheimer decided to abandon it since he was confident that the test would work and did not want the vessel to corrupt measurements of the explosion. This was a wise decision since the blast would have vaporised Jumbo, throwing 214 tonnes of radioactive steel particles into the atmosphere.

The Bomb is a three-headed beast of blast, heat and radiation.* Since no one knew for certain just how devastating the explosion would be, it was difficult to prepare for these calamities. Safety precautions which seemed excessive at the time appear cavalier now. The first observation posts took the form of reinforced bunkers 5,000 yards from ground zero. Most observers were placed well past 10,000 yards. To protect them from the flash, they were advised to put on sun cream and wear dark glasses, or, in some cases, welder's helmets. These precautions were thrown into disarray when the mischievous Fermi began taking wagers on whether Fat Man would ignite the atmosphere and, if so, whether the conflagration

---

* Strictly speaking, the correct word is 'radioactivity'. 'Radiation' in physics means anything that travels at the speed of light. But, since the term is often used to describe the harmful radioactivity emanating from an atomic explosion, it will be used here.

would destroy the entire world or be confined to New Mexico. How he intended to collect on the bet was not entirely clear. When word of it reached Groves, he blew a fuse, fearing that his blissfully ignorant workers would be driven to panic.

Radiation was the most worrying imponderable. Preparations for mass evacuations were made, but no one quite knew exactly how the baby would behave. Fallout would be governed by two great unknowns: the yield of the bomb and meteorological conditions. Groves, worried that uncertainties about radiation might delay the test or cause disquiet about the bomb in general, did his best to curb concern. When the physician James Nolan on 20 June 1945 predicted that the radioactive cloud might rise to 12,000 feet, Groves accused him of intentionally spreading alarm: 'what are you, some kind of Hearst propagandist?'[1]

The possibility of a dud plagued the scientists – about half expected no explosion at all. One pessimist captured the mood:

> From this crude lab that spawned the dud,
> Their necks to Truman's axe uncurled,
> Lo, the embattled servant stood
> And fired the flop heard round the world.[2]

Those who expected success differed widely on the anticipated yield. Around 100 scientists entered a betting pool, at a dollar a bet. Oppenheimer chose 300 tons of TNT, Ulam took 5,000–7,000 tons, and Teller, ever the optimist, took 45,000. Rabi, who joined the pool late, was forced to take 18,000 tons, a much higher figure than he believed possible, but as it turned out a fortunate misfortune.

Oppenheimer preferred a test on 17 July, but the actual date was determined by political events, not technical progress. Truman was due to meet Churchill* and Stalin in Potsdam on 15 July to discuss the postwar configuration of Europe and the completion of the Japanese war. That conference had been delayed by Truman in order to give time to complete the Bomb. It did not take a diplomatic genius to understand that Truman's authority would be strengthened enormously if he went to Potsdam with a Bomb in his pocket. According to his secretary, Groves 'stressed [to] Oppie the importance of trying to arrange for the 14th and . . . told Oppie to tell his people that it wasn't his fault but came from higher authority'.[3] Oppenheimer recalled that his team was 'under incredible pressure to get it done before the Potsdam meeting and Groves and I bickered for a couple of days'.[4]

---

* The British General Election of 5 July 1945 resulted in a victory for the Labour Party and its leader Clement Atlee. Because the results were not announced until 26 July, however, Atlee only attended the final stage of the conference.

The weather did not, however, cooperate. The chief meteorologist at the Trinity site, Jack Hubbard, had earned a reputation for accurate forecasts over the preceding months. He could not promise optimum weather until after 18 July. In the end Groves simply ignored his advice and fixed the date for 16 July, ordering Hubbard to make sure that the weather would be fine.

With that date in mind, Norris Bradbury drew up a schedule for what came to be called the Trinity Hot Run. It set out the precise times that the gadget and its core would be transported to the Trinity site, and detailed the final preparations and inspections. If all went well, the bomb would be hoisted on the tower and ready for detonation by 17.00 on Saturday, 14 July. Bradbury left Sunday clear, with the instruction that staff should 'look for rabbit's feet and four leafed clovers'. The last item on the schedule read, simply, 'BANG!'[5]

The plutonium core, about the size of an orange, was separated into sub-critical pieces and fitted into two special cases for the journey to the Trinity site. The cases were specially constructed to be waterproof, shockproof, heatproof and corrosion resistant – in other words, able to withstand every conceivable calamity that might result when the device itself was shipped to the Pacific theatre.

The bomb mechanism was transported on a large lorry from Los Alamos to Trinity, accompanied by military police. For reasons of security, the convoy travelled at night. Kistiakowsky, who had a macabre sense of whimsy, decided to delay the trip until ten minutes after midnight, so that it started officially on Friday the 13th. Though the journey was supposed to be secret, the convoy did not go quietly in the night. Leo Jercinovic, an SED, recalled:

> every time we went through a town . . . they would turn on the sirens and red lights and we would go through the town raising a raucous din – and of course this was early in the morning. They had hoped to warn off any drunken drivers who might drive into their path – which they succeeded in doing while waking up half the neighbourhood.[6]

Kistiakowsky arrived to find the Trinity team in a state of panic because the firing mechanism had failed its most recent test. He looked it over and discovered that, in the quest for absolute certainty, the device had been tested to destruction. Circuits designed to be used just once had been tested hundreds of times, causing soldered joints to melt. These were repaired and anxieties briefly cooled.

Final preparations were carried out in the open on the tower. Though the core was supposed to be a perfect fit, its receptacle having been tested on innumerable occasions using dummy cores, it could not be inserted.

'We realised that this one was plutonium and was very hot,' recalled Robert Bacher. 'It was producing heat and had expanded a little.'[7] More panic ensued. After a few tense minutes the core cooled sufficiently to be inserted.

On Saturday morning, just two days before the scheduled detonation, word arrived from Los Alamos that last minute tests of scale models had revealed poor implosion results. Oppenheimer, exhausted by the accumulated pressure of the last few years, vented his anger at Kistiakowsky. 'I was accused this time of failing the project, of being the cause of embarrassment to everybody from Oppie upwards. . . . Oppie was very angry, walking up and down desperately and so I said to him, "Look . . . I'll bet one month of my salary against $10 that this bomb will work." Oppie took the bet.'[8] Calm was restored when Bethe found flaws in the methodology of the tests, significant enough to throw doubt on the results.

Meanwhile, the bomb was winched to the top of the tower, an agonizingly slow journey. As it rose, workers stacked mattresses underneath it, to a depth of twenty feet. Their exact purpose was not entirely clear but it seemed the right thing to do. 'If it fell, at least it would have something soft to land on,' Jercinovic explained. Once the bomb was in place and final checks were made, all personnel were ordered to leave the site. But then Groves, in panic, decided that the world's most expensive and secretive weapon could not be left alone. A makeshift guard detail was rustled together, consisting of Kistiakowsky, some other scientists and a few soldiers. They were given a machine gun and told to spend the night under the bomb.

Joe McKibben, one of the chosen few, recalls how, during the night, 'I started dreaming Kistiakowsky had gotten a garden hose and was sprinkling the bomb. Then I woke up and realised there was rain on my face.'[9] And what a rain. On 15 July Hubbard had cautiously predicted that the following morning at 04.00 might prove suitable for the detonation. But then a ferocious thunderstorm arrived, with winds rising to 30 mph. The weather worsened as the appointed hour approached. At 02.00, with the storm in full fury, Groves rounded on Hubbard. 'What the hell is wrong with the weather?' he shouted. Hubbard suggested that the test should be delayed until dawn when conditions were likely to improve. Oppenheimer okayed the delay, but Groves remained livid. 'You had better be right on this, or I will hang you.'[10]

With all the worry and rain, few creatures slept well that night. Emilio Segré was awoken after midnight by a loud din he could not identify. He went outside to find hundreds of frogs mating in the puddles that had suddenly formed. For many, copulation preceded incineration by a matter of minutes.

At around 04.00 the weather improved slightly. Approval was given for firing at 05.30. The arming party at the tower threw switches to activate detonation mechanisms and then made for their vehicles, which fortunately started without any problems. In the bunkers within 10,000 yards from ground zero the men had been instructed to lie on their stomachs with feet facing the blast. They were not to get up or look at the explosion until after the initial flash. Elsewhere, precautions were devised according to the distance from ground zero. All had been instructed not to look at the initial flash and then to gaze at the explosion only through welder's lenses, or similar protection. On a hill twenty miles from ground zero Teller passed around a bottle of suntan lotion. As for the regulations about lying down and looking away from the blast, 'No one complied. We were determined to look the beast in the eye.'[11]

Twenty minutes from detonation, Sam Allison began the countdown. The final switches were thrown at T minus 45 seconds, putting the firing mechanism on automatic. Oppenheimer went rigid with tension, staring straight ahead and hardly breathing. At 05.29.45 the bomb tore the calm, changing the world for ever. 'Without a sound, the sun was shining; or so it looked,' wrote Frisch.

> The sand hills at the very edge of the desert were shimmering in very bright light, almost colourless and shapeless. This light did not seem to change for a couple of seconds and then began to dim. I turned round, but that object on the horizon which looked like a small sun was still too bright to look at. I kept blinking and trying to take looks, and after another ten seconds or so it had grown and dimmed into something more like a huge oil fire, with a structure that made it look a bit like a strawberry. It was slowly rising into the sky from the ground, with which it remained connected by a lengthening stem of whirling dust; incongruously, I thought of a red hot elephant balanced on its trunk. Then, as the cloud of hot gas cooled and became less red, one could see a blue glow surrounding it, a glow of ionized air . . . It was an awesome spectacle . . . And all in complete silence; the bang came minutes later; quite loud enough though I had plugged my ears, and followed by a long rumble like heavy traffic very far away. I can still hear it.[12]

Rabi described the same phenomenon more philosophically:

> Suddenly, there was an enormous flash of light, the brightest light I have ever seen or that I think anyone has ever seen. It blasted; it pounced; it bored its way right through you. It was a vision which was seen with more than the eye. It was seen to last forever. . . . It looked menacing. It seemed to come toward one.
>
> A new thing had just been born; a new control; a new understanding of man, which man had acquired over nature.[13]

The sun had been briefly recreated on earth. A colony on Mars, had such a thing existed, could have seen the flash. Elizabeth Ingram was travelling in a car when her sister suddenly shouted 'What was that light?' Her sister had been blind since childhood.[14] The pressure was measured at over 100 billion atmospheres, enough to create a huge dent in the earth's surface, half a mile across. The sand was fused into glass, later dubbed atomsite or trinitite. The snakes, rabbits, lizards, squirrels and sexually satiated frogs did not have a good morning. All living things within a mile were killed, including all insects.

Kistiakowsky, in a daze, approached Oppenheimer and said: 'Oppie, I won the bet.' Oppenheimer, even more bewildered, reached for his wallet, looked inside and said 'George, I don't have it.'[15] Meanwhile Fermi conducted a makeshift experiment to measure the bomb's power. He dropped small bits of paper from a uniform height before, during, and after the blast wave. He then measured the displacement. 'The shift was about $2^{1/2}$ meters, which, at the time, I estimated to correspond to the blast that would be produced by ten thousand tons of T.N.T.'[16] Later, more precise equipment provided a figure of about 18.6 kilotons.

'The strong, sustained, awesome roar', wrote Brigadier General Thomas Farrell, 'warned of doomsday and made us feel that we puny things were blasphemous to dare tamper with the forces hitherto reserved to the Almighty.' He was struck by the mood among the senior people involved in the project. The tension eased immediately 'and all started congratulating each other. Everyone sensed "This is it!" No matter what might happen now all knew that the impossible scientific job had been done. Atomic fission would no longer be hidden in the cloisters of the theoretical physicists' dreams.' Despite the frightening spectacle, Farrell found reason to be optimistic. He accepted that the Bomb 'was a great new force to be used for good or evil', but added, 'As to the present war . . . no matter what else might happen, we now had the means to insure its speedy conclusion and save thousands of American lives.'[17] The metallurgist Cyril Smith, on the other hand, was deeply worried about this new force. 'This is not a pleasant weapon we have produced . . . a city is henceforth not the place in which to live.'[18]

Some observers tried to capture what seemed a defining moment. 'The Atomic Age began at exactly 5.30 Mountain War Time on the morning of July 16, 1945,' William Laurence, the only journalist to witness the blast, wrote. He described 'an elemental force freed from its bonds after being chained for billions of years. . . . It was as though the earth had opened and the skies had split.' He felt as though he had 'been privileged to witness the Birth of the World – to be present at the moment of creation when the Lord said: "Let There Be Light"'.[19]

Weisskopf witnessed a chain reaction of emotions: 'Our first feeling was

one of elation, then we realized we were tired, and then we were worried.'
But Bradbury thought all the soul-searching rather contrived: 'Some people
claim to have wondered at the time about the future of mankind,' he
remarked. 'I didn't. We were at war and the damn thing worked.'[20]

While the blast was still echoing, Groves barked to his aides: 'We must
keep this thing quiet.' One replied: 'But, sir, I think they heard the noise
in five states.' That was in fact an exaggeration; the noise could be heard
in only three states – New Mexico, Arizona and Texas. Groves nevertheless insisted on secrecy. 'Can you give us an easy job, General, like hiding
the Mississippi River?' an aide replied.[21] An early morning detonation had
been chosen in part to keep curiosity to a minimum. But the rural West
is populated with early risers. A rancher in the process of saddling his
horse for an early morning ride watched helplessly as it bolted in fear. It
took two hours to catch the animal. John Magee and Joseph Hirschfelder,
assigned to track the radioactive cloud, encountered a donkey twenty-five
miles from ground zero which had apparently looked directly at the blast.
It was paralysed with fear, rooted to ground with mouth wide open and
tongue hanging out. A passer-by remarked: 'You boys must have been up
to something this morning. The sun came up in the west and went on
down again.'[22] Rowena Baca recalls how her grandmother 'shoved me and
my cousin under a bed . . . she thought it was the end of the world'.[23]

Rumours spread like tumbleweed. Laurence had been instructed by
Groves to prepare a number of press releases, designed to deal with every
contingency. These were filed in New York, with specific instructions given
on the appropriate conditions for release. One told of a large explosion
which resulted in no loss of life or destruction of property. A second
described an explosion which caused widespread damage in the
surrounding area. The third, and most bizarre, was to be used in the event
of utter catastrophe. While it provided no details of the blast, it contained
obituaries for the major personalities on the project (including Laurence)
who, the story went, were all killed as a result of a freak accident at
Oppenheimer's ranch. The first explanation was eventually used:

Several inquiries have been received concerning a heavy explosion which
occurred on the Alamogordo Air Base reservation this morning.

A remotely located ammunition magazine containing a considerable
amount of high explosives and pyrotechnics exploded.

There was no loss of life or injury to anyone, and the property damage
outside of the explosives magazine was negligible.

Weather conditions affecting the contents of gas shells exploded by the
blast may make it desirable for the Army to evacuate temporarily a few civilians from their homes.[24]

Through careful management of the news, the government kept its secret. A Chicago reporter inadvertently wrote a speculative piece about a huge meteor crash after being relayed information from a man who had witnessed the explosion from a passing train. On the following day two FBI agents paid a visit and grilled the reporter about what she knew. As it turned out, they were as ignorant as she was. The agents nevertheless convinced her that it would not be wise to investigate further.

Groves 'personally thought of Blondin crossing Niagara Falls on his tightrope, only to me the tightrope had lasted for almost three years'.[25] Not long after the blast, he was confronted by a distraught scientist, upset because sensitive measuring equipment had been destroyed. 'Well, if the instruments couldn't stand it', he replied, 'the bang must certainly have been a pretty big one.' As regards the immediate implications, the future seemed clear. 'The war's over,' Farrell remarked. 'Yes,' Groves replied, 'after we drop two bombs on Japan.' He then congratulated Oppenheimer with a simple 'I am proud of all of you'. Oppenheimer replied 'Thank you.'[26]

Groves nevertheless confessed that he was 'fully conscious that our real goal is still before us. The battle test is what counts in the war with Japan.'[27] To that end, he immediately got word to George Harrison (an adviser to Stimson at the War Office), who in turn cabled Stimson, eagerly awaiting news in Potsdam. At 7.30 p.m. on 16 July, Stimson received the following:

> Operated on this morning. Diagnosis not yet complete but results seem satisfactory and already exceed expectations. Local press release necessary as interest extends a great distance. Dr. Groves pleased. He returns [to Washington] tomorrow. I will keep you posted.

A slightly different metaphor was used the next morning: 'Doctor Groves has just returned most enthusiastic and confident that the little boy is as husky as his big brother. The light in his eyes discernible from here to Highhold and I could hear his screams from here to my farm.' Since Harrison's farm was forty miles from Washington and Stimson's farm, Highhold, was 200 miles away, Stimson got a clear indication of the intensity of the blast. Duly impressed, he remarked to colleagues: 'Well, I have been responsible for spending two billions of dollars on this atomic venture. Now that it is successful I shall not be sent to prison in Leavenworth.'[28]

After the explosion, Oppenheimer, a cultured man, chose words from the Bhagavad-Gita:

> If the radiance of a thousand suns
> Were to burst into the sky,

> That would be like
> The splendor of the Mighty One –

Then, when the full enormity of the explosion dawned on him, he chose another line from the same work: 'I am become Death, the shatterer of worlds.'

Just four hours after the Trinity blast, the USS *Indianapolis* sailed from San Francisco harbour, bound for Tinian Island. In its cargo was a 15 foot crate which contained Little Boy.

CHAPTER 5

Decisions

On 1 September 1939, Franklin Roosevelt expressed concern about aerial bombing and the impending war. He feared that, if bombing proceeded unchecked, 'hundreds of thousands of innocent human beings who have no responsibility for, and who are not even remotely participating in, the hostilities . . . will lose their lives'. He appealed to nations 'to affirm [their] determination that [their] armed forces shall in no event, and under no circumstances, undertake the bombardment from the air of civilian populations or of unfortified cities'.[1] Both Britain and Germany replied in the affirmative, the latter as it laid waste to Warsaw.

Both sides argued that their bombing campaigns satisfied Roosevelt's provisos, because neither recognized the existence of an unfortified city or an innocent citizen. Total war meant total involvement; every individual had become a combatant, and a target. Pragmatism smothered morality: bombing was widely condemned but all the powers bombed. All realized that moral platitudes would provide weak armour in an air war. Force begat force.

Evil powers bomb indiscriminately while the righteous conduct 'strategic bombing'. The difference is contrived – a matter of perspective. Indiscriminate bombing means killing civilians for the sake of attrition – the killing is the object. Strategic bombing, on the other hand, arises from the logic that a nation's industry is composed of its factories *and* its workers. Therefore, bombing homes can cripple industry in the same way as bombing plant. In the Second World War, General Curtis LeMay justified the saturation bombing of Tokyo by arguing that there were no civilian areas; the city was one giant factory. Because children made fuses it made strategic sense to kill kids.

The British claimed that Luftwaffe raids on London were barbaric and indiscriminate. But raids by the RAF on German cities, though much more intense, were legitimate attacks upon the enemy's productive capacity. 'Bomber' Harris, the *eminence grise* of British Bomber Command, argued that he who sows the wind should reap the whirlwind. Evil was defined by the first blow struck; guilt lay in the initiative, not the response. Thus, to bomb Germany day and night for four years was fitting retribution for the comparatively short blitz on Britain.

As the war progressed, it grew increasingly difficult for combatants to maintain the pretence that they were bombing military targets. Killing civilians is the last refuge of the desperate, and both sides were desperate. 'When I look around to see how we can win the war I see that there is only one sure path,' Churchill remarked to his Cabinet in 1940. 'That is an absolutely devastating, extenuating attack by very heavy bombers from this country upon the Nazi homeland.'[2] This was a case of forming strategy to fit capability. People became legitimate targets partly because bombers were imprecise. Factories were difficult to hit. Houses, or more precisely neighbourhoods, were, in contrast, impossible to miss.

Air strategists assumed that a sufficient number of bombs would break an enemy's spirit. But how many? When early raids did not cause collapse, larger ones followed. Force inevitably escalated, and each raid provoked exponential retribution. Since the results of a strike were difficult to measure, raids were measured not by what they achieved but by the force deployed – how many bombers, how many bombs.

The addiction to bombing prevented any reasonable assessment of its effects. Strategy was shaped by spite. On 24 August 1940 the Luftwaffe targeted oil storage tanks along the Thames but missed woefully, hitting central London instead. Churchill felt impelled to respond; in the following week the RAF bombed Berlin four times. Hitler, spitting venom, then promised: 'if the British air force drops two or three or four thousand kilograms of bombs, then we will drop in a single night 150,000, 180,000, 230,000, 300,000, 400,000, a million kilograms. If they announce that they will attack our cities on a large scale, then we shall wipe their cities out!'[3]

The vulnerability of their bombers to German defences forced the British to bomb at night, but that rendered precision impossible. The bombing campaign against Germany gradually evolved into a pattern of the British bombing cities indiscriminately at night and the Americans attempting to bomb precise military targets by day. Though the latter were not entirely successful, Americans took some moral pride in the fact that they had not lowered themselves to area bombing.

This strategy did not work in Japan where heavy winds and cloud cover made it virtually impossible for the Americans to carry out high altitude precision bombing. General Hap Arnold, the air commander, grew increasingly frustrated. Anxious for his forces to make an impact on the war, he brought in LeMay. The latter, like Harris, felt no qualms about killing civilians. LeMay decided to bomb Japanese cities with the new B-29s at low altitude at night. This implied an acceptance that the purpose was to kill people. In line with this strategy, a high proportion of incendiary bombs were dropped, the intent being to light fires among the mainly wooden structures. Though this might have seemed a barbaric way to wage war, it was, from the beginning, accepted as preferable to an invasion. 'I had no compunction about participating in the fire bombing raids,' Lt. General James Edmundson reflected.

> . . . by so doing . . . a lot of lives were saved, Japanese lives as well as American lives. Because had we been required to make . . . beachhead assault landings in the home islands of the Japanese, much as we did in Europe and on D-Day, we'd have lost millions of Americans, and probably even more Japanese.[4]

Military necessity was the mother of moral justification. The war had assumed a dynamic of its own which caused men to take actions which, just a few years earlier, would have been considered evil.

The German bombardment of Britain, or the Blitz, lasted about nine months. A total of 18,800 tons of high explosive was dropped by the Luftwaffe. That is 18.8 kilotons in modern parlance, or about the size of the atom bomb dropped on Hiroshima. The campaign caused 20,083 civilian deaths in London and another 23,602 across the rest of the country.* The Blitz was the beginning, Nagasaki was the end.

For most Manhattan Project scientists the Bomb was a deterrent, not a weapon. When, thanks to Alsos, it became clear that Germany was not building a bomb, the need to deter disappeared and the moral justification for the research evaporated. 'During 1943 and part of 1944 our greatest worry was the possibility that Germany would perfect an atomic bomb before the invasion of Europe,' Szilard recalled. 'In 1945, when we ceased worrying about what the Germans would do to us, we began to worry about what the . . . United States might do to other countries.'[5]

Rotblat promptly decided to quit. 'The whole project was taking on a different dimension,' he later remarked. 'It was not anymore something to prepare against the Nazis.'[6] In short, the Bomb had become a weapon. Samuel Goudsmit realized this after chatting with a War Department major. 'Isn't it wonderful that the Germans have no atom bomb?' Goudsmit remarked. 'Now we won't have to use ours.' The major retorted: 'Of course you understand, Sam, that if we have such a weapon we are going to use it.' Roosevelt certainly took that view. In early February 1945, Groves noted that the President 'informed me that if the European war was not over before we had our first bombs he wanted us to be ready to drop them on Germany'.[7] The Bomb was a weapon in search of a role.

---

* As with all cases of mass slaughter, disagreement exists over the precise number killed.

While many scientists were shocked by the idea that the bomb might actually be used, few followed Rotblat. The Sirens of discovery remained irresistible. 'Don't bother me with your conscientious scruples,' Fermi remarked to agonized colleagues. 'After all, the thing's superb physics.' But, science aside, most physicists still sought moral justification. A new line of reasoning became popular:

> If we don't develop this weapon and demonstrate to the world, by public experiment, its appalling nature, sooner or later some other unscrupulous power will attempt, unobtrusively and in all secrecy, to manufacture it. It will be better for the future peace of the world if humanity at least knows where it stands.[8]

In other words, if Pandora's box had to be opened, better that the Americans open it. Others hitched their conscience to nuclear power, which would light the world. Cheap, plentiful energy would wash away evil.

Bohr had never been one to hide in an ivory tower. Having long contemplated the responsibility of the scientist to his world, he was especially vexed by the Bomb which could not, he insisted, be treated like just another weapon. He felt that, for perhaps understandable reasons, the United States had rushed headlong toward construction, without considering the wider implications of atomic power. The Bomb implied new dangers, but also new opportunities. 'It appeared to me', he wrote in 1950, 'that the very necessity of a concerted effort to forestall such ominous threats to civilisation would offer quite unique opportunities to bridge international divergences.'[9] In other words, rather than being a cause of mistrust, the bomb might prove an inspiration for harmony.

After considerable struggle, Bohr secured a meeting with Churchill and Cherwell on 16 May 1944. Churchill was in foul temper. He did not really understand Bohr's concerns, or at least had no patience for them. He listened for half an hour, without interjecting, and then turned to Cherwell and asked: 'What is he really talking about? Politics or physics?'[10] That was a judgement more than a question. Bohr had been told to mind his own business. Churchill told Bohr:

> I cannot see what you are talking about. After all this new bomb is just going to be bigger than our present bombs. It involves no difference in the principles of war. And as for any post-war problems there are none that cannot be amicably settled between me and my friend President Roosevelt.[11]

Bohr next saw Roosevelt. On 26 August 1944, he told the President of the urgent need for international controls on nuclear power. He suggested that the Soviets should be alerted to recent developments. Bohr left the

White House confident that he had made real progress. Roosevelt seemed to suggest that approaches might be made to the Soviet Union and that Churchill might eventually be persuaded to see reason. But much depends on interpretation; Bohr might simply have been fooled by the President's avuncular nature. When Roosevelt met Churchill on 19 September at Hyde Park, the latter's scepticism prevailed. They agreed that

> The suggestion that the world should be informed regarding tube alloys,* with a view to an international agreement regarding its control and use, is not accepted. The matter should continue to be regarded as of the utmost secrecy; but when a 'bomb' is finally available, it might perhaps, after mature consideration, be used against the Japanese, who should be warned that this bombardment will be repeated until they surrender.

The President and Prime Minister also decided that 'enquiries should be made regarding the activities of Professor Bohr and steps taken to ensure that he is responsible for no leakage of information particularly to the Russians'.[12] Privately, Churchill confessed to Cherwell that 'the President and I are seriously concerned about Professor Bohr . . . It seems to me [he] ought to be confined, or at any rate made to see that he is very near the edge of mortal crimes'.[13] Roosevelt subsequently ordered the FBI to tail Bohr.

The politicians did not understand how this weapon differed radically from an ordinary bomb. They were told that it might have a yield equivalent to 20,000 tons of TNT, but force of this magnitude was difficult to comprehend. A more powerful bomb seemed simply a more efficient way to bring pressure to bear on the enemy. It did not seem, at this stage, to raise profound moral issues or to change the nature of war.

Aware of this problem of perception, Szilard advocated a demonstration of the weapon during the war. Without such a demonstration, he argued, 'it will be impossible to have a peace that is based on reality'. He was deeply worried that, within a short time, 'this weapon will be so powerful that there can be no peace if it is simultaneously in the possession of any two powers unless those two powers are bound by an indissoluble political union'.[14] Desperate to persuade Roosevelt to tread carefully, Szilard again called upon Einstein, whose subsequent letter to the President argued that any immediate military advantage gained by using the bomb would be grossly outweighed by the long-term political damage. But neither Szilard's warning nor Einstein's letter came to the notice of Roosevelt, who died suddenly on 12 April 1945.

Szilard immediately tried to see Truman but was refused access. He

---

* The codename for nuclear research.

went instead to James Byrnes, who would shortly become Secretary of State. Byrnes saw no reason for cooperating with the Soviets if, as Groves had advised, the American atomic monopoly would probably last for twenty years. According to Szilard, Byrnes thought the bomb would provide the perfect counterweight to Soviet bullying. 'I shared Byrnes' concern about Russia's throwing around her weight in the postwar period,' Szilard recalled; 'but I was completely flabbergasted by the assumption that rattling the bomb might make Russia more manageable.'[15] Byrnes was not the only one thinking along these lines. In a memo to Truman dated 25 April, Stimson stated that the Bomb might provide 'the opportunity to bring the world into a pattern in which the peace of the world and our civilization can be saved'.[16] Truman was pleasantly surprised that Stimson 'seemed at least as much concerned with the role of the atomic bomb in the shaping of history as in its capacity to shorten this war'.[17]

For Byrnes and Stimson the Bomb was a weapon, perhaps a diplomatic tool, but not a problem. Because the politicians had grown accustomed to mass destruction, they did not entirely appreciate how the Bomb was anything different. On 10 March 1945 a massive B-29 raid was unleashed on Tokyo. Incendiaries started a huge firestorm as oxygen was sucked into the conflagration, causing fierce winds which further fanned the flames. An area measuring sixteen square miles was devastated and over 83,000 people were killed outright, with another 1.5 million left homeless. Germany got similar treatment at Dresden. These raids prepared the way for the atomic bomb in the sense that mass destruction had become commonplace. The Tokyo raid rivalled anything that an atom bomb promised to achieve. But, as Szilard understood, comparison was inappropriate. Tokyo involved hundreds of aeroplanes and thousands of tons of explosives. The atom bomb would achieve similar destruction with one weapon and one plane. The technology was monopolized by one power. Its danger lay in its uniqueness – in the singularly efficient way it destroyed.

But Truman, the straight-talking man from Missouri, had no desire to philosophize about fission. He preferred instead an argument presented by Groves, who visited the White House on 25 April. Groves argued that Japan had always been a legitimate target. With an actor's sense of drama, he then told Truman that dropping the bomb on Japan would nullify the need for an invasion and therefore save perhaps 1.5 million lives. The figure was plucked from mid-air. The invasion plans then taking shape called for an initial attack on Kyushu scheduled for 1 November, followed by an attack on the Tokyo plain commencing on 1 March 1946. No less an authority than Marshall had predicted that the invasion might cost 40,000 American lives.*

---

* Estimates of the number of casualties in an invasion varied, but no one in authority really thought that half a million Americans would die, as Truman later claimed.

But, as Truman saw it, that was 40,000 more than would die if the bomb was used to end the war. Case closed.

Groves later claimed that 'no one who held a position of responsibility in the Manhattan Project could doubt that we were trying to perfect a weapon that, however repugnant it might be to us as human beings, could nonetheless save untold numbers of American lives'.[18] The number of Japanese who would die was not a consideration. This barbaric war had inured all belligerents to the suffering of the enemy. And, deep in the recesses of men's minds, there lurked the notion that the A-bomb was appropriate retribution for Pearl Harbor.

Money was also a concern. Groves and Truman understood that the $2 billion investment would only seem worthwhile if the bomb was used. Men, money and materials had been diverted from other more obvious wartime production. If the war ended without the bomb being dropped, critics would soon argue that Los Alamos had simply been a refuge for liberal intellectuals keen to escape the war. Furthermore, every parent of every GI, soldier or airman killed after the Trinity test would argue that his or her son had died in vain.

Truman would have been quite happy to leave issues relating to the bomb's use to the military. But Bush and Conant, aware of the unease among the scientists, felt that some serious matters needed airing. They pressed Stimson to form a committee to study questions of deployment. Stimson responded positively, despite Truman's lack of enthusiasm. The so-called Interim Committee, formed on 2 May, consisted of Stimson, Bush, Conant, MIT President Karl Compton and a few other senior officials. Truman reluctantly agreed that Byrnes would act as his representative. A scientific panel, consisting of Oppenheimer, Fermi, Arthur Compton and Lawrence, was then formed to advise the main committee.

According to Arthur Compton, the committee never really pondered whether the bomb should be used, only how it should be used. Dropping it on Japan was 'a foregone conclusion'.[19] As for the scientific panel, it stuck strictly to its remit, providing information about the bomb, not advice on deployment. Oppenheimer informed the committee that it would yield between 2,000 and 20,000 tons of TNT, that the radioactivity 'would be dangerous to . . . a radius of at least two-thirds of a mile', and that perhaps 20,000 Japanese would be killed. He did not address whether the bomb was actually necessary to secure victory. 'We didn't know beans about the military situation,' he subsequently claimed.[20]

Lurking in the shadows was Groves. While not an official member of the committee, he was, he admitted, 'present at all its meetings' and considered it his duty 'to recommend that the bomb should be dropped'. He saw himself as an antidote to the moralistic misgivings of the scientists: 'great numbers of our boys were dying every day . . . in the war against the Japanese. So far as I am aware, none of the scientists who opposed the dropping of the bomb had any near relatives in the field. So they could very well afford to be soft.'[21] Groves was naturally delighted when the committee recommended on 31 May that

> we could not give the Japanese any warning; that we could not concentrate on a civilian area; but that we should seek to make a profound psychological impression on as many of the inhabitants as possible. . . . the most desirable target would be a vital war plant employing a large number of workers and closely surrounded by workers' houses.[22]

The recommendation neatly straddles the old world and the new. The committee pretended that the bomb would be used on a military target, but widened the definition of such to include workers' houses. The legitimacy of a target had been stretched to accommodate the power of the bomb. In other words, the committee had approved terror bombing but called it something else.

In 1947, Byrnes explained why the committee had ruled out a warning to the Japanese. It was thought that, if the target was announced in advance, the Japanese would place American POWs in the area as a human shield. More importantly, the committee feared that, if the weapon proved to be a dud, it would embarrass the United States and give heart to the Japanese. Making them surrender would become even more difficult. Truman agreed with this reasoning. The committee had fulfilled its purpose, namely to validate decisions already made. The Japanese fate was sealed a full six weeks before the Trinity test because no one saw fit to alter a pre-determined course toward deployment. At no time did either Truman or the Interim Committee seriously explore the idea of not using the bomb.

The Scientific Panel acknowledged 'our obligation to our nation to use the weapons to help save American lives in the Japanese war'. That ruled out a non-aggressive test, or what Oppenheimer called 'exploding one of these things like a firecracker over the desert'.[23] But the scientists did advise that the USSR should be informed about the Bomb, in order to 'contribute to improved international relations'. Having raised this issue, the panel then quickly backed away, claiming that 'We have no . . . special competence in solving political, social and military problems which are presented by the advent of atomic power.'[24] Prevarication of this sort invited rejection of the panel's views.

Truman was not about to have a cosy chat with the Soviets on the subject of atomic bombs. As Szilard had noticed, the administration hoped that the bomb could be used to manipulate the USSR. Secrecy served this purpose. The extension of Soviet power – particularly in Eastern Europe – deeply worried the Americans. At the Yalta Conference, Roosevelt and Churchill had been keen to secure a promise of Soviet participation in the Pacific War. They had achieved this wish by granting Stalin important concessions including the maintenance of communist rule in Outer Mongolia, the lease of Port Arthur and the annexation of the Kurile Islands. These concessions were regrettable but, at the time, unavoidable. Byrnes privately expressed the view that 'somebody had made an awful mistake in bringing about a situation where Russia was permitted to come out of a war with the power she will have'.*[25] The Bomb, however, offered an escape from commitments. On 14 May, in anticipation of the Bomb, Stimson argued that 'we have got to regain the lead and perhaps do it in a pretty rough and realistic way'. He thought that the US held all the cards. 'I called it a royal straight flush and we mustn't be a fool about the way we play it.'[26]

Stimson felt that, at Potsdam, 'it may be necessary to have it out with Russia'. But timing was unfortunate, since the Bomb was not expected to be ready in time for the summit, then scheduled for the first week of July. 'Over any such tangled wave of problems the S-1 secret [the atom bomb] would be dominant and yet we will not know until after that time probably . . . whether this is a weapon in our hands or not,' he complained. 'We think it will be shortly afterwards, but it seems a terrible thing to gamble with such big stakes in diplomacy without having your master card in your hand.'[27]

Meanwhile, the scientists grew increasingly anxious about the possibility that the Bomb might be used. A group at the Metallurgical Lab in Chicago, headed by James Franck, made a last ditch effort on 11 June to change the government's mind. Their report argued against use of the bomb not only on moral grounds but also because it would be a starter's pistol for a new arms race. They advised instead that the United States should make an overt demonstration of good will by saying to the world: 'You see what weapon we had but did not use. We are ready to renounce its use in the future and to join other nations in working out adequate supervision of the use of this nuclear weapon.'[28] The Interim Committee made note of the Franck report at its 21 June meeting, but simply reiterated its recommendation for deployment 'at the earliest opportunity . . . without warning'.[29]

In one final effort, on 17 July, Szilard sent the government a petition signed by sixty-nine of his colleagues, which argued that the US carried an 'obligation of restraint'. Using the bomb would weaken the American moral position and make it 'more difficult for us to live up to our responsibility of bringing the unloosened forces of destruction under control'.[30] A horribly dangerous arms race would inevitably develop. Conspicuously

---

* Byrnes blamed the British.

absent from the petition was Teller. He claimed that Oppenheimer persuaded him not to sign the petition.

> He thought it improper for a scientist to use his prestige as a platform for political pronouncements. He conveyed to me in glowing terms the deep concern, thoroughness, and wisdom with which these questions were being handled in Washington. Our fate was in the hands of the best, the most conscientious men of our nation. And they had information which we did not possess.[31]

Teller explained his refusal to Szilard:

> First of all let me say that I have no hope of clearing my conscience. The things we are working on are so terrible that no amount of protesting or fiddling with politics will save our souls. . . .
>
> But I am not really convinced of your objections. I do not feel that there is any chance to outlaw any one weapon. If we have a slim chance of survival, it lies in the possibility to get rid of wars. . . .
>
> Our only hope is in getting the facts of our results before the people. This might help to convince everybody that the next war would be fatal. For this purpose actual combat-use might even be the best thing.[32]

Teller's letter to Szilard hit upon a fact which anti-nuclear campaigners have consistently skirted: it is not possible to un-invent a weapon. Szilard's petition did not cause the government to break stride; it was dismissed as the idealistic raving of ivory-tower scientists. Groves in fact began amassing evidence against Szilard, who had not shown 'wholehearted cooperation in the maintenance of security'.[33]

While the scientists fretted, Groves concentrated on practical matters. In order to keep to a tight schedule, the logistics of deployment had to be drawn up long before it was certain that the device itself would work. A bomber with the capacity to carry Fat Man or Little Boy had to be found and adapted accordingly. Special flying techniques had to be devised to allow the crew to drop the bomb without being destroyed by it. Appropriate targets had to be selected. Then there was the problem of final assembly. An atom bomb could not be loaded on a plane fully armed. The job was given to Captain William 'Deke' Parsons, a naval gunnery officer. As he related to Groves, assembling Little Boy would be no more difficult than field-arming a torpedo. But assembling Fat Man would be 'comparable . . . to rebuilding an airplane in the field'.[34] The problem was indeed huge, but in an age of wizardry, mere magic had become commonplace.

In June 1943 Groves asked the Air Force for a plane capable of carrying a bomb 17 feet long. To his horror, it seemed that only a British Lancaster had that capacity. But then someone suggested adapting the bomb bays in the B-29 Superfortress, a brand new craft that had not yet been flown in combat. Eventually, seventeen B-29s were modified to enable them to carry the two different atom bombs. By August 1944, a new unit was established to prepare for the first missions. The 393rd Bombardment Squadron, then stationed in Fairmont, Nebraska, provided the personnel. Command went to Lt. Colonel Paul Tibbets, widely regarded as one of the best bomber pilots in the Air Force. His instructions on assuming his new post were beguilingly mysterious:

> You have to put together an outfit and deliver this weapon. We don't know anything about it yet. We don't know what it can do. . . . You've got to mate it to the airplane and determine the tactics, the training and the ballistics – everything. These are all parts of your problem. This thing is going to be very big. . . . it has the potential and possibility of ending the war.[35]

The operation was codenamed Silverplate. Whatever Tibbets wanted he had only to whisper 'Silverplate', and his wish would be granted. While he understood vaguely that his unit would handle a new weapon of extraordinary power, his men had no such inkling. They nevertheless sensed that there was something special about their assignment, since they practised manoeuvres inappropriate to normal bombing missions.

Groves was determined that, if Truman wanted, the bomb could be dropped on Japan within days of its first test. By preparing for this scenario, he made it more likely. Though he never admitted it, he was probably disappointed that the bomb could not be used against the Germans, who had inspired its development. He certainly feared that the war in the Pacific might end before the bomb was ready. Thus, despite Germany's defeat, he remained a man in a hurry. 'I don't think there was any time when we worked harder at the speed-up than in the period after the German surrender,' Oppenheimer later recalled.[36]

At the beginning of 1945, Marshall ordered Groves to assume responsibility for targeting decisions. Groves responded by gathering a committee to determine criteria for selecting targets. The group, which consisted of physicists, mathematicians, explosives experts, military personnel, meteorologists, and others, met for the first time on 27 April 1945. In other words, over three weeks before the Interim Committee would advise on whether to bomb Japan, the Target Committee was discussing what cities to hit. It came up with four requirements. Firstly, since the effect of the bomb would primarily be blast and, secondarily, fire, the target had to consist of dense, highly flammable construction. Secondly, it should contain a built-up area of at least one square mile, as that would be the area of greatest explosive effect. Thirdly, it should have important strategic and military value. Finally, the target should have escaped earlier bombardment, so as to facilitate measurement of the bomb's effect. Groves added that it should be a place 'the bombing of which would most adversely affect the will of the Japanese people to continue the war'.[37] This implied a large city with a military base or munitions plant within it. The committee discussed 'the possibility of bombing the Emperor's palace' but decided against that recommendation.[38]

Based on these considerations, four cities – Hiroshima, Kokura, Nigata and Kyoto – made the immediate short list and were henceforth omitted from the regular bombing campaign. Of the four cities, Hiroshima was the only one that did not have an allied prisoner of war camp nearby, a fact that caused it to rise to the top of the list. Much to the chagrin of Groves, Stimson removed Kyoto on the grounds that it was important to preserve its ancient temples. He feared that the bitterness caused by 'such a wanton act' would complicate postwar reconstruction efforts.[39]

The 'military value' criterion was loosely applied since, if the target cities had indeed been of great military significance, they would already have been bombed. By this stage in the war, bombing had become a weapon of terror, albeit an inefficient one. It was nevertheless expected that the atomic bomb would kill with such ruthless efficiency that a resurgence of morale among survivors after the raid would be unlikely. Nevertheless, neither the Target Committee nor the Truman administration thought that just one bomb would do the trick. The four cities selected were not a short list from which one would be chosen, but, rather, four cities to be bombed in succession as supplies of the weapon permitted.

The emphasis upon civilian morale is evident in three Target Committee recommendations: (1) that aiming points need not be specified, (2) that industrial targets need not be given high priority because the targets were too small and highly dispersed, and (3) that the bomb should be dropped in the centre of the city (bombing on the outskirts, where militarily important facilities were most likely to be, would waste the power of the bomb on sparsely inhabited areas). In other words, talk of military targets was mere window dressing designed to assuage the guilt of those who found terror bombing unpalatable. This bothered Stimson, who had not fully adjusted to recent trends in aerial warfare. Worried that the United States might 'get the reputation for outdoing Hitler in atrocities', he wanted the bomb used exclusively on industrial targets.[40] Marshall shared Stimson's unease, arguing that the bomb should be used on a specifically military target and then only after a precise warning was given. 'We must offset by such warning methods the opprobrium which might follow from an ill-considered employment of such force,' he argued on 29 May.[41] But their wishes were incompatible with current practice, not to mention with the comprehensive power of the bomb.

Stimson was caught between a rock and a hard place. He hated the idea of bombing civilians indiscriminately, but realized that an invasion of the Japanese mainland might be even more costly and barbaric. The solution to this dilemma seemed to lie in making the Japanese see reason. To this end, he felt that the administration needed to adjust its demands for unconditional surrender:

> I believe Japan *is* susceptible to reason . . . to a much greater extent than is indicated by our current press and other current comment. Japan is not a nation composed wholly of mad fanatics of an entirely different mentality than ours. On the contrary, she has within the past century shown herself to possess extremely intelligent people.

Stimson felt that 'a carefully timed warning' by the United States, Britain, China and the Soviet Union might provide the context for the Japanese to surrender. He added that 'if . . . we do not exclude a constitutional monarchy under her present dynasty, it would substantially add to the chances of acceptance'.[42]

Stimson's argument had strong support from Joseph Grew (Acting Secretary of State), Ralph Bard (Under-Secretary of the Navy) and Major General Clayton Bissell of the Military Intelligence Division. The latter argued that 'If the Japanese become convinced that the only terms they can expect are unconditional surrender, it is quite possible that they will continue the hopeless struggle until their power of resistance is completely destroyed.'[43] But other Truman aides, particularly Byrnes, insisted upon unconditional surrender. He thought Stimson's idea that the Japanese should be allowed to keep their monarchy smacked of appeasement, since monarchy and militarism existed in symbiosis.

Evidence suggests that the Japanese were prepared to end the war if something less than unconditional surrender had been demanded. On 13 July the Americans intercepted a message from Foreign Minister Shigenori Togo to Naotake Sato, the Ambassador in Moscow, to the effect that the Emperor, 'mindful of the fact that the present war daily brings greater evil and sacrifice upon the peoples of all belligerent powers, desires from his heart that it may be quickly terminated'. But the sticking point was unconditional surrender, which was 'impossible for us to accept . . . no matter in what guise'.[44] If those terms were maintained, the Japanese would have to continue fighting. Togo wanted Sato to make peace feelers through the Soviets, to explore the possibility of keeping them out of the war. The messages continued for the next ten days, with Sato repeatedly pouring cold water on the notion that the Soviets might be separated from their allies. These notes might actually have made the Americans less inclined to relax their demands. As Bissell remarked, the administration interpreted Togo's efforts as a cynical scheme to undermine Soviet–American relations, 'whereby they can keep [the Soviets] out of the war and possibly prolong hostilities until the Allies have grown weary of fighting'.[45]

The Japanese were not likely to accept unconditional surrender unless the war was made more horrible. The horror could come through an escalation of conventional bombing or through Russia's invasion of Manchuria. Both were problematic. Escalating the bombing was difficult, firstly due to logistical problems, but mainly because most Japanese cities had already been bombed extensively. Russia's entry into the war might have tipped the balance, but it would have extended Soviet hegemony in the area, a possibility which Truman found unpalatable. In these circumstances the Bomb seemed the perfect solution.

All of these considerations weighed on Truman's mind when he went to Potsdam. Back in New Mexico, Groves was fully aware of the political dynamic:

> I knew the effect that a successful test would have on the issuance and wording of the Potsdam ultimatum. I knew also that every day's delay in the test might well mean the delay of a day in ending the war; not because we would not be ready with the bombs . . . but because a delay in issuing the Potsdam ultimatum could result in a delay in the Japanese reaction, with a further delay to the atomic attack on Japan. Obviously, a reasonable time had to be allowed for the Japanese to consider the ultimatum.[46]

A telegram was sent to Truman on the 16th telling him of the successful test. On the following day he met Stalin for the first time and got a commitment that the Soviets would attack Japan on 15 August. 'I've gotten what I came for,' Truman wrote to his wife. 'We'll end the war a year sooner now, and think of the kids who won't be killed! That is the important thing.'[47] By the 18th, Truman felt confident that the 'Japs will fold up before Russia comes in. I am sure they will when Manhattan appears over their homeland.'[48]

On the 21st, Truman received a detailed report of the Trinity test from Groves. 'The President was tremendously pepped up by [the news], and spoke to me of it again and again,' Stimson recorded. 'He said it gave him an entirely new feeling of confidence.' Churchill was shocked by the effect. 'When [Truman] got to the meeting after having read the [Groves] report he was a changed man. He told the Russians just where they got on and got off and generally bossed the whole meeting.'[49] Assistant Secretary of War John J. McCloy thought that Churchill and Truman 'went to the . . . meeting like little boys with a big red apple secreted on their persons'.[50]

On 24 July, Truman sauntered over to Stalin and announced that the United States had a new, very powerful weapon. No further details were given. Stalin feigned nonchalance – a statue would have been more expressive. He replied that he was delighted to hear the news and hoped the US would make use of the new weapon soon against the Japanese. Churchill wrongly concluded that Stalin 'had no idea of the significance of what he was being told'.[51] In fact, before leaving for Potsdam, Stalin undoubtedly saw a short intelligence report which provided an impressively accurate description of Fat Man and predicted that the first test would take place on 10 July. The information had come from Klaus Fuchs and Theodore Hall, two scientists on the project.

'We have discovered the most terrible bomb in the history of the world,' Truman commented after reading the Groves report.

> It may be the fire destruction prophesied in the Euphrates Valley Era, after Noah and his fabulous Ark.
>
> This weapon is to be used against Japan between now and August 10th. I have told . . . Stimson to use it so that military objectives and soldiers and sailors are the target and not women and children. Even if the Japs are savages, ruthless, merciless and fanatic, we as the leader of the world for the common welfare cannot drop this terrible bomb on the old Capital or the new.*
>
> He & I are in accord. The target will be a purely military one and we will issue a warning statement asking the Japanese to surrender and save lives. I'm sure they will not do that, but we will have given them the chance. It is certainly a good thing for the world that Hitler's crowd or Stalin's did not discover this atomic bomb. It seems to be the most terrible thing ever discovered, but it can be made the most useful.[52]

The entry suggests deep confusion on Truman's part about the power of this weapon and its intended deployment. He seems to have been unaware that, even if a 'purely military' target could be chosen, heavy civilian casualties would result. Or perhaps he needed to believe otherwise.

The Potsdam ultimatum formally demanded 'the unconditional surrender of all Japanese armed forces'. Refusal would lead to 'prompt and utter destruction'. The document, Stimson thought, 'was designed to promise destruction if Japan resisted, and hope, if she surrendered . . . for such a purpose the atomic bomb was an eminently suitable weapon'.[53] Contrary to Stimson's hopes, the ultimatum had no effect. The Japanese Premier Kantaro Suzuki announced that his 'government does not regard [the ultimatum] as a thing of any great value; the government will just

---

* He meant Kyoto or Tokyo.

ignore it. We will press forward resolutely to carry the war to a successful conclusion.'[54] Stimson nevertheless felt satisfied that a warning had been made. Reflecting on the matter after the war, he wrote: 'the only road to early victory was to exert maximum force with maximum speed. It was not the American responsibility to throw in the sponge for the Japanese; that was the one thing they must do for themselves.'[55]

The Soviets sensed that the Americans wanted an early end to the war, one which would allow them to ignore promises made at Yalta. 'Stalin was leaning on our officers to start military actions as soon as possible,' Nikita Khrushchev recalled. '[He] had his doubts about whether the Americans would keep their word. . . . What if Japan capitulated before we entered the war? The Americans might say, we don't owe you anything.'[56]

Soviet troops would enter Manchuria on 15 August. Groves was optimistic that Little Boy might be ready a week before that date. Both the Americans and the Soviets were racing to use their master cards.

CHAPTER 6

Genshi Bakudan

The atom bomb was born out of the marriage of utterly complex science with precision engineering. Two billion dollars were spent on its development. But when Tibbets tried to show a film of the Trinity explosion to his crew prior to the first bombing mission, simple technology failed. The projector jammed.

The 509th Composite Group arrived on Tinian Island on 10 June. The crew practised manoeuvres while remaining ignorant of the bomb's nature. The last practice run, with a dummy Little Boy, was flown by three B-29s on 31 July. It went perfectly. On that same day, the Bomb was ready. Everything was therefore in place for a mission the following day. But then a typhoon intervened. On 3 August, Byrnes surmised that the Japanese were 'looking for peace'. He did not, however, feel inclined to interrupt preparations for the bombing.[1]

On 4 August, Tibbets briefed the seven crews assigned to the first bombing run. Aerial photographs of Hiroshima, Nagasaki and Kokura were shown. Three crews were to fly ahead to scout the weather over the target cities, two would accompany the bombing plane to photograph and observe and the seventh plane would act as a reserve. Parsons then told the crews that the weapon they would deliver was the most powerful bomb ever produced, capable of destroying an area three miles in diameter. After the projector failed, he improvised.

> The film you are not about to see was made of the only test we have performed. This is what happened. The flash of the explosion was seen for more than ten miles. A soldier 10,000 feet away was knocked off his feet. Another soldier more than five miles away was temporarily blinded. A girl in a town many miles away who had been blind all her life saw a flash of light. The explosion was heard fifty miles away. For those of us who were there, it was the beginning of a new age.[2]

'It was like some weird dream', one crewman later recalled, 'conceived by one with too vivid an imagination.' Tibbets then took over.

The colonel began by saying that whatever any of us, including himself, had done before was small potatoes compared to what we were going to do now. Then he said . . . how proud he was to have been associated with us, about how high our morale had been, and how difficult it was not knowing what we were doing, thinking maybe we were wasting our time and the 'gimmick' was just somebody's wild dream. He was personally honored and he was sure all of us were, to have been chosen to take part in this raid, which, he said – and all the other big-wigs nodded when he said it – would shorten the war by at least six months. And you got the feeling that he really thought this bomb would end the war, period.[3]

On the following day, weather reports confirmed an improving trend. That afternoon, LeMay approved plans for a mission on the 6th. While Little Boy was being loaded on B-29 number 82 a painter arrived to put a name on the plane. Tibbets named it after his mother – *Enola Gay*.

Hiroshima was the primary target. The city is shaped like a fan, with the majority of the population residing on six islands formed by the estuarial tributaries of the River Ota. Commercial and residential districts were concentrated in a four square mile section in the centre, where about three quarters of the population lived and worked. Population figures vary greatly due to the evacuation and decentralization of industry during the war. Somewhere between 350,000 and 400,000 were probably resident on 6 August, a figure which included 45,000 Korean slave labourers. There were also nearly 5,000 Americans, mainly children sent to Japan after their parents – US citizens of Japanese origin – had been interned.

Among residents, a feeling of good fortune mingled with trepidation. Of all the major cities, only Kyoto and Hiroshima had escaped visits from the *B-san* or *Mr B*. One rumour held that Hiroshima had been saved because Truman's mother was a prisoner in the city; another claimed that she had been born there. Optimists predicted that the city would be spared, while pessimists feared that some unusually horrible punishment awaited. City officials, inclined toward pessimism, had recently ordered the construction of wide fire lanes from which flammable material had to be cleared. These were designed to act in conjunction with the rivers to limit the spread of fire from an incendiary raid. The priority given to this precaution meant that houses within the designated fire lane were destroyed. On 5 August girls from the local secondary school were released from their studies to help clear these breaks. Residents had also been ordered to construct concrete tanks near their homes, to be filled with water. These would provide a ready water supply for fire fighting and also a shelter for those needing to escape a firestorm.

At the stroke of midnight on 6 August, Tibbets held his final briefing. A Protestant chaplain called upon the Almighty to 'be with those who brave the heights of Thy heaven and who carry the battle to our enemies'.[4]

The men breakfasted, then went out to the *Enola Gay*, where they were photographed before boarding. The plane, with its fuel, crew and cargo, weighed 65 tons, 15,000 pounds overweight. That was ominous, given that B-29 engines had a history of overheating and catching fire. The plane roared to life at 02.27 and lumbered down the runway eighteen minutes later. At about 03.30 Tibbets crawled back to chat with his crew. He asked them if they had any inkling of the bomb's nature. The tail gunner, Robert Caron, guessed that it was either 'a chemist's nightmare' or a 'physicist's nightmare'. Tibbets remained tight-lipped.

> [He] stayed . . . a little longer, and then started to crawl forward up the tunnel. . . . just as the . . . Old Man was disappearing, I sort of tugged at his foot, which was still showing. He came sliding back in a hurry, thinking maybe something was wrong. 'What's the matter?'
>   I looked at him and said, 'Colonel, are we splitting atoms today?'
>   This time he gave me a really funny look, and said, 'That's about it'.[5]

When he got back to the cockpit, Tibbets got on the intercom and explained the bomb to the rest of the crew.

At 07.30 Parsons completed the last stage of the arming process. Tibbets, who had been flying at low altitude to conserve fuel and minimize strain on the engine, began a 45-minute ascent to 31,000 feet. At 08.50 the plane flew over Shikoku, the island east of Hiroshima. Escorts peeled away. A short time later, the bombardier Thomas Ferebee reported the target in sight.

Since Hiroshima lay in a different time zone than Tinian, the time on the ground was 08.00. Three air raid sirens had already broken the calm of that bright summer morning, but that was nothing unusual in a country subjected to relentless bombardment. The last siren was prompted by the weather plane which preceded the *Enola Gay*. When it turned away, the all clear was sounded and the morning bustle quickly resumed. Shortly after 08.00 air defence spotters reported two or three B-29s approaching, but calm prevailed since a really big raid meant a sky crowded with bombers. Radio alerts advised people to watch for the approaching planes but otherwise to go on with their business. A full-scale exodus to the shelters seemed unwarranted.

The bomb bay doors of the *Enola Gay* opened. Ferebee controlled the plane in the bombing run by recalling aerial photos he had studied. He waited for the target to align with his crosshairs and released the bomb at 08.14. Freed of the huge weight, the plane jerked violently upward. Tibbets took over. 'I threw off the automatic pilot and hauled *Enola Gay* into the turn. I pulled antiglare goggles over my eyes. I couldn't see through them; I was blind. I threw them to the floor.'

The bomb, scrawled with messages like 'Greetings to the Emperor', wobbled at first then steadied as it picked up speed. At 5,000 feet, the barometric safety switch operated. Then, at 1,900 feet, the proximity fuse fired. The U-235 bullet shot down the short barrel, hitting the U-235 mass, which went super-critical. In an instant, the chain reaction went through 80 generations before the bomb blew itself apart at 08.16.02. As if to underline the terrible nature of total war, Little Boy exploded directly above Shima Hospital, a spot 550 feet southeast of the actual target.

'A bright light filled the plane.' Caron spotted the approaching shock wave, but was unable to warn the crew. 'We were eleven and a half miles slant range from the atomic explosion, but the whole airplane cracked and crinkled from the blast,' Tibbets wrote. 'I yelled "Flak!" thinking a heavy gun battery had found us.' The navigator, 'Dutch' Van Kirk, thought the sensation was like 'if you've ever sat on an ash can and had somebody hit it with a baseball bat . . . the plane bounced and there was a noise like a piece of sheet metal snapping'.

'No one spoke for a moment,' Tibbets recalled; 'then everyone was talking.' Caron provided a running commentary of events on the ground:

A column of smoke is rising fast. It has a fiery red core. A bubbling mass, purple grey in colour, with that red core. It's all turbulent. Fires are springing up everywhere, like flames shooting out of a huge bed of coals. I am starting to count the fires. One, two, three, four, five, six . . . fourteen, fifteen . . . it's impossible. There are too many to count. Here it comes, the mushroom shape that Captain Parsons spoke about. It's coming this way. It's like a mass of bubbling molasses. The mushroom is spreading out. It's maybe a mile or two wide and half a mile high. It's growing up and up and up. It's nearly level with us and climbing. It's very black, but there is a purplish tint to the cloud. The base of the mushroom looks like a heavy undercast that is shot through with flames. The city must be below that. The flames and smoke are billowing out, whirling out into the foothills. The hills are disappearing under the smoke.

Lewis pounded Tibbets's shoulder, yelling 'Look at that! Look at that! Look at that!' He thought he could taste fission, claiming it tasted like lead. Ferebee wondered aloud whether radioactivity would make them all sterile. Lewis shouted 'My God! Look at that son-of-a-bitch go!' But, in his mission log, he wrote: 'My God, what have we done?'[6]

In the city, few survivors remember hearing the blast – their world was torn apart long before the sound wave arrived. Twenty miles away, sound was the defining element. Closer in, it was an irrelevance. The city had been hijacked by horror.

How could I ever forget that flash of light!
In an instant thirty thousand people disappeared from the streets;
The cries of fifty thousand more
Crushed beneath the darkness.

Yellow whirling smoke became light,
Buildings split, bridges collapsed;
Crowded trams burned just as they were –
Endless trash and heaps of embers,
Hiroshima.

Then, skin hanging like rags,
Hands on breasts;
Treading upon shattered human brains . . .

The conflagration shifts . . .
Onto heaps of schoolgirls lying like refuse
So that god alone knew who they were . . .[7]

Michiko Yamaoka, a middle school student, was walking half a mile from the epicentre.

When I saw a very strong light, a flash, I put my arms over my face uncon-sciously. Almost instantly I felt my face was inflating. I thought I was directly hit by the bomb and was dying. I was proud of myself for dying for my country because we had been educated so. Shortly after, I felt my body flying in the air and then I lost consciousness.[8]

'I just could not understand why our surroundings had changed so greatly in one instant,' another resident recalled. 'I thought it might have been something which had nothing to do with the war – the collapse of the earth which it was said would take place at the end of the world, and which I had read about as a child.'[9]

In another part of the city, Michihiko Hachiya and his wife watched in horror as their house collapsed around them.

The shortest path to the street lay through the house next door so through the house we went – running, stumbling, falling and then running again until in headlong flight we tripped over something and fell sprawling into the street. Getting to my feet, I discovered I had tripped over a man's head.
'Excuse me! Excuse me, please!' I cried hysterically.[10]

For many people, death came with merciful suddenness. Miyoko Watanabe recalls seeing 'a woman lying dead at a house by the river bank – her neck stuck through with a piece of glass blown by the blast. The glass must have cut the artery. Blood was scattered around her. She had been suckling her baby. The baby was still absorbed in sucking the breast.'[11]

At 08.17 an operator at the Japanese Broadcasting Corporation noticed that the Hiroshima station had gone off the air. He tried to contact it, without success. Twenty minutes later the Tokyo railroad telegraph centre noticed that the main line had stopped working ten miles from Hiroshima. Unofficial reports from some railway stops close to the city told of a terrible explosion. This information was transmitted to the General Staff. Officers there were puzzled: they could not raise the Control Station in Hiroshima, yet they knew that the city had not been hit by a large raid. A young staff officer was ordered to fly to the city and assess the damage. Three hours later, he reported that Hiroshima had disappeared.[12]

While the *Enola Gay* travelled to its target, Groves was playing tennis in order to while away the anxious minutes. On returning to his office, he waited impatiently for word from Tinian. Minutes seemed like hours. 'In order to ease the growing tension in the office, I made a point of taking off my tie, opening up my collar and rolling up my sleeves,' he recalled. 'While this was completely out of character for me, I did it for the specific purpose of creating a more informal, relaxed atmosphere.' In fact, fifteen minutes after the drop, Parsons had radioed: 'Results clearcut, successful in all respects'.[13] But for some unexplained reason, the message took a roundabout route to Groves, reaching him around 23.30, four hours after the bomb exploded. On the following afternoon, Groves phoned Oppenheimer:

G 'I'm very proud of you and all of your people.'

O 'It went all right?'

G 'Apparently it went with a tremendous bang.'

. . .

O 'Right. Everybody is feeling reasonably good about it and I extend my heartiest congratulations. It's been a long road.'

G 'Yes, it has been a long road and I think one of the wisest things I ever did was when I selected the director of Los Alamos.'

O 'Well, I have my doubts, General Groves.'

G 'Well, you know I've never concurred with those doubts at any time.'[14]

After hanging up, Oppenheimer called a meeting in the Los Alamos auditorium. 'He entered . . . like a prize fighter,' a colleague recalled. 'As he walked through the hall there were cheers and shouts and applause all round and he acknowledged them with the fighter's salute – clasping his hands together above his head as he came to the podium.'[15] Some staff booked tables for a celebration dinner. 'Of course they were exalted by the success of their work', Frisch thought, 'but it seemed rather ghoulish to celebrate the sudden death of a hundred thousand people, even if they were "enemies".'[16]

Meanwhile, enemies suffered in a city of fire. One resident recalled seeing 'a charred body of a woman standing frozen in a running posture with one leg lifted and her baby tightly clutched in her arms'. The blast had knocked down wooden structures, arranging them into random piles of firewood awaiting ignition. As the fire spread, it generated its own wind, creating a storm of flame. One man recalled:

> In front of the First Middle School there were . . . many young boys the same age as my son . . . and what moved me most to pity was that there was one dead child lying there and another who seemed to be crawling over him in order to run away, both of them burned to blackness.

Dr Mazakazu Fujii was confused. In his area of the city, there were not yet many fires, but a great many burned people. Unbeknownst to him, this was the effect of the massive heat wave. Those within a half mile of the blast were turned instantly into small lumps of charcoal. Thousands of these black lumps dotted the streets and pathways of the area around ground zero. 'A human being who has been roasted becomes quite small, doesn't he?' a patient later remarked to Hachiya.[17]

Kiyoshi Tanimoto, who had been on the outskirts of the city, was worried about the fate of his family and his church. He made his way to the centre, against the tide of shattered humanity.

> hundreds and hundreds . . . were fleeing and every one of them seemed to be hurt in some way. The eyebrows of some were burned off and skin hung from their face and hands. Others, because of pain, held their arms up as if carrying something in both hands. Some were vomiting as they walked. Many were naked or in shreds of clothing. On some undressed bodies, the burns had made patterns – of undershirt straps and suspenders and, on the skin of some women (since white repelled the heat from the bomb and dark clothes absorbed it and conducted it to the skin), the shapes of flowers they had had on their kimonos. Many, although injured themselves, supported relatives who were much worse off. Almost all had their heads bowed, looked straight ahead, were silent, and showed no expression whatever.[18]

'I saw many people coming out of the center of the city,' Kosuke Shishido recalled. 'They were asking for help. Their skin was melted and hung around their arms. I realized something unusual had happened. I cannot describe what I really saw because it was like hell on the earth.'[19]

Michiko Yamaoka regained consciousness to find that she was buried by a pile of bricks.

> I could not move. I heard voices asking for help or asking for water. . . . I heard something burning near me. I do not know how long I was there; it could have been half an hour, it could have been several hours. Suddenly I heard my mother's voice calling my name. I called my mother. I heard someone saying to my mother 'It's too dangerous; it's impossible.' My mother still called my name and I called to my mother. She was trying to rescue me from the fire. Shortly after she found and rescued me. . . . When I was rescued, my hair was burned; my face was inflated like a balloon. . . . I wondered why my shirt had been burnt and hanging around my arms, I soon realized they were pieces of my skin. It was hell.[20]

The need to help the suffering competed with the need to escape the conflagration. Twenty years after the blast, one woman was still haunted by choices made when she was just thirteen:

> I left my mother there and went off. . . . I was later told by a neighbour that my mother had been found dead, face down in a water tank . . . very close to the spot where I left her. . . . If I had been a little older or stronger I could have rescued her. . . . Even now I still hear my mother's voice calling me to help her.[21]

Toshiko Sasaki was trapped for a long time in the wreckage of the tin factory in which she worked. She screamed for help, but no one came. Eventually a group of men pulled her out. Her leg was badly broken and lacerated, hanging at a weird angle below the knee. She was left in the courtyard while her rescuers moved on to other victims. Eventually another man came along and moved her to a sort of lean-to made from a piece of corrugated iron. He then brought two horribly wounded people – a woman whose breast had been sheared off and a man whose face had been burned away. When the sun came out the shelter grew insufferably hot. The three tenants began to stink.

Father Wilhelm Kleinsorge, a German Jesuit priest, found his way to a grove by a river, where many injured people had fled to escape the fire. There, one by one, they slowly died.

The hurt ones were quiet; no one wept, much less screamed in pain; no one complained; none of the many who died did so noisily; not even the children cried; very few people even spoke. And when Father Kleinsorge gave water to some whose faces had almost been blotted out by flash burns, they took their share and then raised themselves a little and bowed to him, in thanks.[22]

In the evening a Japanese naval launch moved up and down the rivers of Hiroshima, between the bloated bodies and burning wreckage. A naval officer stood on the deck repeating vague assurances that help was on the way. In his crisp white uniform he seemed bizarrely incongruous, but also mildly reassuring since he demonstrated that there were limits to the destruction. But the rescue ship he promised never materialized.

Kimiko Takai, five years old at the time, was wandering the streets with her parents and sister, in search of a safe spot to rest:

> we saw soldiers with bloated stomachs floating down the river. They probably had to dive into the river to get away from the flames. A little farther on, we saw many dead people piled up at the side of the road. As we walked on, my father saw a woman whose leg was caught under a large timber. She couldn't get free so he shouted for help but no one came. . . . he got the woman loose by sawing off her leg with a rusty, old saw.[23]

The bomb destroyed everything, including the city's means of coping. In just a few seconds, the majority of doctors and nurses were killed and virtually all hospitals levelled. There were no firemen, no police, no rescue squads. There were only victims, in varying degrees of suffering.

Tanimoto, who found hundreds of heavily wounded people in Asano Park, grew increasingly angry at the failure of doctors to respond. He found an aid station at the East Parade Ground, designated an evacuation area earlier in the war. An Army doctor was working feverishly on a crowd of wounded. 'Why have you not come to Asano Park?' Tanimoto asked. 'You are badly needed there.'

> 'This is my station.'
> 'But there are many dying on the riverbank over there.'
>   'The first duty is to take care of the slightly wounded.'
>   'Why – when there are so many who are heavily wounded on the riverbank?'
>   'In an emergency like this, the first task is to help as many as possible – to save as many lives as possible. There is no hope for the heavily wounded. They will die.'

Tanimoto went back to the park and worked devotedly for the next few days.

Wherever he moved, a twenty-year-old girl lingered nearby, her dead baby daughter in her arms. She held the small corpse close to her for four days, even though it began to smell after the second day. At one point, Tanimoto suggested that she should cremate the baby, but she gripped tighter.[24]

Early on the morning of the 7th, Groves briefed Marshall and Arnold. Marshall cautioned against overt expressions of celebration, in view of the huge number of casualties likely to be involved. Groves replied that 'I was not thinking so much about those casualties as I was about the men who had made the Bataan death march.' Arnold later remarked: 'I'm glad you said that – it's just the way I feel.'[25]

Back in Hiroshima, a bright morning sun shone on the destruction. It was a lovely day, except for the fires, smoke, bodies and rubble. Of the 76,000 buildings in the city, 48,000 were destroyed totally, with another 22,000 suffering serious damage. 'For acres and acres the city was like a desert except for scattered piles of brick and roof tile,' Hachiya wrote. 'I had to revise my meaning of the word destruction . . . Devastation may be a better word, but really I knew of no word to describe the view.'[26] Father John Siemes, a Jesuit priest, was horrified at the carnage which sunrise revealed:

> Where the city stood everything, as far as the eye could reach, is a waste of ashes and ruin. . . . The banks of the river are covered with dead and wounded, and the rising waters have here and there covered some of the corpses. On the broad street in the Hakushima district, naked burned cadavers are particularly numerous. Among them are the wounded who are still alive. A few have crawled under the burnt-out autos and trams. Frightfully injured forms beckon to us and then collapse.[27]

Shock gave way to bewilderment. Within what remained of Hiroshima, explanations of the calamity had a common ring of desperation: how to account for destruction so instantaneous and unimaginable? There was, after all, no real raid, just a single plane. The prevalence of nausea and vomiting suggested that the Americans had dropped poison gas. These suspicions were supported by the strong odour of ionization given off during fission. Others speculated that the widespread fires must have resulted from the Americans spraying the city with petrol. Another rumour held that the single B-29 had dropped magnesium powder, which had ignited when it came into contact with electric tram lines. At the Red Cross hospital, a new clue emerged the day after the bomb. X-ray plates stored in the basement were found to be exposed. But, since no one could explain why, the mystery deepened.

Later on the 7th came the first official acknowledgement. The Japanese government announced that the city had suffered 'considerable damage' as a result of a raid carried out by a few B-29s. A new type of weapon was perhaps involved – 'the details are being investigated'. It was not until a week later that Hiroshima heard a new rumour about a bomb which released power by splitting atoms. The Japanese called it *genshi bakudan* – literally, 'original child bomb'. But this was too much for most people to understand and was given no more credence than the petrol or magnesium explanations.

The Japanese were not unaware of fission. Many of their prominent physicists had been educated in the United States or Europe before the war and had worked with scientists who would eventually join the Manhattan Project. Japan had embarked upon its own exploratory fission project, and the Riken, the renowned Tokyo laboratory, researched isotope separation. The Navy, keen to find a new propulsion for submarines, had thrown its weight behind the work. 'Although it is not expected that nuclear energy will be realized in the near future', a Navy report remarked in 1942, 'the possibility of it must not be ignored.'[28]

Akio Morita, the founder of Sony, was a naval officer assigned to the development of new weapons. On 7 August 1945, he was lunching with colleagues at his office near Kamakura when news of Hiroshima arrived.

> On that hot, humid summer day, we knew nothing of the horror of the bomb that was dropped. The news bulletin we got . . . said only that the bomb that fell was 'a new kind of weapon that flashed and shone', but that description told us this surely had to be an atomic device. . . . My reaction . . . was the reaction of a scientist. Sitting there at lunch, I lost all interest in the rice in front of me, as much of a luxury as it was in wartime Japan. I looked around at my colleagues and said to everyone at the table, 'We might as well give up our research right now. If the Americans can build an atomic bomb, we must be too far behind in every field to catch up.' My superior officer got very angry with me.

Morita's colleagues had been clinging to the hope that a last minute scientific discovery would rescue Japan. 'The bomb took everyone by surprise,' he recalled. 'I knew something about the potential of atomic power, but I thought it would take at least twenty years for an atomic bomb to be developed.'[29] His colleagues nevertheless continued to fantasize.

Father Siemes found a similar inability to confront the truth among the Japanese he encountered:

> A few days after the atomic bombing, the secretary of the University came to us asserting that the Japanese were ready to destroy San Francisco by means of an equally effective bomb. It is dubious that he himself believed what he told us. He merely wanted to impress upon us foreigners that the

Japanese were capable of similar discoveries. In his nationalistic pride, he talked himself into believing this.

Others told Siemes that nuclear power had originally been discovered by the Japanese, but a lack of raw materials had prevented construction of a bomb. He was assured that the Germans had such a bomb and were about to re-enter the war. The Americans, he was told, had stolen the idea from the Germans and had merely built the bomb, not invented it.[30]

On the 7th, Yoshio Nishina, Japan's best known atomic physicist, was summoned to the General Staff. While he was preparing to leave, a reporter arrived and asked him whether he believed American claims that the destruction of Hiroshima had been caused by a single atomic bomb. Nishina had not yet heard of the bombing, so could not comment. When asked in theoretical terms whether a bomb was possible and whether the Americans might have built one, Nishina could only mutter, 'Yes.'

Nishina then proceeded to the General Staff. In a grave voice, he told the senior officers that the Hiroshima blast was very likely an atomic bomb. Someone then asked: 'Could you build an atomic bomb in six months? In favourable circumstances we might be able to hold out that long.' Nishina replied that six years would not be enough. In any case, he added, the question was immaterial since Japan had no uranium. Pressed further, Nishina was asked how to construct a defence against atomic weapons. With stony countenance, he replied: 'Shoot down every hostile aircraft that appears over Japan.'[31]

Nishina, a patriot, dearly hoped he was wrong about Hiroshima. On 8 August he flew over the city. 'As I surveyed the damage from the air, I decided at a glance that nothing but an atomic bomb could have created such devastation.'[32] A ground inspection confirmed this grim conclusion. Roof tiles nearly a half mile from the point of explosion had melted, a heat possible only from splitting atoms. Directly underneath the point of explosion, Nishina found a high level of radioactivity. Four months later, his entire body came out in blotches.

On the same day that Nishina inspected the devastation, Kanji Yamasaki woke up in a Hiroshima park. All around was a sea of misery.

Am I awake? I thought I was dead. Right here in the Park, it was filled with red-black bodies since yesterday. But now it was all white. Just like under the midnight sun in the north pole. Pain was all over my body, and I was wondering if it was still painful after I'm dead? What are those white things? So I crawled toward them and was shocked. They were maggots all over the burnt bodies hatched just in one night. Even on people walking, maggots were clinging on eyes, mouth and ears, and one by one people were collapsing – the most miserable sight right before my eyes.

Soldiers began burning the bodies with wood and oil. Yamasaki drew upon all his energy to move his limbs so the soldiers would not mistake him for dead and burn him. 'I crawled away from the fire, with no hope for living, no strength left, just waiting to die.'[33]

For the Japanese, proper disposal of the dead, through cremation and enshrinement, are hugely important moral responsibilities. Hachiya recalls the fires:

> a light, southerly wind blowing across the city wafted to us an odour sugges-tive of burning sardines. I wondered what could cause such a smell until somebody, noticing it too, informed me that sanitation teams were cremating the remains of people who had been killed. . . . Towards Nigitsu was an especially large fire where the dead were being burned by the hundreds.[34]

Order began slowly to emerge. At the Red Cross Hospital, corpses were piled everywhere, usually not far from where death had occurred:

> whenever a patient appeared to be moribund, a piece of paper with his name on it was fastened to his clothing. The corpse detail carried the bodies to a clearing outside, placed them on pyres of wood from ruined houses, burned them, put some of the ashes in envelopes with the names of the deceased, and piled them, neatly and respectfully, in stacks in the main office. In a few days the envelopes filled one whole side of the impromptu shrine.[35]

A few days after the bomb, Kwak Bok Soon went to the Red Cross Hospital to look for her relatives. Once inside a stranger called her.

> She gave me a pair of chopsticks and asked me to take off the newspaper which covered her back. When I took the paper off I was so surprised to see her back and could say nothing. I saw maggots creeping on her. She asked me to take the maggots off with the chopsticks. I took the worms from her body. I found that the maggots were not just creeping but actually living in her body. I cannot forget this memory.[36]

Luis Alvarez, one of the foremost scientists on the Manhattan Project, observed the Hiroshima blast from one of the B-29s that followed the *Enola Gay*. On the way back from the mission he was moved to write a letter for his four-year-old son. 'What regrets I have about being a party to killing and maiming thousands of Japanese civilians this morning are tempered with the hope that this terrible weapon we have created may bring the countries of the world together and prevent future wars.'[37]

★ ★ ★

Military analysts have precise formulae for measuring a weapon's efficiency. According to the Standardized Casualty Rate, the Hiroshima bomb was 6,500 times more efficient at killing than an ordinary bomb. The exact death toll nevertheless remains elusive. Perhaps 75,000 people died quickly as a result of the blast and fire. Radiation took much longer to kill. In the weeks and months after the blast, those who seemed to have escaped all injury suddenly fell desperately ill. Rumours circulated that the bomb had contained some peculiar poison that would make Hiroshima uninhabitable for seven years. The scientists dispelled these rumours, but people continued to die. After five years, the death toll rose to around 200,000.

It was a season of surprises. The war which most Americans thought would last another year was racing towards an abrupt and incredibly violent end. Sixteen hours after the bombing, Truman confided to the American people about the Manhattan Project. In a prepared statement, he mentioned the work done at Los Alamos, Hanford and Oak Ridge. 'The battle for the laboratories held fateful risks for us as well as the battles of the air, land, and sea, and we have now won the battle of the laboratories as we have won the other battles.'[38] Hearing the news, Willie Schuiten learned for the first time what exactly he had been making at Oak Ridge. 'The people in charge really did a good job of keeping the project a secret.'[39]

A different sort of surprise was evident at Farm Hall in England where the captured German scientists were held. On 6 August, they heard a BBC radio report on the bombing of Hiroshima. Their conversation was secretly recorded by their captors. Astonishment merged with envy and regret. Heisenberg decided that it must not actually be a uranium bomb, since he could not come to grips with the possibility that the Americans might have succeeded where he had failed. 'I am willing to believe that it is a high pressure bomb and I don't believe that it has anything to do with uranium, but that it is a chemical thing where they have enormously increased the whole explosion.' But reality slowly penetrated stubborn egos. After accepting the truth, Weizsäcker decided that the American action was 'dreadful'. Heisenberg disagreed, arguing that the bomb was 'the quickest way of ending the war. If we had all wanted Germany to win the war we could have succeeded.' To that idea, Hahn replied 'I don't believe that, but I am thankful we didn't succeed.'[40]

A rift developed along generational lines. Younger scientists chided their senior colleagues for not pushing harder for a German bomb. If Germany had a bomb, they argued, it would be easier to extract a favourable peace settlement. Older scientists retorted that German physicists would now be able to avoid a moral burden which would weigh heavily upon physicists in America. Weizsäcker reiterated his argument that the Germans had not lost the race, they had merely demonstrated their moral superiority. 'I don't think we ought to make excuses now because we did not succeed, but we must admit that we did not want to succeed.' Karl Wirtz agreed: 'I think it characteristic that the Germans made the discovery and didn't use it, whereas the Americans have used it. I must say I didn't think the Americans would dare to use it.'[41]

Truman returned to Washington from Potsdam at 22.30 on 7 August. That same day his office received a telegram from Senator Richard Russell. 'Permit me to respectfully suggest', the Senator wrote, 'that we cease our efforts to cajole Japan into surrendering in accordance with the Potsdam Declaration. Let us carry the war to them until they beg us to accept the unconditional surrender.'[42] Truman replied on the 9th:

> I know that Japan is a terribly cruel and uncivilized nation in warfare but I can't bring myself to believe that, because they are beasts, we should ourselves act in the same manner.
>
> For myself, I certainly regret the necessity of wiping out whole populations because of the 'pigheadedness' of the leaders of a nation and, for your information, I am not going to do it unless it is absolutely necessary. . . .
>
> My object is to save as many American lives as possible but I also have a humane feeling for the woman and children in Japan.[43]

On the same day, Truman broadcast a long speech to the American people, mainly about the settlement of postwar Germany. He slipped in one paragraph about Hiroshima:

> The world will note that the first atomic bomb was dropped on Hiroshima, a military base. That was because we wished in this first attack to avoid, insofar as possible, the killing of civilians. But that attack is only a warning of things to come. If Japan does not surrender, bombs will have to be dropped on her war industries and, unfortunately, thousands of civilian lives will be lost. I urge Japanese civilians to leave industrial cities immediately, and save themselves from destruction.[44]

The description of Hiroshima as a military base echoes Truman's diary entry before the blast, when he insisted that the bomb would be used on military objectives. Could it be that he did not know that Hiroshima was a city? That seems unlikely. Perhaps he thought he could fool the American people. Perhaps he was trying to fool himself.*

★   ★   ★

---

* On 6 August 1951, Truman claimed that he had been told that the population of Hiroshima was 60,000.

Meanwhile, in Moscow at 5 p.m. on 8 August, Japanese Ambassador Sato met Foreign Minister Vyacheslav Molotov, with a view to enlisting the Soviets to act as mediators between Japan and her enemies, the United States and Britain. Sato was sent packing with the shocking news that the Soviets would enter the war the following day. Given the time difference, this in fact meant that troops would invade Manchuria in two hours.

Everyone was in a hurry. The US wanted to encourage the Japanese (and the Russians) to believe that a virtually unlimited supply of atom bombs existed. Hiroshima alone would not warrant such a conclusion. Dropping a second bomb would drive that message home, even if it was mere bluff. On the 8th, Truman gave the Japanese a second ultimatum: 'Expect a rain of ruin from the air, the like of which has never been seen on this earth.' He told the American people: 'We are now prepared to obliterate more rapidly and completely every productive enterprise the Japanese have above ground in any city. We shall destroy their docks, their factories, and their communications. Let there be no mistake; we shall completely destroy Japan's power to make war.'[45]

When this ultimatum was delivered, the Japanese were still unsure what had happened to Hiroshima. The bomb had destroyed the communications network which might otherwise have spread news of the city's fate across the country. The US tried to speed realization by dropping leaflets:

We are in possession of the most destructive weapon ever devised by man. A single one of our newly developed atomic bombs is actually the equivalent in explosive power to what 2,000 of our giant B-29s can carry on a single mission. This awful fact is one for you to ponder and we solemnly assure you it is grimly accurate.

We have just begun to use this weapon against your homeland. If you still have any doubt, make inquiry as to what happened to Hiroshima when just one atomic bomb fell on that city.

Before using this bomb to destroy every resource of the military by which they are prolonging this useless war, we ask that you . . . petition the Emperor to end the war. . . .

You should take steps now to cease military resistance. Otherwise, we shall resolutely employ this bomb and all our other superior weapons to promptly and forcefully end the war.[46]

Printing millions of leaflets took time, and progress was impeded by a shortage of leaflet bombs. Nagasaki was not leafleted until 10 August, the day after it received an atomic bomb.

As news of the bomb spread, most Japanese would have concluded that their cause was doomed and immediate surrender the only sensible option. A lunatic element still wanted to fight on, but they were slowly melting away. Unfortunately, the process of realization going on in Japan proceeded at a slower pace than the preparations taking place on Tinian. One member of the team assembling Fat Man recalled:

> With the success of the Hiroshima weapon, the pressure to be ready with the much more complex implosion device became excruciating. . . . Everyone felt that the sooner we could get off another mission, the more likely it was that the Japanese would feel that we had large quantities of the devices and would surrender sooner. We were certain that one day saved would mean that the war would be over one day sooner. Living on that island, with planes going out every night and people dying not only in B-29s shot down, but in naval engagements all over the Pacific, we knew the importance of one day.[47]

While Sato was talking to Molotov, a B-29 crew on Tinian was preparing another mission. Norman Ramsey, the senior scientist there, later described how the date for the second strike was decided:

> Our original schedule called for take-off on the morning of the 11th August local time. However, on the evening of the 7th August, we concluded that we could safely advance the date to 10th August. When we proposed this to Tibbets he said it was too bad we could not advance the date still another day since good weather was forecast for 9th August with at least five days of bad weather forecast to follow.[48]

Truman was not part of this decision-making process. In fact, he might not have learned of the Nagasaki bombing until after it occurred. The orders given to the crew on Tinian were to drop the first bomb 'after about 3 August', while second and subsequent bombs would be 'delivered . . . as soon as made ready by the project staff'. In other words, the Tinian crew did not require permission to bomb. Once the process started, it would continue until orders were received to stop it.[49]

The Hiroshima blast is etched in memory; many can easily recall the name of the pilot and the plane. But how many can provide similar details for Nagasaki? For the record, the plane was *Bock's Car*, and the pilot Charles W. Sweeney. The plane's usual pilot, Captain Frederick Bock (thus the name), flew one of the observer planes on this mission. Sweeney renamed the plane *The Great Artiste*, but the original name persists. Just before Sweeney took off, Admiral Purnell asked him: 'Young man, do you know how much that bomb cost?' Sweeney replied: 'About $25 million.' Purnell nodded: 'See that we get our money's worth.'[50]

Flying with Sweeney were two British observers, Group Captain Leonard Cheshire, the famous RAF pilot, and Professor William Penney, who would later become the leading light in the British bomb project. Another passenger was the journalist William Laurence who had observed the Trinity blast. He worshipped the bomb – 'a thing of beauty to behold'. On the flight to the target the radio operator, Sergeant Ralph Curry, asked Laurence, 'Think this atomic bomb will end the war?' Laurence, relaying official opinion, replied: 'There is a very good chance that this one may do the trick, but if not then the next one or two surely will. Its power is such that no nation can stand up against it very long.' The conversation with Curry caused Laurence to reflect:

> In about four hours from now one of [Japan's] cities, making weapons of war for use against us, will be wiped off the map by the greatest weapon ever made by man. In one-tenth of a millionth of a second, a fraction of time immeasurable by any clock, a whirlwind from the skies will pulverize thousands of its buildings and tens of thousands of its inhabitants. . . . Does one feel any pity or compassion for the poor devils about to die? Not when one thinks of Pearl Harbor and the death march on Bataan.[51]

Sweeney's primary target was Kokura Arsenal on the north coast of Kyushu. On approach, he encountered resistance. 'The Japs started to get curious and began sending fighters up after us,' a crewman recalled. 'We had some flak bursts and things were getting a little hairy, so Ashworth and Sweeney decided to make a run down to Nagasaki, as there was no sense dragging the bomb home or dropping it in the ocean.'[52]

'The winds of destiny . . . chose Nagasaki as the ultimate target,'[53] Laurence wrote. That morning, at about 07.50, Japanese time, an air raid alert had sounded in Nagasaki, but the 'All clear' signal was given at 08.30. When two B-29s were detected at 10.53, no further alarm was raised. At that moment, Nagasaki was shrouded in cloud. Sweeney was under strict orders to bomb by sight, but the desire to deliver the bomb was over-whelming. Ashworth decided instead to bomb by radar. Nearly fifty-four years later, the eighty-seven-year-old Ashworth revealed to a Japanese news-paper, the Asahi *Shimbun*, that the plane was so low on fuel that it had to drop the bomb in order to be able to return to base. As it turned out, fuel was so short that the crew had to land on Okinawa, the nearest airfield under American control.[54] The shortage was caused by a defective fuel pump which prevented an 800-gallon bomb bay tank from being used. The problem was discovered prior to take-off but it was decided that, given the mission's importance and the threatening weather, it should not be aborted.[55] When the plane landed at Okinawa there was not enough fuel to taxi off the runway.

At 11.02 *Bock's Car* released its bomb. Fat Man exploded high over the industrial valley of Nagasaki, almost midway between the Mitsubishi

Steel and Arms Works, in the south, and the Mitsubishi-Urakami Ordnance Works in the north. 'A giant flash . . . flooded our cabin with an intense light,' Laurence recalled.

> We removed our glasses after the first flash but the light still lingered on, a bluish-green light that illuminated the entire sky all around. A tremendous blast wave struck our ship and made it tremble from nose to tail. This was followed by four more blasts in rapid succession, each resounding like the boom of cannon fire hitting our plane from all directions.
>
> Observers in the tail of our ship saw a giant ball of fire rise as though from the bowels of the earth, belching forth enormous white smoke rings. Next they saw a giant pillar of purple fire, 10,000 feet high, shooting skyward with enormous speed.
>
> . . . Awe-struck, we watched it shoot upward like a meteor coming from the earth instead of from outer space, becoming ever more alive as it climbed skyward through the white clouds. It was no longer smoke, or dust, or even a cloud of fire. It was a living thing, a new species of being, born right before our incredulous eyes.
>
> At one stage of its evolution . . . the entity assumed the form of a giant square totem pole, with its base about three miles long, tapering off to about a mile at the top. Its bottom was brown, its center was amber, its top white. But it was a living totem pole, carved with many grotesque masks grimacing at the earth.[56]

Dr Raisuke Shirabe was at his desk at the Nagasaki Medical College when he heard a plane overhead. He quickly gathered his things and made for the air raid shelter.

> But just as I reached the door of the office, a silvery purple light flashed in the window on the northern side of the room, followed immediately by a thunderous roar as the building shuddered and the ceilings and walls crashed down around me. Everything became dark, and the debris buried me as I huddled on the floor.
>
> When I regained my senses I could hear a dull drumming noise like the sound of heavy rain. It was probably caused by the falling of soil that had been sucked up into the sky by the explosion. When the sound subsided I tried to stand up. Fortunately the debris on my back was light enough to allow me to struggle to my feet.
>
> I opened my eyes but it was too dark to see anything. Again I crouched down on the floor and waited. I cannot properly describe in words my feelings at this time. It was as though I had been abandoned by humanity to a hell of utter darkness and solitude.

After making his escape, Shirabe found his personal hell multiplied exponentially across the city. Bodies were everywhere. 'I could see . . . people hanging dead from the hospital windows.'[57] The air was poisoned with black smoke and rent by a continuous chorus of screams. From the city below the injured were struggling toward the hospital, to escape the fires and to seek aid. Some made it to the top of the hill, and then, overcome by the effort, died.

In another part of the city, eleven-year-old Koichi Nakajima was playing a game called 'find the bell' with friends in the Ukrami River. He dived to look for the bell on the bottom of the river. When he surfaced, he heard his friends screaming in pain.

> He stared around in fright. There were bodies of his friends on the river-bank, and beyond them he saw that all the houses had been knocked down. What had been a beautiful city a moment before was now a wasteland with a big, black cloud rising above it like smoke from a funeral pyre. Though it was deadly hot, Koichi's teeth began to chatter.[58]

As with Hiroshima, it is difficult to ascertain the exact number of deaths from the second bomb. It is nevertheless safe to surmise that 40,000 were killed outright, 70,000 by the end of the year and perhaps as many as 140,000 in total.

Shirabe managed to locate his wife and his eldest son, but he could not find his younger son, Koji, a medical student at the college. Nineteen days after the blast, his family went to the lecture hall where Koji would have been when the bomb detonated. Only the foundation stones remained. All around them were ashes, charcoal and bones. 'In the sky above the ruins, hundreds of crows soared back and forth searching for the decomposed flesh that had been so plentiful after the bombing. Like screeches from the world of the dead, their raspy cries added to the ghastly atmosphere.' Suddenly Shirabe's daughter cried 'Look at this!'

> Lying in the middle of the former lecture hall was a rectangular slab of metal that had undoubtedly been the door to the room, and stuck to the middle of it was a fragment of cloth. Looking more closely, we realized that it was the front part of the waist of a pair of blue serge trousers with the white lining facing upward. . . . Seeing this, my wife screamed out 'These are Koji's trousers!'

The standard uniform was khaki. On that day, Koji had worn navy blue serge. 'There was no doubt that it was our son who had died on the slab of metal. He had burned to ashes in the fire and only this fragment of cloth . . . remained.'[59]

To allied observers who inspected the damage after the war, it seemed at first that Little Boy had been a great deal more powerful than Fat Man. Hiroshima appeared to have been levelled, while a surprising number of buildings were still essentially intact in Nagasaki. But, further investigation revealed that this had more to do with the nature of the target and the way the bomb was dropped than to actual differences in yield. In fact, further investigation showed that Fat Man was much the more powerful bomb. Roof tiles melted out to 4,000 feet from ground zero in Hiroshima, but out to 6,500 feet in Nagasaki. Large trees were down in both cities, but those in Hiroshima were uprooted, while those in Nagasaki snapped off.[60] While the comparisons fascinated physicists, in truth they yielded a distinction without a difference. The conclusion reached by the British Mission was appropriately simple: 'the impression which both cities make is of having sunk, in an instant and without a struggle, to the most primitive level'.[61]

On Friday morning, 10 August, the Japanese agreed to surrender according to the Potsdam terms, though they refused to accept 'any demand which prejudices the prerogatives of His Majesty as Sovereign Ruler'. In other words, their surrender was not unconditional. On that same morning, Stimson argued that the atomic bombings should stop, regardless of what the Japanese decided. At the same time, Groves announced that components for a third bomb would shortly arrive on Tinian, allowing another drop after the 17th. Truman at first did not agree with Stimson, but then, according to Henry Wallace, his Commerce Secretary, gave orders to stop the bombing. 'He said the thought of wiping out another 100,000 people was too horrible. He didn't like the idea of killing, as he said, "all those kids".'[62] In Los Alamos, Robert Bacher was loading a plutonium core on a truck when Oppenheimer ran up to him and told him to stop. A message had just come from Washington to the effect that the President had ordered that no more bombs were to be shipped to Tinian.[63]

Byrnes drafted an ambiguous reply to the Japanese which suggested that the integrity of the Emperor and the government might survive, but that their 'authority . . . to rule shall be subject to the Supreme Commander of the Allied Powers'.[64] The Japanese continued to deliberate, with some hardliners advocating suicidal resistance. General Carl Spaatz, commander of the US Army Strategic Air Forces, then suggested that the third atomic bomb should be dropped on Tokyo in order to focus minds there. American impatience prompted a resumption of incendiary attacks; 6,000 tons of explosive was dropped by more than a thousand aircraft on the 13th. Around 15,000 Japanese were killed by conventional bombing after the Nagasaki strike. But, as the bombs fell, word came of Japanese surrender.

'We have decided to effect a settlement of the present situation by resorting to an extraordinary measure,' Emperor Hirohito told his people on 15 August.

> We have ordered our government to communicate to the Governments of the United States, Great Britain, China and the Soviet Union that Our Empire accept the provisions of their Joint Declaration. . . . the enemy has begun to employ a new most cruel bomb, the power of which to do damage is indeed incalculable, taking the toll of many innocent lives. Should we continue to fight, it would not only result in ultimate collapse and obliteration of the Japanese nation, but also it would lead to the total extinction of human civilization.[65]

Ordinary Japanese had never before been permitted to hear the voice of the Emperor. Since they had been consistently told that they were winning the war, they were not only surprised at hearing his voice, but also at what he had to say.

A group of soldiers had earlier occupied the Imperial Household Ministry, in an attempt to stop the recording being broadcast. Later, in Tokyo, word of the surrender caused fifty or sixty Japanese soldiers, armed with machine guns, to launch an attack on the Cabinet Offices. They went from there to the home of Prime Minister Suzuki, which they burned to the ground.[66]

Back in America, the news brought profound relief. Most Americans thought not of the dead in Hiroshima and Nagasaki, but of the men from Topeka, Tampa and Tuscon who would live happily ever after. Polls showed about 85 per cent of Americans approved of the bombings, with some expressing a desire for further strikes. 'When one sets out to destroy vermin, does one try to leave a few alive in the nest?' a woman asked in a letter to the *Milwaukee Journal*.[67] Opinion was not, however, unanimous. The leftwing commentator Dwight McDonald regretted America's 'decline to barbarism' while, on the right, David Lawrence argued that 'Military necessity . . . will never erase from our minds the simple truth that we, of all civilized nations . . . did not hesitate to employ the most destructive weapon of all times indiscriminately against men, women and children.'[68] Samuel McCrea Cavert, General Secretary of the Federal Council of the Churches of Christ in America, wrote to Truman on the 9th:

> Many Christians deeply disturbed over the use of atomic bombs against Japanese cities because of their necessarily indiscriminate destructive [effects] and because their use sets extremely dangerous precedent for future of mankind. . . . Respectfully urge that ample opportunity be given Japan to reconsider ultimatum before any further devastation by atomic bomb is visited upon her people.[69]

Truman replied with characteristic bluntness:

> Nobody is more disturbed over the use of atomic bombs than I am but I
> was greatly disturbed over the unwarranted attack by the Japanese on Pearl
> Harbor and their murder of our prisoners of war. The only language they
> seem to understand is the one we have been using to bombard them.
>
> When you have to deal with a beast you have to treat him as a beast. It
> is most regrettable but nevertheless true.[70]

Close on the heels of death and destruction came sick humour. 'Did you
see that Hiroshima?' a radio comedian asks. 'It was a shambles,' his partner
replies. 'Shambles? It looked like Ebbets Field after a doubleheader with
the Giants.'[71]

The Manhattan Project workers, suddenly heroes, were given A-bomb
pins, which bore a mushroom cloud, to commemorate their victory. The
President praised the still anonymous scientists. 'What has been done', he
declared, 'is the greatest achievement of organized science in history. It
was done under high pressure and without failure. We have spent two
billion dollars on the greatest scientific gamble in history – and won.'[72]
Szilard, now tormented with guilt, found Truman's statement grotesque.
'Truman did not understand what was involved,' he later commented. 'You
can see that from the language he used. . . . To put the atomic bomb in
terms of having gambled 2 billion dollars and having "won" offended my
sense of proportions.'[73]

At Los Alamos the pressure finally lifted, replaced by giddy excitement
and relief. Many revelled in their heroic status, growing drunk on pride
and alcohol. Kistiakowsky, having over-indulged on the latter, put together
a twenty-one gun salute. But, since twenty-one guns could not be found,
he instead wired up an equal number of 50-pound cases of TNT. 'It was
quite a show,' he later admitted, 'then I came back to the party and was
told I'd exploded only 20.'[74]

The Bomb was made an honorary citizen of New Mexico. Residents
celebrated the way their two sons had won the war. The *Santa Fe New
Mexican* on 8 August took enormous delight in officially exposing the
great secret. 'Santa Fe learned today of a city of 6,000 in its own front
yard,' the paper announced. 'The Los Alamos bomb . . . lifted the secret
of the community on the Pajarito Plateau, whose presence Santa Fe
ignored, except in whispers, for more than two years.' No mention was
made on the front page of the number of deaths in Hiroshima, but a
short piece on the removal of tomato juice from the ration list was
included.[75]

One month after Hiroshima, listeners to an Albuquerque radio station heard a description of the destruction they had celebrated. Phil Morrison, one of the Los Alamos scientists, described a flight over Hiroshima:

> We . . . stared in disbelief. There below was the flat level ground of what had been a city, scorched red . . . but no hundreds of planes had visited this town during a long night. One bomber and one bomb had, in the time it takes a bullet to cross the city, turned a city of three hundred thousand into a burning pyre. That was a new thing.[76]

The bomb was certainly a new thing. Nowhere was this more poignantly underlined than in the Indian pueblo of San Ildefonso, New Mexico. In December 1945, the pueblo invited the square dance club from nearby Los Alamos to its annual deer dance. Both groups were keenly aware of endings and beginnings. The war was over, ended by a bomb produced locally. The little community which had produced that bomb faced new challenges. So, too, did the entire world. The two groups danced for each other, and then joined in a weird amalgam of accordion and war drum. Cultures mixed, but so too did epochs. At the climax of the proceedings, the pueblo chief climbed on a bench and shouted, with unintentional irony, 'This is the Atomic age!'[77]

It was indeed the atomic age. But whether this was cause for celebration remained to be seen.

> In the place where our city was destroyed,
> Where we buried the ashes of the ones that we loved,
> There the green grass grows and the white waving weeds,
> Deadly the harvest of two atom bombs.
> Then brothers and sisters you must watch, and take care
> That the third atom bomb never comes.[78]

CHAPTER 7

Nuclear Giants and Ethical Infants*

Richard Feynman observed the Trinity blast twenty miles from ground zero. Like so many other scientists, he felt immediate, spine-tingling exhilaration. But then Bob Wilson, who had recruited him for the Manhattan Project, brought him abruptly back to earth. 'It's a terrible thing that we made,' Wilson said. In time, Feynman developed similar misgivings. He came to understand how work on the bomb had been like a powerful drug. 'You see, what happened to me – what happened to the rest of us – is we *started* for a good reason, then you're working very hard to accomplish something and it's a pleasure, it's excitement. And you stop thinking, you know, you just *stop.*'

After the war came time to think. On one occasion, Feynman was sitting in a restaurant in New York, staring out at the buildings. 'I . . . began to think, you know, about how much the radius of the Hiroshima bomb damage was and so forth . . . All those buildings, all smashed – and so on. . . . I would see people building a bridge, or they'd be making a new road, and I thought, they're *crazy*, they just don't understand, they don't *understand*. Why are they making these things? It's so useless.'[1]

In the weeks that followed the war, the Bomb was revealed to be more than a bomb. Fat Man and Little Boy were fearsome enough in their explosive power. But much more sinister was the way they kept on killing. People who had survived the blast and firestorm and seemed perfectly healthy suddenly fell ill weeks after the explosion. One Hiroshima resident watched the slow death of his daughter:

> She was quite all right for a while. But on the 4th of September, she suddenly
> became sick. She had spots all over her body. Her hair began to fall out.
> She vomited small clumps of blood . . . this was a very strange and horrible

* The title is from a comment by General Omar Bradley, who regretted that scientific progress had outpaced moral development. He later pushed vigorously for development of the hydrogen bomb.

disease. We were all afraid of it, and even the doctor didn't know what it was. After ten days of agony and torture, she died on September 14th.[2]

Radiation sickness is generally familiar today. In 1945, it was a mysterious and frightening plague.

Ionizing radiation released in a nuclear explosion passes through the skin without causing external damage. It interacts immediately with tissues within the body, causing an irregular pattern of cell damage. In high turnover tissues, such as those responsible for blood formation and the gastrointestinal tract, the relatively short lifespan of cells leads to rapid depletion, before new cells have a chance to form. In tissues with a slower turnover, such as the brain, liver or thyroid gland, the effects of radiation damage may not become apparent for months or years, and can eventually manifest themselves as cancers. A developing foetus is particularly susceptible to radiation because damage or destruction of cells may impair the development of specific organs or parts of the body. Radiation can also damage DNA in the reproductive system, causing mutation in future generations. While scientists once thought that a 'safe' level of exposure existed, current medical opinion holds that there is no threshold dose below which an effect is not produced.

At Hiroshima and Nagasaki those heavily exposed to radiation, if protected from other injury, showed no immediate ill effect. They seemed fine for about twenty-four hours, whereupon severe nausea, vomiting and fever began. The damage to cells was so widespread that recovery was impossible. Death occurred after about a week, before doctors had any inkling of what was wrong.

Others seemed to recover from the immediate symptoms, but then a second stage of illness set in ten to fifteen days after the blast. This was characterized by bloody diarrhoea, a loss of appetite, general malaise, persistent fever and hair loss. In the most severe cases, symptoms of deficient blood formation were evident. This effect is delayed because gamma rays do not attack the actual blood but rather the bone marrow where blood cells are formed. Serious effects therefore appear only after fully-formed cells already in the blood die off and are replaced by defective cells formed after irradiation.

In the worst cases of radiation poisoning, the gamma rays virtually destroy the entire bone marrow. As a result red cells, platelets and white cells all become deficient. The cessation of red cell formation leads to progressive anaemia. Deficiency of platelet formation causes thin blood to haemorrhage into the skin and the retina of the eye, and sometimes into the intestines and the kidneys. The fall in the number of white cells lowers the victim's resistance to infection. When infection occurred among the Hiroshima and Nagasaki victims, it usually spread from the mouth and was accompanied by gangrene of the lips, tongue and throat. Patients often emitted a terrible smell – they had effectively started to decay from inside. A schoolboy described his mother's illness: '[Her] hair . . . had almost all fallen out, her chest was festering, and from the two-inch hole in her back a lot of maggots were crawling in and out. The place was full of flies and mosquitoes and fleas, and an awfully bad smell hung over everything.'[3] Death resulted from a combination of anaemia, internal bleeding and infection.

Those who survived entered a third stage, in which progressive weakening due to defective white cell formation left the body vulnerable to random diseases and infection. Some recovered, but others grew increasingly debilitated, dying after months of agony. Survivors were then susceptible to a fourth stage many years later when radiation-induced cancers took hold.

Kunizo Hatanaka was on military service elsewhere in Japan on the day of the attack. His wife, at home in Hiroshima, survived the blast, but later suffered badly from radiation sickness. She was three months pregnant. On 14 February 1946, she gave birth to a daughter, Yuriko. 'When she was born she looked just like a normal baby. Although she was a little smaller than other babies, she just looked fine.' By the age of three, however, she could not even crawl. Her parents retained a blind hope that she would catch up to normal children, but she never did. Doctors eventually diagnosed microcephaly, or 'small head disease', and confirmed that she would be severely retarded. 'We still continued to believe that Yuriko would get well soon.' It was not until she was eleven that her parents learned she was a victim of the bomb. Eventually she developed bone-cancer, which killed her in 1978.[4]

William Shawn, managing editor of *The New Yorker*, was struck by the fact that 'in all the millions of words being written about the bomb . . . what had actually happened in Hiroshima . . . was being ignored'.[5] In late 1945, he commissioned John Hersey, the Pulitzer Prize winning novelist and war correspondent, to write an article from the point of view of the victims. Hersey decided that six survivors would tell their own story, with little intervention on his part. Realizing that the impact of the piece would be diminished by serializing it, Shawn devoted an entire issue to it. The magazine, dated 31 August 1946, had the usual light-hearted illustration on its cover (depicting a summer picnic in a park) but inside was a holocaust. The editors explained:

> *The New Yorker* this week devotes its entire editorial space to an article on
> the almost complete obliteration of a city by one atomic bomb, and what

happened to the people in that city. It does so in the conviction that few of us have yet comprehended the all but incredible destructive power of this weapon, and that everyone might well take time to consider the implications of its use.[6]

The bold move received widespread acclaim. The *New York Times* commented:

> Every American who has permitted himself to make jokes about atom bombs, or who has come to regard them as just one sensational phenomenon that can now be accepted as part of civilization, like the airplane and the gasoline engine, or who has allowed himself to speculate as to what we might do with them if we were forced into another war, ought to read Mr. Hersey.[7]

ABC Radio subsequently broadcast the piece in four programmes, with actors reading the parts of the victims. The broadcast was quickly picked up by networks in Britain, Australia and Canada. Within weeks, a book version was rushed into production by Knopf. Over the following year it was translated and distributed around the world – except in Japan, where occupation authorities blocked publication until 1949.

'I wept as I read John Hersey's *New Yorker* account,' a Manhattan Project scientist wrote to his former colleagues on 7 September:

> I am filled with shame to recall the whoopee spirit . . . when we came back from lunch to find others . . . announcing the bombing of Hiroshima. That evening we had a hastily arranged champagne dinner . . . [we felt] relief at the relaxation of security, pride in our part at ending the war, and even pride in the effectiveness of the weapon. And at the same moment, the bomb's victims were living through indescribable horror . . . We didn't realize. I wonder if we do yet.[8]

Hersey's article brought into focus a disparate unease about the bombings. Moral doubt began to seep through the euphoria that had followed the sudden end to the war. Within days of the publication, Admiral William Halsey, commander of the Third Fleet, publicly argued that the scientists 'had a toy and they wanted to try it out . . . The first atomic bomb was an unnecessary experiment. . . . It was a mistake ever to drop it.'[9]

In time, Generals Eisenhower and LeMay, Fleet Admiral Leahy and others joined the chorus of condemnation. Scientists who had felt misgivings before Hiroshima grew more vocal after it. Rotblat called it a 'wanton, barbaric act'.[10] With typical acuity, Szilard proposed a scenario in which Germany beat the Americans to the bomb, dropped two of them, but still managed to lose the war. 'Can anyone doubt that we would then have defined the dropping of atomic bombs on cities as a war crime, and that we would have sentenced the Germans who were guilty of this crime to death at Nuremberg and hanged them?'[11]

Others maintained that the bomb had shortened the war and saved lives. A report by Manhattan Project analysts, dated 29 June 1946, concluded that 'The atomic bomb did not alone win the war against Japan, but it most certainly ended it, saving the thousands of lives that would have been lost in any combat invasion.'[12] In time, this conclusion was supported by prominent Japanese voices. 'I had known that Japan was losing the war and that continuing the battle was futile,' Akio Morita recalled; 'but I also knew that the military would want to fight to the last man.'[13] Taro Takemi, the renowned Japanese scientist, drew a similar conclusion: 'When one considers the possibility that the Japanese military would have sacrificed the entire nation if it were not for the atomic bomb attack, then this bomb might be described as having saved Japan.'[14]

The Strategic Bombing Survey, released in June 1946, cast doubt on these claims. It concluded that 'certainly prior to 31 December 1945, and in all probability prior to 1 November 1945, Japan would have surrendered even if the atomic bombs had not been dropped, even if Russia had not entered the war, and even if no invasion had been planned or contemplated'.[15] If the SBS was right, the bombs shortened the war by at most a few months. In this light, Hiroshima seems unnecessary, perhaps even wanton. Nagasaki seems barbaric.*

It is, however, always hazardous to analyse the urgency of war with the calm reflection possible in peacetime. Those who made the decisions in 1945 did so from a different perspective than those who would eventually judge them. The physicist Herbert York, who built bombs and campaigned for nuclear disarmament, has attacked critics who question Hiroshima from the safe refuge of hindsight. 'The first thing you knew about World War Two is how it came out. And that's the last thing I knew about World War Two . . . The first thing you knew about the atomic bomb is that we used it to kill a lot of people in Hiroshima. And that's the last thing I knew about the atomic bomb.'[16] The urgency to build the Bomb was a self-perpetuating force which carried the project through to its dreadful conclusion. The tail of technology wagged the political dog. Or, to use a metaphor favoured by Groves, Truman was like a boy speeding down a snowy hill on a toboggan, with no real means of stopping or steering. It is easy to judge those who ordered the bombing, but difficult to imagine how they might have acted differently.

---

* Telford Taylor, the former chief prosecutor at Nuremberg, confessed that he had 'never heard a plausible justification of Nagasaki'. He felt it qualified as a war crime (Lifton and Mitchell, p.162).

In 1949, the British physicist Patrick Blackett called the bombings 'not so much the last military act of the second World War, as the first major operation of the cold diplomatic war with Russia'. That was certainly Stalin's interpretation. 'Hiroshima has shaken the world,' he remarked. 'The balance has been destroyed.' Molotov later commented that the bombings 'were, of course, not against Japan, but against the Soviet Union'. He thought Truman was essentially saying 'see, remember what we have. You don't have the atomic bomb, but we do.'[17]

Churchill sensed ulterior motives. 'It is quite clear that the United States do not at the present time desire Russian participation in the war against Japan,' he remarked on 23 July after a conversation with Secretary of State Byrnes.[18] As has been seen, Stimson saw the Bomb as a 'master card' and Truman delighted at the chance to swagger at Potsdam. But die-hard Truman supporters strenuously reject the notion of a hidden agenda. Blackett found this insistence rather strange, 'a curious preference to be considered irresponsible, even brutal, but at all costs not clever'.[19] Perhaps indeed the bombing was clever. Soviet involvement in the war would have meant Soviet involvement in the peace, thus rendering the reconstruction of Japan a great deal more complicated.

The deaths in Hiroshima and Nagasaki were a huge tragedy. But, had the war lasted until November (as the SBS proposed) many more would have been killed by conventional means – as a result of the Russian invasion and American bombing raids. While postwar commentators agonize endlessly about the moral difference between atomic and conventional weapons, those differences matter only to survivors. Those who die care not for the manner of death.

Truman appears not to have been bothered by ethical issues. During a meeting at the White House in October 1945, Oppenheimer tried to convey his deep moral crisis. 'Mr President, I have blood on my hands,' he remarked. 'Never mind,' Truman replied, 'it'll all come out in the wash.' (According to some accounts he offered Oppenheimer a handkerchief.) 'Don't you bring that crybaby in here again,' Truman later told an aide. 'After all, all he did was make the bomb. I'm the guy who fired it off.'[20]

Those who questioned the bombings were brushed away like annoying flies. Truman answered dissent with a standard refrain: 'Dropping the bombs ended the war [and] saved lives.' As for ulterior motives, he insisted that 'My objective was . . . a military blow to create a military surrender . . . That is all I had in mind.'[21] As the years passed, the number of lives saved steadily increased. 'I knew what I was doing when I stopped the war that would have killed a half million youngsters on both sides if those bombs had not been dropped,' Truman wrote in 1963. 'I have no regrets and, under the same circumstances, I would do it again.'[22] The justification was repeated so many times it wore a groove in his mind. Most

Americans nevertheless welcomed this easy escape from moral torment. As the *Chicago Tribune* put it: 'Being merciless, [we] were merciful.' A cartoon showed a dove flying over Japan, an atom bomb in its beak.[23]

On 16 October 1945, while thousands were suffering a slow death in Hiroshima and Nagasaki, Groves presented the Los Alamos laboratory with an Army Certificate of Appreciation. When Oppenheimer took the podium to accept the award, he spoke more freely than he had been able to for years:

> If atomic bombs are to be added to the arsenals of a warring world, or to the arsenals of nations preparing for war, then the time will come when mankind will curse the name of Los Alamos and Hiroshima.
> The peoples of this world must unite, or they will perish. This war, that has ravaged so much of the earth, has written these words. The atomic bomb has spelled them out for all men to understand.[24]

Alfred Nobel worried about what the world would do with dynamite. Oppenheimer worried about what it would do with the Bomb. Not long after the Japanese surrender, he confessed that he was 'a little scared of what I have made'. Critics might argue that this was a bit like shutting down the reactor long after the neutrons had escaped.

Oppenheimer took refuge in the technological imperative: 'A scientist cannot hold back progress because of fears of what the world will do with his discoveries.'[25] When he spoke about the reasons why the bomb was developed, he touched upon the fear of Germany, the desire to shorten the war, and the sense of adventure which all scientists feel. But,

> When you come right down to it the reason we did this job is because it was an organic necessity. If you are a scientist you cannot stop such a thing. If you are a scientist you believe that it is good to find out how the world works; that it is good to find out what the realities are; that it is good to turn over to mankind at large the greatest possible power to control the world and to deal with it according to its lights and its values.[26]

On occasion, however, Oppenheimer found he could not keep guilt at bay. 'In some sort of crude sense', he once wrote, 'which no vulgarity, no humour, no overstatement can quite extinguish, the physicists have known sin.'[27] Some colleagues found the Faustian turmoil annoying. How, they wondered, could the Oppenheimer who strutted like Gary Cooper in *High Noon* after Hiroshima coexist with the man so eager to broadcast his angst? Stanislaw Ulam thought that he 'perhaps . . . exaggerated his role when he saw himself as the "Prince of Darkness, the destroyer of Universes"'. Fellow mathematician John von Neumann was more cutting: 'Some people', he remarked, 'profess guilt to claim credit for the sin.'[28]

Oppenheimer was not, however, the only one to worry. Scientists who felt no qualms about their work during the war did so immediately afterwards. Like the child who lights a match and transforms his home into an inferno, they were shocked at the power they had unleashed. 'The lesson we should learn from all this', Isidor Rabi thought, '[is] . . . how easy it is to kill people when you turn your mind to it. When you turn the resources of modern science to the problem of killing people, you realize how vulnerable they really are.'[29]

Thanks to the Bomb, nuclear physicists, once the practitioners of an obscure science, were suddenly celebrities. No Washington guest list was complete without one. They were described in the press as titans, lab-coated warriors who had won the great scientific war. Comparisons were made to Prometheus and Zeus. 'Before the war we were supposed to be completely ignorant of the world and inexperienced in its ways,' one commented. 'But now we are regarded as the ultimate authority on all possible subjects, from nylon stockings to the best form of international organization.'[30] Because of this new celebrity, the scientists' moral concerns drew wide exposure.

The post-atomic age seemed a world in which the old certainties had been destroyed. Einstein saw some hope amidst the destruction. The Bomb, he thought, might force men to find peace. In 1947 he warned that atomic power 'cannot be fitted into the outmoded concept of narrow nationalisms. For there is no secret and there is no defense; there is no possibility of control except through the aroused understanding and insistence of the peoples of the world.'[31] Many scientists shared this desperate desire to find a silver lining in the mushroom cloud. Oppenheimer, for instance, thought that the bomb 'is not only a great peril, but a great hope'.[32] Bohr had long dreamed that the bomb might be big enough to destroy war itself.

Scientists hoped that life might imitate art. In *The World Set Free*, H. G. Wells wrote of a hugely destructive nuclear conflict forcing nations to realize that 'war was becoming impossible'.[33] The Bomb set the world free from the prison of primal aggression, pointing the way to a higher ethical state. For Wells, the solution lay in world government. Previously, such a notion had seemed impossible because of the manifold differences that divided people. It eventually became possible because of the one thing that united them – the threat of a world destroyed. 'The atomic bombs had dwarfed the international issues to complete insignificance,' Wells wrote. 'The old tendencies of human nature, suspicion, jealousy, particularism and belligerency were incompatible with the monstrous destructive power of the new appliances.'[34]

Well before Hiroshima, the Interim Committee was directed to consider 'atomic energy not simply in terms of military weapons but also in terms of a new relationship of man and the universe'.[35] While it hardly lived up to this Wellsian remit, it did occasionally acknowledge that the Bomb would change the world. At a meeting on 31 May, attention was directed towards the political aftermath of the Manhattan Project. Oppenheimer proposed that the United States should 'offer to the world free interchange of information with particular emphasis on the development of peace-time uses'. While some support for this view was voiced, mention of international cooperation made Byrnes squirm. He insisted that the only option was 'to push ahead as fast as possible . . . to make certain that we stay ahead'.[36]

Truman agreed with Oppenheimer, but also with Byrnes. Atomic energy, he remarked in October 1945, 'constitutes a new force too revolutionary to consider in the framework of old ideas – the hope of civilization lies in international agreements'.[37] But he could not see how to achieve these agreements in the short term, while the US retained a monopoly on atomic power and the Soviet Union was bitterly jealous of that monopoly. In the meantime, he felt obliged to guard the secret of the bomb 'pending further examination of possible methods of protecting us and the rest of the world from the danger of sudden destruction'.[38] Therein lay the difference: while many scientists thought that sharing secrets was the surest road toward international cooperation, Truman felt that the mechanisms for cooperation had to be established before secrets could be shared. Popular opinion agreed with the President. Around 66 per cent of respondents polled in February 1946 rejected any notion of sharing secrets, but a similar percentage wanted the UN to prohibit production of atomic bombs. In other words, the public, like Truman, wanted international control but felt that, in the meantime, the US should guard its secret and make more bombs.[39]

At Potsdam, Truman and Stimson briefly considered using atomic knowledge as a carrot to persuade the Soviets to liberalize their government. But, by September 1945, Stimson had cooled on the idea. Any attempt to strike such a deal might, he warned, render the Soviets more intransigent. If the administration insisted on dealing with the Soviets with 'this weapon rather ostentatiously on our hip, their suspicions and their distrust of our purposes and motives will increase'. He had come to the conclusion that secrets should be shared. 'The chief lesson that I have learned in a long life is that the only way you can make a man trustworthy is to trust him; and the surest way to make him untrustworthy is to distrust him and show your distrust.' Echoing Wells, he argued that the Bomb had rendered irrelevant the old patterns of international affairs. A new approach was needed:

Unless the Soviets are voluntarily invited into the partnership upon a basis of cooperation and trust, we are going to maintain the Anglo-Saxon bloc over against the Soviet in the possession of this weapon. Such a condition will almost certainly stimulate feverish activity on the part of the Soviets toward the development of this bomb in what will in effect be a secret armament race of a rather desperate character.

Stimson did not think it remotely relevant whether the Soviets developed the bomb in four years or in twenty. The crucial issue was to ensure that, when they did develop that power, they are 'willing and cooperative partners among the peace loving nations of the world'. Given the dangers of mutual distrust, it seemed sensible to take risks in order 'to get the best kind of international bargain that we can – one that has some chance of being kept and saving civilization not for five or for twenty years, but forever'.[40]

Stimson's argument was idealistic – an unusual quality in a Secretary of War. More typical of the American mood was the Agriculture Secretary, Clinton Anderson, who remarked: 'we could not trust Russia when she was our ally in the war. I wonder why we feel we can trust her when she is our competitor in the peace.'[41] In the end Truman rejected Stimson's advice on the simple grounds that it was always safe to keep a secret and because Groves had told him that it would take the Russians a very long time to develop a Bomb. In the meantime, the Bomb would be used as a master card to extract concessions.

On 7 October, Truman formally announced that, if other nations wanted to 'catch up' with the United States, 'they will have to do it on their own hook, just as we did'. When his friend Fyke Farmer asked: 'Then, Mister President, what it amounts to is . . . that the armaments race is on, right?' Truman nodded. He added, however, that the US would 'always stay ahead'. As for the crazy notion of world government, 'maybe we could get [that] in a thousand years or something like that, but . . . it was nothing more than a theory at the present time'.[42]

Truman's hardline attitude was apparent when Foreign Ministers met in London to discuss the postwar settlement. Before the conference, Stimson regretted that Byrnes '[has] the bomb in his hip pocket, so to speak, as a great weapon to get through the thing'.[43] With strange synchronicity, at the conference Molotov asked Byrnes whether he had 'an atomic bomb in his side pocket'. Byrnes reacted with characteristic swagger. 'You don't know southerners. We carry our artillery in our pocket. If you don't . . . get down to work, I'm going to pull an atomic bomb out of my hip pocket and let you have it.'[44] Molotov, under strict instructions from Stalin not to show fear, simply chuckled. A short time later, he warned the US that 'there can be no large-scale technological secrets that can remain the property of any one country . . . therefore the discovery of atomic energy must not encourage . . . enthusiasm for using this discovery in a foreign-policy power game'.[45]

Mutual intransigence guaranteed that the London conference ended without significant agreement. Byrnes nevertheless learned an important lesson: the Soviets would not be intimidated. As a result of this realization, he moved closer to Stimson, and further away from the President and Congress. At a subsequent conference in Moscow, a more conciliatory Byrnes found himself out on a limb, while Truman stood by with sharp saw. Some progress on nuclear issues was made, but not in a direction Truman wanted. Afterwards he berated Byrnes for conducting his own foreign policy. 'I'm tired of babying the Soviets,' he barked. When Truman later announced that he would not be bound by the Moscow decisions, the limb holding Byrnes was severed. He later announced his retirement. It is uncertain whether a more conciliatory approach would have improved relations with the Soviets. What is certain is that such an approach was never tried.

The desire to preserve secrets inspired the May-Johnson Bill, introduced on 3 October 1945. Congress proposed stringent controls over nuclear knowledge and harsh penalties for passing on secrets, thus confirming the deepest worries of the scientists, namely that America would remain highly possessive of her secrets, and that the military would control atomic research. Scientists at Chicago and Oak Ridge protested vehemently, with Szilard again leading the way. Though their objections were at first treated with contempt by legislators, the physicists managed to capitalize on their considerable public esteem. Embarrassed by the Bill's many weaknesses, legislators killed it.

The energy generated from opposition to the May-Johnson Bill found outlet in the formation of the Federation of Atomic Scientists (FAS) at George Washington University in December 1945.* Around the same time, in Chicago, the physicists Eugene Rabinowitch and Hy Goldsmith met regularly with the social scientist Edward Shils at the fountain of the Stineway Drug Store to drink coffee and save the world. Out of their intellectual meandering came the *Bulletin of the Atomic Scientists of Chicago*, first published on 10 December 1945. It quickly became a moral forum for the atomic community, and before long shortened its name to the *Bulletin of the Atomic Scientists* to reflect its wider constituency. The *Bulletin* is most famous for its Doomsday Clock, a simple, but graphic assessment

---

* The name was later changed to the Federation of American Scientists, in recognition of its members' broad expertise.

of the risk of nuclear war. The Clock first appeared on the cover of the June 1947 issue, when it was set at seven minutes to midnight, an entirely arbitrary decision based on matters of design. The last quadrant seemed to evoke the urgency the editors wanted to convey. The clock's impact was dramatically increased when the editors decided periodically to adjust the 'time' according to the state of nuclear tension.

Both the FAS and the Chicago scientists were hampered by the naïve innocence associated with their profession. That stereotype was justified; many scientists *were* politically naïve.* The real world did not quite conform to their idealistic visions. When debating Armageddon, they were always outgunned because they could not effectively answer the argument that the best protection against nuclear calamity was more and better weapons and tighter secrecy. For most people, the bomb was a problem but also a solution.

The urgency evoked by the first Doomsday Clock seemed entirely appropriate. Many people assumed that a Third World War would follow quickly upon the Second. Cold hard reality suggested that talk of international cooperation would prove futile – a confrontation between capitalism and communism was inevitable. The mood can be gauged by Churchill's speech at Westminster College in Fulton, Missouri on 5 March 1946. He warned of an 'Iron Curtain' descending across Europe and of a relentless Communist advance around the world. Given this danger, Churchill argued, 'It would . . . be wrong and imprudent to entrust the secret knowledge or experience of the atomic bomb . . . to the world organization while it is still in its infancy. It would be criminal madness to cast it adrift in this still agitated and un-united world.' (Truman enthusiastically applauded this passage.) The Bomb offered the best protection at a time of high danger: 'From what I have seen of our Russian friends and Allies during the war, I am convinced that there is nothing they admire so much as strength, and there is nothing for which they have less respect than for weakness, especially military weakness.'[46] Churchill could make these statements precisely because he no longer held public office. But he was not simply a private citizen, nor a loose cannon. His value lay in his ability to voice the pessimism Truman and Attlee shared, but which neither could openly express.

While debate raged about the post-atomic world, the US decided to pump up the volume by testing bombs. The precise purpose of these tests was

---

* One satirist cruelly, but accurately, characterized the scientist's typical reaction to the bomb as 'just too terrible, too dreadful, too everything. We must do something about it. What are you doing? What I am doing? We must all get together right away and do more.' (Herken, p.71.)

unclear. The official explanation was that they were designed purely to amass data about the new weapon. But cynics suspected the real purpose was swagger and intimidation. Several members of Congress openly condemned the plans, and the FAS criticized the government for flexing its nuclear muscle at a particularly sensitive time. Byrnes warned, to no effect, that they would render negotiation all the more complicated.

The Crossroads tests were ostensibly inspired by the US Navy's desire to enter the nuclear arena. 'We are seeking primarily to learn what type of ships, tactical formation and strategic disposition of our own naval forces will best survive attack by atomic weapons should we ever have to face them,' Vice Admiral William Blandy explained.[47] In truth, the exercise seems to have been motivated primarily by an eagerness to blow something up. The US had a huge flotilla of surplus ships (many of them Japanese) which made for convenient targets. But, while ships were plenty, ports on which an atom bomb could be dropped were not. Bikini Atoll, in the Marshall Islands, seemed to fit the Navy's needs perfectly since the area was sparsely populated and a long way from the US.

Exploding bombs in paradise did not seem remotely ironic to self-righteous Americans. The idea did, however, cause some disquiet among the natives, who feared that the Americans had come to kill them. 'We were elated when we discovered that [they] . . . weren't going to hurt us', Emso Leviticus recalled;

> in fact, the Navy men were very kind and gave us big bins filled with all kinds of food that we had never seen or eaten before like C-rations, chocolates, corned beef and other wonderful things. They took some of us to the ship to get medical attention. One woman named Tamar was very sick, and when she returned, she was all better again.

First the bribe, then the revelation. On 10 February 1946, Commodore Ben Wyatt, military governor of the Marshall Islands, informed the 167 residents that they would have to leave. 'I can still recall the day when the more important looking Americans came to ask us to move from our islands,' Leviticus remarked. 'All of these new men were wearing beautiful uniforms.'[48] Wyatt told the islanders that they were like the children of Israel whom God had led to the Promised Land; their sacrifice would bring peace and prosperity to all men. Leaving the island was 'for the good of mankind and to end all world wars'.[49] Though the islanders in truth had no choice, most of them accepted their fate out of religious duty. Their Chief, Juda Kessibuki, told Wyatt: 'If the United States government and the scientists of the world want to use our island and atoll for furthering development, which with God's blessing will result in kindness and benefit to all mankind, my people will be pleased to go elsewhere.'[50]

The official government film of the test claimed: 'The islanders are a nomadic group and are well-pleased that the Yanks are going to add a little variety to their lives.'[51]

Around 42,000 military and civilian personnel were sent to the atoll for the tests, which cost $50 million to administer. The Americans brought 242 ships, 156 aeroplanes, 25,000 radiation-recording devices, 5,400 rats, goats and pigs – and 170 journalists. The USS *Appalachian* was turned into a floating newsroom, providing text transmission and photographic development for the international press corps. A team of interpreters translated reports into five languages. In the main, the media cooperated, since trust in the military remained high in the immediate aftermath of war. It also helped that the Navy was footing the bill for the reporters' junket in paradise. Journalists dutifully described the tests as 'benign, circumscribed and well-meaning'. *US News and World Report* explained that they were necessary to 'give the final answer to the main question of how today's modern warship can stand up in combat in an age of atomic warfare'.[52] The effect upon Soviet–American relations was conveniently ignored.

H. S. Uhler, emeritus professor of physics at Yale, predicted that the bombs would crack the earth's crust, causing seawater to rush into the resultant crevasse. Huge explosions and tidal waves would follow. Uhler also warned that the bombs might upset the gyroscopic balance of the earth, causing violent earthquakes on this 'sorely stricken human carrousel'. Blandy was quick to rebut:

> The bomb will not start a chain reaction in the water converting it all to gas and letting all the ships in all the oceans drop to the bottom. It will not blow out the bottom of the sea and let all the water run down the hole. It will not destroy gravity. I am not an atomic playboy as one of my critics labelled me, exploding these bombs to satisfy my personal whims.[53]

Fears were calmed, but then a temporary panic in the press corps arose when the Johns Hopkins seismologist Anatol Schneiderov warned that all the ships in the Bikini flotilla would be swamped, leaving no survivors. The university quickly retorted that Schneiderov was 'only a student' and furthermore 'of Soviet origin'. Some people nevertheless decided there was no point in taking chances. Of the sixty members of Congress invited to observe the tests, only twelve attended. In Los Angeles, San Francisco and San Diego an unusual enthusiasm for a walk in the mountains was evident on the day of the test.[54]

In Test ABLE, on 1 July 1946, a bomb named 'Gilda' (after a Rita Hayworth movie) was dropped from a B-29, exploding 1,000 feet over the lagoon in which eighty-eight ships and small craft were moored. The target was supposed to be the battleship *Nevada*, but the bomb missed by half a mile. Nevertheless, five ships sank immediately, six were immobilized and others suffered a range of damage. The official report submitted by the US Strategic Bombing Survey concluded that the bomb had little value in naval actions and was ineffective against submarines.

This result disappointed military personnel who had imagined a weapon of unlimited omnipotence. But, as William Laurence, who had witnessed Trinity and Nagasaki, found, one man's worry was another's relief:

> Before Bikini the world stood in awe of this new cosmic force. Since Bikini this feeling of awe has largely evaporated and has been supplanted by a sense of relief unrelated to the grim reality of the situation. Having lived with a nightmare for nearly a year, the average citizen is now only too glad to grasp at the flimsiest means that would enable him to regain his peace of mind.[55]

One reporter compared the sound of the explosion to that of a 'discreet belch' from the far end of a bar, a Boston journalist claimed that 'there were more explosions in the first game at Fenway yesterday'.[56] The *Chicago Tribune* argued that the test had demonstrated that the power of the Bomb had been exaggerated by 'internationalists' who wanted the weapon outlawed.[57]

On the evidence of Bikini, the Bomb seemed survivable. The tests facilitated a process of accommodation; Americans were learning to live with the weapon. In the *Saturday Review*, Norman Cousins lamented the fact that 'the atomic bomb is no longer a novelty on the face of the earth, no longer a phenomenon. After four bombs, the mystery dissolves into a pattern. By this time there is almost a standardization of catastrophe.'[58] *Newsweek* encouraged this process by commenting: 'Man . . . set off his fourth atomic bomb this week. . . .Yet . . . he could sigh with relief. Alive he was; given time and the sanity of nations, he might yet harness for peace the greatest force that living creatures had ever released on this earth.'[59]

The star of the propaganda show was Patty the piglet, one of the thousands of animals brought to Bikini. Found swimming in the radiated waters of the lagoon after the blast, she was rescued by the Navy. At this point it becomes difficult to separate truth from propagandistic fantasy, but, according to *Colliers*, Patty was taken to the Naval Medical Research Institute in Bethesda, Maryland, where she ate like, well, a pig, and grew into a happy, 600-pound paragon of porcine perfection, never for a moment showing any ill effects of her extended swim in radioactive soup. She ended up a VIP (very important pig) at a local zoo, testament to the benign nature of the bomb and proof that, though pigs cannot perhaps fly, they can swim.

Bikini demonstrated that a single, poorly aimed, bomb had limited potential against a flotilla of warships. But that could have been predicted beforehand. Journalists, politicians and ordinary folk continued to think of the bomb in conventional terms, in other words as a powerful explosive. The radiation problem was conveniently forgotten. Amidst the chatter, a study by the Joint Chiefs Evaluation Board went largely unnoticed:

> Measurements of radiation intensity and a study of animals exposed in ships show that the initial flash of principal lethal radiations, which are gamma-rays and neutrons, would have killed almost all personnel normally stationed aboard the ships centered around the air burst and many others at greater distances. . . . it is clear that vessels within a mile of an atomic bomb air burst would eventually become inoperative due to crew casualties.[60]

A Strategic Bombing Survey report subsequently confirmed that 'Efforts to decontaminate these ships have thus far emphasized the difficulties of the problem and the necessity for further experiment.'

In the second test, BAKER, the weapon was exploded underwater, to measure its effect against the hulls of ships and submarines. This had a predictable effect:

> At the moment of explosion, a dome, which showed the light of incandescent material within, rose upon the surface of the lagoon. The blast was followed by an opaque cloud which rapidly enveloped about half of the target array. The cloud vanished in about two seconds to reveal, as predicted, a column of ascending water. From some of the photographs it appears that this column lifted the 26,000-ton battleship ARKANSAS for a brief interval before the vessel plunged to the bottom of the lagoon.

A huge column, containing 'roughly ten million tons of water', rose into the air, with spray rising even higher. About half the target flotilla was engulfed. Evaluators were fully aware of the significance of this effect:

> The explosion produced intense radioactivity in the waters of the lagoon. . . . Great quantities of radioactive water descended upon the ships from the column or were thrown over them by waves. . . . These contaminated ships became radioactive stoves, and would have burned all living things aboard them with invisible and painless but deadly radiation.[61]

Prior to the test, one medical specialist warned that the ships would not be safe to re-board for months. In fact, sailors were sent to clean them four days after the blast, armed only with mops, soap and water. When this proved ineffective, crews were instructed to sandblast the paint from the ships. Frank Karasti, who boarded one of the target destroyers a day after the blast, recalled that 'Out of the four hours we spent on her, two were spent vomiting and retching as we all became violently ill.' Another sailor recalled, 'At no time did I or anyone working with me – that is, naval personnel – have a Geiger counter, nor any other testing device to measure the danger of radiation.' A Navy diver remarked how the scientists were 'dressed like for outer space, with instruments like I had never seen', while 'all we had were skin and tanks'.[62]

Dr David Bradley, one of the chief radiation monitors, later remarked that, if the safety of personnel had been the first priority, 'nothing at all could have been done and the experiment would have been a total failure'. Stafford Warren, a medical adviser, condemned this 'blind, hairy-chested approach to the matter of radiological safety'.[63] He managed to convince commanders to abandon some ships due to the extreme health risk to sailors, but at the cost of being labelled a crank by Los Alamos scientists. Their official report boasted: 'As a result of carefully planned operating procedures and radiological safety measures, no casualties resulted from . . . radiation during, or after, either test.'[64] That was a rather hasty conclusion, but, in 1946, long-term effects were not widely understood. In any case, the US felt herself at war, and in war people get hurt.

In early 1946, the Acheson-Lilienthal report came out heavily in favour of international control of nuclear energy, based upon 'an acceptance . . . that our monopoly cannot last'. The authors (Dean Acheson, the Under-Secretary of State, and David Lilienthal, formerly director of the Tennessee Valley Authority) called for a system of safeguards which would outlaw 'certain well-defined activities' which might lead to the production of atomic bombs.[65] Oppenheimer, who advised the authors, had a profound influence on the tone of the report.

Dissenting scientists were pleased, and some even convinced themselves that their agitation had succeeded. But it soon became clear that Truman would pay little heed to the report. The President's hard-nosed attitude was signalled when Bernard Baruch was appointed US spokesman on the newly formed United Nations Atomic Energy Commission. 'When I read the news', Lilienthal remarked, 'I was quite sick. . . . We need a man who is young, vigorous, not vain, and who the Russians would feel isn't out simply to put them in a hole, not really caring about international co-operation. Baruch has none of these qualifications.'[66] Baruch, a hardline anti-Communist, had a twenty-kiloton ego. He had no intention of listening to scientific opinion. 'I knew all I wanted to know,' he confessed. 'It went boom and it killed millions of people and I thought it was an ethical and a political problem and I would proceed on that theory.'[67] Like Truman, he saw the Bomb as a 'winning weapon'. 'Before a country is ready to relinquish any winning weapon', he once remarked, 'it must have more than words to reassure it.'[68] The news of Baruch's appointment plunged Oppenheimer into deep depression. 'That was the day I gave up hope.'[69]

'We are here to make a choice between the quick and the dead,' Baruch told the UN Commission on 14 June 1946. Like a latter day Moses he would lead a frightened world to the promised land. 'Behind the black portent of the new atomic age lies a hope which, seized upon with faith, can work our salvation. If we fail, then we have damned every man to be the slave of Fear. Let us not deceive ourselves: We must elect World Peace or World Destruction.' He explained that he did not see any merit in 'simple renunciation, unsupported by effective guarantees of security and armament limitation'. The world deserved something more substantial. 'If I read the signs aright, the people want a program not composed merely of pious thoughts but of enforceable sanctions – an international law with teeth in it.'[70]

The Soviets found the teeth too sharp. They objected in particular to two proposals: the Security Council veto would not apply in questions relating to the violation of future nuclear treaties, and inspection of nuclear facilities would be unrestricted. Baruch's plan was fatally ambitious and cynically one-sided. All other nations were essentially asked to give up nuclear weapons even before they had developed them. Sceptics saw a clever trap: a proposal designed to fail and, in the process, to cast the Russians as villains. Given that the talks occurred against the backdrop of the Bikini tests, America seemed at best schizophrenic, at worst two-faced.

At the UN meeting, American and Soviet representatives met like two heavyweight prize-fighters – big on muscle but short on subtlety. The pacifist A. J. Muste felt that both sides assumed an attitude of 'I cannot trust you and will not take any risks, but I ask you to trust me and take the risks involved'.[71] Baruch used the American nuclear monopoly like a fearsome club, while the Russians played innocent martyrs, threatened by a nuclear-mad America. In fact, the Russians could afford to be uncooperative, since their own atomic programme was much more advanced than America realized. For Stalin, the Bomb was a hugely important status symbol; he did not think the device itself was dangerous, but the American monopoly was. He wanted to break that monopoly, while the Baruch Plan seemed to reinforce it. For this reason, the Soviet reception was as cold as a Siberian wind. Impasse was apparent long before Baruch resigned in January 1947. The UN failure convinced Americans that there was no sense in sharing secrets and that security would henceforth be measured by the size of their arsenal.

Meanwhile, Congress looked again at nuclear regulation. The McMahon Bill, or Atomic Energy Act of July 1946, seemed to take nuclear power out of the hands of the military, passing it instead to an Atomic Energy

Commission (AEC). But a last minute amendment by the conservative Senator Arthur Vandenburg put real power in the hands of a military liaison committee which would review AEC decisions. The AEC henceforward danced to the military's tune. During the first fifteen years of its life, 70 per cent of its budget went to weapons-related projects.

The Act codified into law Truman's cautious instincts. Nuclear cooperation was placed on indefinite hold, while efforts were directed toward improvement and expansion of the American arsenal. The Americans were not only disinclined to share secrets with the Russians, they were also no longer willing to confide in the British. Much to the dismay of the Attlee government, the Act stipulated that the 1943 Quebec Agreement no longer applied. The doors to the laboratories were slammed shut, bolted and barred. But, if polls are accurate, this is what most Americans wanted. After the Bikini tests, support for secrecy grew. Most people agreed with the *Arizona Republic* that the Bomb was America's 'ace in the hole'.[72]

A second series of tests, codenamed Sandstone, was approved in June 1947. Since the planned tests were land-based, and therefore unsuitable for Bikini, the task force decided instead to use Eniwetok Atoll. Some 142 residents were moved to a less desirable location over one hundred miles away, after being assured that they were making an important contribution to world peace. Three devices of 37, 49 and 18 kilotons were eventually exploded. Much had changed in a year. This time, there was no great public relations effort; in fact, new designs meant secrecy was paramount. The public was nevertheless assured that the tests would 'provide new fundamental data and a broader understanding of the phenomena of nuclear fission, for peaceful as well as military application of atomic energy'.[73]

After Hiroshima, an enthusiasm for world government burst forth like a mushroom cloud, and then quickly dissipated. The idea attracted an impressive array of supporters, including Harold Urey, Norman Cousins, Sumner Welles, and E. B. White, not to mention a significant section of the Los Alamos community. The interest was motivated mainly by a fear that the terrible weapon the Americans had invented would someday be used on them. No one ever explained how common ground might be found to accommodate the world's competing ideologies. Much of the talk was in truth inspired by a deluded hope that the entire world might be recreated in the American image – a *Pax Americana* forged by the Bomb.

By 1947, the 'revolt' of the scientists was virtually dead, though a few lonely voices howled from the wilderness. Many of those who had left the laboratories immediately after the war returned, either out of a desire to be part of cutting edge research, or simply for a job. A smug Groves commented: 'What happened is what I expected, that after they had this extreme freedom for about six months their feet began to itch, and as you know, almost every one of them has come back into government research, because it [is] just too exciting.'[74] A poll of FAS members revealed a large majority in favour of weapons research, though whether this was simply self-justification is not clear. There might indeed have been a genuine political conversion, inspired by growing fears about a nuclear arms race and a feeling that the United States, in order to protect herself, had to stay ahead.

It is easy to exaggerate the importance of the brief revolt of the scientists. Moral protest always attracts attention, even when the number of protestors is puny and their effect minuscule. The life of the Bomb reveals one consistent trend: a few scientists write agonized letters to the *New Statesman* or the *Nation* while thousands of others take the government's money and make its weapons. Bohr once remarked that scientists had become both spectators and actors in the great drama of being. But therein lay a danger. They exhibited the actor's egotism – drawn to the big part, blinded by the footlights and intoxicated by celebrity.

Victor Weisskopf thought that the Bomb was 'the first serious encounter of physicists with the problems of responsibility'.[75] In truth, most of them gave guilt a wide berth. David Hawkins, the Berkeley philosopher who followed his friend Oppenheimer to Los Alamos, was disturbed by the 'manic, joyous, delirious' enthusiasm there. The scientists 'seemed to have lost sight of the grave consequences of doing this job'.[76] 'They had come through the war without scars,' Freeman Dyson said of his colleagues. 'Los Alamos had been for them a great lark. It left their innocence untouched.'[77] When Oppenheimer left Los Alamos, his staff formally thanked him for the atmosphere he had helped to create. 'We drew more satisfaction from our work than our consciences ought to have allowed us,' they admitted somewhat guiltily.[78] Creating havoc had been great fun. For most scientists the intense excitement of nuclear research would continue to smother moral scruples. It is perhaps possible that the guilt many felt arose not from the bomb itself, but from the enjoyment derived in making it.

CHAPTER 8

On a Russian Scale

In 1991, a bizarre argument erupted in the Russian press. Ultra-patriotic rightists, threatened by the disintegration of the Soviet bloc, launched a blistering attack on the scientific community, in particular the physicists. In magazines like *Molodaya Guardia*, they claimed that Russian spies, not scientists, were chiefly responsible for breaking the American nuclear monopoly. 'There was no "Russian" atomic bomb', one author proudly asserted. 'There was only an American one, masterfully discovered by Soviet spies.' Since physics is 'a Jewish science', the physicists could not, by definition, be patriots.

Lurking in the shadows was the KGB. Disgruntled spies complained that their contribution to the development of the first Soviet bomb had not been adequately recognized. Among the discontented was Lt. Colonel Anatoly Iatskov, the former chief spy in New York who had supplied a sketch of Fat Man to comrades back home. Iatskov was awarded the Combat Red Banner Order for his efforts, but that failed to satisfy him. The award rests a number of rungs down the ladder of prestige from the top honour – the Hero of Socialist Labour. Six atomic physicists had been made Heroes no less than three times each.*

Hell hath no fury like a spy scorned. In an effort to set the record straight, the KGB opened its files to historians in the hope that they would reveal just how much had been stolen from the Americans and, by implication, how little was owed to Soviet science. Since they could no longer derive credit from the survival of the state they had served, the spies sought the next best thing: personal glory.

The historians were all set to publish their findings in the journal *Issues in the History and Methods of Natural Science*. But, at the last moment, publication was blocked on the recommendation of senior physicists, who argued that the articles revealed sensitive nuclear secrets of benefit to an aspiring nuclear power. Publication was cancelled, leaving the world a slightly safer place.

Or so it seemed. Sergei Leskov, a journalist at *Izvestia*, believes that the

---

* Only Leonid Breshnev was more often honoured – he gave himself the award five times.

embargo on publication had nothing to do with nuclear secrets. The dispute was instead 'part of the struggle for a place on the Mount Olympus of history'. Having consulted 'experts' about the banned material, Leskov concluded that 'even Edward Teller and Andrei Sakharov would not have been able to build a bomb based on the information it contained'.* While that might be true, David Holloway, an expert on Russian atomic physics, argues that a cautious line is always merited. In any case, he contends, the documents that were released adequately demonstrate the KGB's point about the debt owed to espionage.[1] Unconvinced, a disgruntled Leskov feels that, after political and economic disintegration, 'no great new feats are being performed. The heirs of history have no choice but to divide what was achieved by previous generations. The sons now divide the glory of their fathers.'[2]

But how great was that debt? When Stalin learned, at Potsdam, that the US had developed a powerful new weapon, he immediately relayed the information to Molotov. The latter replied: 'We'll have to talk it over with Kurchatov and get him to speed things up.'[3] Igor Kurchatov was the USSR's chief nuclear scientist. In other words, Stalin understood precisely what Truman meant and, in fact, knew about atom bombs well before the man from Missouri. Some time before Roosevelt's death, Stalin had seen the sketch of Fat Man supplied by Iatskov.

One of the middle-ranking scientists on the British team at Los Alamos was Klaus Fuchs, the son of a German Protestant pastor. While still in Germany, Fuchs had dabbled in communist politics. He fled to Britain in 1933 to escape arrest and, eight years later, was invited by Peierls to join a team working on gaseous diffusion. Shortly after the German invasion of the USSR, Fuchs decided to pass secrets to the Soviets. 'I had complete confidence in Russian policy and I believed that the Western Allies deliberately allowed Russia and Germany to fight each other to the death,' he later revealed. 'I had therefore no hesitation in giving all the information I had.'[4] He eventually managed to pass on what amounted to a blueprint for the implosion bomb. Treason was committed not out of cynicism, self-aggrandisement or any particular hatred of the capitalist world, but rather out of loyalty to mankind. Fuchs thought that the monopolization of the weapon by one power endangered world peace. In this view, he had many supporters, but was unusual in his reaction.

According to Colonel Vladimir Barkovski, one of the KGB conduits for Manhattan Project secrets, at least ten members of the British contingent supplied information to the Soviets. He claims that they did so for no financial reward.[5] Since Barkovski has refused to name the other spies, it

---

* In any case, he pointed out, an 'internal' KGB journal (circulation 150,000) had already published the disputed material.

is impossible to tell whether his claims are true, or simply another example of KGB kite-flying. But we do know that Fuchs was not the only leak. As has been discussed, the technician Harry Greenglass passed sensitive information to his brother-in-law, Julius Rosenberg. Far more important was Ted Hall, a boy genius who joined the project in January 1944 at the age of eighteen. Hall used his friend and fellow traveller Saville Sax as a courier to pass information to the Soviets. Reflecting on his action in 1997, Hall admitted that he was

> immature, inexperienced, and far too sure of myself. I recognize that I could easily have been wrong in my judgment of what was necessary, and that I was indeed mistaken about some things, in particular my view of the nature of the Soviet state. The world has moved on a lot since then, and certainly so have I. But . . . I still think that brash youth had the right end of the stick. I am no longer that person; but I am by no means ashamed of him.[6]

Hall's crimes were never punished. He was interviewed by the FBI, but, for reasons which remain mysterious, was never arrested.

Hans Bethe once remarked that 'Klaus Fuchs is the only physicist that I know who really changed history.'[7] Some veterans of the Soviet bomb project have claimed that espionage material saved them 'at least two years'.[8] 'The information we received was always precise and, most of the time, complete,' Abram Ioffe confessed. 'Of course access to such a complete source of information reduces the volume of our work by many months, facilitates the choice of direction, and frees us from extended searches. Never have I encountered one false instruction.'[9] At Los Alamos, Hall, Fuchs and Greenglass all worked on implosion, which meant that the Soviets were doubly fortunate in the intelligence they received. Implosion was far more difficult to engineer than the gun-bomb, but the nuclear fuel, plutonium, was much easier to obtain than Uranium-235.

Andrei Sakharov always downplayed the significance of espionage. 'There was only one secret', he argued, '[and that is] that it is possible to make the nuclear bomb.'[10] Implementing the stolen plans still required immense technical skill and a deep understanding of atomic processes. In addition, though the information was, as Ioffe claimed, always precise, Soviet scientists could not assume that it was. An immense amount of checking had to be done, since it was always possible that the Americans had intentionally released carefully constructed disinformation. And, in order to protect the secret of the stolen secrets, only the most senior scientists were aware that designs had been pilfered. Most scientists went to their grave believing that their bomb was distinctively Russian.

In 1994, the former spy Pavel Sudoplatov claimed, in a sensational memoir, that a number of eminent scientists on the Manhattan Project,

1. DOG test, 1 November 1951: US Army soldiers wait before 'attacking' an objective 500 metres from ground zero.

2. The Alpha-1 racetrack at the Oak Ridge separation plant. The wire for the magnets was made with 6,000 tons of silver obtained from the Treasury.

3. Oak Ridge: hundreds of buildings were needed to make a substance measured in grams.

4. Lecture at Los Alamos: Enrico Fermi is second from left in the front row, Robert Oppenheimer is behind him.

5. Trinity: Oppenheimer and Groves inspect the remains of the tower after the first atomic test.

6. Hiroshima: an allied correspondent looks over the remains of a city.

7. The *Enola Gay*:
Lt. Col. Paul Tibbets
prepares to embark for
Hiroshima.

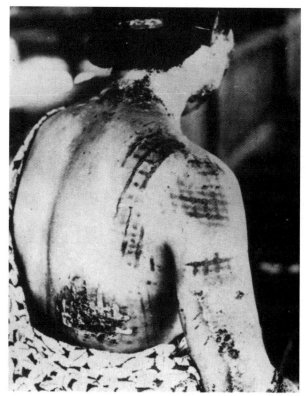

8. Hiroshima:
the victim's skin is burned in
a pattern corresponding to the
dark portions of the kimono
she was wearing.

9. Technicians assemble the Soviet Union's first atomic reactor, 1946.

10. Igor Kurchatov and Yuli Khariton in Central Asia, 1953.

11. A model of the Fat Man bomb exploded at Trinity and Nagasaki.

12. Yuli Khariton posing in front of a model of the Soviet Union's first atomic bomb. Note the similarity to Fat Man.

including Oppenheimer, Szilard, Fermi and Bohr, passed secrets to the Soviets. The best explanation for these ludicrous claims seems to be that the ageing Sudoplatov was keen to leave his family a sizeable legacy courtesy of an unscrupulous American publisher. But, while the allegations are largely without foundation, those concerning Bohr have basis in fact. In mid-November 1945, the physicist Yakov Terletskii met Bohr at the Institute of Theoretical Physics in Copenhagen. Terletskii pretended that the visit was simply an intellectual encounter between two scientists. In fact it was a carefully organized KGB mission arranged by Lavrenti Beria, head of the Soviet secret police (NKVD). Terletskii arrived with a set of questions prepared beforehand by Kurchatov.

Transcripts of the interview suggest that Bohr willingly answered Terletskii's questions without concern for the secrets he might have been divulging. Beria certainly presented the information to Stalin as an intelligence coup. But Bohr's answers did not in fact go beyond anything available in the Smyth Report, the US government's account of the Manhattan Project, which was already in Soviet hands. In any case, it is unlikely that Bohr, so keen to limit the spread of nuclear weapons, would have consciously done anything to assist their proliferation.

In truth, the visit was more important for what Bohr decided to tell the Soviets than for what the Soviets learned from Bohr. Aware that he was being manipulated, he cleverly turned the situation to his own advantage. He gave Terletskii the same lecture earlier delivered to Roosevelt and Churchill:

> All mankind must understand that with the discovery of atomic energy the fates of all nations have become very closely intertwined. Only international cooperation, the exchange of scientific discoveries, and the internationalization of scientific achievements, can lead to the elimination of wars, which means the elimination of the very necessity to use the atomic bomb. This is the only correct method of defense. . . . Either reason will win, or a devastating war, resembling the end of mankind.[11]

Bohr's rather idealistic reply was given in answer to Terletskii's practical question about possible defences against nuclear attack. Since Beria sent a record of the interview to Stalin, Bohr had succeeded in communicating his views to all of the Big Three leaders.

But Stalin was no more receptive than Roosevelt or Churchill. In fact, he was initially much more enthusiastic about the Bomb than they had been. The Soviet failure to develop a Bomb during the war was due to a lack of resources, not a lack of commitment. But while Stalin was intrigued by nuclear physics, he was not very fond of physicists, whose liberal views seemed to threaten his orthodoxy. The party had always been deeply suspicious of scientists even while it recognized their crucial importance. In March 1919, the Bolsheviks' Second Party Program recommended that great use should be made of scientists, 'in spite of the fact that in most cases they have inevitably been nourished upon capitalist ideology and have been trained in bourgeois habits'. These 'bourgeois habits' caused Soviet physicists to suffer badly in the 1930s. Investigating the theory of relativity or the concept of fission carried the risk of political persecution. But the greatest impediment to scientific progress in the Soviet Union was not the fact that scientists were too bourgeois, but rather that they were not bourgeois enough. The state encouraged research, but not as well as private industry might have done. 'The capitalist looks after his own pocket very well, and knows perfectly well how to buy scientists and make them work for him,' the Academician Dmitrii Rozhdestvenskii complained. 'Here, in a socialist country, what collective will take the place of the capitalist's ability to use science?'[12]

The first cyclotron built in Europe was Russian. By the outbreak of war, two more were under construction. Despite meagre support, a small group of outstanding Russian physicists worked energetically on bomb construction, isotope separation and the design of a reactor. The 'disappearance' from physics journals of Western scientists convinced them that both the United States and Germany were racing to build an atomic bomb.

On 5 May 1940, William Laurence, who had been following atomic research closely, published an article in the *New York Times* designed to alert the US government to the possibility that the Germans might be surging ahead. The article was spotted by George Vernadsky, a historian at Yale, who sent it to his father, the prominent Russian physicist Vladimir Vernadskii. The latter in turn wrote to the Academy of Sciences, urging an immediate survey of uranium deposits. Vernadskii also alerted the Deputy Premier, Nikolai Bulganin, about the importance of fission research.

Vernadskii subsequently led a team surveying uranium supplies, while Yuli Khariton and Iakov Zel'dovich investigated chain reactions. In early 1941 they produced a paper remarkably similar to the Frisch-Peierls Memorandum, though probably not the fruit of espionage. While Frisch-Peierls had led to the establishment of the MAUD committee, no similarly active response occurred in the Soviet Union. Though Soviet physicists were not far behind their Western colleagues at this stage, progress stalled when the Germans invaded on 22 June 1941. Laboratories were disbanded and equipment moved out of the way of the invading armies. The physicists themselves were either drafted or forced to concentrate their research in areas likely to produce immediate benefit.

In the spring of 1942, Georgi Flerov, a brilliant young physicist, sent a memo to Kurchatov proposing, essentially, a gun-type bomb. Dissatisfied with Kurchatov's response, the impulsive Flerov then wrote directly to Stalin, promising 'a genuine revolution . . . in military technology'.[13] He warned that work was probably proceeding apace in Germany, Britain and the United States. 'The results will be so huge that there will be no time to decide who was guilty of the fact that we abandoned this work here.'[14] A month earlier, Beria had informed Stalin about the Bomb, utilizing the top secret MAUD Report, which probably came to him via John Cairncross, private secretary to Lord Hankey, chairman of the Cabinet Scientific Advisory Committee.* Eventually, the steady stream of information making its way to Stalin convinced him that a formal project should be commissioned. On 11 February 1943, the State Defence Committee sanctioned an atomic energy initiative with Kurchatov in charge. Beria was appointed as an overseer to keep the scientists in line.

Stalin had merely commissioned a modest investigation of the possibilities for a Bomb, not a Soviet-style Manhattan Project. By this stage he had received intelligence that his enemy would not be able to build a bomb and that his allies might be able to do so. A full-blown Soviet project therefore seemed superfluous to the task of defeating Germany. The wartime Soviet programme existed almost entirely on paper. Scientists did not have the resources to move beyond theoretical calculations to practical experiments.

By February 1943 Kurchatov understood in a basic sense how to build a reactor and that the product of doing so would be element 94, or plutonium. But building a reactor was out of the question, in part because uranium stocks were so low. In January 1943 the Soviet government formally asked the United States, under the Lend-Lease agreement, for 10 kilograms of uranium metal and 100 kilograms each of uranium oxide and uranium nitrate. Since Groves did not want to arouse Soviet suspicions, not to mention those of Washington legislators, he granted the request. Similar shipments followed over the duration of the war.[15] But Groves gave with one hand and took with another. When Alsos found 1,200 tons of ore hidden in a German salt mine in April 1945, the team managed to spirit it away just before the area came under Soviet occupation.

Espionage provided Soviet scientists with a steady stream of information about the Manhattan Project, but the experience was rather like listening to a tennis match on the radio. The signal was clear, but the game itself existed only in the mind. A sense of helplessness was apparent when Kurchatov wrote to Beria on 29 September 1944:

---

* Spymaster Guy Burgess had recruited Cairncross as a Soviet agent while the latter was at Cambridge in the 1930s.

there has been created abroad a concentration of scientific and engineering-technical power on a scale never . . . seen in the history of world science, and which has already achieved the most priceless results. In our country, despite major improvement in work on uranium in 1943-44, the situation remains completely unsatisfactory. Though I know that you are extremely busy, in view of the historic meaning of the uranium problem I . . . ask you to order an effort which would correspond to the potential and significance of our Great State in world culture.[16]

In truth, there was little Beria could do. The American experience demonstrated that it was not sufficient merely to understand how to build the Bomb – a huge industrial effort was also essential. This was not remotely possible during the war.

After the meeting at Potsdam when Truman taunted Stalin with the Bomb, the Soviet premier immediately summoned Molotov and foreign minister Andrei Gromyko. 'The USA has a new weapon,' he announced. 'The real question is should countries which have the Bomb simply compete with one another or . . . should they seek a solution that would mean prohibition of its production and use?' He surmised that the US and Britain 'are hoping we won't be able to develop the Bomb ourselves for some time [and] . . . want to force us to accept their plans. Well that's not going to happen.' According to Gromyko, the Stalin diatribe was punctuated with some 'ripe language' directed at the 'allies'.[17]

For Stalin, the surprise of the Bomb lay not in its existence, but in its use. After Potsdam he had expected that his country would play its part in the final defeat of Japan and derive political advantage from doing so. But then the war ended abruptly, before Soviet forces could play a part. Alexander Werth, the *Sunday Times* correspondent in Moscow, recalled that Hiroshima

had an acutely depressing effect on everybody. It was clearly realized that this was a New Fact in the world's power politics, that the bomb constituted a threat to Russia, and some Russian pessimists . . . dismally remarked that Russia's desperately hard victory over Germany was now 'as good as wasted'.[18]

To Stalin, bombing Hiroshima seemed unnecessary and unscrupulous – a calculated effort to deny the USSR the spoils of victory. Perhaps understandably, the Soviets decided that Fat Man and Little Boy had been directed as much at them as at the Japanese. Hiroshima and Nagasaki demonstrated that the Americans had no qualms about using this terrible new weapon, and might therefore do so again. Stalin understood that the atomic bomb was a political weapon from which the Americans would try to extract maximum advantage. Truman seemed to be saying, 'behave yourself or you will be next'. According to former KGB officer Oleg Tsarev, Stalin convinced himself, on the basis of intercepted British intelligence documents, that the US and UK were preparing for an attack on the Soviet Union.[19]

Stalin played a clever game. The Americans thought that the Bomb would frighten him, and that fear would render him malleable. He, however, correctly calculated that the Americans did not have enough bombs to destroy the Soviet Union. 'They cannot decide the outcome of a war,' he argued. 'Atomic bombs are quite insufficient for that.'[20] He thought that the Americans would instead use the Bomb to manipulate him – exactly what they tried (unsuccessfully) to do at the London conference. Stalin told Werth that atom bombs were 'meant to frighten those with weak nerves' – clearly indicating that he was made of sterner stuff.[21]

In the end, the Americans derived very little advantage from their atomic monopoly. They could not, for instance, use the Bomb to stop the blockade of Berlin in 1948. The Berlin incident was carefully engineered by Stalin to show the West that the USSR could not be bullied. He simply ignored the Bomb. 'I believe that Stalin . . . embarked on that affair in the certain knowledge that the conflict would not lead to nuclear war,' Gromyko later commented. 'He reckoned that the American administration was not run by frivolous people who would start a nuclear war over such a situation.'*[22]

Meanwhile, the Americans whistled in the dark. They assured themselves that their nuclear monopoly would be long-lasting. On 1 June 1945, industrialists from Du Pont, Union Carbide, Westinghouse and Tennessee Eastman, the major contractors on the separation plants, were asked by Truman to estimate how long it might take the Russians to build a Bomb. Men with little experience of Russian industry spoke with supreme authority about her capabilities. Myths about Russian industrial incompetence were taken for fact. James White, of Tennessee Eastman, 'doubted whether Russia would be able to secure sufficient precision in its equipment' to construct a separation plant. According to Walter Carpenter of DuPont,

> it would take Russia at least four or five years to construct this type of plant even assuming that they had the basic plans. Russia's greatest difficulty would be in securing the necessary technicians and adequate production facilities. If Russia were able to secure the services of a large number of German scientists . . . they would be able to proceed much more rapidly.[23]

---

* Thanks to his spies, Stalin probably had a clear idea of his enemy's strength. At the time of the London Conference, the US had just nine atomic bombs. By the Berlin Crisis, the American arsenal stood at fifty bombs, still not sufficient to intimidate the Soviets.

These views harmonized with the accepted folklore about the Soviet Union. On 25 September 1945, the Agriculture Secretary Clinton Anderson counselled Truman not to worry about a Soviet bomb:

> It is not a question of cold science, or the application of certain mathematical laws. We know that in the production of the atomic bomb there was a certain element of American mathematical and mechanical genius which has given us the automotive industry, the great development of the telephone industry, and countless other inventive processes which are not always developed in every land, and which seem to be peculiarly the result of long years of mechanization of industry within the United States. . . . [the Russians] had copied all they could copy, but they couldn't copy our minds.[24]

The US was aware of Soviet efforts, during the final stages of the war, to commandeer German atomic research facilities, including, where possible, technicians and scientists. In December 1945, an attaché at the US embassy in Moscow warned that the Russians were determined to build a Bomb as quickly as possible. But, though the Truman administration was fully aware of Stalin's desire for a Bomb, no alarm bells rang. 'Experts' blithely assumed that it would take the Russians years, even decades, to duplicate the American effort. Leading the doubters was Groves who confidently predicted that, even if the Russians could steal the complete design for a bomb, they would not be able to make one because 'there is no uranium in Russia'.[25]

Exactly two weeks after Hiroshima, Stalin turned the makeshift wartime operation into a crash programme to build a Bomb. A short time later he told Kurchatov: 'If a child doesn't cry, the mother doesn't know what it needs. Ask for whatever you like. You won't be refused.'[26] The fact that he could even contemplate this while his country lay devastated is testimony to his determination.

Stalin's resolute mood provides effective rejoinder to those who have argued that the Americans should have shared their nuclear secrets. If Truman had confided in Stalin, it would not have altered the fact that the Bomb had become a vital component in the balance of power. As a demonstration of American technological and industrial might it had completely neutralized the cachet the Soviets hoped to gain from their remarkable victory over Germany. Since Stalin was desperate to restore the balance, he had to have the Bomb. Nothing was more important.

Stalin at first intended to give the project to Molotov, but his plate was already full. A better option materialized when Beria offered to put it under the auspices of the NKVD, which also ran the gulags. This had the advantage of opening access to hundreds of thousands of slave labourers who, because they were expendable, need not be protected from nuclear dangers.

In addition, the NKVD's inherent secrecy lent itself well to the Bomb project. All this seemed attractive to Stalin, but he still doubted that the NKVD could provide the level of management required. He therefore decided to graft Beria's network onto that of Georgii Malenkov, the chief of all Party cadres.

Beria was not remotely moved by the ideals that motivated his scientists. His was not an esoteric voyage of discovery but a practical quest to build a bomb in the shortest possible time. Therefore, he simply told his scientists to build an exact copy of the American bomb, the specification of which had been supplied by Fuchs and others. A specifically Russian design was cast aside even though it offered more promise than Fat Man.*

On the Manhattan Project, the forced alliance between scientists and the government had produced inevitable friction. In the Soviet Union, state authority had a much more sinister side, rendering the alliance even more fraught. 'When we Bolsheviks want to get something done, we close our eyes to everything else,' Beria warned a scientist who had displeased him. The cold menace in his voice made most men tremble. 'You've lost your Bolshevik edge. We won't punish you now, and I hope you'll correct the error. But don't forget – we have plenty of room in our prisons.'[27]

Many scientists found Beria intolerable, in part because a high proportion were Jewish and the NKVD was notoriously anti-Semitic. But few were in a position to complain. One exception was Peter Kapitsa, the 1978 Nobel laureate. Having been at Cambridge from 1921 to 1934, he understood what it was like to work in a liberal environment. After the war he became head of the Institute for Physical Problems and was expected to play a prominent role in the Soviet bomb project. But, in a rather rash move, he wrote to Stalin on 3 October 1945, asking to be allowed to resign on the grounds that he could not work with Beria. He explained:

> Comrades Beria, Malenkov, and Voznesensky conduct themselves in the Special Committee as if they were supermen. Especially Comrade Beria. To be sure, he holds the baton in his hands. This is not bad, but the scientist nonetheless should play first violin. . . . Comrade Beria's basic weakness consists in the fact that the conductor must not merely wave the baton, but also understand the score. In this Beria is weak.[28]

Kapitsa attacked the agreed strategy of copying the American bomb, arguing that a distinctly Russian approach would produce a bomb more quickly and cheaply. Stalin was never likely to be moved by such a letter. The Bomb was more important than any scientist, therefore dissension

---

* When finally built and tested in 1951 (the second Soviet atomic test) it produced twice the yield, at half the weight.

was intolerable. The American way might not have been the best, but it did guarantee results. Kapitsa aroused further displeasure by adding his weight to the moral debate then raging in the United States, urging friends in Europe and America to pressure their governments to outlaw the use of atomic weapons. A short time later, he was placed under house arrest for treasonous views and fired from his directorship. Under the circumstances, his treatment was remarkably lenient. A lesser scientist would have been shot.* That was certainly what Beria wanted.

Beria was probably well suited to a crash programme designed to build a bomb whatever the cost. He had no qualms about using slave labour, nor of working men to death. A genius at manipulation, his cruelty was used with precise calculation. Given the fear he inspired, his orders usually had immediate effect. But his sinister side has, according to two scientists who worked under him, clouded his real contribution:

> Beria understood the necessary scope and dynamics of the research. This man, who was the personification of evil in modern Russian history, also possessed great energy and capacity for work. The scientists who met him could not fail to recognize his intelligence, his will power, and his purposefulness. They found him a first-class administrator who could carry a job through to completion. It may be paradoxical, but Beria – who often displayed great brutishness – could also be courteous, tactful, and simple when circumstances demanded it.[29]

Beria, like Groves, eventually learned that he had to treat his senior scientists with some respect. Though cruelty and menace were standard NKVD procedure, most officials understood that creative energy had to be encouraged, not simply coerced.

On 25 January 1946, Kurchatov met Stalin, Molotov and Beria at the Kremlin. According to Kurchatov's notes, Stalin was keen to impress upon his chief physicist the importance of the project: 'Viewing the future development of the work, Comrade Stalin said that it is not worth spending time and effort on small-scale work, rather, it is necessary to conduct the work broadly, on a Russian scale, and that in this regard the broadest, utmost assistance will be provided.'[30] Stalin wanted the project to be massive, like the country itself. '[He] said that it is not necessary to seek out the cheapest paths' – instead, Kurchatov should spend, spend, spend. The huge cost became a metaphor for the Bomb's importance. Kurchatov was encouraged to be selfish, grasping, ambitious, a message all the more

---

* Beria met personally with Kapitsa after the latter's letter to Stalin. He gave the scientist a gift of a double-barrelled shotgun. The precise meaning of this gift remains obscure, but one can safely assume it was not given in a spirit of friendship.

profound given the deprivation then gripping the Soviet Union. By 1950, around 400,000 people were working in some capacity on the project.

During a speech at the Bolshoi Theatre in February 1946, Stalin revived the old Leninist line that there would always be war as long as imperialism existed. The Second World War had not eradicated imperialism; a clash between capitalism and communism was inevitable. Stalin used this speech as a warning to the West, but also as a prelude to the announcement of a new industrial programme to equip the country for the challenges ahead. He announced three more five-year plans, news which alarmed those Russians who, in the 1930s, had become intimately familiar with his industrial programmes. There would be no waiting, no period in which the people would be allowed to lick their wounds and enjoy the fruits of victory. Granted, a great leap forward was essential if communism was to compete with the capitalist world. But the strategy was also designed to provide a foil behind which the massive bomb programme could proceed. 'I do not doubt', Stalin told the audience gathered at the Bolshoi, 'that if we render the proper help to our scientists they will be able not only to catch up, but also to overtake in the near future the achievements of science beyond the borders of our country.' In the following month, pay rises for scientists were announced, and the science budget for 1946 was trebled.[31]

The Bolshoi speech was not meant as a direct challenge to the capitalist world, but rather as a stern demand to be left alone. Unfortunately, the Truman administration read it as a threat. While Stalin did not actually want war, that was how the Americans interpreted his message. Their reaction eventually provoked Stalin to adopt the script Truman had written for him. Each side saw the other as a dangerous threat and, by reacting aggressively, became just that. All possibility of understanding quickly evaporated. The Soviets saw America and her allies as intolerant. The Americans, on the other hand, thought the Soviets had willingly entered a fight to the death.

The five-year plans, and indeed the Bomb, would be paid for by the sacrifices of ordinary Russian people. They were used to that. But, unlike during the war, they had no precise idea as to what the sacrifices were supposed to achieve, beyond the vague promises of an industrial surge. Stalin realized that, in order to get his Bomb, his people would have to freeze and starve. Estimates suggest that about two million people died of famine in the Ukraine, while throughout the country countless others suffered serious malnutrition. In some places electricity was cut off so that nuclear facilities could get all the power they needed. Nor did nature cooperate. The winters of 1945 to 1947 were terrible across Europe, but especially so in the Soviet Union.

The nerve centre of the Soviet project was 'Laboratory Number Two' or LIPAN – aliases for the Kurchatov Institute, located on the outskirts of Moscow. The proximity of the lab to the capital made it impossible for anything more than theoretical experiments to be conducted. The Bomb itself would be built at a remote location. By the spring of 1946 development was centred on the provincial town of Sarov, on the Sarovka River. Direction of the new facility was given to Yuli Khariton, Kurchatov's trusted associate. Before the Communist Revolution the town had been a popular pilgrimage destination since its waters were supposed to have healing powers. Communists had closed the Sarova monastery in 1923, executed many of the priests and destroyed most of the religious buildings, including a splendid cathedral. From the moment the nuclear facility was established, Sarov disappeared from unclassified maps. It was instead given a series of codenames, the most well known being Arzamas-16, after the town located 60 kilometres to the north. It was sometimes known as 'the Volga office', while scientists jokingly called it 'Los Arzamas'.

Sarov seemed an unlikely place to build an immensely powerful weapon. Scientists who regretted its isolation were consoled somewhat by its great scenic beauty. Lev Altshuler recalled his arrival in December 1946:

> We made this journey in a bus which had been thoughtfully provided with sheepskin coats. Past the windows flashed villages which recalled the settlements of pre-Petrine Russia. On our arrival at the place we caught sight of the monastery churches and farmsteads, the forest, the Finnish houses nestling in the woods, the small engineering plant, and the inevitable companions of that period – the 'zones' [prison camps] populated by representatives of all the regions of the country . . . The columns of prisoners passing through the settlement in the morning on their way to work and returning to the zones in the evening were a reality that hit you in the eyes. Lermontov's lines came to mind, about 'a land of slaves, a land of masters'.

For the masters, life was good – certainly a marked improvement on conditions in Moscow. 'All material questions were removed,' Altshuler remarked. 'Leading researchers were paid a very large salary for those times. Our families experienced no needs. And the supply of food and goods was very different.' One Politburo member in fact complained that the atomic cities were like health resorts.[32]

The atmosphere was not unlike Los Alamos. Brilliant scientists were gathered together in a small close-knit community, united by what seemed a worthy cause. V. A. Tsukerman and S. M. Azarkh recalled how, 'in the first, most romantic years of our work in the institute a wonderful atmosphere of good will and support was created around the research. We worked selflessly, with great enthusiasm and the mobilization of our spiritual and physical forces.'[33]

Scientists did not choose to work on the Russian bomb; they were instead chosen. Summoned by the Ministry of Medium Machine Building, Vladislav Nikitin was offered either a Siberian plant or a mysterious research institute in the Urals. He naturally took the latter. 'The manager had a ready-made document – they knew my decision.'[34] Shortly before Yuri Smirnov's graduation in 1960, two men arrived at his university and mysteriously started looking through student records. 'They . . . [wore] the badges of Lenin prize laureates. They had excellent suits on. All of this made an irresistible impression on us.' They selected a few of the most promising students for interview and then whittled their choice down to just two, one of whom was Smirnov.

> I was curious where the organization for which we would have to work was located and what we would be working on. Instead of answering my question about the location of the organization, one of them took out his passport. We have this phenomenon of registering our residential address. That is, our passports have stamps of the geographical places where we reside. And he opened the appropriate page and I read 'Moscow, Center, 30.' And I, an absolutely uninformed person, immediately believed that this geographical spot was in Moscow, first of all, and, second of all, apparently not far away from the Red Square, because it said 'center'. This satisfied me and I did not ask any additional questions.

As for the nature of the work, Smirnov's interviewers remained tight-lipped; they merely said, 'You won't be sorry, you will be working on the most current questions of physics and you [will] find it an engrossing task.'

Attracted to the idea of performing cutting edge research in Moscow, Smirnov dutifully signed a contract. A few months later he was sent money for travel to his new place of employment. It seemed an unnecessarily large sum. Like a typical student, he spent the money on a party, saving only enough to get to Moscow. When he arrived at a mysterious office in Moscow, he was told that he would shortly be travelling to a lab 400 miles away. Smirnov protested, whereupon he was shown his contract and told to do as he was told. When he mentioned that he had already spent his travel money, the understanding official gave him more.

He was instructed not to talk on the train. 'They told me, when you get to the spot, you will find out everything.' When the train reached the destination stated on his ticket, Smirnov found that he was not allowed to leave. 'It turned out that I was in a special sleeping-car; there were many passengers in it, but they all turned out to be connected to Arzamas-16.' The train continued for another seventy kilometres until it reached a heavily guarded frontier, where soldiers conducted the most thorough search Smirnov had ever experienced. After the train crossed the frontier, the passengers suddenly became very talkative. 'They began to congratulate us, saying, you guys are getting into a very interesting place and that you would be shocked.'[35]

The scientists were Stalin's new warriors. 'I regarded myself as a soldier in this new scientific war,' Andrei Sakharov wrote. Indeed, Kurchatov referred to his team of scientists as soldiers and sometimes signed his correspondence 'Soldier Kurchatov'. The top personnel were treated like national heroes. Kurchatov recalled how, at the 25 January meeting,

> Comrade Stalin was preoccupied by thoughts of how to . . . make it easier, help [the scientists] in their material-living situation. And in prizes for great deeds, for example . . . He said that our scholars are very modest, and they never notice that they live badly – that is bad in itself, and he said that although our state also had suffered much, we can always make it possible for several thousand persons to live well, and several thousand people better than very well, with their own dachas, so that they can relax, and with their own cars.[36]

Kurchatov was asked to prepare a report cataloguing the kinds of inducements necessary to 'speed up the work'. Addressing this problem, Beria decided 'we will build fully furnished dachas for them at state expense. We will build cottages or give them apartments, whichever they wish. We will give them cars.'[37]

Though the scientists were aware of the sacrifices the programme imposed upon ordinary people, this awareness did not make them any less inclined to contribute. While many were placed under great pressure to join the project, it is foolish to assume that they worked against their will. Had this been the case, there is no way the project could have been completed so quickly. Speed required enthusiasm, which was in plentiful supply. Some were motivated by the same quest to discover which had driven the Manhattan Project scientists. But most were inspired out of a patriotic belief that the Soviet Union needed a Bomb to protect itself from the Americans. According to Altshuler:

> Our consent [to work on the bomb] was determined . . . by an inner feeling that our confrontation with a very powerful opponent had not ended with the defeat of Fascist Germany. The feeling of defencelessness increased particularly after Hiroshima and Nagasaki. For all who realized the realities of the new atomic era, the creation of our own atomic weapons, the restoration of equilibrium became a categorical imperative.

The work was simply a continuation of the Great Patriotic War. The only difference was that the enemy had changed. Viktor Adamski, who worked in the theoretical department, felt:

all scientists held the conviction – and it now seems right for that time – that the state needed to possess atomic weapons, that one could not allow one country, especially the United States, to hold a monopoly on this weapon. To the consciousness of performing a most important patriotic duty was added the purely professional satisfaction and pride from work on a splendid task in physics – and not only in physics. Therefore we worked with enthusiasm, without taking account of time, selflessly.[38]

Sakharov felt 'committed to the goal which I assumed was Stalin's as well: after a devastating war, to make the country strong enough to ensure peace'.[39] Stalin encouraged the scientists to think this way and they measured the importance of their work by the unlimited resources he provided. 'We saw ourselves at the center of a great enterprise on which colossal resources were being expended,' Sakharov wrote. 'We never questioned the vital importance of the work. And there were no distractions. The rest of the world was far, far away, somewhere beyond the two barbed wire fences.'[40]

'We never had a moral problem with what we were doing,' Nikitin recalls. 'It was a sacred thing.'[41] The moral burden was lessened significantly by the fact that the Americans had already taken the crucial first steps – they had made a bomb *and* used it. Nikolai Dollezal, the chief designer of the first reactor, felt that the bombing of Hiroshima was 'a repulsive act of cynical anti-humanism'. Yet he did not hesitate to lend his expertise to the Soviet project. Like his American counterparts, he took refuge in the technological imperative, passing the moral burden to the soldiers and politicians who would make use of his research. Nor was he bothered that the state to which he entrusted his research was responsible for terrible crimes against its own people. These, Dollezal felt, were internal issues. In international affairs, he felt, the Soviet Union had acted morally – certainly more so than the United States or Germany during the Second World War. He placed his faith in deterrence, echoing the Manhattan Project scientists.

> The security of the country and patriotic duty demanded that we create the atomic bomb. And these were not mere words. This was objective reality. Who would forgive the leadership of the country if it began to create the weapons only after the enemy had decided to attack? The ancients had a point when they coined the phrase 'If you want peace, prepare for war.'

'We knew nothing of those horrors of Stalinism which are today generally known,' Altshuler claimed. 'You can't jump out of your own time.'[42] That was perhaps true, but only in terms of degree and detail. They may not have known about the Stalinist purges nor about the full extent of the gulag system. But no scientist could completely ignore the fact that suffering in the labour camps made their work possible. Arzamas-16 was built by slave labour; the gulag was adjacent to the nuclear facility. The scientists would have seen prisoners march in and out. When Kurchatov ran into an obstacle, or when progress slowed, he simply asked Beria for another 10,000 slave labourers.

'Of course there was little joy in watching the columns of prisoners who built the installation initially,' Khariton and Smirnov have written. 'But all that receded into the background, and people had little regard for the difficulties of everyday life – they were trying to achieve success in the best and quickest way. They knew that the country was in danger and they understood that the state was relying on them and giving them everything necessary for their work and their daily life.'[43] The sacrifices made – by the people of the gulag and those who went without food or power – merely confirmed how big and important the project was.

'On the one hand', German Goncharov recalled, 'we were surrounded by barbed wire and were not allowed to leave; on the other hand, this helped our complete concentration on the work.' Exposure to the suffering in the rest of the country might have caused the scientists to question Stalin's genius. Isolation also meant that they fed on their own enthusiasm – an effect not unlike Los Alamos. But, at times, Arzamas seemed like a prison. Goncharov recalled:

> what struck me as very unpleasant and what weighed heavily on me for the first year was the realization that we were not allowed to leave the place even for a vacation. So, even during my vacations I couldn't visit my parents and relatives, you see? That was a heavy burden and it simply tormented me at first. But the contact with Sakharov, Tamm, Zel'dovich quickly relieved some of the tension; I got involved in interesting, absorbing work.[44]

The nuclear facilities were called 'closed' towns for good reason. In order to minimize contact with the outside and the potential for leaks, goods consumed by the community were usually produced there. Holidays outside were strongly discouraged, if not prohibited. In some cases, bonuses were paid to those who agreed to take their holidays within the centre.

The scientists were young romantics, in love with their country and inebriated by the idea that they would save it. The project provided an opportunity to prove themselves and to assert the right of their country to strut on the international stage. The Bomb was a challenge, a challenge inadvertently set by the Americans, who made no secret of their disdain for Soviet science and industry. Russian scientists eagerly joined the contest to prove the Americans wrong. But it was a high stakes venture. Though they were well treated, all scientists understood that the privileges they enjoyed were entirely dependent upon quick results. '[We] all felt the prickly chill of retribution when a device refused to work.'[45]

The Bomb was a secret project carried out within a secret society. It is no wonder, then, that security, a multi-headed fiend, always lurked in the shadows. Scientists were instructed to write their reports in longhand since typists were not trusted. Codes were widely used. Knowledge was strictly compartmentalized and doled out on a 'need to know' basis. Very senior scientists often had no idea about the precise nature of the project on which they worked. Granted, Groves instituted a similar scheme, but Beria did it so much better, if judged by the fact that no serious leaks occurred and the Americans remained blissfully ignorant of Soviet progress.

At one point a chief of the atomic bomb design bureau was talking to a colleague on the eve of the first Soviet hydrogen bomb test. He was leaning against the actual device when he said:

> It is incredible how far secrecy goes in our country! Somewhere there is another centre where they also work on weapons, and we don't even know about it! Yesterday Malenkov delivered a speech and said that hydrogen weapons had been created in our country. And we don't even know who did it and where!

When Sakharov joined the project in 1949, he was told by Zel'dovich that 'There are secrets everywhere and the less you know that doesn't concern you, the better off you'll be.' All this was somewhat ironic, given that the Soviets were protecting a secret they had themselves stolen from the Americans. But the security apparatus was not solely concerned with keeping secrets. Beria's regime was also designed to frighten workers – to motivate through intimidation. He encouraged the impression that his spies were everywhere and that, at any moment, a scientist might be wrenched from the project and thrown in the gulag. It was an open secret that under-studies were in place to take over key positions if any of the leading scientists disappointed the state. Ambitious individuals used gossip to get ahead, often accusing colleagues who stood in their way of 'political errors'. Ordinary failures, entirely normal in an experimental project, were often alleged to be evidence of sabotage or political deviancy. Jewish scientists and technicians, in particular, endured relentless intimidation.

The war had been a time of relative freedom for scientists — the struggle for survival had left little time for persecuting intellectuals. But, after the war, official paranoia resurfaced. Stalin needed scientists, but did not remotely admire them. The cosmopolitan nature of the profession, with scientists of different nationalities borrowing freely from each other, did not sit well with the Soviet system; Stalin suspected them of being more loyal to science than to the state. A worried Beria once asked Kurchatov if quantum mechanics and relativity theory were inimical to Stalinist thought. With admirable frankness, Kurchatov replied that if relativity theory and quantum mechanics were rejected by the state, the Bomb would also have to be rejected. Given a stark choice between politics and physics, Beria wisely chose the latter, an indication of just how important the Bomb had become. Stalin agreed with this relaxation of principles. 'Leave them in peace,' he remarked. 'We can always shoot them later.'[46]

The physicists, though they had to endure repression and intimidation, were ultimately protected by their knowledge. The worst accusation that could be levelled against a physicist was that he was cosmopolitan, in other words that he had borrowed too heavily from foreign, capitalist intellectuals. Yet the Soviets had no qualms about borrowing heavily from the Manhattan Project to build their Bomb. Copying foreign plans for bombers and missiles was also encouraged by the state. While ideologues dominated the USSR, the Bomb was a uniquely pragmatic venture.

At 6 p.m. on Christmas Day, 1946, Kurchatov's first nuclear reactor, built at Laboratory No. 2, went critical. 'Atomic energy', he pronounced, 'has now been subordinated to the will of Soviet man.' Beria could not, however, rid himself of doubt. Since nothing dramatic was apparent, he remained suspicious that his scientists were fooling him.

A short time later, construction of the first production reactor began in the Urals, fifteen kilometres east of the town of Kyshtym – a site subsequently dubbed Chelyabinsk-40. At a ceremony to mark the final assembly of the core in March 1948, Kurchatov referred to a Pushkin poem about the establishment of St Petersburg, built 'to spite our arrogant neighbour' Sweden. 'We still have arrogant neighbours,' Kurchatov warned.

> And to spite them [a town] will be founded. In time your town and mine will have everything – kindergartens, fine shops, a theater and, if you like, a symphony orchestra! And then in thirty years' time your children, born here, will take into their own hands everything that we have made. And our successes will pale before their successes. The scope of our work will pale before the scope of theirs. And if in that time not one uranium bomb explodes over the heads of people, you and I can be happy! And our town can then become a monument to peace.[47]

On 19 June the reactor reached full power and began producing plutonium for Russia's first bomb.

Construction of the bomb proceeded at breakneck pace. By June 1949 the Soviets had sufficient plutonium. The core was taken to Arzamas-16, where the mechanism awaited. When Zel'dovich saw the core, he felt that thousands of lives had been squeezed into a tiny mass – those of the uranium miners, the nameless project workers and the possible future victims of atomic war.[48] While Zel'dovich struggled to come to terms with what he had built, back in Washington the director of the CIA, Admiral R. H. Hillenkoeter, told Truman that the most likely date for a Soviet nuclear explosion would be mid-1953. Groves still insisted that it would be fifteen years before the Russians got the bomb.

By mid-August 1949, the device was nearly ready. A test site was constructed on the river Irtysh, 140 kilometres north-west of Semipalatinsk. At 06.00 on 29 August 1949 the device was detonated.

> On top of the tower an unbearably bright light blazed up. For a moment or so it dimmed and then with a new force began to grow quickly. The white fireball engulfed the tower . . . and, expanding rapidly, changing colour, it rushed upwards. The blast wave at the base, sweeping in its path structures, stone houses, machines, rolled like a billow from the center, mixing up stones, logs of wood, pieces of metal, and dust into one chaotic mass. The fireball, rising and revolving, turned orange, red. Then dark streaks appeared. Streams of dust, fragments of brick and board were drawn in after it, as into a funnel. . . . A strong wind muffled the sound, and it reached us like the roar of an avalanche. . . . the atomic mushroom was blown away to the south, losing its outlines, and turning into the formless torn heap of clouds one might see after a gigantic fire.[49]

Beria raced over to the bunker where Michel Yakow was sheltering. Yakow had been one of the invited guests at Bikini in 1946. With a mixture of nervousness and impatience, Beria demanded to know whether the Soviet blast looked exactly like Bikini. When Yakow replied 'Yes, Sir,' Beria finally felt satisfied.[50] The chief intimidator undoubtedly realized that a dud would have been deadly. He rushed to a phone to ring Stalin but, when he got through, the Premier simply replied 'I know' and abruptly hung up. Beria found the General who had deprived him of his moment of triumph and punched him. 'You've put a spoke in my wheel, traitor, I'll grind you to a pulp.'[51]

Khariton's relief was different from Beria's. 'In possessing such a weapon', he wrote, 'we had removed the possibility of its being used against the USSR with impunity.'[52] Another scientist, Igor Golovin, wrote:

> When the physicists who had created the bomb saw the blinding flash, brighter than the brightest sunny day, and the mushroom cloud rising into the stratosphere, they gave a sigh of relief. They [had] carried out their duties. No one became frightened like the physicists in the USA . . . The Soviet physicists knew they had created the weapon for their own people and for their own army which was defending peace. Their labor, their sleepless nights,

and the huge effort that had constantly increased in the course of those past years had not been in vain: they had knocked the trump card from the hands of the American atomic diplomats.[53]

If Golovin was telling the truth, it merely shows that naïveté was a characteristic shared by scientists on both sides of the Iron Curtain.

Stalin wanted to keep his Bomb a secret, since he did not want to provoke an aggressive American response before the USSR was able to build up its arsenal. But this proved impossible. Shortly after the test, a USAF B-29, equipped as a flying laboratory, found traces of radioactive matter in the atmosphere, in places where it was not supposed to be. A radiation detection aircraft subsequently confirmed that the source had to be a recent atomic explosion somewhere in Soviet Asia. The Americans dubbed the new baby Joe I. Official American acknowledgement came on 23 September in a terse statement from Truman. Two days later came a brusque denial from the Soviet news agency TASS:

> In the Soviet Union, as is known, building work on a large scale is in progress – the building of hydroelectric stations, mines, canals, roads, which evoke the necessity of large scale blasting work . . . Insofar as this blasting work has taken place frequently in various parts of the country, it is possible this might draw attention beyond the borders of the Soviet Union.[54]

Rather bizarrely, TASS went on to argue that the explosion in question could not have been the first Soviet atomic bomb, since the USSR had tested its first bomb nearly two years before.

In his statement, Truman neglected to mention that the Russian bomb had taken him by surprise. 'The eventual development of this new force by other nations was to be expected,' he claimed. 'This probability has always been taken into account by us.'[55] Bluster aside, the failure to predict how quickly the Soviets would develop the Bomb was probably the greatest blunder of Western Intelligence during the entire Cold War. Complacent assumptions about lumpish Russian technology had caused most analysts to assume that the American monopoly would survive for at least a decade. A handy explanation for this failure arrived when Fuchs was arrested in March 1950. But Fuchs himself did not believe that his contribution was crucial. In his interrogation, he remarked that he was 'extremely surprised that the Russian explosion had taken place so soon'. In common with other analysts, he had assumed that the information he had given 'could not have been applied so quickly and that the Russians would not have the engineering, design and construction facilities that would be needed to build large production plants in such a short time'.[56]

It was indeed an incredible achievement. On 29 October 1949, Stalin signed a secret decree rewarding the atom scientists. Khariton and Smirnov recall a lavish distribution of prizes:

> several particularly distinguished participants in the research, led by Kurchatov, were named 'Hero of Socialist Labor', awarded bonuses, and given ZIS-110 or Podeda cars, the title of the Stalin Prize Laureate of the First Degree, and dachas. Their children were to receive a free education in any educational establishment at state expense. The recipients and their wives were awarded free and unlimited transportation . . . anywhere in the Soviet Union, for as long as they lived, a privilege shared by their minor children.[57]

According to one account, Beria used a rather macabre method to decide the distribution of rewards. Those who would have been shot if the test had failed were given the accolade of 'Hero of Socialist Labour'. Those who would only have been given a long prison term were given the Order of Lenin, and so on to lesser punishments and more modest rewards.

In 1949, after the successful Soviet test, the *Bulletin of the Atomic Scientists* moved the Doomsday Clock from seven to three minutes to midnight. The world seemed more dangerous, but the Soviets felt more secure. Mark Hibbs, an expert on the nuclear industry in present-day Russia, has witnessed a surprising attitude among workers at a uranium mine, where at least 5,000 have died from cancer.

> the people who worked in this mine . . . said, 'It's true that it caused enormous suffering. But that shows just how valuable this activity was.' . . . [they] were intensely proud of the fact that their activity, their energy, their suffering, allowed the Soviet Union to make sure that the West would not invade their country.[58]

The bomb, Khariton argued, allowed 'Our country . . . to defend itself from really threatening mortal danger'.[59] That is perhaps true, but it also triggered an arms race that would eventually lead to bankruptcy and disintegration. The Bomb did not need to explode in order to destroy.

CHAPTER 9

Embracing Armageddon

On 21 May 1946 in Los Alamos, Lewis Slotin, a young Canadian physicist of Russian parentage, was performing an experiment designed to measure criticality. The process involved pushing two hemispheres of plutonium into close proximity with nothing more sophisticated than a pair of screwdrivers. At the precise moment of criticality, Slotin was supposed to pull the hemispheres apart, in order to avoid a massive radiation release. The process, called 'chasing the dragon's tail', appealed to young men with a taste for danger. Fermi had previously warned Slotin that he would not last a year if he kept doing the experiment.

Slotin's screwdriver slipped and a blinding blue flash illuminated the laboratory. Instead of instinctively ducking down, he reached in and tore the hemispheres apart with his bare hands. By doing so, he saved the lives of his colleagues, but condemned himself to an agonizing death. Raemer Schreiber, standing 20 feet away, saw the flash and heard Slotin say 'Well, that does it.'[1] As he was helped from the lab, he said to a co-worker: 'You'll be OK, but I think I'm done for.'[2] He died nine days later and was buried in a lead-lined casket.

Slotin was one of the last American casualties of the Second World War and one of the first of the Cold War. He was, in essence, a warrior – in different circumstances of brain and brawn he might have been a pilot or a commando. To men like him, fighting fascism had rendered danger irrelevant. The bomb was built by a team of young adventurers who thought in heroic terms of saving the world. Like all heroes, they cared little for their own fate and took huge risks. But by 1946, their carefree gallantry had become old fashioned. A new age had dawned. The Bomb, which a year earlier was a single weapon designed in haste to win the war, was now an arsenal carefully constructed to keep the peace. Slotin's approach, and indeed his character, was out of place in the new ethos of sophisticated bomb production. After the accident, Los Alamos switched to remote control critical assembly equipment. Operators were separated from the radioactive substances they controlled by hundreds of metres. Adventurers gave way to technicians. The factory replaced the laboratory.

★   ★   ★

In late September 1945, experts from various fields gathered at the University of Chicago to discuss the post-atomic world. Apocalyptic forecasts mixed with predictions more suited to Polyanna. One of the more clear-sighted participants, Jacob Viner, an economist, surmised that the world would be dominated by two superpowers, both of which would eventually have nuclear weapons. This would change the nature of war. 'The atomic bomb makes surprise an unimportant element of warfare. Retaliation in equal terms is unavoidable and in this sense the atomic bomb is a deterrent, a peace-making force.'[3] Conflict would take the form of a battle of nerves between superpowers. Later, the naval historian Bernard Brodie echoed Viner's remarks about deterrence. 'Thus far the chief purpose of our military establishment has been to win wars,' he later wrote. 'From now on its chief purpose must be to avert them. It can have almost no other useful purpose.'[4]

The effect of the Bomb was also analysed by the Strategic Bombing Survey, in a report published on 30 June 1947. *The Evaluation of the Atomic Bomb as a Military Weapon* foretold the way the United States, and indeed other powers, would react to the brave new world. To the SBS the Bomb was, quite simply, a 'threat to mankind'. For the first time, man held the ability to 'depopulate vast areas of the earth's surface, leaving only vestigial remnants of man's material works'. The Bomb was therefore cause for regret, but it could not be uninvented. The SBS placed little faith in international control – 'this nation can hope only that an effective deterrent to global war will be a universal fear of the atomic bomb as the ultimate horror in war'. In other words, the best defence against the Bomb was more bombs.

The report argued that conventional standards of threat assessment had been completely altered. In contrast to Viner, the SBS felt that a huge advantage lay in striking first with nuclear weapons. This implied

a consequential revision of our traditional attitudes toward what constitutes acts of aggression . . . Our policy of national defense must provide for the employment of every practical means to prevent surprise attack. Offensive measures will be the only generally effective means of defense, and the United States must be prepared to employ them before a potential enemy can inflict significant damage upon us.

In the past, American military power was deployed in response to actual attacks. But now a single attack could kill 100,000 people in seconds. Defence had therefore to be more proactive. 'It is necessary that, while adhering in the future to our historic policy of non-aggression, we revise past definitions of what constitutes aggression.' The duty of the military would henceforth be to 'to defend the country against imminent or incipient atomic weapon attack'. The mere manufacture of nuclear weapons by another power, or even the procurement of fissile materials, might constitute grounds for action. A JCS document, published around the same time, maintained that 'forebearance in the future will court catastrophe. Offensive measures will be the only generally effective means of defense and the United States might be prepared to employ them before a potential enemy can inflict significant damage on us.'[5] In line with this thinking, Groves advocated pre-emptive nuclear strikes against any hostile power about to develop a nuclear capacity.

Within two years of the first atomic blast, defence against nuclear attack had been categorically defined as a capacity for overwhelming offence – with all the expense that implied. The SBS report provided a blueprint for nuclear deterrence:

> An adequate program of defense . . . must have as a goal, the possession of a superior striking power and the ability to explode at will, with greatest effectiveness, such a number of suitably designed atomic weapons as will: (a) Deter a potential enemy from attack, or, (b) If he prepares an attack, overwhelm him and destroy his will and ability to make war before he can inflict significant damage upon us.

Even though the United States perceived no scenario in which she might use the weapon for conquest, she had to build a huge arsenal and sophisticated system of delivery purely to keep the peace.

The SBS accepted that 'the development of these weapons by others is inevitable'. Nor could it be assumed that, because the US had a head start, she would for ever maintain her lead. 'It is the lesson of history that new inventions may at any time vastly accelerate presently known methods and thus make it possible for a potential enemy of the United States, starting late, to outstrip us quickly in atomic weapon production.' Since the consequences of being left behind were so great, research (the SBS report argued) could never cease. 'Dominance in the ability to wage atomic warfare, the loss of which might be fatal to our national life, can be retained only by unflagging effort to hold that leadership in science and engineering which made the atomic bomb possible.'

With obscene understatement, the SBS concluded that 'From a military viewpoint, the atomic bomb's ability to kill human beings or to impair, through injury, their ability to make war is of paramount importance.' In other words, the Bomb implied an acceptance of the notion that civilian populations were legitimate targets. To this end, the Bikini tests provided direction on how to maximize kill potential:

> TEST BAKER gave evidence that the detonation of a bomb in a body of

water contiguous to a city would vastly enhance its radiation effects by the creation of a base surge whose mist, contaminated with fission products, and dispersed by wind over great areas, would have not only an immediately lethal effect, but would establish a long term hazard through the contamination of structures by the deposition of radioactive particles.

The advantage of radiation, the report suggested, was not just that it killed, but also that it demoralized those it did not immediately kill. Analysts cast a cold eye on the new warfare:

We can form no adequate mental picture of the multiple disaster which would befall a modern city, blasted by one or more atomic bombs and enveloped by radioactive mists. Of the survivors in contaminated areas, some would be doomed to die of radiation sickness in hours, some in days, and others in years. But, these areas, irregular in size and shape, as wind and topography might form them, would have no visible boundaries. No survivor could be certain he was not among the doomed and so, added to every terror of the moment, thousands would be stricken with a fear of death and the uncertainty of the time of its arrival.

The difficulty of providing relief would compound suffering and spread the demoralizing effect of the weapon:

Rescue parties could not enter any part of the city, except at the hazard of life, until the contaminated areas had been established and delimited. When this had been done, relief might be brought to those remaining in lightly contaminated areas, but the dead would remain unburied and the wounded uncared for in the areas of heaviest contamination where certain death would lurk for many days and, in which, for many years to come, continuous habitation would be unsafe.

The Bomb's effect would quickly spread to areas not immediately affected by blast or heat. Panic and illness would extend inexorably outward on a tide of shattered refugees. 'Thousands, perhaps millions . . . would rush from the city in panic, breaking down remaining transportation facilities, congesting highways, and creating in their flight new hazards to life.' These fugitives would expand the chaos; their 'contaminated clothing and any goods they carried could establish in others the fear of dangerous radioactivity, thus creating a unique psychological hazard'.

Throughout the report, strategies of defence and attack were interwoven. Strategic possibilities were discussed with respect not only to the action American forces might take but also to the kind of attack Americans might expect. Most striking is the chillingly dispassionate way in which mass extermination was discussed. It is not entirely clear, for instance, whether the following paragraph sought to expose a potential danger or to explore a strategic option:

> It cannot be assumed that in a future war, a participant, with a range of choice, will rely altogether upon a single weapon of mass destruction. Driven by the necessity of overwhelming his adversary, lest he himself be overwhelmed, a combatant might well choose to compound the horror of an atomic bomb attack with the simultaneous delivery of pathogenic agents which would insure that frightened fugitives would spread, not only their panic, but epidemic disease as well.

Psychological implications were discussed at length, with a view to formulating strategies accordingly. In a massive nuclear attack, the report concluded, 'of primary military concern will be the bomb's potentiality to break the will of nations and of peoples by the stimulation of man's primordial fears, those of the unknown, the invisible, the mysterious'.

Not long after the release of the SBS report, the JCS approved the Joint Emergency War Plan, codenamed Halfmoon. The plan, finalized in January 1948, called for 'a powerful air offensive designed to exploit the destructive and psychological power of atomic weapons against the vital elements of the Soviet war making capacity'.[6] Truman, who still had not given up on the idea of international control of nuclear weapons, rejected the plan and called for one based exclusively on conventional weapons. But matters of economy thwarted this effort. A conventional strategy implied a massive expansion of the military. At least seventy divisions would be needed to stand ready in the event of a Soviet invasion of Western Europe. Truman, unwilling to fund such a force, returned to the atomic option by default.

The United States Air Force was made an independent service in 1946, thus underlining the heightened importance of air power in the post-atomic age. The new service was organized into three units. Strategic Air Command (SAC) was given the bombardment capability; Tactical Air Command (TAC) the ground support capability; and Air Defense Command (ADC) the job of defending American skies from invading bombers.

SAC's role was simple and clear: in the event of hostilities it would carry out long range bombing missions against the Soviet Union. But it was initially ill-equipped for this remit. Lt. General James Edmundson recalled 'a hodgepodge of people and airplanes'; aircraft constantly broke down, and personnel were woefully under-trained. But then LeMay took over in 1948. A self-made man, he trained as a civil engineer but found his calling in the military. Returning to his native Midwest in late 1945, he was amazed at the 'difference between the bomb-blackened ruins of our enemies' cities and the peaceful Ohio landscape, untouched and

unmarred by war'. The lesson was clear: 'If you love America, do everything you can to make sure that what happened to Germany and Japan
will never happen to our country.'[7] For him, 'making sure' meant building
a military force which had no equal. He retained the engineer's tendency
to approach problems structurally; solutions lay in a consideration of time,
energy and space – a coldly rational approach that left no room for moral
nuance.

In mid-1945, LeMay had predicted that the Japanese would surrender
on 1 September 1945. He had arrived at this conclusion by counting the
number of targets in Japan and dividing that by the number his men could
destroy each day. In other words, there was nothing subtle about his
approach to war: victory came when everything was destroyed. LeMay
loved his bombs and his bombers. 'That beautiful devilish pod underneath, clinging as a fierce child against its mother's belly carries all the
conventional bomb explosive force of World War II and everything which
came before,' he once wrote. 'One B-58 can load that concentrated fire-
power and convey it to any place on the globe, and let it sink down, and
let it go off, and bruise the stars and planets and satellites listening in.'[8]

LeMay embarked upon a mission to turn SAC into a highly polished
fighting unit, enormously powerful and totally reliable. 'My determination
was to put everyone in SAC into this frame of mind: We are at war now!
. . . so, if we actually did go to war the very next morning, or even that
night, no preliminary motions would be wasted.'[9] He impressed upon his
forces the need to be vigilant, warning them about the 'gnome' in the
Kremlin basement who was waiting for the perfect moment to attack.
Most days the gnome would say 'No, we won't attack today.' But some
day, the gnome would announce 'Yes, the correlation of forces is right
today. Let's go.'[10]

LeMay was convinced that, in the nuclear age, the only intelligent war
strategy was to apply overwhelming force immediately. Speed was the
essence. He surmised that the Soviets would not have enough fighter,
radar, or anti-aircraft guns to handle a massive strike. So, in the event of
a Soviet threat, SAC would overwhelm Russian air defences with an insurmountable number of attackers. His idea was 'to deliver the entire stock-
pile of bombs . . . in a single massive attack'.[11] 'There must be no ceiling,
no boundaries, no limits to our air power,' he declared. 'The Air Force
must be allowed to develop unhindered and unchained.'

By 1949, his first plan for nuclear war was ready. On command, his
crew would deliver 133 atomic bombs to seventy Soviet cities in just a
few days. LeMay dubbed this 'killing a nation'.[12] But the Harmon
committee, commissioned by the JCS, found the plan insufficiently
comprehensive to ensure victory. Hitting seventy cities would kill perhaps
2.7 million people and destroy up to 40 per cent of industrial capacity,

but it would not '*per se*, bring about capitulation, destroy the roots of communism, or critically weaken the power of the Soviet leadership to dominate the people'.[13] It would not stop a Soviet invasion of Europe and might even make the Soviet people more determined to resist.

The Harmon Committee was probably right to conclude that LeMay's planned strike would not defeat the USSR. In the Second World War, the Soviets lost perhaps as many as 25 million people. Sixty per cent of their coal, iron, steel, and aluminium production was captured or destroyed in the first four months of the war with Germany. By this standard, LeMay's strike was survivable.

But, for better or worse, the US was wedded to a nuclear strategy – the cheapest option available. Since the strategy could not be abandoned, it had to be improved – or, more precisely, expanded. The Harmon Report advised that 'Every reasonable effort should be devoted to providing the means to be prepared for prompt and effective delivery of the maximum numbers of atomic bombs at appropriate target systems.'[14] In other words, in the event of war, the US should hit early, hit fast and hit hard.

Under this strategy, the US would go to war not in response to an attack but rather in anticipation of one. The consequences of misinterpretation were therefore potentially catastrophic. Such a strategy also required turning a blind eye toward the moral reckoning which would inevitably occur after such a gargantuan act of destruction. In addition, it ignored the simple fact that dropping hundreds of nuclear weapons on the USSR would produce fallout which might eventually poison the air over America. But LeMay was untroubled by these considerations. His goal, he later explained, 'was to build a force so professional, so strong, so powerful that we would not have to fight. In other words, we had to build a deterrent force. And it had to be good.'[15]

Each SAC crew was assigned a very specific target in LeMay's general plan. 'Each crew slept with [their] target,' Edmundson commented. Since the crews could not practise their designated missions by flying over the Soviet Union, they instead staged elaborate simulations over friendly or neutral territory.

We constantly flew what were called profile missions, where a guy and his airplane would take off . . . and would fly as nearly identical a mission as you could make it to what his war plan called for him to do. Distances were the same. Takeoff weights were the same. The type of target that he was given to hit at night was similar to the type of target that he was going after in Russia. You would hit refueling tankers at the same time. Everything would be the same as a wartime mission, except the geography that he flew over – He'd be up over Canada or up someplace else.

Steadily shrinking response times meant that SAC crews lived life on a hair trigger. They had to be available at any moment to fly to the Soviet Union and launch Armageddon. 'The biggest thing in your life was your wartime mission,' Edmundson felt.

> You were held for that. You lived for it. You knew that they might blow the whistle at any time, and when they did, that's where you were going. Unit commanders, group commanders, wing commanders, were never permitted to be more than three rings away on the telephone. . . . So this was . . . a pretty controlling way to live.

Bomber crews had to live every day knowing that they might be the ones to initiate utter destruction. They were taught to act upon a simple order and never to question the consequences of their action. 'It was a very fine line,' Edmundson felt. 'Athletes don't peak and stay that way forever. They peak and then they sit back and rest, and then they peak for another game. . . . this was peaking once and then staying that way . . . for 10 years, and living at the peak . . . and feeling the pressure . . . that goes with it. . . . It was a tough life.'[16]

Soviet military planners would not have been surprised by the Harmon Report or by LeMay's plans. They assumed that a future conflict with the US would begin with an American nuclear offensive which would cause immense destruction but would not be decisive. A massive land campaign in Europe and Asia would then follow, with the Soviet Union prevailing due to her huge conventional military forces. But the confidence that these assumptions encouraged was shaken by the rapid expansion of American nuclear capability.

Stalin nevertheless refused to be intimidated. In response to SAC's expansion, he built up an enormous armoured force in Eastern Europe, which stood poised to invade westward should the Americans misbehave. Soviet armed forces doubled from 2.8 million men in 1948 to 5.7 million in 1955. Granted, this was not a direct response to the American nuclear threat, but it was the best that Stalin could manage at the time. He even organized a strike group in Siberia, to enable an invasion of Alaska. Neither side wanted to appear intimidated, so both reacted by intimidating.

Once the Soviets developed their own nuclear capability, they too began to gather an arsenal to enable them to land a massive blow. But, while the Americans could hit Soviet targets with planes mobilized from European bases, or those fuelled in mid-air, Soviet bombers could not reach targets within the continental United States. Attention instead focused on American bases in Europe, North Africa and the Middle East, which were within Russian bomber range. What resulted was a hugely tense situation in which both sides understood the importance of landing the first blow but neither had an arsenal sufficiently large to guarantee that such a blow would prove decisive. Yet effective deterrence depended upon the capability of each side to destroy the other. The Cold War was at its most dangerous when both sides were able to maintain the fantasy that a nuclear conflict was survivable.

In September 1949, Stalin remarked to an aide about the new world order that would arrive with nuclear parity. 'If war broke out, the use of A-bombs would depend on Trumans and Hitlers being in power. The people won't allow such people to be in power. Atomic weapons can hardly be used without spelling the end of the world.'[17]

The Americans would probably have been surprised by that statement, and would probably have discounted it. They have always believed that their possession of atomic bombs does not endanger the world, because they do not consider themselves warlike people. But, while they did not consider themselves a danger, they did consider a nuclear-armed Soviet Union dangerous. They took seriously Leninist claims about inevitable communist expansion. Occasionally, Stalin provided justification for their fears, as at the Bolshoi in 1946. But, while Soviet aggressiveness seemed manageable before 1949, this changed fundamentally once the Russians got the Bomb. In early 1950, an internal policy document entitled 'Soviet Intentions and Capabilities' drew on commonly held American assumptions:

> The USSR is motivated by a combination of factors springing from its unique world position. As a state in a system of states, the USSR pursues a policy conditioned by the need to safeguard its national interests. As the successor to the Russian Empire, the USSR inherits a tradition of expansionism apparently inherent in its historical and geographic position. As a totalitarian dictatorship, the USSR is ever driven to new conquests, internal and external. As the center of the world Communist movement, the USSR is irrevocably identified with an increasing struggle for world revolution.

This led to a stark assessment: 'The avowed basic intention of the USSR is to engage in "competition" with the US until the US is destroyed, or forced to capitulate.' The Soviets would 'wage a relentless, unceasing struggle in which any weapon or tactic which promises success is admissible'. Any hints of peaceful coexistence should not be allowed to deceive: 'In the eyes of the Kremlin, it is war in the broadest sense of the term, a war to the death.'[18] In other words, the Americans were certain that, in contrast to themselves, the Soviets were ideologically inclined to go to war *and* to use the Bomb.

Americans thought not in terms of if, but when. In February 1950 the Pentagon released a report by the Joint Intelligence Committee exploring the probable timetable for a Soviet nuclear attack. The report accepted that, given the overwhelming American advantage in nuclear weaponry, an immediate attack was unlikely. 'However, with the progressive increase in their atomic capability, their attitude may become more truculent, thus increasing the risk of war. . . . if at any time they assessed that it was to their advantage to initiate military action against the United States and/or its Allies, they would do so.' The size of the Soviet arsenal would determine the moment for attack:

> Whether or not the Soviets would consider that a stockpile of 25-45, 45-90, 70-135, or 120-200 atomic bombs constituted a decisive atomic capability against the Allies is problematical. It is, therefore, uncertain if the Soviet planners would consider mid-1951, 1952, 1953, or 1954 as an opportune time to initiate an all out offensive against the United States and its Allies. In this connection . . . the surprise use of a relatively small number of bombs would be more effective than the expected use of a much larger number.

The report contained a number of other assertions that would become abiding truths of American Cold War policy. For instance, it argued that 'The Soviets will continue to try to stir up mass opinion in the West for disarmament and against the use of atomic weapons in the event of war. In this way it may hope to create sufficient public pressure on the Western governments to neutralize the United States bomb.' The idea that disarmament campaigns were Soviet-inspired would prove durable. In the American view, any proposal for arms reduction had to be treated with suspicion, because, given Soviet superiority in conventional arms, 'the elimination of the atomic bomb as a weapon of war would be militarily advantageous to the USSR'.[19]

Similarly gloomy predictions were made in NSC-68, written in large part by Paul Nitze, head of the Planning Division at the State Department. The document, released in April 1950, argued that when the USSR 'calculates that it has sufficient atomic capability to make a surprise attack on us, nullifying our atomic superiority and creating a military situation decisively in its favor, the Kremlin might be tempted to strike swiftly and with stealth'. The crucial year, the document argued, was 1954, when the USSR was expected to have 200 bombs. These assumptions were based on the 'fact' that the USSR is 'inescapably militant . . . because it possesses and is possessed by, a worldwide revolutionary movement, because it is the inheritor of Russian imperialism, and because it is a totalitarian dictatorship'.[20]

The American attitude deeply worried their most loyal allies, the British.

In October 1951, Vice Admiral Eric Longley-Cook warned the British government that 'Many responsible and influential Americans are obviously convinced that war with Russia is inevitable.' He thought the decisive point would come in mid- or late-1952 and doubted whether, 'in a year's time, the US will be able to control the Frankenstein monster they are creating'. A year later, though the attack had not materialized, Longley-Cook was still convinced that the American attitude remained one of 'we have the bomb; let us use it now while the balance is in our favour. Since a war with Russia is inevitable, let's get it over with now'. Ironically, British intelligence feared that the Soviets might be similarly inclined to go to war soon in order to avoid a worse war later. 'We cannot exclude the possibility', the Joint Intelligence Committee reported in February 1951, 'that the Soviet leaders may consider the immense scale of American rearmament and the rearmament of Western Germany to be a direct threat to the security of the Soviet Union and may decide their best course is to start a total war before Western rearmament becomes effective.'[21]

The Americans might not have wanted to destroy the USSR, but that is not the same as saying they were never a threat to do so. Because the US assumed that the Soviets wanted to destroy them, and because the American response was to prepare for all-out nuclear war, the risk that the Americans would attempt to obliterate the USSR with a pre-emptive strike was very real.

The new vision of war, as set out in the SBS report and eventually implemented by LeMay, had a huge impact upon the nuclear industry, particularly in New Mexico. Immediately after the war, many scientists were inclined to 'hand back Los Alamos to the desert foxes', a sentiment encouraged by the misguided hope that the nuclear genie might be squeezed back into the bottle. Most wanted to return to the cosy comfort of academia. Groves, however, was determined that the facility should continue. Seclusion, he thought, was the lab's greatest strength. Oppenheimer agreed. 'No government can adequately meet its responsibilities for defense if it rests content with the wartime results of this project,' he warned.[22] The importance of sustained research became undeniable after the American monopoly disappeared. '[If] there are to be atomic weapons in the world', Groves argued, 'we must have the best, the biggest and the most.'[23]

But, while Oppenheimer felt that Los Alamos remained essential, he no longer coveted its directorship. Determined to return to academia, he left as quickly as he could. Escape was not, however, quite as easy for the hundreds of less illustrious scientists. They were told that the work would go on and that the frenzied wartime pace could not slacken. Due to the highly sensitive nature of this work, Los Alamos would remain a prison in which knowledge was incarcerated.

For many scientists, staying in Los Alamos seemed a cruel form of servitude. Even those who agreed with the need for continued research wanted out of the New Mexico environment. The high desert had been tolerable when the war had provided justification for sacrifice. Now, with the threat of Germany and Japan lifted, the harsh climate, substandard accommodation, isolation and strict secrecy grew tiresome. David Lilienthal found that when he visited in February 1946

> Deterioration had set in . . . Scientists had left the project in large numbers. Contractors had declined to go forward . . . There was great uncertainty. Morale was badly shot. At Los Alamos we found the most serious situation because although some very able men remained, the top management of the project had left for the universities. We found a great many health hazards and fire hazards that were very damaging to morale . . . The net effect of that was a very depressed state of mind.[24]

A psychiatrist was called in to advise the government on creating a better working environment. Norris Bradbury, who succeeded Oppenheimer as director, brought in various entertainments, including touring jazz bands and professional wrestlers. But all this had limited effect. With the wartime excitement gone, Los Alamos seemed rather too much like a New Deal work camp.

Money, however, eventually proved an antidote to discontent. In 1946, half of the papers delivered at the conference of the American Physical Society arose from military projects. During the Second World War, military-funded research averaged $245 million per year. By 1957, that figure had risen steadily to $1.5 billion, with indirect research totalling an additional $3.6 billion.[25] The new generation of scientists enjoyed high quality facilities and virtually limitless research grants. But, with the dollar now the main motivator, the atmosphere in the laboratories was distinctly different from that which had prevailed during wartime, when scientists were driven by patriotism, fear and the quest for discovery. They looked nervously over their shoulders, cognisant of how fickle their paymaster could be. In the *Herald Tribune*, Philip Morrison complained that science had been 'bought by war on the instalment plan'. Before long, he predicted,

> The now amicable contracts will tighten up and the fine print will start to contain talk about results and specific weapon problems. . . .The physicist knows the situation is a wrong and dangerous one. He is impelled to go along because he really needs the money. It is not only that the war has taught him how a well-supported effort can greatly increase his effectiveness, but also

that his field is no longer encompassed by what is possible for small groups of men. There is a real need for large machines – the nuclear chain reactors and the many cyclo-, synchro- and beta-trons – to do the work of the future. He needs support beyond the capabilities of the university. If the [military] comes with a nice contract, he would be more than human to refuse.[26]

Labs were now subjected to timetable and productivity assessments, while clock and calendar entered every equation. Though theoretical research was not exactly discouraged, theories that seemed to have no practical application withered on the vine.

The old liberal ethic vanished and with it the ideal of an international scientific community freely exchanging ideas. Armed guards and sophisticated alarm systems regulated access to labs. 'The creation of new barriers, restricting the free flow of information between countries, further increased distrust and anxiety,' Bohr complained. 'The continued secrecy and restrictions . . . split the world community of scientists into separate camps.'[27] Scientists looked nostalgically to the pre-war period when borders were unknown. Now, out of self-protection, they were suspicious of foreigners working in their field. Instead of the free exchange of ideas there were secrets and whispers.

Under the terms of the Atomic Energy Act anyone working for the AEC or its contractors had to be vetted. A new category of 'restricted data' was established, while the death penalty could be imposed if anyone disclosed sensitive material 'with intent to injure the United States or secure an advantage to a foreign power'.[28] On 21 March 1947 a new 'loyalty order' provided for a comprehensive investigation of the political and moral reliability of all government officials. Though scientists did not, strictly speaking, fall into this category, paranoid authorities were not too interested in technicalities when national security seemed at stake.

'I am of the opinion we'll never obtain international control,' Truman told his advisers in July 1949. 'Since we can't obtain international control we must be strongest in atomic weapons.'[29] In the following month, the Soviets exploded their first atomic bomb. Being strongest was no longer a question of maintaining the monopoly; it was now a simple matter of having more bombs than the Russians. In response to the Harmon Report, the JCS called for a significant expansion of nuclear weapons production. Still smarting from news of the Soviet bomb, Truman approved the recommendations on 19 October 1949. As part of this expansion, the AEC established a new bomb factory at Kirkland Air Force Base near Albuquerque. This would become the Sandia Corporation, its purpose being to mass manufacture deliverable nuclear weapons according to designs supplied by Los Alamos.

In June 1949, a Soviet military analyst confidently predicted that the number of atomic bombs needed in order to defeat the millions of troops that the USSR could muster was more than a capitalist state could possibly make. That was a stupid prediction, given the might of American industry. In 1950, the Americans had 298 atomic bombs. Three years later they had 1,161. In the same period, the number of bombers quadrupled from 250 to 1,000.

The US had hitched her fate to the atomic bomb. The enthusiasm for all things nuclear could be measured at the Hanford Engineering Works, where a brief postwar recession gave way to incredible growth. Immediately after the war the workforce had been cut in half from 10,000 to 5,000, a disaster for private businesses that had sprouted in the Bomb's early light. But, then, in August 1947, the AEC announced an expansion plan – the largest peacetime construction project ever. Nearly 10,000 new residents moved permanently to Richland, while temporary housing was erected for 12,000 construction workers and their 13,000 family members. In 1948, over 2,000 babies were born at Kadlec Hospital in Richland. The area around the Hanford site had the highest birth rate in the nation. By 1955, federal investment topped $1 billion and 9,000 permanent employees earned a payroll of $55 million.[30] The nuclear boom was also apparent among the fish in the nearby Hanford Reach. Tests revealed levels of radioactivity in their tissues 170,000 times higher than in the surrounding water.[31]

Out in Los Alamos, seemingly limitless government money soothed moral qualms and made the desert seem attractive. From its low point in early 1946 the facility experienced a rapid resurgence. Gone was the wartime attitude of 'making do' for the duration; paint here and paving there made a huge difference to morale. Los Alamos quickly evolved from camp, to town, to city. Officials were no longer reluctant to provide amenities essential to peacetime life – cinemas, sports halls, shops, schools, etc. Everything assumed an air of permanence. The local sports club was christened the Los Alamos Atomic Bombers, and a small stadium was dedicated in honour of Lewis Slotin.

CHAPTER 10

To Little Boy, a Big Brother

When Neils Bohr visited Los Alamos in 1943 he asked his friends: 'Is it enough?' What he meant was, would the atom bomb be powerful enough to vaporize war itself? At the time, no one was sure whether Fat Man would be fat enough. But a different sort of bomb might be.

While chatting with Teller in September 1941, Fermi pondered whether a fission explosion might be used to trigger a thermonuclear reaction in deuterium, an isotope of hydrogen. The process, similar to the production of energy in the sun, promised virtually limitless explosive power. Teller took to the idea like a dog to a bone. While walking with Bethe in the majestic beauty of Yosemite National Park in the summer of 1942, he mused about an explosion powerful enough to destroy the earth. Bethe found the prospect terrifying, but thought that research was justified since 'the Germans were probably doing it'.[1]

Here comes the science, so pay attention. It's easy to understand Teller's excitement: not only did the 'Super' promise a big bang, it also seemed, on paper, easy to build. A thermonuclear reaction is, as the name implies, a very hot fire. Under intense pressure the nuclei of two light atoms (usually isotopes of hydrogen) can fuse to form a heavier nucleus (usually helium). The surplus mass is released as energy – a lot of energy. The size of the explosion is determined not by a critical mass – as in a fission bomb – but by the amount of fuel. The more fuel, the more powerful the explosion. In the early days, the most promising fuel seemed to be deuterium, which was much easier to procure than enriched uranium or plutonium. One kilo of deuterium consumed in a thermonuclear reaction promised 85 kilotons of blast. Thus, a one megaton blast (1,000,000 tons of TNT) could theoretically be produced with a mere 11.76 kilos of deuterium.

It sounds easy, but it's not. The protons in the nuclei of hydrogen have no desire to combine. They're like two partners in an arranged marriage who are certain they'll hate each other and therefore resist every matchmaking effort. But then, when they're finally forced together, they discover an enormous attraction. Their love is inseparable, and the sex positively explosive.

The difficult part is to squeeze the partners hard enough. Prior to 1945, that kind of pressure was present only in the interior of stars; it had never been produced artificially on earth. But the fission process (in other words the atom bomb) promised temperatures exceeding 100,000,000 degrees, which, if contained, seemed sufficient to create the pressure necessary to allow fusion to occur. The problem lay in containing the pressure long enough, in other words before the device blows itself apart with the force of the fission reaction alone.

Teller recognized the need for intense pressure, but underestimated the difficulty of achieving it. His conception of a hydrogen bomb was beautifully simple. Take one tube of deuterium and attach to one end of it an atom bomb. Detonate the bomb. This would pressurize the deuterium, causing it to fuse into helium, releasing an enormous amount of energy. The idea came to be known as the 'classical' or 'tube' design. But though the process seemed simple, making it happen was a great deal more complicated than Teller appreciated. Since complexity was not welcome at Los Alamos during the war, the idea was shelved. Or, more precisely, Teller was put away in a lab of his own, while others got on with the job of making a fission bomb. Neither isolation nor adversity discouraged him; the Super remained his abiding passion.

The wizards at Los Alamos saw the Super as the logical successor to Fat Man. But just because it was logical did not mean it was right. After the government had demonstrated its willingness to use the atomic bomb aggressively, enthusiasm for fusion waned. At a meeting with Acheson on 25 September 1945, Oppenheimer warned that there was 'a distinct opposition' among his colleagues 'to doing any more work on any bomb – not merely a super bomb, but any bomb'.[2]

This reluctance annoyed Teller. 'I knew that at that time, by splitting the uranium nucleus, we [had] only barely started . . . much more could be done in the hydrogen bomb and I was unhappy to stop it. It was unnatural to stop it.'[3] He was optimistic that progress would be swift. 'It is my belief that five years is a conservative estimate,' he wrote in October 1945. 'This assumes that the development will be pursued with some vigor. The job, however, may be much easier than expected and may take no more than two years.' The political implications of a bigger bomb did not worry him. 'If the development is possible', he argued, 'it is out of our powers to prevent it.'[4]

Teller was one of the few senior scientists inclined to stay at Los Alamos after the war, in part because he coveted Oppenheimer's job. When the directorship was instead given to Bradbury, he did not immediately resign, since he still hoped to be given overall control of thermonuclear research. When Bradbury offered him the directorship of the Theoretical division, Teller replied that he would accept only if 'we were to have a vigorous program for refining fission weapons which included at least twelve tests a year, or if we were to concentrate on the hydrogen bomb. In other words, I was fully willing to participate if our work could make a comprehensive contribution to the nation's military strength.'[5] When Bradbury replied that he could not meet these conditions, Teller skulked off to Chicago.

He returned to Los Alamos to promote his tube design at a secret conference on the Super held from 18–20 April 1946. Though the idea sparked some interest, it was generally felt that the process would prove more complicated than Teller appreciated. Teller, still insisting that the Super could be built in two years, bitterly objected to his colleagues' pessimism. Employing the same reasoning used by Szilard five years earlier, he argued that it was again necessary to build a horrible weapon because an evil power might otherwise do so first. Furthermore, he maintained, the only defence against a hydrogen bomb was another hydrogen bomb. Though Teller gave lip service to the idea of international control of nuclear research, he was pessimistic of progress. For this reason, he thought it ludicrous to place limits on research. 'It won't be until the bombs get so big that people will really become terrified and begin to take a reasonable line in politics,' he argued. 'Those who oppose the hydrogen bomb are behaving like ostriches if they think they are going to promote peace in that way.'[6] Teller also hid behind the physicist's favourite blind, arguing that it was not for him or his colleagues to decide whether a hydrogen bomb should be constructed or used. Those decisions had to be made by the American people through their chosen representatives.

Throughout his life, Teller consistently maintained that nay-sayers at Los Alamos delayed development of the hydrogen bomb. Yet the pessimists were right: the problem was immensely complicated. While controlled fission experiments had pointed the way to the atom bomb, controlled fusion was not possible, given the intense heat that was a necessary pre-requisite. The physical processes had instead to be simulated mathematically, yet computers to do so had not been invented. 'In those days', one scientist recalled, 'computers were mostly young women who would take a problem and fill in a spreadsheet with one number after the other, using hand-cranked Marchant or Friden calculators.'[7]

In attendance at the Los Alamos conference was Fuchs, who had recently been working on a new theory with John von Neumann. In 1944, the latter had proposed placing a capsule of D-T (deuterium and tritium – another isotope of hydrogen) inside a fission bomb. (A mixture of equal parts deuterium and tritium reacts 100 times faster than pure deuterium.) This would ignite when the bomb exploded. The consequent thermonuclear reaction in the D-T would release fast neutrons increasing the yield of an ordinary atom bomb. The concept was eventually incorporated into what became known as boosted fission weapons. Early in 1946 Fuchs took von Neumann's idea a stage further, proposing to put the D-T mixture in a beryllium oxide tamper, outside the enriched uranium core. The entire configuration would then be encased in a radiation-impervious shell. According to Fuchs, the uranium core would explode, releasing radiation which, contained by the shell, would compress and ignite the D-T, causing a sustainable thermonuclear reaction. In other words, both implosion *and* ignition would occur at the same time – the D-T would be squeezed and burned, thus increasing the intensity of the reaction and containing it for long enough to prevent premature explosion. The key was that implosion would occur by radiation, not by an explosive shock wave, as had been the case in Fat Man. Fuchs and von Neumann applied for a patent on 28 May 1946.

After the conference, Fuchs returned to Britain, to take up a post as a division head at the Atomic Energy Research Establishment. He undoubtedly briefed his British colleagues on the Los Alamos proceedings and also on his own work with von Neumann. Over the next two years, he also provided the Soviets with a steady stream of information. In other words, the first three powers to develop a hydrogen bomb – the United States, the Soviet Union and Great Britain – had a single common denominator in Fuchs.

In August 1946, Teller came up with a new design for the Super, which he dubbed the 'Alarm Clock'. Its distinguishing feature was alternating layers of fissionable and thermonuclear fuel. This idea, and that of the classical Super, were investigated at Los Alamos over the next three years, without much progress. To most of the team, the pessimism which had so annoyed Teller seemed perfectly justified. The AEC was likewise unenthusiastic.

The Soviet atomic test of August 1949 threw scientists, soldiers and politicians into a spin. Many who had previously expressed moral qualms about the Super turned into advocates overnight. On 5 October 1949 Alvarez speculated in his diary that 'the Russians could be working hard on the Super and might get there ahead of us. The only thing to do seems to be to get there first – but hope that it will turn out impossible.'[8] He contacted Lawrence, who felt the same. Alvarez and Lawrence then sought out Teller who now felt vindicated. The three began lobbying key politicians. On 17 October, Senator McMahon warned the AEC that the Soviets had probably already embarked on a hydrogen bomb and that the consequences would be fatal if they were to develop one before the United States. He nevertheless admitted that the weapon had limited strategic utility, since there were only two or three urban targets in the Soviet Union which merited power of that magnitude, and they could be destroyed as efficiently with a few atomic bombs.

Those who argued for a crash programme relied on fallacious logic. They held that the only adequate defence against a thermonuclear device was another thermonuclear device, a hopelessly narrow interpretation of deterrence. In fact, a one-megaton Super bomb could be deterred with a 100-kiloton atom bomb since the potential destruction in each case was so great that the difference in yield was immaterial. Recent developments in fission technology had yielded weapons immensely more powerful than Little Boy. Given such potential, what justification was there for a Super? Though Oppenheimer reluctantly accepted that 'It would be folly to oppose the exploration of this weapon,' he regretted the way it had become a panacea. 'This thing appears to have caught the imagination both of the Congressional and of military people, as the answer to the problem posed by the Russian advance. . . . that we [should] become committed to it as the way to save the country and the peace appears to me full of dangers.'[9]

Fears of a Soviet thermonuclear project had some foundation. In September 1945, Iakov Frenkel wrote to Kurchatov proposing that an atomic bomb might be used to initiate a thermonuclear reaction. Unbeknownst to Frenkel, Fuchs had alerted his Russian handlers to this possibility seven months earlier. According to Goncharov, Fuchs returned to the subject after the war, periodically sending observations and documents concerning American research on a deuterium-based bomb. This material 'provided a basic diagram of the bomb . . . and . . . described several potential alternatives, but it was indicated that all the diagrams were quite preliminary. And, of course, this material did not contain any evidence of its feasibility.'[10]

During his visit to Bohr in Copenhagen in November 1945, Terletskii (on Beria's instruction) asked about the Super. 'I believe that the destructive power of the already invented bomb is already great enough to wipe whole nations from the face of the earth,' Bohr replied. 'But I would welcome the discovery of a super-bomb, because then mankind would probably sooner understand the need to cooperate.' This answer was rather too esoteric for KGB tastes, but they were at least reassured when Bohr added that there was 'insufficient basis' for reports that the Americans had embarked on a hydrogen bomb.[11] On 17 December, Zel'dovich told Kurchatov that the thermonuclear idea seemed plausible. Though the Soviets were preoccupied with producing a fission device as quickly as possible, Kurchatov was sufficiently interested in fusion to direct Zel'dovich, in June 1946, to explore it further.

Later that year, a team which included Khariton, Zel'dovich, Isaak Gurevich and Isaak Pomeranchuk proposed using an atomic detonator to trigger an explosive reaction in deuterium. Though the idea was remarkably close to what Fuchs had been thinking, Gurevich insists they were unaware of any intelligence material. In any case, the idea generated little enthusiasm. 'We were simply waved away at the time,' Gurevich recalls. 'Stalin and Beria put nothing above the creation of the atomic bomb, and without even an experimental reactor gone critical, here are these high-brow pundits pestering people with projects whose feasibility is anybody's guess.'[12]

On 13 March 1948, Fuchs handed over some astonishing material, including the work done with von Neumann on radiation implosion. In quick succession, the information was seen by Molotov, Beria and Stalin. By 10 June, at the government's behest, two new groups were set up to explore the feasibility of a thermonuclear bomb. The first group, under Zel'dovich, worked at Arzamas-16, the second, headed by Igor Tamm, at the Physics Institute of the Academy of Sciences in Moscow. Included in the 10 June resolutions were very specific directives to improve the living conditions of the project participants and, specifically, to provide a private room for a promising young disciple of Tamm's named Andrei Sakharov.[13] 'In 1946 and 1947, I twice rejected attempts to entice me away,' Sakharov recalled. 'But the third time, nobody bothered to ask my consent. . . . I had no real choice in the matter.'[14]

Goncharov also joined the new team. He has fond memories of 'the healthy moral climate' created by Sakharov and Tamm.

> They exhibited scientific honesty, i.e., everyone could count on objective recognition of his work. There wasn't anything extraneous, any distortions, any subjective attitudes . . . that someone was favored while someone else was not . . . In general, everything was determined by one's real capacity for work, one's merits, one's contribution, an atmosphere of utmost fairness.[15]

While Zel'dovich set to work on the classical Super (called the *truba*), the Tamm group maintained an open mind. They did not have access to espionage, and therefore had to think creatively. By the autumn of 1948, they concluded that the classical Super had little promise. Sakharov instead proposed a radically new design which he called *sloika* – or Layer Cake.* Layers of light and heavy elements would be covered with an 'icing' of high explosives, which would implode the cake, causing an atomic bomb at the centre to explode. This would then ignite a fusion reaction in the light elements (deuterium and tritium). The proposal was similar to Teller's Alarm Clock, but Sakharov conceived of the sloika without knowledge of Teller's idea. The process came to be known within the community as

_____

* A loose translation, in fact, since a sloika is actually a cheap pastry.

'Sakharization'.* Later in the year, Vitalii Ginzburg, another member of the Tamm group, proposed using lithium deuteride instead of deuterium and tritium. It was much easier to handle, and much less costly to produce.

By early 1949, the Soviets had a design for a bomb that would actually work. All they had to do now was make it. Sakharov was sent to a secret weapons lab to plan construction of the sloika. Kurchatov seems to have been sufficiently committed to the idea to make sure that lithium deuteride production would be on stream by the time the fuel was needed. Ironically, at one point, Sakharov proposed that the initial compression of the sloika could be brought about by the fission of plutonium instead of by high explosives – an idea very close to the configuration that would eventually lead to a genuine hydrogen bomb. But at the time this was just another theory, one that would not be revived for another five years.

After the August 1949 atom bomb test, Russian scientists were exhausted. 'Everyone was longing for the holiday they had not had for five years,' Igor Golovin recalled. 'But before letting people go to their well-deserved rest, Kurchatov kept everyone for a week, let the excitement calm down, and directed them to the next stage – the creation of a hydrogen bomb.'[16]

While Sakharov was musing about layer cakes, back in the United States the General Advisory Committee met to consider the Super question. On 30 October 1949, the eight members, chaired by Oppenheimer, expressed a unanimous moral opposition:

> It is clear that the use of this weapon would bring about the destruction of innumerable human lives; it is not a weapon which can be used exclusively for the destruction of material installations of military or semi-military purposes. Its use therefore carries much further than the atomic bomb itself the policy of exterminating civilian populations.

The GAC warned that, while the Super might be feasible, its construction would probably be so complicated that it would adversely affect production of fission bombs, thus weakening America's defences. In addition, the Super seemed strategically unsound since the Soviet Union had only two cities – Moscow and Leningrad – of sufficient size to justify such a large bomb. In other words, nothing the Super could achieve could not be done more effectively by smaller atomic weapons.

The GAC also argued that the moral reputation of the US would be significantly damaged if it embarked upon such a project.

---

* Since the Russian word *sakhar* means sugar, this was in fact a pun suggestive of caramelization. In other words, the sloika was toffee-flavoured. The Soviet physicists obviously had sweet tooths.

Let it be clearly realized that this is a super weapon; it is in a totally different category from an atomic bomb. . . . reasonable people the world over would realize that the existence of a weapon of this type whose power of destruction is essentially unlimited represents a threat to the future of the human race which is intolerable. Thus we believe that the psychological effect of the weapon in our hands would be adverse to our interest.

The group carefully rebutted the argument that it was essential to pre-empt Soviet development of such a weapon. 'Our undertaking it will not prove a deterrent to them. Should they use the weapon against us, reprisals by our large stock of atomic bombs would be comparably effective to the use of a super.' The GAC members perceived a sublime opportunity to reject escalation of the arms race – to provide 'by example some limitations on the totality of war and thus of limiting the fear and arousing the hopes of mankind'.

In their minority opinion, Rabi and Fermi voiced these moral objections more forcefully. Since 'no limits exist to the destructiveness of this weapon', it would be 'a danger to humanity' and 'an evil thing considered in any light'. 'By its very nature', they argued, the Super 'cannot be confined to a military objective but becomes a weapon . . . of genocide'. For that reason, it 'cannot be justified on any ethical ground . . . Its use would put the United States in a bad moral position relative to the peoples of the world.' They implored the President 'to tell the American public, and the world, that we think it wrong on fundamental ethical principles to initiate a program of development'. An American refusal to begin development might, they thought, kick-start arms control negotiations. They proposed inviting 'the nations of the world to join us in a solemn pledge not to proceed in the development or construction of weapons of this category'.[17]

The GAC's logic was unattractive to those who preferred their politics simple and saw security in ever-bigger bombs. In the climate of the early 1950s, opposition to a more powerful weapon was often interpreted as an attempt to emasculate America. Amidst growing anti-communist tension, the Super was a shibboleth used to test loyalty. For those who had always been suspicious of Oppenheimer, his opposition seemed further proof of perfidy.

In the midst of the GAC debate, General Omar Bradley argued that, while he could not vouch for the military necessity of the H-bomb, he thought it would be a bad thing psychologically if the Soviets had it and the Americans did not. In effect, a commander had advocated the development of a weapon for which he could perceive no use. The JCS chimed in by arguing that 'it is folly to argue whether one weapon is more immoral than another . . . in the larger sense it is war itself which is immoral'.[18] Oppenheimer was right in arguing that the weapon had no strategic purpose; it was far too powerful to fit into a strategy for winning a war. Since the Americans had plenty of smaller atomic bombs, which had some strategic utility, there was no *military* need for the hydrogen bomb. The importance of the weapon, as Bradley understood, rested solely in its psychological impact. Even though Americans would not actually be more vulnerable, they would feel more vulnerable if the Soviets had a monopoly on the hydrogen bomb.

Teller, disgusted with the GAC, mused that if the US did not immediately embark on a crash programme to build the Super, he would end up a prisoner of war of the Russians. 'Scientists naturally have a right and a duty to have opinions,' he later reflected. 'But their science gives them no special insight into public affairs. There is a time for scientists and movie stars and people who have flown the Atlantic to restrain their opinions lest they be taken more seriously than they should be.'[19] In fact, Teller needn't have worried. Momentum in favour of the Super was building on Capitol Hill and at the Pentagon. McMahon warned that a failure to develop it might mean 'unconditional surrender . . . to alien forces of evil'.[20] On 25 November, Lewis Strauss, an AEC commissioner, urged Truman to ignore the GAC, arguing that it had gone beyond its remit of providing opinion on the feasibility of weapons. Only the Department of Defense could advise on issues of deployment and only the State Department could provide guidance on how a weapon might affect international relations. Strauss then added tactical justifications, which, technically speaking, were not within his remit. He claimed that the weapon 'may be critically useful against a large enemy force both as a weapon of offense and as a defensive measure to prevent landings on our own shores' – a rather dubious argument. As for the moral issues, 'a government of atheists is not likely to be dissuaded from producing the weapon on "moral" grounds'.[21] Equally enthusiastic was Paul Nitze who argued that a belief in the superiority of American technology was essential to world security and domestic harmony. The estimated $500 million dollar cost seemed small price for that kind of security.

Truman wanted to disregard the GAC, but found it difficult to ignore a group of highly respected men who had voiced a unanimous opinion. Instead, he asked a Special Committee of the NSC, consisting of Louis Johnson, Acheson and Lilienthal, to consider the issue. The committee was chosen in the expectation that it would confirm Truman's own inclinations. It did not disappoint. After only two meetings, the group resolved by two to one (Lilienthal the dissenter) to recommend a crash programme. This was reported to Truman in a brief meeting on 31 January 1950. When Lilienthal tried to express reservations, Truman interrupted by asking if the Russians could build an H-bomb. When all three guests nodded, he replied: 'What the hell are we waiting for. Let's get on with it.'[22]

Truman saw the Super in terms of strategic necessity and cost. Morality was not an issue. It seemed strategically sensible to have a weapon more powerful than the Soviets possessed. Financial considerations were immaterial since the project was supposed to eat up only $70–$100 million of a defence budget then totalling $14 billion per year. Once Truman received assurances that the US could have an improved atomic arsenal, an adequate conventional force *and* the H-bomb, there seemed no reason to prevaricate.

'It is part of my responsibility as Commander in Chief of the Armed Forces to see to it that our country is able to defend itself against any possible aggressor,' Truman told the American people on 31 January. 'Accordingly, I have directed the Atomic Energy Commission to continue work on all forms of atomic weapons, including the so-called hydrogen or super bomb. . . . This we shall continue to do until a satisfactory plan for international control of atomic energy is achieved.'[23]

Four days earlier, Fuchs had been arrested for espionage. On the 28th the AEC confirmed that he had recently attended meetings relevant to the construction of the Super. It was therefore safe to assume that thermonuclear research had been passed to the Soviets. While Truman would undoubtedly have decided in favour of the Super with or without the Fuchs revelations, the news convinced Americans that their President knew what he was doing.

Back in the USSR, the work of Tamm and Zel'dovich had not generated much enthusiasm, and had even encountered hostility from those who felt the Super superfluous. Proposals to invigorate the project had been put forward in the summer of 1949, but Beria refused to support them. But then, four days after Truman's announcement, Beria issued Protocol No. 91 commanding Kurchatov to submit within five days a report on the progress of thermonuclear research. On the 26th, Beria sent this material to Stalin and urged him to approve an accelerated programme of research, for the very simple reason that the Americans were doing so. On that very same day, Stalin signed decrees authorizing construction of the Super and production of tritium. Goncharov is 'sincerely convinced that these were forced measures . . . taken in response [to US action] . . . There was no attempt of revanchism, of getting ahead of the United States.'[24] In other words, the Americans decided to build the Super because they thought the Soviets were doing so. And the Soviets did so because they were certain the Americans were building one.

Truman's decision was applauded by Congress and most sections of the press. But there were significant dissenters. Some journalists, churchmen, academics and politicians criticized the way the US had escalated the arms race without justification. Einstein felt that arms proliferation had assumed 'an hysterical character', with the effect that radioactive poisoning of the atmosphere and hence annihilation of any life on earth has been brought within the range of technical possibilities. The ghostlike character of this development lies in its apparently compulsory trend. Every step appears as the unavoidable consequence of the preceding one. In the end there beckons more and more clearly general annihilation.

Bethe, who had wavered about whether to participate in thermonuclear research, was now firmly opposed. He attacked Truman's decision in *Scientific American*:

> The usual argument . . . is that we are fighting against a country which denies all the human values we cherish and that any weapon, however terrible, must be used to prevent that country and its creed from dominating the world. It is argued that it would be better for us to lose our lives than our liberty; and this I personally agree with. But I believe that . . . we would lose far more than our lives in a war fought with hydrogen bombs, that we would in fact lose all our liberties and human values at the same time, and so thoroughly that we would not recover them for an unforeseeably long time.
>
> We believe in peace based on mutual trust. Shall we achieve it by using hydrogen bombs? Shall we convince the Russians of the value of the individual by killing millions of them? If we fight a war and we win it with H-bombs, what history will remember is *not* the ideals we were fighting for but the method we used to accomplish them. Those methods will be compared to the warfare of Genghis Khan, who ruthlessly killed every last inhabitant of Persia.[25]

These criticisms were voiced against a backdrop of virulent anti-Communism. Open debate could not thrive. Several thousand copies of the *Scientific American* issue were confiscated and subsequently destroyed, on the grounds that the article revealed nuclear secrets.

The Nobel prize winning physicist Arthur Compton argued that 'This is not a question for experts: either militarists or scientists. All they can do is explain what the results will be if we do or do not develop such destructive weapons. The American people must themselves say whether they want to defend themselves with such weapons.'[26] In truth, the arguments were too complex for the average American, who craved security and measured safety by the size of his country's arsenal. So, while experts fretted over the implications of the project, the public remained remarkably silent. Its silence was an expression of support for the hydrogen bomb. Not for the first time Truman's government found itself in tune with the public mood on the subject of nuclear weapons. Both president and people adhered to an equation in which size mattered most.

Resigning themselves to the decision, the dissenters desperately counselled restraint. Along with twelve other eminent scientists, Bethe sent an open letter urging the President to make a solemn declaration never to use the weapon first. 'The circumstance which might force us to use it would be if we or our allies were attacked by *this* bomb. There can be only one justification for our development of the hydrogen bomb and that is to prevent its use.'[27] Argument had come full circle: Bethe's line of reasoning was rather close to Teller's original justification. No one really proposed that the bomb should be used for offensive purposes. But, as the mathematician Norbert Wiener recognized, a similar argument had been used during the Second World War to justify construction of the atom bomb, only to be cast aside when an opportunity to use it arose. The scientist, he argued, puts 'unlimited powers in the hands of the people whom he is least inclined to trust with their use. . . . to disseminate information about a weapon in the present state of our civilization is to make it practically certain that that weapon will be used'.[28] Wiener argued that, if a scientist objected to the possible use of the weapon, the only option was to refuse to take part in the research. Unlike Teller, Wiener drew a direct line of guilt from the suffering a weapon caused to the laboratory in which it was devised. Most scientists preferred to reject that logic since it forced them to tear down the curtain of innocence that separated them from the real world.

The greatest weakness of the dissenters' argument was that they willingly worked on projects they implored the government to end. The lure of cutting edge work drove them to moral contortion. Fermi went to Los Alamos for the summer of 1950, fascinated by the research, but praying it would not succeed. Another contortionist was Bethe, who decided eventually to join the project. Like Fermi, he hoped that research would lead to failure. He nevertheless remained tormented by moral doubt: 'I wish I were more consistent an idealist. . . . I still have the feeling that I have done the wrong thing. But I have done it.' Still seeking validation, he argued, rather weakly, that '[in] Los Alamos I might still be a force for disarmament'.[29] And pigs might fly.

The decision to embark upon the Super brought new urgency to Los Alamos. Scientists and technicians went on a six-day week, a return to wartime conditions. In the computer section, technicians willingly acceded to double shifts so that calculations could proceed day and night. But the work did not progress smoothly and pessimism prevailed. The problem was still one of computations – without computers, the necessary simulations could not proceed. But then Stanislaw Ulam embarked on an ambitious and painstaking venture to carry out these calculations by hand. In the end he succeeded, but not in the way Teller hoped.

Ulam's calculations revealed that a fission reaction could not produce the heat necessary to produce a sustained thermonuclear reaction in deuterium. One solution proposed was to use a deuterium-tritium combination as a trigger; the two isotopes fuse at a lower temperature than is required to ignite deuterium alone. An atomic explosion would provide the heat to start the D-T thermonuclear reaction, which would then ignite the rest of the deuterium in the tube. But tritium, unlike deuterium, is both costly and difficult to make. The effort required to produce one kilogram of tritium in a reactor can be used to produce 70 kilograms of plutonium, or enough for around a dozen atomic bombs. In other words, as the GAC had warned, construction of a hydrogen bomb threatened to impede atom bomb production – with as yet no guarantee that the H-bomb would even work. In response to this snag, Teller desperately assured all who would listen that the amount of tritium needed was very small.

Ulam's calculations suggested otherwise, rendering the project immensely expensive. He and Fermi also surmised that a thermonuclear reaction in deuterium would be difficult to sustain because the fission trigger would blow the bomb apart before the fusion reaction could take place properly. The energy had to be delivered to the D-T mixture at velocities approaching the speed of light, which seemed impossible, since the energy would take the form of conducted heat, which travels too slowly. 'All of the calculations were showing that the existing ideas about how you would introduce the energy led to a situation where it fizzled,' Herbert York recalled. 'And not just marginally so . . . it never got started at all.'[30]

For Teller the hydrogen bomb was personal, a way to settle old scores. His super-ego released only slightly less energy than the super-bomb he envisaged. He stubbornly insisted that since his idea was sound, there must be something wrong with Ulam's calculations. But, in truth, the classical Super was dead. 'We were on the wrong track,' Bethe recalled. 'The hydrogen bomb design we thought would work best would not work at all.'[31]

After carrying out his gargantuan calculations, Ulam set to work trying to build more efficient atomic bombs. The problem was again one of speed. Ordinary explosives, used in implosion, could not crush plutonium quickly enough to derive the utmost energy from it. The core blew itself apart before it could be sufficiently squeezed. But Ulam surmised that using a nuclear explosion to crush the core might perhaps yield the required rapidity of compression. He envisaged a chain of explosions (what he called an iterative scheme), each producing a higher yield. In early 1951, while making these calculations, he essentially solved the problem plaguing the Super. His wife recalled:

Engraved on my memory is the day when I found him at noon staring intensely out of a window in our living room with a very strange expression on his face. He said: 'I found a way to make it work.' 'What work?' I asked. 'The super,' he replied. 'It's a totally different scheme, and it will change the course of history.'[32]

Ulam had in mind not just ignition, but also implosion. The thermonuclear fuel would be compressed to high density before being ignited, thus achieving the elusive pressure essential for fusion to take place. Ulam took this idea to Teller who was at first deeply suspicious. But, after being taken through the calculations, he quickly changed his mind. Teller modified the idea somewhat by suggesting that radiation, not blast, would produce the necessary implosive force – and the essential speed. Blast involves matter moving through space. Ionizing radiation, on the other hand, involves waves travelling at the speed of light.

In the meantime, a series of tests, codenamed Greenhouse, took place in the spring of 1951. These had been scheduled a year before and had gone forward in spite of the failure of the tube design. The most important of these, nicknamed George, occurred on 8 May and involved a tiny D-T core being compressed and ignited by a fission explosion. The physicist Robert Jastrow called the George test 'more a way to impress the public than a real experiment, because everyone knew beforehand that it was pretty certain to work; using a huge atomic bomb to ignite a little vial of deuterium and tritium was like using a blast furnace to light a match'.[33] The test was nevertheless hugely important because, according to Bethe, 'the energy was conducted by radiation from a fission bomb . . . and the radiation was used not only to heat but also to compress the T-D'.[34] In other words, the test provided proof of the Teller-Ulam scheme. That proof was entirely accidental, since the test itself had been planned well before Teller and Ulam proposed their design.

Radiation implosion had, it will be recalled, been proposed by Fuchs in 1946. Teller and Ulam took the idea a step further by devising an actual configuration in which this could occur. The radiant energy from an atomic explosion would be used to compress and ignite a physically isolated thermonuclear core. This would become known as a 'two-stage' weapon – the fission primary separated from the thermonuclear fuel. 'I have this vivid memory of Teller going to the blackboard and just with a few strokes drawing a cartoon that was: "This is how you make a hydrogen bomb",' York recalled. 'And I remember, either at the time or that evening, getting a little bit of the shivers because I realized: That was it.'[35] Ulam henceforth came to be called the 'father of the H-bomb'. 'I am the father in [the] biological sense that I performed a necessary function and let nature take its course,' he later remarked. 'After that a child had to be born. It might be robust or it might be stillborn, but *something* had to be born.' Bethe elaborated: 'it is more precise to say that Ulam is the father, because he provided the seed, and Teller is the mother, because he remained with the child. As for me, I guess I was the midwife.'[36] The man who despised thermonuclear research helped deliver the hydrogen bomb.

Scientific possibility once again smothered moral doubt. 'My feeling about development became quite different when the practicabilities became clear,' Oppenheimer later confessed.

> When I saw how to do it, it was clear to me that one had at least to make the thing. . . . The program we had in 1949 was a tortured thing that you could well argue did not make a great deal of technical sense. It was there-fore possible to argue also that you did not want it even if you could have it. The program in 1951 was technically so sweet that you could not argue about that. It was purely the military, the political, and the humane problem of what you were going to do about it once you had it.[37]

A fresh spirit of endeavour enlivened the laboratories. 'Everyone . . . was enthusiastic now that you had something foreseeable,' Gordon Dean, the AEC chairman, recalled. 'There was enthusiasm right through the program for the first time. The bickering was gone.'[38] The once-tormented souls were now intoxicated by success. Politics also proved persuasive. 'The possibility that the Russians might obtain an H-bomb was of course the most compelling argument for proceeding with our thermonuclear program,' Bethe thought. 'It was, in my opinion, the *only* valid argument.'[39]

But some friction remained. Residual ill-feeling existed between Teller and the established scientists at Los Alamos, many of whom remained loyal to Oppenheimer. Teller thought that because he had solved the mystery of the bomb's design, he deserved to be placed in charge of building it. But his patent unsuitability as a manager ruled out that possi-bility. The fact that he was not chosen convinced him that a conspiracy existed to make the project fail. 'It was an open secret, among scientists and government officials, that I did not agree with . . . Bradbury's admin-istration of the thermonuclear program at Los Alamos,' Teller later remarked.

> Bradbury and I remained friends, but we differed sharply on the most effec-tive ways to produce a hydrogen bomb at the earliest possible date. . . . The dissension with Bradbury crystallized in my mind in the urgent need for more than one nuclear weapons laboratory.[40]

In February 1952, Lawrence tried to lure Teller to Berkeley. 'I said I would come on one condition – that I could work in a laboratory devoted to the development of thermonuclear weapons.'[41] That was precisely what Lawrence had in mind. He asked Herbert York, then a postdoctoral researcher, to make soundings among the physics community. A few months later York reported enthusiastic backing for a second lab. Meanwhile, Teller lobbied for funding in Washington by making grandiose promises about what could be achieved once the Los Alamos monopoly was broken. Strong support came from Air Force Secretary Thomas Finletter, in addition to Lewis Strauss, Senator McMahon and William Foster, Under-Secretary of Defense.

A small facility in Livermore, not far from Berkeley, was found to house the lab. It quickly expanded to meet the needs and ego of Teller, who moved there in July 1952. York, just three years out of graduate work, was named the first director of what was then called Project Whitney. At first, Livermore seemed a return to wartime austerity. The decrepit wooden buildings were cold in winter and stiflingly hot in summer. At the first meeting of the administrative committee the team was told that 'there will be fewer telephones than promised . . . The desk lamp situation is very bad.'[42] Recruitment also proved a problem since scientists were less willing to make personal sacrifices than they had endured during the war. 'It was not an easy task attracting talent to a laboratory housed in old wooden buildings with poor heating and no air conditioning, located near a town of not yet 5,000 situated in a small rural valley noted mainly for its wine, roses, cattle and gravel,'[43] one of the early recruits recalled. But before long Livermore achieved critical mass; in the six years that York was director, the staff grew from 100 to 3,600 and the budget from $3.5 million to $45 million. For Teller, the move completed a personal transformation. He no longer gave lip service to international control, nor did he speak of the bomb as an agent of peace. An unrepentant worshipper of power, he defined security in terms of bigger, more powerful weapons. America's safety provided justification for his megalomania.

The first bona fide thermonuclear device was born in 1952. It was not a bomb in the conventional sense but more like a factory for producing an explosion. Nicknamed 'Mike', it weighed 65 tonnes and was two storeys tall. Most of its bulk was devoted to the refrigeration unit needed to keep the thermonuclear fuel at -250 degrees centigrade. Anyone familiar with American refrigerators should not be surprised at its dimensions nor at the capacity of the US to build it.

Everything about Mike was big. Since it could not be dropped, it had instead to be transported by ship to the islet of Elugelab and placed in position with huge cranes. A massive rectangular-shaped building was specially constructed to house the device and its refrigeration unit. Over 300 kilograms of liquid deuterium was held in a cryogenic tank the size of a railroad car. The tank was kept cool with huge quantities of liquid hydrogen – more of the substance than anyone had ever worked with before. Surrounding the liquid deuterium and its insulation was a huge uranium canister, the largest such casting ever made. This would serve as a tamper to hold the whole device together, rather like a shell casing. The uranium was supposed to undergo fission – only a thermonuclear reaction would cause non-enriched uranium to do this. The inside of the casing was covered with gold foil, the better to keep cold in and heat out. An Albuquerque sign painter was contracted to apply the gold leaf which came in little books (twenty-five sheets to a book) – certainly the strangest job he ever landed.

After Mike was assembled and set in place the technicians burned off the excess liquid hydrogen, venting it from an open chimney. Hydrogen burns with no visible flame, which was unfortunate for the local bird population. Totally oblivious to the threat, they flew straight into the flame and were instantly turned into toast.

All of the islands in close proximity were evacuated. Most technicians and scientists were taken by ship to designated points of safety at least forty miles away, while a small core stayed behind to perform the final preparations. Though their calculations suggested that they would be safe in specially constructed bunkers on the atoll, the possibility remained that the device would turn out to be many times more powerful than anticipated. In truth, the team had no clear idea how powerful it would be. They sought the biggest possible blast, engineering every constituent to ensure maximum yield.

The test was scheduled for 1 November 1952. In the official newsreel, an Army spokesman calmly explains the purpose of the test, presenting it as a scientific experiment, rather than as a precursor to the most fiercesome weapon ever devised. Midway through his commentary from the deck of a destroyer on peaceful seas, he lights a pipe, as if to underline the benign intent of the project. 'You have a grandstand seat here for one of the most momentous events in the history of science,' he announces. 'In less than a minute you will see the most powerful explosion witnessed by the human eye. For the sake of all of us and for the sake of our country I know you wish this expedition well.'[44]

As the countdown proceeded, Teller waited in a laboratory at Berkeley, over 5,000 miles away. He had been invited to observe the test but, still in a huff, had declined. At the moment of detonation, he watched a highly sensitive seismograph capable of picking up the vibration from the explosion:

> about the time of the actual shot . . . nothing happened or could have happened. About a quarter of an hour was required for the shock wave to travel, deep under the Pacific basin, to the Californian coast. I waited with

little patience . . . At last . . . the luminous point appeared to dance wildly and irregularly. . . . It was clear and big and unmistakable.

With fatherly pride Teller wired a friend: 'It's a boy!'[45]

The explosion exceeded even the most optimistic predictions. Mike yielded 10.4 megatons, producing a fireball three and a half miles across and gouging a crater one mile in diameter and 175 feet deep. 'Observers . . . saw millions of gallons of lagoon water, turned to steam, appear as a giant bubble,' wrote Leona Marshall Libby. 'When the steam evaporated, they saw that the island of Elugelab, where the bomb had been, had vanished, vaporized also.'[46] Harold Agnew, on a ship twenty-five miles away, found it a frightening experience:

> something I'll never forget was the heat. Not the blast. . . . the heat just kept coming, just kept coming on and on and on. And it was really scary. . . . It's really quite a terrifying experience because the heat doesn't go off. . . . on kiloton shots it's a flash and it's over, but on those big shots it's really terrifying.[47]

Where the island once was one now finds a crater of melted coral, a mile in diameter, several hundred feet below the surface of the water. Fly over the area today and all that is evident is a perfectly circular deep blue hole.

Mike terrified the Soviets, who found themselves again threatened by an American nuclear monopoly. Stalin had died the previous March, after thirty years in power. His death left his people feeling vulnerable. 'There was this perception on many levels that without Stalin other great powers might crush us and might use some chink in the armor to penetrate,' the historian Vladislav Zubok recalls.[48] That chink was, perhaps, the hydrogen bomb. On 2 December Beria sent Kurchatov a memo emphasizing that 'the solution to the problem of the construction of RDS-6s [the sloika] is of paramount importance . . . we need to marshal every effort to ensure the successful completion of scientific-research and experimental-design operations'.[49]

On 3 July 1953, Avraami Zavenyagin, deputy head of the Ministry of Medium Machine Building, proudly informed the Central Committee of the Communist Party that the Soviet Union would soon respond dramatically to the American hydrogen bomb.

> The Americans . . . at Truman's order began the work on the hydrogen bomb. Our people and our country are no slouches. We took it up as well and, as far as we can judge, we believe we do not lag behind the Americans.

The hydrogen bomb is tens of times more powerful than a plain atomic bomb and its explosion will mean the liquidation of the second monopoly of the Americans . . . which would be an event of ultimate importance in world politics.[50]

A few weeks later, Nikita Khrushchev publicly proclaimed: 'The United States is said to have a monopoly on the hydrogen bomb. Apparently it would be of comfort to them, if that were the truth. But it is not.'[51] The announcement was designed as much to calm fears within the Soviet Union as it was to frighten the Americans. Khrushchev, still consolidating his hold on power, could not afford to seem vulnerable.

Khrushchev was bluffing, but only technically so. Since 1948, two teams had been pursuing different designs – the truba and the sloika. Because of the arrest of Fuchs, the Soviets were not alerted to the fact that the truba was a dead end – they had to come to that conclusion by themselves. The sloika, on the other hand, had progressed well and was scheduled for testing just four days after Khrushchev's pronouncement.

Beria wanted a dramatic demonstration of Soviet power. Shortly before the scheduled test date, he attended a meeting about preparation of the site. Scientists discussed the placement of measurement equipment, the building of structures and the disposition of experimental animals. 'Suddenly, Beria became incensed,' one witness recalls. 'He interrupted angrily, moving from one briefer to another, asking strange questions which were not easy to answer.' Then he completely lost his temper. 'He screamed: "I will tell you myself!" Then he started to talk nonsense. It gradually became clear from his stormy monologue that he wanted everything at the test site to be totally destroyed in order to provide the maximum terror.'[52]

A few weeks earlier, the CIA had confidently announced that there was no evidence that thermonuclear weapons were being developed in the USSR. That impression had been supported by senior physicists, including Bethe, who surmised that, if the Soviets had started from information supplied by Fuchs, they would inevitably have failed. But Teller warned against complacency, arguing that it was entirely possible that the Soviets were forging ahead. He feared that Fuchs might have relayed ideas about radiation implosion mooted at the 1946 conference which would have pointed the way to the Teller-Ulam configuration.

On 12 August 1953, the Soviets exploded the sloika at their test site in Kazakhstan. 'The earth trembled beneath us', one observer recalled, 'and our faces were struck, like the lash of a whip, by the dull strong sound of the rolling explosion. From the jolt of the shock wave it was difficult to stand on one's feet.' All around were dying birds writhing on the grass, their wings scorched and eyes burned. 'The impact of it apparently transcended some kind of psychological barrier,' a scientist wrote. 'The . . . first atomic bomb had not inspired such flesh-creeping terror.'[53] Though not nearly as powerful as Mike, the sloika had the great advantage of being a deliverable bomb. Its dimensions were roughly similar to the first Soviet atomic bomb, but its yield was twenty times higher – about 400 kilotons. Thermonuclear reactions contributed 15 to 20 per cent of that yield. Though it was not a bona fide hydrogen bomb, it was a significant step in that direction.

Americans reacted with deep shock at how their monopoly had been shattered so quickly. But much more worrying was the realization that the Soviets had constructed a 'dry bomb' that needed no refrigeration. After Elugelab, the Americans had turned their attention to a 'dry bomb', but they had not remotely considered that the Soviets might beat them to it. By examining fallout data, Bethe correctly surmised that the Soviet device consisted of alternating layers of uranium and lithium deuteride, compressed by high explosive. He argued that the weapon was merely a boosted fission device which could not be made much more powerful than 400 kilotons. 'This was not a true H-bomb,' he concluded.[54] The reader can complete this paragraph, using the words 'whistling' and 'dark'.

Far from Kazakhstan, equally explosive developments were occurring at the Kremlin. After Stalin's death, a power struggle inevitably developed between Khrushchev, Molotov, Beria and Malenkov. The first casualty was Beria who had wrongly assumed that his leadership of the NKVD and his accomplishments in the nuclear field would provide a platform for supreme power. But, with Stalin gone, he had few friends left. Khrushchev launched a vicious attack that others eagerly joined. They alleged that Beria was excessively ambitious and had 'positioned himself above the party'. He was specifically accused of renouncing socialism in the GDR and of carrying out a secret rapprochement with Tito's Yugoslavia. Words like 'imperialist' and 'bourgeois' were thrown in for good measure. The critics also derided Beria's accomplishments in atomic weaponry. At a party plenum in July 1953 Vyacheslav Malyshev accused him of making important decisions regarding nuclear technology without informing the Central Committee. He was criticized for turning the nuclear project into his own personal fiefdom, probably an accurate accusation. But the cruellest blow came when Zavenyagin alleged that 'Beria had a reputation of organiser, but in reality he was a die-hard bureaucrat. . . . Decision-taking dragged on for weeks and months.' Granted, Beria had many faults, but bureaucratic indecision was not one of them. A more clear-sighted organizer would have been difficult to find. In truth, the allegations were simply window dressing for decisions already made. Beria was doomed the moment Stalin took his last breath. He was executed in December 1953.[55]

For a brief period in late 1953 the Soviets held an advantage over the

United States. Because they were ahead in weapon design, not in the size of their arsenal, this advantage had no strategic significance. But it was hugely important psychologically. The Soviet leadership was fully aware to whom gratitude belonged. Malenkov conveyed a message of congratulation to Kurchatov, who in turned thanked Sakharov, calling him the 'savior of the Soviet Union'. A short time later, he was awarded the Stalin Prize and made a 'Hero of Socialist Labour'. Just thirty-three, he was appointed head of the theoretical division at Arzamas-16.

The United States was in no greater danger because of the sloika, but the Soviet weapon did mean that the Americans could no longer indulge in nuclear swagger. More important, the new weapon was proof that the Soviet system worked, that it could compete with the Americans in scientific development. This was immensely valuable for a country keen to teach the non-aligned world a lesson about the benefits of Communism. The sloika was a symbol of Soviet virility.

Goncharov insists that the driving force behind the arms race was the United States. The Americans, he argues, continually sought new developments and always gave the impression that they were prepared to devote limitless resources to their nuclear arsenal. As a result, scientists in the Soviet Union felt themselves under siege.

> We were always told that we must not lag behind. . . . an absolutely insane task was set for us . . . We must have everything Americans have. There must not be a slightest gap. And it was considered that as soon as . . . new information about . . . work in this or that direction became known, we absolutely had to do the same thing . . . That's what happened. And it resulted in the mindless arms race. The leadership lost their sense of reality. Everyone forgot that our whole country almost turned into a military plant. But it is clear that our resources were always smaller than the resources of the United States. . . . And that also led us into crisis.[56]

The implication of Goncharov's statement is that an opportunity to slow down the arms race was missed when Truman decided in 1950 to proceed with development of the Super. A refusal to proceed would not have weakened American defences; security could easily have been maintained with fission weapons. Vannevar Bush was thinking along precisely these lines when he urged the government not to go ahead with the Mike test, warning that it would escalate the arms race. He also feared that fallout from Mike might lead the Soviets to the secrets of thermonuclear weapons.

> I felt strongly that that test ended the possibility of the only type of agreement that I thought was possible with Russia at that time, an agreement to make no more tests. . . . I still think we made a grave error in conducting

that test at that time, and not attempting to make that type of simple agreement with Russia. I think history will show that was a turning point . . . those who pushed that thing through to a conclusion without making that attempt have a great deal to answer for.[57]

But Truman was still racing downhill on his toboggan. The Mike test had effectively been approved two years earlier when he had decided that the US needed a hydrogen bomb.

Though Sakharov also felt that the US was the driving force in the escalation of the arms race, he rejected the notion that Stalin would have responded positively to a symbolic gesture by Truman not to develop the hydrogen bomb.

> Stalin, Beria and company already understood the potential of the new weapon, and nothing could have dissuaded them from going forward with its development. Any US move toward abandoning or suspending work on a thermonuclear weapon would have been perceived either as a cunning, deceitful maneuver or as evidence of stupidity or weakness. In any case, the Soviet reaction would have been the same: to avoid a possible trap and to exploit the adversary's folly.[58]

In 1953, after the Americans and Soviets had both tested a version of the hydrogen bomb, the Doomsday Clock was moved from three to two minutes to midnight. Speaking to the House of Commons in March 1955, Winston Churchill commented on the threat now facing the world:

> The atomic bomb, with all its terror, did not carry us outside the scope of human control or manageable events in thought or action in peace or war . . . With the hydrogen bomb, the entire foundation of human affairs was revolutionized, and mankind placed in a situation both measureless and laden with doom. . . . I find it poignant to look at youth in all its activity and ardour and, most of all, to watch little children playing their merry games, and wonder what would lie before them if God wearied of mankind.[59]

Teller saw things differently: 'I believe that having argued for the hydrogen bomb in 1949 at an important juncture helped keep the world safe. I'm proud of it.'[60] Khariton and his friends agreed. They thought the Super marked the stage at which Oppenheimer's vision of a bomb big enough to eradicate war had been achieved. 'It is the possession of these weapons by both the Soviet Union and the United States that made a war between the two superpowers impossible.'[61]

Apparently the bomb that could destroy the world destroyed war instead.

CHAPTER 11

The New Look

In Nevada, the holes in the earth are so big they have names. One of the biggest is called Sedan. It was formed on 6 July 1962 when a 104 kiloton thermonuclear device was detonated, leaving a crater 1,280 feet in diameter and 320 feet deep. Twelve million tonnes of earth was displaced. The seismic energy equalled an earthquake of 4.75 on the Richter scale.

Granted, there's nothing particularly unusual about this; there are plenty of big holes in Nevada. But Sedan is special – not because of its size, but because of its purpose. The test was part of Operation Plowshare, a biblical reference designed to bathe the blast in moral virtue. Originally part of Eisenhower's 'Atoms for Peace' programme, Plowshare explored peaceful uses for atomic explosions, in particular their applicability to large-scale construction projects.

The guide on the Test Site tour, a retired AEC engineer, assumes a fatherly pride when he shows off Sedan. He stands taller, thrusts out his chest and comes very close to saying 'I made this'. The crater is impressive, but mainly as a huge metaphor for the gargantuan naïveté of those years. Sedan was an experiment to explore whether a second Panama Canal could be made with nuclear explosions. Atomic devices would be stretched across the isthmus like a string of pearls and, presto, a big explosion would achieve in seconds what previously took decades of digging. When Teller (CEO of Bombs R Us) explained the idea to an unenthusiastic President Kennedy, he boasted: 'It will take less time to complete the canal than for you to make up your mind to build it.'[1]

'Why didn't the project go ahead?' someone asks. The guide shrugs. 'Tastes change. We did not know then what we know now.'[2]

The Mike test preceded the 1952 American presidential election by a matter of days. In that election the American people chose Dwight Eisenhower, in part because his glittering military career suggested a man who would not neglect the nation's defence. Yet Eisenhower was frightened by Mike's strength. 'The promise of this life is imperilled by the very genius that has made it possible,' he warned in his Inaugural Address.

'Science seems ready to confer upon us, as its final gift, the power to erase human life from this planet.'[3]

When the first atomic bomb exploded at Alamogordo, some observers decided that the world had been changed beyond recognition. Man now possessed seemingly limitless destructive powers. But how, then, does one react to the hydrogen bomb? Hiroshima had been levelled by one atomic bomb, yet within ten years the two superpowers possessed weapons 100 times more powerful. Mike had caused an island to disappear. Lewis Strauss, the AEC chairman, discussed the new power with alarming frankness at a press conference on 31 March 1954:

A Well, the nature of an H-bomb . . . is that, in effect, it can be made as large as you wish, as large as the military requirement demands, that is to say, an H-bomb can be made as large as – large enough to take out a city.
(*A chorus of 'What?'*)
To take out a city, to destroy a city.
Q How big a city?
A Any city.
Q Any city, New York?
A The metropolitan area, yes.[4]

American and Soviet scientists were engaged in a Faustian struggle, building ever more powerful weapons not to destroy, but supposedly to protect. They were driven forward by a very real fear that to fall behind might mean annihilation. Destructive power seemed the best way to preserve the common good. Perhaps the clearest expression of this logic came from Teller, who was least tormented by its ironies: 'I don't like weapons. I would like to have peace. But for peace we need weapons and I do not think my views are distorted. I believe I am contributing to a peaceful world.'[5] Out of faith or desperation, scientists on both sides believed that the immense power of their inventions would prove a bar to their use – that restraint would grow in proportion to payload.

Eisenhower wanted international controls on the Bomb, but, like Truman before him, maintained that the United States must first have a nuclear arsenal with which it could feel secure. Though he feared the power of the new weapons, he felt compelled to collect them. The same could be said of Khrushchev. Each new development merely increased their feeling of vulnerability. The quest for security encouraged mutual insecurity. Oppenheimer likened the situation to that of 'two scorpions in a bottle, each capable of killing the other, but only at the risk of his own life'.[6]

Eisenhower inherited the Korean War, which tested his nuclear policy. The dynamic of deterrence suggested that bombs were protection against an enemy's bombs and were not supposed to be used. That is how most scientists saw things – the belief in deterrence permitted participation in an otherwise morally reprehensible venture. But the military envisaged a different Bomb. Soldiers could not conceive of a weapon not meant to be used. The same could be said for the eggheads at RAND. Project RAND was formed on 1 October 1945 in order to provide research for the Air Force. Originally under special contract to the Douglas Aircraft Corporation, it became an independent, non-profit corporation in May 1948, concerned primarily with issues of national security. In real terms this meant that RAND analysts concentrated on the development of nuclear strategy – they became the thinkers of the unthinkable. On joining RAND in the late 1950s, Daniel Ellsberg and Alain Enthoven decided not to sign up to the corporation's deluxe retirement plan, for the very simple reason that they did not think the world would last long enough for them to enjoy its benefits.

'All the gasping of horror which occurs every time the use of the atomic bomb is mentioned', the RAND strategist Bernard Brodie remarked during the Korean War, 'is extremely harmful to us politically and diplomatically.'[7] Some thought Korea provided the perfect opportunity to test its utility. Shortly after North Korea invaded the South on 25 June 1950, Truman asked the JCS to explore the use of atom bombs in the event that the Soviet Union entered the war. Two weeks later, General Douglas MacArthur, the commander in Korea, intimated his desire to have nuclear weapons at his disposal. He thought they might be useful to 'isolate the battlefields' by hitting the routes that led into North Korea from Manchuria and Vladivostok.[8] The JCS concurred and on 5 August ten B-29s with unarmed nuclear weapons were despatched to Guam.* They remained there throughout 1951 but were never used.

After the Chinese intervention led to stalemate and American casualties passed the 30,000 mark, pressure to use the Bomb intensified. Since it had ended the war with Japan, surely it could be used for the same purpose in Korea? In 1951, Gallup found that a slight majority of Americans favoured use of the bomb in Korea on 'military targets'. Country music star Roy Acuff thought Moscow seemed a better target:

> You will see lightning flashing, hear atomic thunders roll
> When Moscow lies in ashes, God have mercy on your soul
> There's a question, Mr Stalin, and it's you who must decide
> When atomic bombs start falling, do you have a place to hide?[9]

---

* Only nine planes and bombs made it to Guam. One B-29 crashed shortly after takeoff from Fairfield-Suisun Air Force Base near San Francisco. One of the passengers, General Robert Travis, was killed in the crash. The base was subsequently renamed in his honour.

But Korea, like Berlin, revealed that the Bomb was an inadequate instrument of manipulation. Mao Zedong, like Stalin, answered the nuclear threat with contempt. 'The atom bomb is a paper tiger which the US reactionaries use to scare people,' he boasted in 1947. 'It looks terrible, but in fact it isn't. Of course the atom bomb is a weapon of mass slaughter, but the outcome of a war is decided by the people, not by one or two new types of weapon.'[10]

In November 1950, Truman conceded that 'there has always been active consideration of its use', but then added, 'I don't want to see it used. It is a terrible weapon and it should not be used on innocent men, women and children who have nothing whatever to do with this military aggression.'[11] LeMay agreed, but for different reasons, arguing that Korea did not provide the right theatre for deployment. Using the Bomb 'would not be advisable . . . unless undertaken as part of an overall atomic campaign against Red China'.[12] That idea also appealed to MacArthur, who drew up a list of 'retaliation targets' in China and North Korea which would require up to twenty-six atomic bombs.

When the war began to bog down, and the Soviets and Chinese proved unreceptive to peace feelers, Truman began to have second thoughts. On 27 January 1952 he fantasized about using the bomb to forestall further interference by China and the USSR. Mao and Stalin would be given a ten-day ultimatum to cease aiding the North; if they failed to respond adequately, 'Moscow, St Petersburg, Mukden, Vladivostok, Peking, Shanghai, Port Arthur, Darien, Odessa, Stalingrad, and every manufacturing plant in China and the Soviet Union will be eliminated.' Privately, Truman mused about the message he might send to his adversaries: 'Now do you want an end to hostilities in Korea or do you want China and Siberia destroyed? You may have one or the other; whichever you want, these lies of yours . . . have gone far enough. You either accept our fair and just proposal or you will be completely destroyed.'[13] Musings of this sort are always serious when they are punctuated with nuclear weapons. But, in truth, Truman's diatribe seems evidence more of frustration than intent. He was annoyed that the war was not going his way and that his nuclear arsenal was not providing the authority he had hoped.

By January 1953 the US had tested its first tactical nuclear weapon. The pressure for its use in Korea intensified, with the JCS actively considering targets for deployment. In February, Eisenhower, now president, suggested to the NSC that the Kaesong area of North Korea 'provided a good target for this type of weapon'.[14] On 19 May the Joint Chiefs recommended direct air and naval strikes against China, including the use of nuclear weapons, a recommendation endorsed by the NSC.

Korea provided a unique opportunity for deployment without the risk of escalation – since the Soviet arsenal was still minuscule, it is highly unlikely that the action would have triggered a catastrophic nuclear contest. But caution eventually prevailed, a result that still intrigues historians. The best explanation seems to be that Korea was the wrong war. It was a limited war; the US had not yet worked out how to fight such a contest, much less how nuclear weapons might play a part. Within the American administration, deep unease was felt about the consequences of using nuclear weapons in Korea. Frank Pace, the Secretary of the Army, gave three reasons why the Bomb was not used:

> The first, that it would not be productive, that this was not the kind of war in which the use of the atomic bomb would be effective. . . . Second, was the concern about the moral use of weapons of this nature against a smaller country in this kind of war, and the third was that if it proved ineffective then its function as a shield for Europe would be either minimized or lost.[15]

Nitze worried in particular about what might happen if the Bomb was used but did not achieve its purpose. The failure, he feared, would undermine the very foundations of American strategic policy which rested so heavily on the weapon's omnipotence. In other words, the only way to maintain the credibility of the bomb was not to use it. Deployment meant running the risk that its mysterious power might be revealed as a sham – that the Emperor might be discovered to have no clothes.

In 1945 a degree of atomic innocence had existed. Five years later, that innocence had evaporated. Using the Bomb against Korea would therefore have been perceived as more wilful and reprehensible than had been the case at Hiroshima. A moral Rubicon would have been crossed. Truman and Eisenhower came to understand the Stygian symbolism of the weapon – that its evil lay not in the destruction caused but in its nature. 'This isn't just another weapon, not just another bomb,' Truman once remarked. He had come to this conclusion not because of moral scruples but because of a cold hard realization that nuclear war would be disaster. 'War today . . . might dig the grave not only of our Stalinist opponents but of our own society, our world as well as theirs,' he confessed just before leaving the White House in 1953. 'Such a war is not possible for a rational man.' But this realization was not in itself enough to bring a sense of reason to the arms race, since Truman did not believe that the Soviets followed a similar logic. 'We . . . dare not assume', he concluded, 'that others would not yield to the temptation science is now placing in their hands.'[16]

Korea convinced Eisenhower that a new approach to the Cold War was essential. Faced with a dangerously spiralling defence budget and the real threat of superpower confrontation, he sought ways to create a peaceful world in which American commerce could flourish. Two policies were formulated in tandem to promote peace and prosperity. The first was the New Look. Eisenhower was keen to avoid protracted, indecisive and expensive engagements like Korea. 'I can conceive of no greater disadvantage to America than to be employing its own ground forces, or any other kind of forces, in great numbers around the world,' he told a reporter. 'What we are trying to do is make our friends strong enough to take care of local situations by themselves.' Military power would be deployed only when 'vital interests demand'.[17]

Yet Chinese aggression, when combined with the development of the Soviet nuclear arsenal and the escalating crisis in Europe, made the dangers facing the US seem hugely threatening. Eisenhower knew that the Communists would have to be confronted, but wanted to choose the circumstances in which he did so. Toward this end, the New Look would rely more heavily upon nuclear weapons, either for deterrence or actual attack, instead of expensive ground troops. In line with this policy, Eisenhower cut Truman's 1954 defence budget from $41.3 billion to $36 billion. Secretary of State John Foster Dulles formally unveiled the strategy on 12 January 1954. 'It is not sound policy', he argued, 'permanently to commit United States land forces . . . to a degree that gives us no strategic reserve.'[18] Instead, America would use nuclear weaponry to achieve her aims. Dulles hoped to break the psychological taboo against nuclear weapons; he wanted to treat them like any other weapon, using them where appropriate. The Bomb would become 'a normal part of the arsenal of war'. Eisenhower agreed that henceforward the administration would 'regard . . . these weapons as "conventional"'.[19]

As Dulles admitted, the policy was driven by economic considerations. In the 1952 presidential election Eisenhower stressed that 'the foundation of military strength is economic strength . . . a bankrupt America is more the Soviet goal than an America conquered on the field of battle'.[20] The magical solution to tight budgets was the Bomb. 'The basic decision is to depend primarily on a greater [nuclear] capacity to retaliate instantly by means and at places of our choosing,' he explained. 'As a result it is now possible to get and to share more basic security at less cost.'[21] Beyond the matter of cost, the policy also addressed the basic dilemma that would plague the US throughout the Cold War, namely the fact that the Chinese and Soviets 'can pick the time, place and method of aggression'. Since it was impossible for the US to keep, in a permanent state of readiness, a force capable of countering the huge Communist armies, the only answer was air power, backed by nuclear weapons.

But this meant using a large sledgehammer to crack what might be a small nut. 'Massive atomic and thermonuclear retaliation is not the kind of power which could most usefully be evoked under all circumstances,'

Dulles admitted.[22] He failed, however, to clarify what sort of problem would merit such a response. According to its exponents, this uncertainty was the beauty of the New Look: adversaries would be kept in line because they could never be certain when the Bomb might fall.

The idea was tested when, toward the end of the Korean War, Eisenhower and Dulles used the threat of a nuclear strike while negotiating a ceasefire. Then, during the treaty discussions, threats were again used to keep Russia and China in line. In August 1953, LeMay was ordered to take twenty B-36s loaded with nuclear weapons to Okinawa – an operation appropriately dubbed 'Big Stick'. Keen that the message would not go unheeded, LeMay invited the press to record the force's arrival. 'We stayed . . . on the alert, crews at the airplanes, while the hostility cessation papers were being signed,' Edmundson recalled. 'The B-36s . . . with atomic weapons . . . ready to go, was a warning to the North Koreans and the Russians and the Chinese not to try anything funny when we were sitting around the peace table.'[23]

The successful negotiations convinced Eisenhower and Dulles that the strategy had worked. In fact, it now appears that the Chinese were not remotely affected – they subsequently claimed they were unaware of the nuclear threat. As for the Russians, their support for the ceasefire seems to have been affected more by the death of Stalin in March 1953 than by Big Stick. The war came to an end not because of the bomb, but rather because all sides had tired of the contest.

In Europe, the New Look seemed to offer a solution to the Soviet's conventional force superiority. There was no escaping the fact that, if a Russian premier ordered his troops westward, NATO forces would be quickly overrun. In response to this threat, NATO adopted the policy of 'massive retaliation', in which nuclear weapons would be used in response to conventional attack. According to a plan formulated in March 1954, 'SAC could lay down an attack . . . of 600-750 bombs by approaching Russia from many directions so as to hit their early warning screen simultaneously. . . . virtually all of Russia would be nothing but a smoking, radiating ruin at the end of two hours.'[24] The strategy called for 118 major cities to be hit, killing around 80 per cent of the population in those cities, or around 60 million in total. In late 1954, General Bernard Rogers, the deputy supreme commander in Europe, explained: 'I want to make it absolutely clear that we . . . are basing all our operational planning on using atomic and thermonuclear weapons in our own defense. With us it is no longer "they may possibly be used", it is very definite "they will be used, if we are attacked".'[25] As part of this plan, a huge effort was devoted to the development of tactical nuclear weapons – small yield bombs, artillery shells and mines. By December 1954, NATO ministers felt sufficiently confident in the plan to reduce the force level objective from ninety-six to thirty active divisions.

In line with the new policy, the US began in 1954 to place its bombs in allied countries. Four years later there were nearly 3,000 American nuclear weapons deployed in Western Europe. This suited European governments since it seemed the best way to guarantee that the US would come to their aid if the Soviets attacked. It also suited the Americans, who were keen to place their forces as close to their adversary as possible, and as far from the homeland as practicable. But some Germans grew concerned that their country had become the chosen site for nuclear apocalypse. In 1955, in an exercise called Carte Blanche, NATO simulated an attack against Warsaw Pact forces which involved the detonation of 335 nuclear weapons, mainly tactical devices to halt Soviet conventional forces. Eighty per cent of these were deployed on German soil. Immediate casualties were estimated at around 1.5 million dead and 3.5 million wounded in just two days of war. Analysts neglected to count the number likely to die from radiation poisoning. On hearing the results of the exercise, the German politician Helmut Schmidt remarked that tactical nuclear weapons 'will not defend Europe, but destroy it'.[26]

Massive retaliation also worried those at RAND. With admirable succinctness, Brodie warned: 'National objectives cannot be consonant with national suicide.'[27] He realized that, in the age of the H-bomb, a mutual exchange of nuclear weapons was indeed suicide. His colleague William Kaufman, in *The Absolute Weapon*, argued that using nuclear weapons to deter a conventional military threat might not work if both superpowers possessed huge atomic arsenals. 'Despite our best efforts, the antagonist will challenge us to make good on our threat. If we do so, we will have to accept the consequences of executing our threatened action.' In other words, the other side would respond with a nuclear attack. 'If we back down and let the challenge go unheeded, we will suffer losses of prestige, we will decrease our capacity for instituting effective deterrence policies in the future, and we will encourage the opponent to take further actions of a detrimental character.' In short, the US was back where she started, with no dependable way to meet the conventional threat posed by the Soviets or Chinese. Absolute power meant absolute impotence.

This lesson should not have surprised the US, for it was essentially what Stalin had taught them since 1945. He had assumed that, since the US would resort to nuclear weapons only under the most extreme circumstances, he was safe to take whatever action short of that extreme. The possibilities for brinkmanship were huge precisely because the nuclear brink was so far away. If this was true when the US held a nuclear monopoly, it was even truer when there were two well-armed nuclear powers. At that very moment the Communists were demonstrating the principle in Vietnam. Contrary to what Dulles suggested, there were very few issues worthy of nuclear war.

The second aspect of Eisenhower's nuclear policy, 'Atoms for Peace', was unveiled to the UN on 8 December 1953. 'My country wants to be constructive, not destructive,' he began. 'It wants agreement, not wars among nations. It wants itself to live in freedom, and in the confidence that the people of every other nation enjoy equally the right of choosing their own way of life.' Toward this end, Eisenhower sought to move the world 'out of the dark chamber of horrors into the light, to find a way by which the minds of men, the hopes of men, the souls of men everywhere, can move forward toward peace and happiness and well being'. This meant the 'reduction or elimination of atomic materials for military purposes', but much more than that. 'It is not enough to take this weapon out of the hands of the soldiers. It must be put into the hands of those who will know how to strip its military casing and adapt it to the arts of peace.' He proposed that the nuclear powers would donate fissionable materials to an agency which would allocate them in ways calculated to 'serve the peaceful pursuits of mankind'. He had in mind the provision of 'abundant electrical energy in the power-starved areas of the world'. Eisenhower wanted, literally, to bring light to the world.[28]

The Atomic Energy Act was revised to enable 'the development, use, and control of atomic energy . . . so as to promote world peace, improve the general welfare, increase the standard of living, and strengthen free competition in private enterprise'.[29] On the surface, the new law seemed close to what morally tormented scientists had long demanded. But qualification for nuclear munificence was strictly limited – to Eisenhower 'the world' meant 'the free world'. Since the technology was supposed to strengthen 'free competition in private enterprise', that ruled out the Communist bloc. In other words, Atoms for Peace was designed to strengthen America and her allies in the protracted Cold War struggle. Electricity was the power behind propaganda; the light shining in the dark corners of the world would illuminate capitalism.

Because security remained the 'paramount objective', the lion's share of funding and effort would continue to go toward bombs. In fact, the reason why Eisenhower could contemplate generosity with fissionable material was precisely because the nuclear industry had been so successful. In January 1947, when the AEC took control of the Manhattan Project, the US had no stockpiles of plutonium or enriched uranium. Six years later, when Eisenhower announced 'Atoms for Peace', the US had enough fissionable material to make five thousand bombs.[30]

Meanwhile, the arms race continued at frenetic pace. On 1 March 1954, the Americans again edged ahead when the Bravo test took place on Bikini Island. The device used lithium deuteride instead of deuterium, thus

pointing the way to a deliverable bomb. Marshall Rosenbluth, on a
destroyer thirty miles away, saw the fireball

> rising and rising, and spreading . . . It looked to me like what you might
> imagine a diseased brain, or a brain of some mad man would look like.
> . . . And it just kept getting bigger and bigger, and eventually got right over-
> head of us, and the air started getting filled with this gray stuff, which I
> guess was somewhat radioactive coral coming down, and I remember every-
> body was shooed . . . below decks, or in below the water line to cut down
> the radiation, but then the temperature got to be like a hundred and fifty,
> or something, and we didn't have air conditioning, so it was pretty brutal.[31]

The explosion was twice as large as expected, and forty times more powerful
than Sakharov's sloika. Alarmed by the way the Soviet lead had been rudely
erased, Khrushchev demanded a weapon like Bravo. Sakharov, feeling the
pressure, recruited additional scientists.

At a meeting in early 1954, the truba's progress was officially reviewed.
The big names of Soviet nuclear research all attended and listened to an
extended tale of woe. Tamm spoke last, delivering, in essence, the funeral
oration for the truba. Its potential was so low, he argued, that it was pointless to discuss modifications. With the truba dead and the sloika a dead
end, Soviet scientists found their minds cleared. Within weeks of the Bravo
test, they began brainstorming the idea of radiation implosion. Viktor
Davidenko proposed using an atomic explosion to compress and ignite
thermonuclear fuel. Others took up the idea and developed it, giving rise
to a new spirit. An atmosphere of 'complete self-denial' was apparent, one
scientist recalled:

> everyone contributed to the general progress and participated in the discus-
> sion of the problem as a whole. A 'people's project', Zel'dovich jokingly
> called it, repeating the all-too-familiar catchword for irrigation canals and
> similar public construction projects that usually demanded an assault-style
> effort on the part of a large number of people.

Sakharov called radiation implosion the 'Third Idea'* – essentially the
Teller-Ulam concept, but arrived at without their help. Though he admitted
that he played an important role, Sakharov insisted it was a group discovery.
'We were all too busy . . . to worry about who got credit. Any assigning
of honors . . . would have been "skinning the bear before it was killed".
Now it is too late to recall who said what during our discussions. And
does it really matter?'[32]

---

* The sloika was the first idea, the use of lithium deuteride the second.

The Soviet's first genuine thermonuclear device was tested on 22 November 1955 at the Semipalatinsk site. It was, significantly, an air-dropped bomb, the first of its kind in the world.* The bomb was designed to yield three megatons, but some fuel was replaced by a passive substance in order to halve its power. 'The . . . bomb made a greater impression on me than anything else in my entire life,' Goncharov felt.

> Immediately, it felt as if you had put your head into an open oven. The heat was unbearable. Then we had this impressive view of the fireball, the mushroom cloud, all of it on a huge scale. What was shocking was that this great scene was unfolding in absolute silence. And when the shock wave approached us, we dropped to the ground. Thunder. Stones were flying. Someone was hit by a large rock. There were several claps of thunder and the ground was shaking.

Due to a temperature inversion, the blast was even more powerful than anticipated, causing damage in towns fifty miles away. 'I remember when we arrived back at our hotel, the windows and doors had been blown out,' Goncharov recalled.

> It felt as if the place had been hit by an air raid. But our joy was indescribable. We started celebrating immediately. We took out all our supplies. Someone brought alcohol. There was a sense of fulfilment, of having completed our task. That this beautiful, complex device – and that's what it was from a physicist's point of view – had worked was a triumph of science, of course. We all understood that.[33]

Excitement mingled with fear. Two people, a soldier and a two-year-old girl, were killed as a result of the test. After the initial exhilaration, a sombre mood descended.†

Kurchatov and Sakharov were taken aback by the destructive power they had created. 'We were stirred up', Sakharov recalled, 'but not just with the exhilaration that comes with a job well done. For my part, I experienced a range of contradictory sentiments, perhaps chief among them a fear that this newly released force could slip out of control and lead to unimaginable disasters.'[34] He later reflected:

---

* The US did not test an air-dropped thermonuclear bomb until the following year, though the Bravo bomb was adaptable to air delivery.
† Conspicuously absent from the scientists' grief were the thousands who died in the gulag in order to make the bomb. Stalin once said that one death is a tragedy, a million deaths a statistic.

When you see all of this yourself, something in you changes. When you see the burned birds who are withering on the scorched steppe, when you see how the shock wave blows away buildings like houses of cards, when you feel the reek of splintered bricks, when you sense melted glass, you immediately think of times of war . . . All of this triggers an irrational yet very strong emotional impact. How not to start thinking of one's responsibility at this point?[35]

'That was absolutely terrible,' Kurchatov remarked to a colleague; 'we have to make sure that that weapon is never used.'[36]

At the subsequent celebration, Sakharov proposed a toast: 'May all of our devices explode as successfully as today's, but always over test sites and never over cities.' He had stepped too far. Scientists, servants of the state, were not supposed to concern themselves with how their discoveries might be used. Marshall M. I. Nedelin, who had been in charge of the test, publicly upbraided Sakharov by telling an off-colour joke:

he rose, glass in hand, and said: 'Let me tell a parable. An old man wearing only a shirt was praying before an icon. "Guide me, harden me, guide me, harden me." His wife, who was lying on the stove said: "Just pray to be hard old man, I can guide it in myself." Let's drink to getting hard.'

First there was an uncomfortable silence, then the rattle of nervous chatter. Sakharov went pale.

I drank my brandy in silence and didn't open my mouth again for the rest of the evening. Many years have passed, but I still feel as if I had been lashed by a whip. Not that my feelings were hurt; I am not easily offended, especially by a joke. But Nedelin's parable was not a joke. He wanted to squelch my pacifist sentiment, and to put me and anyone who might share these ideas in our place.

Sakharov clearly understood what Nedelin meant. 'We, the inventors, scientists, engineers and craftsmen, had created a terrible weapon, the most terrible weapon in human history; but its use would lie entirely outside our control.' Sakharov knew this already, 'but understanding something in an abstract way is different from feeling it with your whole being, like the reality of life and death'. Nedelin's comments struck him to the quick; the seeds of his dissidence were sown at that moment of celebration. 'The ideas and emotions kindled . . . have not diminished to this day, and they completely altered my thinking.'[37] Like the scientists at Los Alamos, he had been pulled along by the euphoria of discovery and by the national crisis. But, like them, success tormented him.

For some Soviet scientists, however, abstraction still provided a handy refuge. Goncharov confessed that, in order to protect their sanity, his colleagues viewed the hydrogen bomb as a physics problem, not a military weapon.

> I . . . was never interested in questions of (weapons) effects. That is, I felt an aversion to everything that was outside the boundaries of . . . the physical picture . . . All the questions relating to the impact . . . the applied side of it, were very disagreeable to me. I always tried to remove myself from them. And I think that many experienced the same feeling. . . . During many of the tests we would stop at the strictly physical questions . . . we would not develop it into a military model.[38]

Goncharov's statement is remarkable only for its honesty. Scientists on both sides of the Iron Curtain took the same blinkered view. How else to explain the surprised sense of betrayal many felt when soldiers and politicians began to consider military uses for these weapons?

Abstract unreality was briefly interrupted by the Bravo test. The Americans had advised all vessels in the predicted vicinity of fallout to vacate the area. But then the wind shifted. The test went ahead even though it was known that the fallout would travel toward areas that had not been swept of shipping, and also toward islands that had not been evacuated. A Japanese trawler, the *Fukuryu Maru* (*Lucky Dragon*), found itself in the wrong place on the wrong day.

> Suddenly the skies in the west lighted up and a great flare of whitish yellow light splashed against the clouds and illuminated the water. The startled seaman grasped the rough wood of the cabin with his hands and gazed in awe at the spectacle in the west. It seemed like minutes, but it was really only for seconds that he was transfixed by the dazzling light. It changed to a yellow-red and then to a flaming orange before Suzuki came to his senses and dashed back to his cabin to tell his mates what he had seen. As he entered the cabin, Takagi, a cabin mate, was humming a song. Suzuki blurted out, 'The sun rises in the West!'[39]

A strange cloud overtook the ship, dropping radioactive ash like snow. The crew reached the port of Yaizu thirteen days later suffering from advanced radiation poisoning, unwilling martyrs to the cause of arms control.

On 31 March 1954, Strauss rejected allegations that the Americans had lost control of their test. He nevertheless admitted that 'the yield was about double that of the calculated estimate, a margin of error not incompatible with a new weapon'. He accepted that the fallout had not travelled in the predicted pattern, but blamed rogue weather. He was lying. A 1982

Defense Nuclear Agency study found that officials knew precisely where the fallout would travel, but refused to postpone the test.[40] As for the Japanese, Strauss insinuated that they had ignored warnings to stay out of the danger area, another lie.

Strauss was studiously vague about the fate of the Japanese fishermen, blaming his lack of hard information on the fact that American doctors were denied access to them. He nevertheless mentioned that their blood count did not give cause for alarm. The Japanese government reacted angrily: 'These simple fishermen . . . resent and refuse the type of clinical examination which they feel might place them in the position of experimental objects.' Then, on 23 September, Aikichi Kuboyama died. The AEC refused to accept responsibility, claiming that he was making a full recovery when 'he developed hepatitis . . . of infectious type caused by a filterable virus. . . . After a prolonged illness, he died from the effects of the hepatitis. Such hepatitis is not in itself a direct consequence of radiation injury and does not constitute a part of such injury.'[41]

A similar policy of denial was maintained with respect to the poisoning of the fish in the area. Though some 457 tonnes of tuna eventually had to be destroyed, the AEC vehemently maintained that only those in the hold of the *Lucky Dragon* were poisonous and that the hazard for other stocks caught in the area was 'negligible'. Meanwhile, the US Food and Drug Administration banned importation of tuna from the region. Only after severe pressure did the US agree to pay $2 million compensation to the Japanese for injuries or damage sustained as a result of the blast.

The Japanese were only the most visible victims. The huge cloud of radioactive coral travelled in the direction of Rongerik, Rongelap and Utirik islands, where 28 Americans and 236 islanders were subjected to a shower of fallout. According to a 1982 study, fallout on Rongerik 'gathered to a depth of $1/4$ to $1/2$ inch (0.6 to 1.2 cm) deep in places and left a visible layer on tables in the mess hall and barracks'. American personnel nevertheless 'continued normal activities during the remainder of the day', though they did change to 'long sleeves and long pants'.[42] Since no prior warning was given to the islanders about the dangers of fallout, they carried on with their lives as usual, consuming irradiated food and water. Children on Rongelap played in the dust, which seemed like snow. By nightfall, they began to show the first signs of radiation poisoning – severe vomiting and diarrhoea. Before long, their hair began to fall out. The islanders, who did not remotely understand what had happened, were thrown into terrified panic. Some were not evacuated until three days after the blast.

Strauss again downplayed the dangers. Those exposed were 'well and happy . . . the medical staff on Kwajalein have advised us that they anticipate no illness'. An AEC film, kept secret for decades, told a different story: 'A majority of those receiving the heaviest radiation reported some transient nausea on the first or second day and some loss of hair was a frequent symptom. Most . . .developed multiple skin lesions.'[43] Rumours circulated that the islanders had been intentionally used as guinea pigs to measure the radiation effects of the new bombs, an allegation Strauss called 'utterly false, irresponsible and gravely unjust to the men engaged in this patriotic service'.[44] He saw a silver lining in the radioactive cloud:

> one important result of these hydrogen bomb developments has been the enhancement of our military capability to the point where we should soon be more free to increase our emphasis on the peaceful uses of atomic power at home and abroad. It will be a tremendous satisfaction to those who have participated in this program that it has hastened that day.[45]

The Utirik islanders were allowed to return within two months, even though the radiation danger had not dissipated. Rongelap, on the other hand, remained dangerously contaminated for three years, preventing reoccupation. Ten years after the test came the first thyroid tumours and other cancers.

In the weeks that followed the Bravo test, traces of radioactive fallout were found on the Japanese mainland, in Australia, India, parts of Europe and even the United States. The fate of the Japanese fisherman focused attention on the hidden dangers of these bombs. Among those sounding a warning was Kurchatov:

> Aside from the destructive impact of atomic and hydrogen bombs there is another threat for mankind involved in atomic war – poisoning the atmosphere and the surface of the globe with radioactive substances . . .There is no hope that organisms, and the human organism in particular, will adjust themselves to higher levels of radioactivity on earth. This adjustment can take place only through a prolonged process of evolution. So we cannot but admit that mankind faces the enormous threat of an end to all life on earth.[46]

Originally a secret test, Bravo turned into a massive international incident. One of the Japanese fishermen, while still receiving treatment in hospital, sent a message to the world: 'Our fate menaces all mankind. Tell that to those who are responsible. God grant that they may listen.'[47] 'The world understood the difference,' Goncharov remarked. 'The fishermen were 220 km away. So the difference between the hydrogen and atomic bomb became absolutely clear. . . . authorities everywhere were greatly alarmed. . . . It became clear that Americans had created something.'[48] The US soon found itself having to defend its testing programme against criticism from around the world. At the UN, India became the first country to call for a ban on atmospheric testing.

★　★　★

While the Americans were poisoning the Marshall Islanders, the Soviets were busy poisoning their own people. Russia's weapons development complex eventually dwarfed its American counterpart. The main laboratories and factories were located in ten 'nuclear cities' – fortresses designed to exclude those from outside and to restrict the movement of those who lived and worked within. Arzamas-16 and Chelyabinsk-70 contained the weapons design laboratories, with the former also housing a warhead production plant. Penza-19, Sverdlovsk-45 and Zlatoust-36 contained the main warhead production plants. Krasnoyarsk-26, Krasnoyarsk-45, Tomsk-7, Chelyabinsk-65 and Sverdlovsk-44 produced fissile materials.

Chelyabinsk has been dubbed 'the most contaminated spot on the planet'. From 1949 to 1956, around 76 million cubic metres of radioactive waste was dumped into the Techa River, resulting in an epidemic of various illnesses downstream from the site where around 124,000 people lived. Eventually, twenty-two villages along the riverbank had to be evacuated, but, for some reason, Muslyumovo, in which contamination was especially high, was never abandoned. Since the village had no well, the 4,000 residents depended entirely on river water for their needs.

Alarm bells were raised when radioactivity carried by the Techa was found in the Arctic ocean in 1951, but it was not until 1956 that measures to clean up the river were implemented. The dumping problem was 'solved' by diverting radioactive waste into self-contained lakes – Lake Karachay for high-level waste and Lake Staroe Boloto for medium-level waste. During hot summers, however, the lakes dried up whereupon winds blew radioactive dust over the surrounding countryside. In 1967, the dust blew over an area totalling 2,200 square kilometres.

An explosion in a nuclear waste storage tank on 29 September 1957, equivalent to 70 tons of TNT, resulted in a radioactive cloud over the provinces of Chelyabinsk, Sverdlovsk and Tyumen. Around 80 metric tonnes of waste was ejected, discharging 20 million curies of radioactivity. Plutonium and strontium were released across 60,000 square kilometres, an area now called the East Ural Radioactive Trace (EURT). The intensity of the radioactive release was double that which would be released in the 1986 accident at Chernobyl. Some 10,700 people were evacuated, but the incident was otherwise kept secret from the outside world. 'When they evacuated us', one woman recalled, 'they made us sign a form saying that we wouldn't reveal state secrets. Of course, we knew what that meant.' Since 1957 there has been a 21 per cent increase in the incidence of cancer in the area, a 25 per cent increase in birth defects and 50 per cent of the population of child-bearing age are sterile.[49]

* * *

Since fallout victims are usually poor or anonymous, it is easy to ignore their plight. A more prominent casualty of the hydrogen bomb was Robert Oppenheimer. Many Americans interpreted Soviet progress in nuclear technology as evidence that traitors had infiltrated the highest echelons of government, science and the military. The Fuchs case provided grist to the paranoia mill. Since many assumed that Fuchs must have had an accomplice at Los Alamos, focus centred on Oppenheimer, who had made a nuisance of himself by opposing development of the hydrogen bomb. With anti-communism growing hysterical, trivialities from his distant past seemed more important than recent sublime service. Convinced of Oppenheimer's guilt, Strauss waged a vicious vendetta against him. Matters reached a climax when Oppenheimer's security clearance came up for review. Most of his colleagues, including Groves, testified to his loyalty and dependability. But Teller, still smarting from being snubbed over the Super, had no qualms about knifing his 'friend' in the back. When asked if Oppenheimer was a security risk, Teller replied: 'I would feel personally more secure if public matters would rest in other hands.'[50] Though not a direct condemnation, it was sufficient to destroy Oppenheimer. Teller's testimony was crucial, but that of General Kenneth Nichols, who had succeeded Groves, demonstrated how times and priorities had changed:

> through World War II [Oppenheimer] was of tremendous value and absolutely essential. . . . since World War II his value to the Atomic Energy Commission as a scientist or as a consultant has declined because of the rise in competence and skill of other scientists and because of his loss of scientific objectivity probably resulting from the diversion of his efforts to political fields . . . I doubt that the Atomic Energy Commission, even if the question of his security clearance had not arisen, would have utilized his services to a markedly greater extent during the next few years.[51]

In other words, Oppenheimer was expendable. He had not changed, but his country had. With access to sensitive documents henceforth blocked, he could no longer work in, or wield influence over, the Bomb's development. Oppenheimer lost his work and Teller his friends.

The matter of J. Robert Oppenheimer is incidental to the life of the bomb and has, in any case, been adequately covered elsewhere. But one aspect of that case, namely the extent to which the Soviets stole nuclear technology to develop their H-bomb, deserves attention. Fuchs supplied comprehensive information on the 'classical' Super, but that design proved futile, as the Americans and then the Soviets eventually discovered. The Americans then turned to the Teller-Ulam configuration, and the Soviets, three years later, produced a version of it. But therein lies the question: did the Soviets steal the Teller-Ulam secrets, or did they discover them independently?

Bethe thought that since the American hydrogen bomb 'came about by a series of accidents . . . It would be a most remarkable coincidence if the Russian project had taken a similar course'.[52] In 1990 nuclear analysts Daniel Hirsch and William Matthews argued that the Soviets unlocked the American secret by analysing fallout from Mike. Radionuclides released into the atmosphere would have demonstrated that Mike involved extremely high compression of thermonuclear fuels. From this evidence, the Soviets would have been able to deduce the process by which high compression was achieved. But the Brahmins of the Soviet project – Khariton, Smirnov, Goncharov, Adamski, et al. – dismiss this argument as simple American prejudice, an inability to accept that Soviet scientists might be sufficiently skilled to discover a process on their own. As Teller once admitted, the laws of physics operate on both sides of the Atlantic.

Khariton and his friends insist that their hydrogen bomb resulted from an independently creative process – 'perhaps the brightest page in the history of the Soviet atomic project'. Their argument is bolstered by the fact that the Soviets did not have the technical capacity at the time of Mike's detonation to collect and analyse fallout.* In any case, Soviet scientists already knew that high compressions were necessary to achieve thermonuclear explosion, what they didn't know was how to achieve them. Goncharov insists that his colleagues had reached a critical state of understanding, so that, once the idea of radiation implosion was proposed, progress was swift. 'All the processes had been already deeply understood. So as soon as the idea [of radiation implosion] was born, it immediately began to be realized.'[53]

The Soviets had spent eight years enduring the bitterness of atomic inferiority. Though they had survived that period with their integrity intact and had not, in fact, made many concessions to the Americans, they still viewed the bomb much as they had in 1945 – in other words as a weapon of manipulation. As a result, once they attained rough parity with the United States, they were keen to turn the tables, to frighten their adversaries with their power.

The Americans hardly behaved better. Central to the New Look was the idea that the bomb was a lever and that, given its power, few adversaries would refuse to bend. In April 1954, the Americans briefly considered using nuclear weapons to break the Viet Minh stranglehold upon French forces at Dien Bien Phu. But the idea was abandoned when it was realized that while such a weapon might defeat the Viet Minh, it would

---

* In fact, Sakharov and Viktor Davidenko did collect newly fallen snow a few days after the Mike explosion, but a colleague poured the water down the drain before it could be analysed.

also annihilate the French. In any case, Eisenhower found the idea morally repugnant. 'You boys must be crazy,' he said to an adviser who suggested the possibility. 'We can't use those awful things against Asians for the second time in less than ten years.'[54] This reveals the weakness of the New Look: there were actually few Cold War contests in which using a Bomb seemed credible.

Taken in tandem, 'New Look' and 'Atoms for Peace' envisaged a world tamed by nuclear weapons and civilized by nuclear power. Cheap energy from nuclear generation would, the propaganda claimed, 'warm the cold . . . feed the hungry . . . [and] alleviate the misery of the world'. Like some 1950s equivalent of *Tomorrow's World*, boffins promised an atomic locomotive, nuclear greenhouses and endless medical advances. Newspapers forecast that 'Atomic Rays will Cut Lumber Instead of Saws' and celebrated a 'Nuclear Device in Fight Against Cancer'. The US Postal Service commemorated the initiative with a new stamp: 'Atoms for Peace: To Find the Way By Which the Inventiveness of Man Shall Be Consecrated to New Life'.[55] Plowshare explored ways to use nuclear devices in the construction of canals, roads, reservoirs and harbours, not to mention oil and gas exploration. In March 1955, engineers exploded a one-kiloton device at the Nevada Test Site (NTS), to see whether bombs might be used for demolition purposes. The big obstacle, however, was fallout. Investigating this problem, the AEC at one point intentionally contaminated an area in the Arctic with radioactive isotopes in order to measure how they might disperse in the environment after a peaceful explosion. In all, twenty-six Plowshare tests were conducted between 1957 and 1973. Aside from the practical benefits (which proved non-existent), the government hoped that the tests would improve the respectability of nuclear power.

Teller was head cheerleader for the programme. One of his more imaginative schemes was Project Chariot, a plan to detonate six thermonuclear devices at the mouth of the Ogoturuk Creek in Alaska, the purpose being to develop a major international harbour. Conveniently ignoring the fact that such a harbour would be ice-bound for a good part of the year, Teller saw it as a clever way to transport coal from Alaska's interior to Japan. 'The Japanese might become the first beneficiaries of atomic explosions as they have been the first victims,' he mused. The tests were also designed to study the effect of radiation on the ecosystem – an ecosystem which included human beings. That purpose, however, was not widely publicized.[56]

A similar programme took place within the Soviet Union, though without the self-righteous claims about bringing light to the dark corners of the world. Always fascinated by big projects, the Soviets were drawn to the idea of using this huge explosive force to re-design their landscape. At one point a large bomb was placed under a river in Kazakhstan and, presto, the explosion created a sizeable lake. Vladislav Trutnev recalls that 'In a year or two we could swim and fish there.' In all, 156 'peaceful' detonations were conducted. Scientists at Chelyabinsk worked on atomic explosions designed to extinguish oil fires, extract ore deposits and, bizarrely, investigate the composition of the earth. In Siberia, 500 detonations were to take place at precise points on a grid, supposedly to study the earth's crust. The project was halted after around 100 charges were detonated.[57]

In 1955, the first International Congress on Peaceful Uses of Atomic Energy was attended by over 3,500 representatives from politics, commerce, industry, and academia. This led in turn to the establishment of the International Atomic Energy Agency in October 1956. As a symbol of his support, Eisenhower donated 100 kilograms of U-235, to be used for peaceful purposes. But, far from developing into a self-sustaining organization for the development of benign atomic energy, the IAEA instead became a group of nations feeding off American nuclear technology and dependent upon the US for fissionable material. Since membership was the only qualification necessary in order to receive American largesse, the US ended up supplying the raw materials for bomb-making to countries whose interest in power plants, atomic locomotives or nuclear saws was not exactly genuine.

A case in point was South Africa, where a nuclear programme started innocently as part of Atoms for Peace in 1957. The US supplied a reactor and fuel, in addition to training personnel. South Africa was interested in part because she had huge reserves of uranium and fancied becoming a supplier of fissionable materials. But nuclear ambitions and apartheid politics proved a volatile mix. As the country grew ever more isolated because of international contempt, she became ever more covetous of her nuclear capacity, in part to become self-sufficient in enriched uranium, but also to develop bombs. An atomic capacity was seen as a potentially useful bargaining counter with an otherwise disdainful West. A top secret programme of weapons development began in 1971.

Atoms for Peace and the New Look caused turbulence in the Soviet Union where the leadership was still in turmoil after Stalin's death. His orthodox vision of international affairs held that capitalism would eventually be destroyed by the communist revolution. But this apocalyptic vision did not accord well with a world of atomic weapons, especially not thermonuclear devices. Despite his tough talk, Khrushchev was genuinely concerned about the power of the new weapons and their implications for superpower confrontation. 'When I was appointed First Secretary of the Central Committee and learned all the facts of nuclear power I couldn't sleep for several days,' he recalled. 'Then I became convinced that we could never possibly use these weapons, and when I realised that I was able to sleep again.'[58]

The impossibility of using nuclear weapons did not, however, harmonize well with communist dogma. On 1 April 1954, Vyecheslav Malyshev, the Minister of Medium Machine Building, sent an article by four senior atomic scientists (of whom Kurchatov was one) to the ruling Soviet troika (Khrushchev, Malenkov and Molotov). Entitled 'The Danger of Atomic War and President Eisenhower's Proposal', it was intended as a direct answer to Atoms for Peace. The article mirrored the scepticism already felt by the Soviet leadership, but did so on technical, not political, grounds, thus making it all the more powerful. The scientists warned that the spread of nuclear technology would inevitably result in a proliferation of atomic weaponry, since expertise in atomic energy 'can also serve as a means for the further perfection of methods . . . for military purposes'. They maintained that a power plant with a 10,000-kilowatt capacity could, for instance, produce about 130–200 kilograms of plutonium annually, enough to create a sizeable nuclear arsenal. Speaking from experience, they added that 'the production of atomic bombs from these materials . . . can be accomplished within a very short period of time'. In other words, Eisenhower's proposals, far from diminishing the danger of atomic war, had the opposite effect. Atoms for Peace, they alleged, was designed to neutralize negative reaction to the *Lucky Dragon* incident. 'The world community is concerned. Such concern is entirely understandable.'[59]

The article constituted a genuine expression of fear. Leaving politics aside, the authors warned that

> use of atomic weapons on a mass scale will lead to devastation of the warring countries. . . . Aside from the destructive impact of atomic and hydrogen bombs, there is another threat for mankind involved in atomic war – poisoning the atmosphere and the surface of the globe with radioactive substances, originating from nuclear explosions. . . . So, we cannot but admit that mankind faces an enormous threat of the termination of all life on Earth.[60]

This doomsday scenario ran counter to the traditional Soviet notion of capitalism's inevitable destruction. Since, in a contest with communism, capitalists would undoubtedly defend themselves with nuclear weapons, the destruction of the entire world (not just capitalism) might result. The article therefore challenged orthodox Soviet thinking, even though that was not the precise intent.

Malenkov agreed with the scientists. He had responded to news of Bravo by publicly stating that, 'considering the modern means of warfare', a war with the US 'would mean the end of world civilization'. The Politburo reaction was quick and severe. In a direct rejoinder to Malenkov, Anastas Mykoyan reasserted the standard line that nuclear weapons were 'a means for deterring aggressors and for waging peace'. In truth, the issue was not about weapons, but about who would eventually lead the Soviet Union. Malenkov had essentially gifted Molotov and Khrushchev the perfect opportunity to attack him for deviation. Publication of the article was vetoed. Malenkov was forced into a public repudiation of his views at the subsequent Communist Party plenum, offering instead a canned statement that American aggression would be crushed by nuclear weapons, leading to the 'collapse of the capitalist social system'.[61]

Over the following year the Bomb was repeatedly used as a stick with which to beat Malenkov. At the plenary meeting on 31 January 1955, Khrushchev called his warnings about the possible destruction of civilization 'theoretically mistaken and politically harmful'. Molotov's rebuttal was even more vicious: 'A communist should not speak about the "destruction of world civilisation" or about the "destruction of the human race"'. He should instead concentrate on 'the need to prepare and mobilize all forces for the destruction of the bourgeoisie'. Molotov continued:

> How can it be asserted that civilization could perish in an atomic war? . . .
> Can we make the peoples believe that in the event of war all must perish?
> Then why should we build socialism, why worry about tomorrow? It would
> be better to supply everyone with coffins now. . . . You see to what absurd-
> ities, to what harmful things, mistakes on political issues can lead.[62]

Less than a month later, Malenkov was formally ousted from the post of head of state. The outcome was all the more ironic given that Khrushchev, as will be seen, was actually in sympathy with much of what he had argued.

At the Geneva summit in July 1955, a profoundly important conversation took place between Eisenhower and Soviet Defence Minister Georgi Zhukov – both allied commanders in the Second World War. Eisenhower spoke openly about his fears of nuclear weaponry, arguing that 'many notions that were correct in the past have changed'. War, he felt, had become 'even more senseless than ever before'. Zhukov agreed, remarking that 'if in the first days of war the United States would drop 300-400 bombs on the USSR', and the Soviet Union retaliated in kind, 'then one can imagine what would happen to the atmosphere'. Zhukov, whose candour must have received prior approval from Khrushchev, confided that he 'personally favors the liquidation of atomic and hydrogen weapons'.

Khrushchev felt that the summit 'convinced us once again, that . . . our enemies were afraid of us in the same way as we were of them'. After the summit he presented his vision of deterrence: 'Let these bombs lie. Let them get on the nerves of those who would like to unleash war. Let them know that war cannot be unleashed, because if you start a war, you will get the proper response.' At the Twentieth Congress of the CPSU in January 1956, the inevitability of a catastrophic war with capitalism was quietly set aside, replaced by a new vision of 'peaceful coexistence'. 'Either peaceful coexistence or the most destructive war in history,' he warned Party colleagues. 'There is no third way.'[63]

Malenkov had been attacked for failing to support the traditional line. In the next phase of Politburo intrigue, Molotov was derided for upholding it. At the Party plenum in June 1957, he desperately tried to straddle two stools. 'We all understand and consider it to be necessary to conduct, promote and stimulate such measures which are conducive to the reduction of international tension,' he proclaimed. 'This is the foundation of our work on the strengthening of peace, on the postponement and prevention of a new war.' War, in other words, was still inevitable, though not perhaps imminent.[64] But then Molotov attacked peaceful coexistence, arguing that the Soviet Union 'must take special care to broaden every fissure, every dissent and contradiction in the imperialist camp'. Mykoyan, supporting Khrushchev, derided Molotov as 'a dyed-in-the wool conservative'.[65] He was accused of 'dogmatic deviation' – an interesting oxymoron that encapsulates the turbulence within the Kremlin.

Malenkov's position had been too pessimistic, Molotov's too inflexible. In contrast, Khrushchev established a pragmatic policy that recognized the dangers of nuclear weaponry but still managed to make use of them politically. His approach was a carbon copy of Eisenhower's. Both men uttered anguished warnings about the threat to mankind, but both amassed huge arsenals and occasionally threatened to use them. Both advocated a test ban and arms limitations, but neither would compromise defence priorities in order to achieve those goals.

While the Soviets were tailoring their dogma to suit the H-bomb, American strategists were stubbornly searching for a solution to atomic impotence. In a 1953 article entitled 'Must We Shoot from the Hip?', Brodie explored ways to use nuclear weapons while avoiding catastrophic escalation. The RAND team objected to the Air Force's stubborn adherence to LeMay's idea of killing a nation. 'Godammit,' General Jim Walsh, director of SAC Intelligence, screamed when a RAND egghead questioned the plan. 'There's only one way to attack the Russians and that's to hit them hard with everything we have – knock their balls off!'[66] Brodie, Kaufman, and others at RAND retorted that the strategy would inevitably provoke a similar act of castration from the Soviets. There had to be a better way. They began thinking in terms of a 'counter-force', as opposed to the prevalent 'counter-city' strategy. Nuclear weapons would be used in precise attacks upon the Soviet offensive capability, thus defining the limits of the conflict and at the same time limiting the Soviet capacity to respond. Brodie, a victim of too much Freud, likened the SAC plan to full-blown sex, while his idea was like withdrawal before ejaculation.

Kaufman believed that counterforce would allow the US to win a nuclear contest. According to his scenario, if the Soviets attacked Western Europe, the US would respond by hitting hard targets – missile pads, submarine pens, control facilities and bomber bases. The Soviets, in retaliation, would honour the limits which the Americans had set and confine themselves to hard targets. But their response would be restricted due to the damage already caused by the American first strike. They would therefore be unable to eliminate all remaining American nuclear forces. With what remained of their forces, the Americans could then knock off Soviet cities one by one until the Soviets, unable to respond in kind, surrendered and withdrew from Western Europe. Such an encounter, Kaufman surmised, would result in perhaps three million Americans dead, and five million Russians.

Some strategists were bothered by the fact that counterforce was still likely to kill eight million people. But in stepped Herman Kahn, the thinker of the unthinkable. Suffering, he insisted, was always relative. 'The survivors will not dance in the streets or congratulate each other if there have been 20 million men, women and children killed; yet it would have been a worthwhile achievement to limit casualties to this number.'[67] Kahn also thought that positive steps could be taken to limit casualties the US might suffer. In other words, civil defence played a prominent part in his vision of war. Protecting the American people would allow greater strategic flexibility. His ideas were set forth in *On Thermonuclear War* (1960), a huge book dedicated to making nuclear war seem logical, palatable and winnable.

The book is a massive window into a warped mind. Critics who deplored the long-term genetic effects of nuclear fallout were reminded that four per cent of children are born with genetic defects in 'normal' circumstances. 'War is a terrible thing, but so is peace,' Kahn concluded. 'The difference seems in some respects to be a quantitative one of degree and standards.' He went on to argue that a bit of nuclear destruction might in fact benefit society: 'We can imagine a renewed vigor among the population with a zealous, almost religious, dedication to reconstruction, exemplified by a 50- to 60-hour work week.'[68] James Newman, who reviewed the book for *Scientific American*, wrote: 'This is a moral tract on mass murder: how to plan it, how to commit it, how to get away with it, how to justify it.'[69]

In the bizarre logic of nuclear strategy, massive retaliation seemed more civilized than counterforce because the level of destruction was so catastrophic that war was self-negating. The prospect of 100 million dead was sufficient deterrent. In contrast, the limited war idea of Kahn and Kaufman, by restricting fatalities to less than twenty million, was barbaric since it made nuclear war seem winnable and the weapons themselves usable.

For the moment, however, SAC wanted nothing to do with limited war. In 1956, in a speech at the National War College, LeMay gave a chilling summary of SAC's capabilities:

> Let us assume that the order had been received this morning to unleash the full weight of our nuclear force. . . . Between sunset tonight and sunrise tomorrow morning the Soviet Union would likely cease to be a major military power or even a major nation: the bulk of its long-range air power would be shattered, its centers of industry and control devastated. Communications would have been disrupted and much of their economic strength depleted. Dawn might break over a nation infinitely poorer than China – less populated than the United States and condemned to an agrarian existence perhaps for generations to come.[70]

General Tommy Power, who took over in 1960, adhered to the 'hit them with everything you've got' theory devised by LeMay. 'Why do you want us to restrain ourselves?' Power angrily interrupted when Kaufman tried to explain his plan. 'Restraint! Why are you so concerned with saving *their* lives? The whole idea is to *kill* the bastards! . . . Look. At the end of the war, if there are two Americans and one Russian, we win!' A somewhat shaken Kaufman replied: 'Well, you'd better make sure that they're a man and a woman.'[71]

An entirely different view of SAC was presented to the American people by Jimmy Stewart. In 1955, Stewart, the most trusted actor in Hollywood, took on the role of bomber pilot Dutch Holland in *Strategic Air Command*. In the film, Holland gives up professional baseball, the national pastime, to join the 'war effort', thus underlining the sublime nature of his patriotic act. He repeatedly enjoins his crew to remind themselves that the country is at war. His newly-wed wife (June Allyson) at first complains about being a service widow, but eventually she too realizes that sacrifices are necessary for the US to prevail.

A clutch of similar films were made, all with the same basic message. In these films, pilots and crew are often seen running. The klaxon sounds, they drop what they are doing, and run to their planes. Running is a substitute for fighting, an implication of urgency in a war that remained stubbornly cold. Once airborne, the planes themselves provide little sense of drama. The sleek aluminium craft cut through the stratosphere like sharp knives slicing air. They are motionless against a featureless landscape; war and conflict have been cleaned of dirt and blood. The bomber is stationary yet travels at immense speed; it is benign yet menacing. But nothing ever explodes. Nothing ever happens.

Theories of confrontation replaced actual conflict. An entirely new nomenclature evolved to express nuclear strategy. A first-strike capability implied the ability to destroy an enemy's capacity to respond to attack. This in turn led to an emphasis on a second-strike capability, in other words the capacity to survive an attack sufficiently to deliver devastating retaliation. Deterrence depended on both sides maintaining a second-strike capability. This might be achieved either by producing so many weapons that it was impossible for the enemy to destroy them all, or by rendering them less vulnerable to attack, for instance in submarines or hardened silos. To be safe, the superpowers adopted both approaches.

Proliferation carried an enormous price. In order to make the sacrifice seem necessary, both the American and Soviet governments had to make their people feel vulnerable. They had to be reminded continually that there was a war on, even if no fighting occurred. As Dulles confessed, 'In order to make the country bear the burden we have to create an emotional atmosphere akin to wartime psychology. We must create the idea of a threat from without.'[72]

In response to the bomber, both superpowers developed air defences. The American Nike missile system went operational in 1954 and was eventually deployed at some 250 sites around the United States, in addition to other locations in allied countries. 'We lived as though we were never more than three hours from war and possible Armageddon,' Gary Stephens, who joined a Nike unit as an eighteen-year-old, recalled.[73] Nike inspired the Soviets to embark upon their own defence system, at considerable sacrifice. So great was the need for alcohol for missile fuel that in 1961 a temporary but crippling shortage of vodka developed. Guns and butter was within the capacity of the Soviet system; guns and booze was not. In truth, however, while air defences could be highly effective against individual bombers, they could never guarantee complete protection. In practice, they encouraged further proliferation, since deterrence was calculated not according to the gross number of bombs, but rather on the percentage of bombers likely to penetrate enemy defences.

Competition within the American military contributed to further proliferation. The Navy did not believe that it was well served by SAC's targeting plan. It demanded its own nuclear capability in order to hit specifically naval targets – facilities within the Soviet Union that seemed a threat to American ships. Since no President wants to annoy the Navy, its wishes were granted. But this resulted in two battle plans and the problem of 'deconfliction' – literally, pilots getting in each other's way in their effort to destroy the Soviet Union. Routing of missions and selection of targets became, by the late 1950s, too complex for the human mind. Edmundson remembers a huge room at SAC full of bulky computers which generated an immense amount of heat.

> We'd crank into the computers the weather program for that month (winds aloft and target visibility), and would adjust the timing on the takeoff of the airplanes . . . A computer would enable us to route them so they wouldn't fly into somebody else's bomb blast, or if there was somebody else's radio-active cloud from a target that had been hit someplace else.[74]

In 1960 all nuclear forces were amalgamated into a Single Integrated Operating Plan, formulated and administered by the joint strategic target planning staff headquartered deep underground at SAC headquarters in Omaha, Nebraska. It was called 'single' for good reason – there was no other plan. SIOP became known as the 'doomsday machine' – within twenty-eight hours of a threat being confirmed, the US would deliver over 3,000 weapons to around 1,000 targets in the Soviet Union, China and Eastern Europe. According to reliable estimates, such an attack would kill 285 million people.

The Russians had their own plan. Their prevailing objective was to limit the damage caused to the USSR and its allies. This sounds simple and self-evident, but in practice it meant attempting to destroy American nuclear forces before they could be launched, essentially a first-strike strategy. In a Soviet military journal, Colonel M. Shirokov explained that the objective 'is not to turn the large economic and industrial regions into a heap of ruins (although great destruction, apparently, is unavoidable), but to deliver strikes which will destroy strategic combat means . . . and sharply reduce the enemy capability to conduct strikes'. Another Soviet paper described the strategy more succinctly: 'victory over the forces of the enemy Coalition is possible only under conditions of a decisive offensive directed at his total destruction'.[75] Though analysts liked to draw distinctions between American and Soviet strategy (and still do), it is hard to see how LeMay was thinking any differently. But while the above quote might seem aggressive, it was in truth (and perhaps inadvertently) an admission of the impossibility of victory. Since destruction of an enemy's forces could never be 'total', winning a nuclear war was never possible.

All plans depended upon the willingness of pilots to act according to pre-determined routines, without questioning the destruction they would cause. The pressure they felt was compounded by the strange nature of the Cold War. In most wars, combat enables a release of tension – waiting to fight is much more unsettling than actually fighting. During the Cold War the military waited to fight for forty years. Members of the nuclear strike force had to be on constant alert in order for deterrence to have credibility. Whereas most soldiers prepare physically for war, mental preparation was immensely more important during the Cold War. 'We have two tasks,' one American soldier remarked. 'The first is not to let people go off their rockers. That's the negative side. The positive side is to ensure that people act without moral compunction.'[76] 'Yeah, we thought about it,' Edmundson recalled. 'Certainly, I didn't have any . . . regrets . . . because we knew that at the time we were doing that, they would be doing the same thing to us. . . . No, I had no compunction about going after any target they gave me to go after.'[77]

James Lees-Milne recalls a party in September 1957 at Lord Beaverbrook's villa in the South of France. Talk turned to Nevil Shute's *On the Beach*, a haunting novel about the slow death of the world seen from the point of view of Australians who await the approach of a cloud of fallout produced from a catastrophic war in the northern hemisphere. Churchill, a guest at the party, said that he was going to send a copy to Khrushchev. When asked whether he would also send one to Eisenhower, he replied: 'It would be a waste of money. He is so muddle-headed now. . . . I think the earth will soon be destroyed. . . . And if I were the Almighty I would not recreate it in case they destroyed him too the next time.'[78]

Those who believed in deterrence measured safety in the size of an arsenal and worried little about the inexorable proliferation of weapons. But others felt concern at the seemingly inevitable approach of Armageddon. On 9 July 1955, eleven high profile individuals (including nine Nobel prize winners) issued a warning to the world. Included in their number were Einstein, Pauling, Frédéric Joliot-Curie, Rotblat and Bertrand Russell. 'We are speaking on this occasion not as members of this or that nation, continent, or creed, but as human beings, members of the species Man, whose continued existence is in doubt.' The danger of the hydrogen bomb, the Russell-Einstein Manifesto argued, went far beyond its immediate explosive potential:

> the best authorities are unanimous in saying that a war with H-bombs might possibly put an end to the human race. It is feared that if many H-bombs are used there will be universal death, sudden only for a minority, but for the majority a slow torture of disease and disintegration.

The document called upon governments to renounce thermonuclear weapons and 'to find peaceful means for the settlement of all matters of dispute between them'.[79] This meant an entirely new approach to international affairs:

> We have to learn to ask ourselves not what steps can be taken to give military victory to whatever group we prefer, for there no longer are such steps; the question we have to ask ourselves is: what steps can be taken to prevent

a military contest of which the issue must be disastrous to all parties? . . .
Shall we put an end to the human race; or shall mankind renounce war?[80]

The manifesto caused a brief stir, given the status of its signatories. But
its most profound effect was more internal than external. The Pugwash
movement (named for the small Canadian village in which the dissenters
first met) was established to provide an intellectual forum to discuss the
threat posed by nuclear weapons. A core of dedicated pacifists had established a centre toward which others of similar persuasion would migrate.

A short time later, a grass roots movement gradually took shape in the
United States. In November 1957, the National Committee for a Sane
Nuclear Policy was formed. At the end of its first year it claimed 25,000
members, a conveniently round figure which invites doubt. As with other
dissident groups, counting members was always problematic: is such a
group defined by the number who attend rallies, those who sign petitions
or those who are card-carrying members? In truth, most local associations
consisted of no more than a few dedicated diehards in a dingy office
equipped with a dilapidated mimeograph machine. Their dedication and
concern occasionally erupted in protest events, such as sit-ins at missile
bases or marches in favour of disarmament. These gained fleeting attention, more for their novelty than their impact. In early 1958 a group of
Quakers attempted to sail from Hawaii to Eniwetok to protest against the
H-bomb testing programme. The press, which labelled the protesters 'atom
lopers', took great delight when the peace boat managed to travel only
two miles from Hawaii before it was stopped and turned around by the
Coast Guard. At no time did the AEC or the American government worry
that pacifists might threaten the viability of the nuclear weapons
programme.

Opinions about nuclear weapons were nevertheless changing, though
whether this can be attributed to the peace movement is open to doubt.
By the time of his re-election in 1956, Eisenhower felt frightened awe at
the sheer power of the hydrogen bomb. Referring to the possibility of using
nuclear weapons aggressively, he remarked: 'Surely no sane member of
the human race could discover victory in such desolation. Could anyone
wish his name to be coupled by history with such degradation and destruction?'[81] General Andrew Goodpaster, an Eisenhower aide, recalled that
'Once the hydrogen weapon was available . . . you began to hear from
him that any idea of nuclear war would be . . . an absurdity or a form of
insanity. That no longer was war an extension of policy by other means,
but it was a form of mutual . . . suicide.'[82] Toward the end of his administration, Eisenhower

would say, you know, we are coming to a time when the only thing worse

than losing an atomic war would be to win it, and to have the responsibility
for attempting to restore civilized life afterwards. Or in a more graphic way,
on occasion he said, you know what we would need, we would need bull-
dozers to push the bodies off the streets. And repeatedly said, this just makes
no sense at all.[83]

The songwriter Tom Lehrer expressed this same sentiment in his macabre
'We Will All Go Together When We Go', released in 1959:

> Oh we will all fry together when we fry
> We'll be french fried potatoes by and by.
> There will be no more misery
> When the world is our rotisserie,
> Yes, we will all go together when we fry.[84]

Teller, the high priest of nuclear weapons, was annoyed by all this hand-
wringing. He feared that the end result might mean an emasculation of
American power. 'In a dangerous world we cannot have peace unless we
are strong,' he argued in 1962. 'We cannot be strong unless we are fully
prepared to exploit the biggest modern power, nuclear explosives.
Nuclear weapons can be used with moderation on all scales of serious
conflict. . . . World War III would be much worse than anything we can
remember. But it would not destroy mankind.'[85] In truth, Teller needn't
have worried, since fear of the bomb did not inspire arms reduction.
Eisenhower spoke increasingly about the futility of nuclear war, yet
continued to expand his arsenal.

Khrushchev behaved in a remarkably similar fashion. He encouraged
the publication of articles by Sakharov on the dangers of fallout and talked
of the need for a test ban, but, like Eisenhower, he could not resist engaging
in nuclear swagger. During the Suez crisis, Moscow threatened a nuclear
strike if the British and French did not withdraw from Egyptian territory.
At the 24 June 1957 Party plenum, Mykoyan boasted: 'We were strong
enough to keep troops in Hungary and to warn the imperialists that, if
they would not stop the war in Egypt, it might come to the use of missile
armaments from our side. All acknowledge that with this we decided the
fate of Egypt.'[86] While both leaders played the game of atomic bluff, both
also developed a healthy fear of nuclear war.

Preventing war meant making sure that the enemy did not obtain a
first-strike capability. Both sides therefore expanded their arsenals in order
to bolster deterrence. Unfortunately, the quest for security was interpreted
as aggressive by the other side, thus stimulating a desire for more bombs.
The pace of proliferation was governed partly by the way the weapons
industry continually developed new systems that inspired new feelings of

vulnerability and an even greater appetite for weapons. Lord Zuckerman felt that scientists had a heavy guilt to bear:

> It is the man in the laboratory, not the soldier or sailor or airman, who at the start proposes that for this or that reason it would be useful to improve an old or devise a new nuclear warhead; and if a new warhead, then a new missile; and, given a new missile, a new system within which it has to fit. . . . The men in the nuclear laboratories of both sides have succeeded in creating a world with an irrational foundation on which a new set of political realities has in turn to be built. They have become the alchemists of our times, working in secret ways which cannot be divulged, casting spells which embrace us all.[87]

In his farewell address, Eisenhower warned:

> We have been compelled to create a permanent armaments industry of vast proportions . . . We must not fail to comprehend its grave implications . . . In the councils of government we must guard against the acquisition of unwarranted influence, whether sought or unsought, by the military-industrial complex. The potential for the disastrous rise of misplaced power exists and will persist.[88]

The 'military-industrial complex' was a new term invented to identify a new threat. Never before, in peacetime, had the military and the arms industry wielded so much power in the everyday life of nations and in the determination of government policy.

'In holding scientific research and discovery in respect', Eisenhower warned, 'we must also be alert to the equal and opposite danger that public policy could become captive of a scientific technological elite.'[89] Herbert York, who met with Eisenhower around the time of the speech, later commented that the President seemed to be referring specifically to the danger posed by the duumvirate of Teller and the rocket scientist Werner von Braun. Eisenhower, according to York, 'regarded both of them as super-salesmen who would say anything, invent any threat, to sell their idea of the moment'.[90]

In a September 1945 article, *Aviation News* predicted that the next revolution in military science would be a 'V-2 type rocket with an atomic bomb in the nose'. The author argued that 'With such weapons . . . war may be concluded overnight.' Soldiers, ships, tanks, etc. would become obsolescent.[91]

When it came to rocketry, the Soviets initially had more thrust than the Americans. In April 1947 Stalin gathered together rocket scientists and military leaders and ordered them to develop missiles capable of hitting the US. 'Do you realise the tremendous strategic importance of machines of this sort?' he asked. 'They could be an effective strait jacket for that noisy shopkeeper Harry Truman. We must go ahead with it, comrades.'[92] The Soviets decided that deterrence could best be assured through rapidly mobilized missiles capable of quick, accurate strikes. Rocketry provided a way of countering the geographic isolation of the US and the numerical superiority of American nuclear forces. 'The Soviet Union felt naked, unprotected, surrounded everywhere by American nuclear forces,' Nikolai Detinov, formerly of the Soviet Defence Ministry, recalled. 'It was very difficult to protect the Soviet Union. When we . . . developed our own ballistic missiles, although we had very few, we realized that it . . . acted as a counterbalance.'[93] Rockets were also cost effective – less expensive, easier to maintain and less vulnerable than bombers. To Khrushchev, the bomber seemed a decidedly old fashioned way to deliver death.

The first Soviet long-range rocket, the R-1, tested in October 1947, was unashamedly copied from the German V-2. Three years later the R-2, with a range of 600 kilometres, was successfully fired and work on the R-3 had begun. As A. N. Pilyugin, the Chief Designer of Control Systems, remarked, the pace of development was breathtaking: 'one rocket is being tested, the next modification is on the drawing board, while the third is being conceived'.[94] The SS-6 ICBM (Intercontinental Ballistic Missile), which had the capacity to hit the United States, was first tested in August 1957.

These developments frightened the Americans, who had placed too much confidence in their bomber force. Though they had their own rocket programme, it was an embarrassment compared to that of the Soviet Union. Fear, however, proved an effective spur to progress. On 31 October 1953, the Strategic Missiles Evaluation Committee (better known as 'Teapot'), chaired by John von Neumann, recommended a crash programme to develop ICBMs. By May 1960, $43 billion had been invested, making it the largest single military programme up to that point. Progress was rapid, with the first Atlas ICBMs entering service in October 1959. While the Soviets had been the leaders in rocket development, the Americans proved most adept at mass-producing them.

Missiles meant that warning times were shortened still further. 'That's when SAC went to the 15-minute alert for one-third of the force,' Edmundson recalled of the advent of Soviet ICBMs. Eventually, SAC implemented airborne alert – 'a certain number of them would be in the air with [nuclear] weapons all the time, around the clock. . . . this meant that even if [the Soviets] hit the United States, we would have a certain number of aircraft already airborne with weapons on board, the target material they needed, and halfway to Russia'.[95] The shortening of the alert time meant that the period available to analyse threats was also drastically reduced. Each side had only minutes to decide whether a threat was real. If it did launch its forces, perhaps mistakenly, that action would in turn be interpreted by the other side as an act of war.

Technology continued to torment. When the Soviets launched Sputnik in October 1957, sending a satellite into earth's orbit, they destroyed at a stroke the American assumption of technological superiority upon which security in the arms race was based. The former Congresswoman, Clare Booth Luce called Sputnik's beep from space 'an inter-continental outer-space raspberry to a decade of American pretensions that the American way of life was a gilt-edged guarantee of our national superiority'. Teller declared on national television that the United States had lost 'a battle more important and greater than Pearl Harbor'.

'The Russians have left the earth and the race for control of the universe has started,' George Reedy commented in a memo to his boss, Senator Lyndon Johnson.[96] In desperation, a secret government study was commissioned at the Armour Research Foundation in Illinois. The physicist Leonard Reiffel was asked to look into the feasibility of exploding a nuclear weapon on the moon, simply as a publicity stunt. From May 1958 to January 1959, Reiffel's team (which included the young astronomer Carl Sagan) studied the likely effect of a Hiroshima-sized bomb on the moon's surface, particularly the visual effect of such an explosion. 'As these things go, this was small,' Dr Reiffel said of the project. 'It was less than a year and never got to the point of operational planning. We showed what some of the effects might be. But the real argument we made, and others made behind closed doors, was that there was no point in ruining the pristine environment of the moon. There were other ways to impress the public that we were not about to be overwhelmed by the Russians.'[97]

As wacky ideas go, this was not the most bizarre. Paul Nitze, the prolifically imaginative Cold Warrior, at one point in the 1950s came up with the idea of a 'love gas' which could be sprayed over the Soviet Union, with particularly high concentration around the Kremlin. The gas would instantly render the Russians more loving, unassertive and nice. It was, perhaps, a more humane idea than blowing the enemy to smithereens, or cutting off his balls.

CHAPTER 12

Symbols, not Weapons

'It is said that three [nuclear powers] is better than four or five,' John Horner of the Fire Brigades Union told the 1960 Labour Party Conference during a debate on Britain's nuclear deterrent.

> I put it that two is better than three. But, if the possession of the bomb has advantages for us, what right have we to declare to other nations that they should not also possess the advantage we claim for ourselves? . . . Indeed, if there is a single ounce of logic in the argument that somehow there is an advantage for Britain in having the bomb, we should be welcoming and not deploring extension of the Nuclear Club because everybody would deter everybody else.[1]

Horner's argument was perfectly logical. For that reason, it was roundly rejected. Logic was never allowed to stand in the way of the British Bomb.

Britain's right to membership in the nuclear club was based on two assumptions. The first was that, despite the decline of her Empire, she was still a superpower with a right to dine at the top table with the Soviet Union and the United States. On becoming Prime Minister, Sir Alec Douglas-Home argued that Britain needed the hydrogen bomb 'to secure our place above the salt at the negotiating table'. Status gave Britain the right to a Bomb, and the Bomb underlined that status. It was a symbol, not a weapon.

The second assumption held that Britain was morally superior to any other nation and therefore that she alone could be trusted with nuclear weapons. Right of ownership was based not upon need, but rather upon the promise of sensible stewardship – rather like the man who adopts a scorpion not because it will make a good pet, but because he will look after it properly. The danger of nuclear weapons, so the argument goes, lies in the character of those who possess them.

A nuclear capability seemed the perfect response to the problems facing Britain in the aftermath of the Second World War, namely an uncertain relationship with the US, the threat of the Soviet Union, an unstable Empire, a shattered economy and a new strategic environment dominated by the Bomb. Even before Trinity, the British government held that 'the only answer that we can see to the atomic bomb is to be prepared to use it ourselves in retaliation. A knowledge that we were prepared, in the last resort, to do this might well deter an aggressive nation.'[2] As for Britain's role in the world, Attlee felt:

> We had to hold up our position *vis-à-vis* the Americans. We couldn't allow ourselves wholly to be in their hands, and their position wasn't awfully clear always. At that time we had to bear in mind that there was always the possibility of their withdrawing and becoming isolationist once again. The manufacture of a British atom bomb was therefore at that stage essential to our defence.

The Bomb also seemed cheap. Massive power would be obtained at relatively low cost, an attractive proposition during a period of austerity. The Chiefs of Staff advised the government that atomic weapons would make possible 'consequential reductions in other forms of armament production'.[3] In other words, Britain would be able to maintain her influence without the large troop deployments or huge Navy that power had once implied.

On 29 August 1945, less than three weeks after Nagasaki, Attlee convened a secret Cabinet committee to decide upon nuclear policy. Called GEN 75, it was better known as the Atom Bomb Committee. By the end of the year, approval had been given for the construction of at least one nuclear reactor, but a commitment to a bomb programme had not been made. In January 1946, Air Marshal Lord Portal was made Controller of Production of Atomic Energy – essentially a British Leslie Groves. A site at Harwell, on the Berkshire Downs, was selected as the location for the Atomic Energy Research Establishment.

The government had always assumed that Britain would take advantage of the 1943 Quebec Agreement which stipulated that research would be shared. But, in the tense atmosphere of the Cold War, the Americans grew very possessive of their knowledge. In August 1946, the McMahon Act essentially rescinded the Quebec Agreement. While this was a blow to the British, at the same time it seemed to underline the fact that they could not rely on the Americans for their defence. But the ruling did make the British Bomb much more complicated and expensive. At a meeting of GEN 75 in the autumn of 1946, the Chancellor Hugh Dalton and Sir Stafford Cripps, President of the Board of Trade, questioned 'whether we could afford to divert from civilian consumption and the restoration of our balance of payments the economic resources required for a project of this scale'. They were making some headway when suddenly the Foreign Secretary Ernest Bevin stumbled in, apologizing that he had fallen asleep after a heavy lunch. After being told of the Cripps/Dalton objections, he went ballistic:

> No, Prime Minister, that won't do at all. We've *got* to have this. I don't mind for myself, but I don't want any other Foreign Secretary of this country to be talked at, or to, by the Secretary of State in the United States as I just have in my discussions with Mr Byrnes. We've got to have this thing over here, whatever it costs. We've got to have the bloody Union Jack on top of it.[4]

On 8 January 1947, GEN 163, an even more secret subset of GEN 75, was formed, with Cripps and Dalton conveniently excluded. The new committee decided to proceed with development, but kept the decision from Parliament until 12 May 1948.

Responsibility for construction was given to William Penney, a veteran of the Manhattan Project implosion team. For most of 1946, he took part in the Crossroads tests, an assignment completed just before the McMahon Act closed the door on collaboration. In May 1947 Portal formally asked Penney to head the development effort. Penney immediately began assembling his team, relying heavily on veterans of the British Mission. The project, called BHER (for Basic High Explosive Research), was at first scattered around various locations but on 1 April 1950 a single site was established at Aldermaston in Berkshire. Construction of a plutonium production reactor and processing plant began in September 1947 at Sellafield in Cumbria, a site renamed Windscale.* Perhaps because the emphasis was on speed, safety standards were compromised in the construction of the reactor.

As stubby cylinders of plutonium emerged from the processing plant, they were loaded into the boot of a taxi and driven to Aldermaston. In the end, some of the plutonium had to come from Canada, since Sellafield was unequal to the task. A target date was set for the autumn of 1952 and all efforts were devoted to meeting that deadline by whatever means. Given that a domestic test was clearly out of the question, the British looked to their former colonies for help. Sites in Canada, South Africa and British Somaliland were all considered. Eventually, the Monte Bello Islands off northwestern Australia were selected for the test codenamed Hurricane. Recruiting civilian staff for the long sea journey in cramped ships to an island with an inhospitable climate and shark-infested seas proved a challenge. In an attempt to sugar the pill, Air Vice-Marshal E. D. Davis claimed that 'any right-minded man would regard these trials as a grand experience combined with the fun of a picnic'. The mission would be like a 'prolonged rest cure'.[5]

---

* It is now called Sellafield again.

After its journey to Australia, the bomb was positioned inside the hull of the frigate HMS *Plym*, anchored 400 metres off Trimouille Island. By 30 September 1952 everything was in place and detonation was scheduled for the morning of 3 October. At 9.15 a.m. the chemist Alfred Gavin Maddock began the countdown, a task which earned him the nickname Count of Monte Bello. As a result of the explosion, the ship essentially disappeared, leaving a crater in the seabed 30 feet deep and 1,000 feet across.

The British are experts at understatement. If catastrophe strikes, it is described as 'rather unpleasant'. No wonder, then, that the first British atomic blast inspired neither celebration nor agonized soul-searching. Personal recollections, if available at all, are conspicuously muted. But, then, Britain did come in third in the nuclear race, and who celebrates a bronze medal? While Trinity had been a miraculous achievement, and Joe I an equally stupendous response, the blast at Monte Bello was something of an anti-climax – just another bomb. Winston Churchill, never one to shun hyperbole, was remarkably subdued when he announced the successful test in the Commons:

> Technical descriptions of the performance of the Bomb cannot, of course, be given. It may, however, be said that the weapon behaved exactly as expected and forecast in many precise details by Dr W. G. Penney, whose services were of the highest order. Scientific observations and measurements show that the weapon does not contradict the natural expectation that progress in this sphere be continual. . . .
>
> All those concerned in the production of the First British atomic bomb are to be warmly congratulated on the successful outcome of an historic episode and I should no doubt pay my compliments to the Leader of the Opposition and the party opposite for initiating it.[6]

In the now customary fashion, Penney was awarded a knighthood for his service to British defence.

The official film of the test, *This Little Ship*, captured the finality of the explosion:

> ADMIRALTY LONDON:
> PLYM, OBLIVION.
> REPEAT, OBLIVION.
> OBLIVION.

The film is a typical example of official British dissimulation – propaganda skills learned during the Second World War were applied to a new, cold, conflict. Instead of a film about a bomb, it is the heroic little story of the life and death of a ship – as if *Thomas the Tank Engine* had been written by Edward Teller. Narrated by Jack Perkins, the film takes the ship along its path toward noble sacrifice. The air of inevitability suggests that the British bomb project was part of some inexorable tide, rather than a conscious act. The film presents a sense of finality – the death of the ship – rather than of beginning – the dawning of a new age of nuclear uncertainty. Indeed, the explosion is presented as solution rather than problem. The penultimate line in the film asks, 'For now war is self destruction, and who will dare attack?'[7]

After the Hurricane test, a deliverable weapon was incorporated into the UK arsenal in November 1953. The Blue Danube bomb initially had a yield of 15 kilotons, but it was eventually beefed up to 40 kilotons. Plans at first called for 200 bombs by 1957. Toward this end, two new MAGNOX reactors were built at Calder Hall. In fact, when production halted in 1958 only twenty Blue Danube weapons had been manufactured.

By the time the British exploded their first fission bomb, fashion had already changed – Mike had vaporized an entire island and the Soviets were busy making layer cakes. In February 1953, Churchill, the new Prime Minister, asked his friend and scientific adviser Lord Cherwell whether Britain possessed the technical knowledge and economic resources to build a hydrogen bomb. Cherwell replied: 'we think we know how'[8] – an answer based more on wish than reality. Though Churchill had expressed dismay at the terrible power of the hydrogen bomb, he still coveted one. As he reflected to Eisenhower, 'the few men upon whom the supreme responsibility falls . . . have to drive their minds forward into these hideous and deadly spheres of thought'.[9] To his own colleagues, he remarked: 'We must do it. It's the price we pay to sit at the top table.'[10]

The H-bomb was intended as much to impress Britain's ally as her enemy. According to Cabinet minutes, the government was worried that America might plunge the world into nuclear holocaust 'either through a misjudged intervention in Asia or in order to forestall an attack by Russia'. The British saw themselves as a potentially calming influence. But, in order to play this role, they would have to impress the Americans with their willingness to defend themselves, rather than cowering under the American nuclear umbrella. Financial considerations also played a part, as Churchill made clear to the Defence Policy Committee on 20 May 1954:

the problem was to decide what practical steps could be taken to effect the savings of £200 million a year, with the least risk of weakening our influence in the world, or endangering our security. Influence depended on possession of force. If the United States were tempted to undertake a forestalling war, we could not hope to remain neutral. Even if we could, such a war would in any event determine our fate. We must avoid any action which would weaken our power to influence United States policy. We must avoid anything which might be represented as a sweeping act of disarmament. If, however, we were able to show that in a few years' time we should be possessed of great offensive power, and that we should be ready to take our part in a world struggle . . . it would not be impossible to reconcile reductions in defence expenditure with the maintenance of our influence in world councils.

In other words, the H-bomb promised power on the cheap. The British, Churchill confidently predicted, would increase their influence *and* cut their defence spending. The Chiefs of Staff agreed. 'Our scientific skill and technological capacity to produce the hydrogen weapon', they argued, 'puts within our grasp the ability to be on terms with the United States and Russia.'[11]

On 16 June 1954, the Defence Policy Committee gave its approval to a thermonuclear programme. The decision was ratified by the full Cabinet on 26 July, though some moral reservations were voiced. In response to these objections, someone (probably Churchill) argued that there was 'no difference in kind between atomic and thermo-nuclear weapons' and that, if there was a moral principle at issue, 'it had already been breached by the decision of the Labour Party to make the atomic bomb'. While the Super Bomb seems to accord well with Churchill's megaton personality, it would be wrong to blame the decision in favour of thermonuclear weapons on him. Churchill simply reiterated logic first expressed by Attlee and repeated by every Prime Minister since. Love of the bomb was not specific to party or personality. Harold Macmillan, for instance, thought Britain's 'independent nuclear capability' would provide the opportunity 'to retain our special relation with the United States and, through it, our influence in world affairs, and, especially, our right to have a voice in the final issue of peace and war'. Hydrogen bombs would 'enable us, by threatening to use our independent nuclear power, to secure United States co-operation in a situation in which their interests were less immediately threatened than our own'.*[12] For all postwar Prime Ministers, the bomb was a magic key to the corridors of power.

Wanting an H-bomb was one thing, building it another. While a fission device had been relatively easy, thanks to what the British had learned on the Manhattan Project, a thermonuclear programme was uncharted territory. The course the British took was similar to that traversed by the Soviets and the Americans, in other words, an initial period in which the influence of Fuchs was evident, followed by a gradual realization that the tube

---

* Ironically, Macmillan penned that view *after* the Suez Crisis patently demonstrated that the bomb had no such effect upon American behaviour.

design held no promise, followed by hopeless uncertainty and then, the sudden discovery of radiation implosion. Running parallel to this process was work on a boosted fission weapon – a layer cake, a sloika or (given British tastes) a trifle.

The British discovered radiation implosion with plenty of help from their friends. Penney, who remained friendly with his former Los Alamos colleagues, probably gathered a great deal of useful information when he visited them, particularly during late night chats lubricated with whiskey and wine. Changes to the McMahon Act also removed many of the barriers to collaboration. From March through May 1954 the UK was allowed to observe the Castle tests at Bikini and fly sampling aircraft in the vicinity. The Americans also supplied debris from Soviet thermonuclear explosions. While data of this sort would not have pointed directly to the correct design for a hydrogen bomb, it would have enabled the British to derive a reasonably clear picture of what they were supposed to build, in particular the importance of high compression produced by radiation implosion.

The Soviet explosion of a true thermonuclear device on 22 November 1955 raised the stakes in the nuclear game. In addition, the fact that pressure was building for a halt to atmospheric testing added urgency to the British programme, since there was not much sense in developing a multimegaton weapon without showing it off to the world. By April 1956, plans for a two-stage weapon were complete and construction had commenced.

Tests began on 15 May 1957 on Christmas Island. 'We still haven't got it right,' Bill Cook, deputy head of the atomic weapons programme, admitted after the first two tests yielded just 300 and 200 kilotons. Further modifications increased the yield to 1.8 megatons on 8 November and 3 megatons the following April. By the end of the test series the British had proven to the world that they had mastered the art of designing thermonuclear weapons. 'We have made a successful start,' Macmillan commented. 'When the tests are completed, as they soon will be, we shall be in the same position as the United States or Soviet Russia. We shall have made and tested the massive weapons. It will be possible then to discuss on equal terms.'[13]

Up to this point, each new British nuclear weapon had been smoothly incorporated into NATO's deterrence strategy. But the development of the hydrogen bomb coincided with two events which convinced the government that the independent deterrent remained a good idea. The first was the Suez Crisis, which demonstrated that there were limits to American friendship. The second, the launch of Sputnik, suggested that American technological might was by no means invincible.

★ ★ ★

While British engineers built the Bomb, British civil servants planned for Armageddon. Unlike the Americans, they did not waste much effort devising schemes to protect ordinary people. Attlee decided early on that civil defence was pointless. 'The modern conception of warfare to which in my lifetime we have become accustomed is now completely out of date,' he concluded in August 1945. 'It would appear that the provision of bomb-proof basements in factories and offices and the retention of ARP [Air Raid Precautions] and Fire Services is just futile waste . . . The answer to an atomic bomb on London is an atomic bomb on another great city.'[14] This belief was reiterated by every subsequent British government.

The Women's Royal Voluntary Service had different ideas. In 1956, it launched the One in Five lectures with the aim of instructing 20 per cent of the female population about preparedness. WRVS volunteers visited schools to talk specifically to girls about what to do in the event of nuclear attack. They came armed with leaflets offering advice on stockpiling food, building a shelter under the dining room table, and covering windows with brown paper to prevent flying fragments of glass. Elizabeth Trueland remembers the WRVS in their pseudo-military uniforms visiting her school in 1964. 'Though it was a "nice" girls' school, we weren't completely out of touch with reality. It was the mid 1960s after all! I do remember that we were all very sceptical, and well read in the doom and gloom scenarios popular at the time. No-one had the slightest intention of sticking brown paper to the windows and we all assumed that it would be much better to die than to try to survive.'[15]

The bulk of government effort was devoted to protecting politicians. 'Although it seemed like Never-Never Land at the time, we did work out these theoretical methods of keeping on the government,' Philip Allen, under-secretary responsible for home defence in the 1950s, recalled. 'One had a feeling that, if it came to it, nothing would quite work out the way one was planning. But, nevertheless, one simply had to have a plan.'[16] The plan they settled on divided the country into regions, each of which would act as an autonomous unit in the aftermath of nuclear attack. Regional governments, and their attendant civil servants, would retreat to underground bunkers at the first indication of hostile action. Meanwhile, the Royal Family, time permitting, would escape to sea on the royal yacht *Britannia*.

The plans were based on the assumption that the UK would be reduced to a scorched ruin within hours of war starting. 'We believe that the Russians will regard the UK as such a threat that they will aim to render it unusable for a long period, and will not hesitate to destroy great parts of the UK to achieve this plan,' the JIC pronounced in 1955. The advent of deliverable thermonuclear weapons made this scenario seem all the more grim – and possible. Experts calculated that ten hydrogen bombs exploded over Great Britain would kill 12 million people instantly. The survivors would envy the dead. In such an event, regional governments, safe in their boltholes underground, would be left with only themselves to govern. 'I never really ever believed in it,' Sir Frank Cooper, a senior civil servant at the Ministry of Defence, confessed. 'It was going to be such a shambles if anything like that did happen. And a picture of chaps sitting underground thinking calmly and clearly in the depths of some country shire just doesn't seem likely.'[17]

British officials worried endlessly about the 'headless chicken' scenario: an unexpected nuclear strike finds the Prime Minister in a situation where he or she cannot easily be contacted. In anticipation of such an event, the Commander-in-Chief of Bomber Command was given authority to order a nuclear attack. Meanwhile, communication systems were improved in order to reduce the likelihood of this scenario, but they merely underlined the British talent for half measures. A two-way radio was installed in the Prime Minister's car, but it relied on transmitters already part of the Automobile Association roadside assistance network. If a message about nuclear war needed to be sent to the Prime Minister, civil servants would have to wait for the AA to finish helping the bloke on the M-1 whose fan belt had broken.

The advent of nuclear submarines brought forth the possibility that Britain's deterrent might survive long after Britain herself was destroyed. Who, then, might decide whether to unleash the nuclear missiles? The problem was complicated by the fact that, while the submarines could receive radio communications, they could not send them. Commanders were given a precise procedure for determining whether the UK had been destroyed, one element of which was whether the BBC's *Today* programme was no longer being broadcast. In such an event, the commander was to go to his safe and retrieve a sealed envelope containing handwritten instructions from the Prime Minister. (Each Prime Minister completes these instructions on taking office.) The note will probably contain one of four orders:

1. Put yourself under the command of the United States, if it is still there.
2. Make your way to Australia, if it is still there.
3. Retaliate.
4. Use your own judgement.[18]

Logic suggests that option four is the only credible one, since there's no point in following the orders of a government which has been vaporized. But one should never underestimate the British respect for authority.

★ ★ ★

On 8 October 1957, while tests were proceeding on Christmas Island, a technician back at Windscale was heating up the reactor to release energy accumulated in the graphite blocks (called Wigner energy). This should have been a routine operation, but, due to faults in the instrumentation, control room staff were misled about the temperature of the reactor. Oblivious to the approaching crisis, they continued to add heat. At 11.05, control rods were withdrawn in order to start what should have been a routine chain reaction. But, since the heat in the reactors was already far too high, an intense fire erupted. The uranium and graphite quickly ignited, sending temperatures to 1,300 degrees centigrade.

Blue flames shot out of the back of the reactor. The cooling fans, woefully inadequate for this level of heat, served only to fan the fire and blow radioactive contamination out the chimneys. No plans for dealing with a fire of this magnitude had been arranged. Workers armed with scaffolding poles were sent in relays to push the fuel cans out of the pile, but this had no significant effect. The reactor was then pumped full of carbon dioxide, but, in the intense heat, oxygen was produced, which simply encouraged the fire. The crew then had to gamble on a measure they hoped never to employ, namely flooding the reactor. If the water failed to smother the fire, it would be converted to hydrogen and acetylene gas by the heat, causing a massive explosion. But, since the temperature was rising at 20 degrees per minute, that risk had to be taken.

The water brought the fire under control, but forty years later the crippled reactor was still generating heat from the molten uranium contained within. As a result of the fire, around 20,000 curies of radioactive iodine, plutonium, caesium and polonium were released into the atmosphere, travelling in a southeasterly direction toward population centres. At the time, the government claimed that the radiation did not pose a threat, but in 1987 the National Radiological Protection Board estimated that at least thirty-three people would die prematurely from cancers because of the accident.

While chasing nuclear parity the British took enormous risks. In the late 1950s, a 500-kiloton weapon was rushed into production so that Britain could keep abreast of the Russians and the Americans. Unfortunately, the weapon, codenamed Violet Club, relied on a crude safety mechanism consisting of 450 kilos of steel balls which kept two pieces of U-235 apart. The massive amount of fissile material (70 kilograms) rendered the weapon highly volatile. When the balls were removed upon arming, there was a high risk that the weapon could go super-critical even without the explosive charge usually required to detonate. There was also no way to de-arm the bomb by re-inserting the balls. The weapon was hurried into service in 1958 and about a dozen were eventually deployed, much to the annoyance of RAF officers, who hated it. The Violet

Club problems were kept tightly under wraps for over forty years until declassified documents were discovered in the Public Records Office.

Windscale and Violet Club demonstrate the difficulty the British experienced in trying to maintain an independent deterrent. In reality, it was not in their power to keep pace with the Americans and Soviets – neither qualitatively nor quantitatively. The speed of technological change in the 1950s and the sheer cost of new weapons systems thwarted the British. For instance, when they developed their V-bomber force (Vulcan and Victor), they thought that the combination of long-range bombers and free-fall nuclear bombs would provide reasonable security for the foreseeable future. In fact, that combination was virtually obsolete even before the squadrons were operational. By the time the RAF got its shiny new bombers, the Soviets and Americans had moved on to missiles.

The only logical solution was to borrow American technology. Such an opportunity arose on 2 July 1958, when a major revision of the Atomic Energy Act made collaboration on weapons development possible again. In Los Alamos in mid-September detailed designs of American weapons were passed to the British, who decided to abandon their independent line of development.* But, collaboration carried a cost: the increasingly American character of their arsenal rendered it difficult for the British to claim that their deterrent was truly independent. Government spin doctors worked overtime in April 1960 when the much-trumpeted Blue Streak missile programme was cancelled in favour of the American Skybolt. Because Blue Streak used liquid fuel, it took dangerously long to prepare for launch and was therefore vulnerable to a first strike by Soviet missiles, which used solid fuel. Skybolt, it was presumed, would allow the British to make better use of their V-bombers. But, as US Defense Secretary Robert McNamara soon discovered, Skybolt was 'an absolute pile of junk'.[19]

With Blue Streak abandoned and Skybolt a turkey, a forlorn and embarrassed Macmillan was forced to go cap in hand to the Americans. In November 1962, he travelled to Nassau with the goal of persuading Kennedy to give him a system which would allow Britain to destroy the 'forty largest cities' in the USSR – an eventuality thought to be 'quite unacceptable to the Russians'. Kennedy offered the Polaris submarine system – the boats and their weaponry would be built in Britain according to American designs. An internal defence memo made the best of a bad job by arguing that, though the design was American, its character was British: 'there is very much to be said for a system which is quietly unobtrusive, secure in a

---

* Cooperation had limits, however. When British variants of American weapons were developed, they were give silly British names suggestive of household cleaning products. Thus, the British MK-28 was called Yellow Sun.

relaxed way and ultimate in its bulldog-like determination to retaliate if the homeland is attacked. The submarine system seems in every way compatible with the British character. Let us have it.'[20] While Polaris meant that the V-bombers would decline in importance, the government had no alternative but to accept. Had Macmillan returned from Nassau empty-handed, his government might not have survived.

Macmillan wanted Polaris so that (in the words of an aide) 'we should have enough nuclear power to prevent some foolish decisions being made to our detriment on the other side of the Atlantic'.* During the negotiations, he insisted that while the British nuclear force would become part of the NATO defence package, Britain reserved the right to withdraw its forces from NATO responsibilities in such circumstances 'where Her Majesty's Government may decide that the supreme national interests are at stake'. This concession was granted without any specific mention of what those interests might be. But, in the following year, when a similar offer was made to France, Kennedy

> cited Suez or Kuwait [Iraq had threatened invasion in 1961] as examples of how the 'supreme interests' formula might be invoked. If some action on the part of the British or French, not directly affecting the United States, led to the Russians threatening either country with missiles, they would be in a position to decide to use their own Polaris missiles against say Moscow or Kiev.[21]

Still bruised by Suez, this offer appealed to Macmillan. He feared that, despite its NATO commitments, America would always act in her own interest and therefore might not come to Britain's aid if the US was not itself threatened. That possibility had been underlined a few years earlier when Christian Herter, Eisenhower's Secretary of State, admitted he could not 'conceive of any President engaging in all-out nuclear war unless we are in danger of all-out nuclear destruction ourselves'.[22]

Since the British independent deterrent now relied on American weapons, it would for ever be held captive by inverted commas. Furthermore, in exchange for Polaris, the US gained the right to establish military bases on British soil during peacetime – including nuclear bases. During the debate on the Nassau Agreement in the House of Commons, the Labour leader Harold Wilson probed the weaknesses of the deal:

> the government have presented their case in terms of an answer to the question of whether the missile we should have from the Americans should be Skybolt or Polaris . . . Our criticism is not of the answer, but that the

---

* That desire had some poignancy given that the statement was made one month after the Cuban Missile Crisis.

question is wrong. How can one pretend to have an independent deterrent when one is dependent on another nation . . . to supply one with the means of delivery?[23]

In the 1964 election Labour campaigned on the premise that Polaris 'will not be independent and it will not be British and it will not deter'. But, lacking a better idea, Wilson made no promises about scrapping the deal.[24]

While the British might have been able to threaten a nuclear strike independently, it is difficult to imagine how they could have acted on such a threat without American approval. Russian radar would not be able to tell whether a Polaris missile launched from somewhere in the Baltic was American or British. Therefore any such launch would inevitably mean a Soviet counter-response against both the US and Britain. That being the case, one suspects that, regardless of the Nassau agreements, any Polaris strike would always have required American approval.

After Labour won the 1964 election Wilson too found that nuclear sirens sing sweetly. He could not bring himself to abandon Polaris, nor did he deliver on promises to renegotiate Nassau. When the Defence Secretary Denis Healey told him that it would be possible to convert Polaris subs into hunter-killer submarines without additional cost, Wilson advised against telling the rest of the cabinet, since he wanted to make it seem that Polaris was 'past the point of no return'.[25] Wilson later confessed that, though he did not really believe the British deterrent was independent, he 'didn't want to be in the position of having to subordinate ourselves to the Americans when they, at a certain point, would say, "We're going to use it" . . . We might need to restrain the Americans.'[26]

While Labour gained some mileage from the nuclear issue in 1964, that issue usually brought the party more grief than gain. At the 1957 party conference a motion was tabled calling for the adoption of a policy of unilateral nuclear disarmament. Aneurin Bevan, hitherto a stalwart of the Left, attacked it, in the process alienating many of his erstwhile supporters:

I know that you are deeply convinced that the action you suggest is the most effective way of influencing international affairs. I am deeply convinced that you are wrong. It is therefore not a question of who is in favour of the hydrogen bomb, but a question of what is the most effective way of getting the damn thing destroyed. It is the most difficult of all problems facing mankind. But if you carry this resolution and follow out all its implications and do not run away from it you will send a Foreign Secretary, whoever he may be, naked into the conference chamber.[27]

They were fine words, impressively delivered, but they did not convince those on the left to give up their struggle. Unilateral disarmament, a many-headed hydra, preyed on the party for the next forty years. The alliance between the Labour left and the anti-nuclear cause did huge damage to both Socialism and disarmament.

Outside Parliament, the anti-nuclear movement coalesced in the Campaign for Nuclear Disarmament (CND), formally launched on 17 February 1958 at the Central Hall, Westminster. CND was originally intended to be a high-level pressure group, rather like the Federation of Atomic Scientists. The membership included some impressive names: Bertrand Russell, Michael Foot, A. J. P. Taylor, J. B. Priestley and Joseph Rotblat. 'We were an odd collection', wrote Taylor, 'appointed by nobody and convinced that we could change the fate of the world by our own unaided efforts.'[28] Priestley's wife Jacquetta Hawkes, one of the few women on the executive, described the group as 'a compact sort of little campaign [which] depended very substantially on friends'.[29]

Contrary to the intentions of that group, ordinary people soon looked to CND to give focus to their fears about nuclear weapons. The group's appeal was demonstrated by the positive reaction to the four-day march on Aldermaston at Easter in 1958.* Before starting out, Foot told some 4,000 people gathered at Trafalgar Square: 'This can be the greatest march in English history.' The *Manchester Guardian* wrote:

> It was a happy crowd, a London holiday crowd, in benign mood . . . no more combative than the empty London streets through which the long procession made its way . . . The nearest thing to an incident was the cheerful booing as a policeman stopped a troop of folk-dancers from entertaining the lunch-time picnickers with an eightsome reel in front of Albert's statue.[30]

Marchers carried placards with slogans like 'Which is to be banned, the H-bomb or the human race?' A jazz band started to play, but was politely told by the organizers to remain silent until lunchtime, in respect to those observing Good Friday.

Behind the walkers came a convoy of vans, cars and coaches, 'one of them bearing that essential morale-builder, the tea urn'. The group brought 500 mattresses, the better to sleep on hard church hall floors. A passing motorist shouted 'Ostriches!, Ostriches!', but at no time did the marchers allow themselves to be distracted by hecklers. They kept their spirits up by singing 'That Bomb has Got to Go!' by Ewan MacColl and Peggy Seeger and by chanting

---

* In subsequent years, CND reversed the direction of the march (going from Aldermaston to Trafalgar Square) in order to emphasize that its beef was with politicians, not nuclear workers.

> We're going to stop the loonies and preserve the human race
> We're going to save our country for we like the dear old place.[31]

It was all terribly well-mannered, quiet and civilized. The bomb, apparently, would be defeated by English politeness, English principles and English morality. 'Alone, we defied Hitler,' Priestley commented. 'And alone we can defy this nuclear madness into which the spirit of Hitler seems to have passed.'[32] Behind the protests lurked a gargantuan national ego. Activists wanted Britain to 'give a moral lead to Russia and America' and convinced themselves that British unilateralism would lead inexorably to world disarmament. 'The force of our example might be great . . . there may be other chain reactions besides those leading to destruction; and we might start one.'[33] Both advocates and opponents of the bomb started from the assumption that Britain was uniquely well placed to provide moral example.

The crowd had a half-life of one day; when the procession reached Hounslow, the first stop, only 2,000 remained.[34] But Foot was right; the march did become one of the most famous in British history, creating a myth that would last for ever. From myth grew nostalgia. There were 4,000 protesters on that first day, but at least 40,000 now recall setting out from Trafalgar Square.

Capitalizing on the march's publicity and public sympathy, CND transformed itself into a mass movement, against the wishes of some original members. By the end of 1958 it had nearly 300 affiliated groups. The second Aldermaston march attracted perhaps 100,000 total participants, though there was never, at any single time, that many people marching. The final rally in Trafalgar Square drew a crowd of perhaps 20,000. This quick and unexpected growth left the organizers unprepared. The more 'members', the more unwieldy the organization became and the more diluted the message.

Labour leftists interpreted the Aldermaston marches as evidence of widespread public discontent with nuclear weapons. At the 1960 party conference, a resolution from the Transport and General Workers Union supporting CND's policy of unilateral nuclear disarmament was passed, despite protests by the party leadership. Hugh Gaitskell, the party leader, reacted angrily to the decision, vowing to 'fight, fight and fight again to save the Party we love'. CND saw the resolution as a huge victory and as an endorsement of its tactics. But triumph was short-lived. By the following year, Gaitskell had managed to mobilize sufficient trade union votes to reverse the decision. The party had rediscovered pragmatic good sense, recognizing that there were certain issues which, no matter how noble and well meaning, were vote-losers. Nevertheless, there were always some who would find ideological purity and hopeless causes irresistibly attractive.

In 1961 the CND activist Merfyn Jones warned followers of the need for sustained commitment. He told them that politicians 'don't intend to argue with you – they're waiting for you to get tired'. By late 1962 most dissenters were exhausted and CND itself was a spent force. Already severely weakened by the 1961 Labour conference decision, the organization found that its argument was nearing the end of its shelf-life. It had attracted followers by promising doom, but doom did not come. Every year that passed without nuclear war seemed proof that deterrence worked and that CND pointed the wrong way toward peace. Rather than a liability, the weapons seemed a blessing. Nor did it help that CND repeatedly attacked nuclear weapons as immoral. Though Foot has always defended this strategy, accusations of immorality alienated the honest, God-fearing people who sincerely believed that bombs were the best way to defend their country.

In reality, CND was never a truly popular movement. According to the opinion polls, support for unilateral nuclear disarmament peaked at 33 per cent in April 1960 and declined steadily thereafter. What CND saw as apathy was in truth silent support for Britain's nuclear weapons. This was especially true in the case of the working class, and, as such, reveals the problem of CND hitching its star to the Labour Party. British workers are highly patriotic and tend to see a strong defence capability as essential to the protection of their way of life. Like Bevin, they saw the bomb as a symbol of British greatness. The debate over nuclear policy was yet another manifestation of the acrimony between the middle-class left and the workers, both of whom sought refuge within the dysfunctional Labour Party. As an indication of the uneasy relationship between CND and the labour movement, the list of sponsors in 1958 included over 100 prominent artists, academics, writers, scientists, members of the clergy and politicians, but only two trade unionists.

What then did CND achieve during this, its first phase? Nothing concrete, though it made a lot of noise. Foot took pride in that fact. CND 'made our country the most active and vocal in the world in attempting to arouse mankind to an awareness of the nuclear horror'.[35] That might have been true but behind that assessment lurked a painful truth. Advocates and critics of the Bomb shared one misconception: that Britain was important. 'We made one great mistake which ultimately doomed CND to futility,' Taylor admitted. 'We thought that Great Britain was still a great power whose example would affect the rest of the world. Ironically, we were the last Imperialists. . . . No one cared in the slightest whether Great Britain had the bomb or did not have the bomb. The Russians were not frightened because we had it. The rest of the world would not be impressed if we gave it up.'[36]

While the Labour left and CND struggled to get rid of the Bomb, across the English Channel the French celebrated obtaining one. On 13

13. Publicity still from MGM's 1946 film *The Beginning of the End*, which demonstrated that the Bomb posed no threat to monogamous relationships.

14. Mannequins from Penney's department store being dressed for their starring role in a Doom Town test, April 1958.

15. Turning the Cold War into cold, hard cash: business card from an enterprising construction company.

16. Miss Atomic Bomb, 1957, selected at the Sands Hotel, Las Vegas.

17. Doom Town test: though American authorities sometimes pretended otherwise, atomic bombs could in fact destroy houses.

18. TRUCKEE test, 9 June 1962: a 210 kiloton thermonuclear bomb (a prototype for the Polaris missile) was air-dropped 10 miles south of Christmas Island.

19. A pause in the arms race: Andrei Sakharov (*left*) and Igor Kurchatov (*right*), 1959.

20. Reykyavik, October 1986: Mikhail Gorbachev assures Ronald Reagan that there's plenty of time left before the end of the world.

21. The first Aldermaston March, Easter 1958.

22. Greenham Common: sisters doing it for themselves.

23. Edward Teller embraces the Russian Tsar Bomba, the largest bomb ever built, in 1994.

February 1960, the French detonated a device, codenamed Gerboise Bleue, at Reggane in Algeria. It yielded an incredible 60 kilotons, far more than any other nuclear power has ever achieved in its first test. Though the French justification for having nuclear weapons was similar to that of the British, ego figured more prominently. For this reason, protest was virtually non-existent and celebration intense. No power is more proud to be nuclear than the French.

France, like Britain, was desperate to demonstrate her greatness in a postwar world dominated by two superpowers. Although French nuclear physicists were highly respected before the Second World War, the circumstances of the conflict left them isolated. Unlike their British colleagues, they did not join the Manhattan Project and therefore were ill equipped to embark upon an atom bomb at the war's end. But that did not stop the French provisional government under Charles de Gaulle from issuing a decree on 18 October 1945 establishing the French Atomic Energy Commission (Commissariat à l'Energie Atomique, or CEA). Raoul Dautry was appointed Administrator-General and Frédéric Joliot-Curie, France's leading nuclear scientist, became High Commissioner.

De Gaulle's enthusiasm was not enough to sustain momentum. The influence of French communists within the political system brought a swing toward non-proliferation, in line with Soviet directives. In addition, the fact that Joliot-Curie was an ardent communist ruled out any sharing of American, British or Canadian knowledge. But, then, in 1951, Joliot-Curie was dismissed and Dautry died. The new High Commissioner Francis Perrin and the new Administrator-General Pierre Guillaumat brought fresh energy to the project. The government also showed renewed enthusiasm, as evidenced by the appointment of Félix Gaillard as Secretary of State for Atomic Energy. In July 1952 a five-year plan was approved by the National Assembly and plutonium production facilities were built. Though no firm commitment to making a bomb had been made, a military application was implicit in the project. The last sentence in the preamble to the plan made intentions clear: 'It depends on us, today, that France be still a great modern country in ten years.'

In April 1954, French forces were humiliated by Viet Minh rebels at Dien Bien Phu. Defeat in Vietnam was a huge blow to French esteem, especially since, during the last years of the war, the Americans had paid 80 per cent of the war's expense. Like a jilted lover, France turned from Empire to the Bomb. On 26 December 1954, the cabinet of Prime Minister Pierre Mendes-France officially authorized construction of an atomic device. He argued that

> The guidance of strategy will henceforth increasingly belong to powers that have the atomic weapon. . . . It is therefore essential for France to embark

on a military programme. Otherwise, its security will be assured entirely by the Anglo-Saxons. . . . Perhaps never has France's position as a world power, or even simply as an independent nation, been so threatened as it is today by the fact of progress in military technique.[37]

The bomb would allow France to remain the predominant continental power, setting her apart from Germany. Furthermore, as Second World War veteran General Catroux argued, possession of the bomb was the only way to ensure France's future safety. 'There will be states that have the atomic bomb (and will not use it among themselves). There will be States without the bomb, which will be the battlefields. We need our atomic weapons.'[38]

Bearing these benefits in mind, the anticipated cost of 125 billion francs seemed a bargain. Indeed, as with the British, nuclear weapons were thought to be the cheapest way to maintain national status – cheaper certainly than conventional forces. The wisdom of a bomb programme seemed to be reinforced when, in 1956, the US pulled the plug on the Anglo-French adventure in Egypt. Like the British, the French interpreted Suez as proof that the Americans could not be relied upon for support. In fact, French alienation ran deeper, as evidenced by their decision to withdraw from NATO ten years later.

On 11 April 1958, Gaillard, by this stage Prime Minister, signed an official order for the manufacture and testing of a nuclear device. But a more important development occurred later in the year when de Gaulle returned to power as the first President of the Fifth Republic. For him the weapon had always been seen as symbolic of French greatness and for him French greatness was unlimited.

The French believed in deterrence, but trusted only themselves to provide it. 'To possess the atomic weapon . . . is . . . to deter any nation that possesses it from acting against [us] with atomic aggression,' de Gaulle argued.[39] The actual size of the French nuclear force did not matter: the strategy came to be known as proportional deterrence, or 'the deterrence of the strong by the weak'.[40] France sought a nuclear capability which would allow her to inflict 14 to 20 million deaths on the Soviet Union and measured deterrence as the ability to inflict pain proportionate to the gain that the USSR might derive from defeating France.

Like the British, de Gaulle feared that American strategic plans were designed to quarantine a nuclear conflict within Europe. A French nuclear weapon seemed the best way to guarantee full American participation in a war from the outset. But this meant that the French would have to be prepared actually to use their weapons. 'Should the United States abstain from acting immediately with all its intercontinental forces', de Gaulle wrote in May 1963, 'it is necessary to use [our] nuclear weapons in the

European theatre as soon as the aggressor commences his offensive.'[41] A few months later he elaborated: 'If France is attacked, it is certain that the Americans will intervene. But when and how? Their interest might not coincide with ours. The alliance does not oblige them to be at our side right away, with all their weight and all their weapons. That is why our atomic force is necessary. It is a triggering and entangling force. It is the starter.'[42]

After the first test in 1960, three more followed over the next three years, much to the dismay of the African nations. Though the French usually take great delight in causing nuclear annoyance, they eventually agreed to carry out further tests underground. When blowing up bits of newly independent Algeria grew too controversial even for them, testing moved to Mururoa and Fangataufa Atolls in the South Pacific.

The French bomb was eventually mated with the Mirage IV bomber. Ballistic missile development began in 1959, with the first tests five years later. After the successful atomic test, the French embarked on a thermo-nuclear project, which culminated in the Canopus test of 24 August 1968 at Fangataufa. That meant full membership of the nuclear club. 'We have accomplished it all by ourselves,' de Gaulle boasted, 'entirely on our own.'[43]

In 1962, the American Defense Secretary Robert McNamara tried to reassure America's allies that they were safe under the American nuclear umbrella, even if this meant sacrificing some of their symbolic sovereignty. He assured them that there was still a great deal that could be accomplished in the way of a conventional military contribution. But,

> if, despite all our efforts, nuclear war should occur, our best hope lies in conducting a centrally controlled campaign against all of the enemy's vital nuclear capabilities, while retaining reserve forces, all centrally controlled.
>
> More specifically, the US is as much concerned with that portion of Soviet nuclear striking power that can reach Western Europe as with that portion that also can reach the United States. In short, we have undertaken the nuclear defense of NATO on a global basis. This will continue to be our objective.[44]

While the British continued the pretence of independence, the Americans simply incorporated British weaponry into NATO strategy. At no point during the Cold War was it ever conceivable that Britain might use her nuclear weapons independently, against the wishes of the United States. Yet, if a country needs an ally's permission to use its weapons, those weapons are hardly independent.

The French case was slightly different. Her eventual withdrawal from NATO and her refusal to have American forces (including nuclear forces) stationed on her soil provided more credence to her claim to independence. But the same objections raised by McNamara nevertheless applied. Though the French had an independent deterrent, they could never independently deter, since they never possessed the capacity to destroy their enemy. As with the British, issues of national prestige led to muddled strategic thinking and a failure to explain clearly the logic of the nuclear arsenal.

To accept the logic of the British Bomb required ignoring the acknowledged conventions of deterrence. If the Soviets attacked first, the British could not really manage a second strike of any credibility. Thus, the tiny British arsenal could not by itself deter the Soviets from attacking and yet deterrence was supposed to be the justification for the weapons. The British might respond to an attack by hitting the Soviets with a few of her own weapons, but they could not achieve much beyond spite. That was apparently enough to satisfy both the British and the French – it was, after all, implicit in the latter's principle of 'proportional deterrence'. 'Nuclear deterrence', Mrs Thatcher proclaimed (in Moscow, no less) on 31 March 1987, 'is the only means allowing small countries . . . to stand up to big countries'.[45]

In 1961, the Foreign Secretary Alec Douglas-Home claimed that 'The British people are prepared if necessary to be blown to atomic dust.'[46] If the lack of protest against nuclear weapons is taken as a measure of support, then Douglas-Home was perhaps correct. But what was it they were supporting? They had been sold a deterrent which could not deter. All they got was some flimsy notion of status. The bomb was like one of those magical devices advertised in 1950s magazines which promised to turn an eight stone wimp into Charles Atlas within a fortnight, but never quite delivered. For £50 billion the British (and French) bought themselves a ticket to the top table and then found themselves ignored by the other two occupants.

CHAPTER 13

Testing Times

In the spring of 1954, twelfth century Mongolia was recreated in the Escalante Desert of southwestern Utah. A film called *The Conqueror*, loosely based on the life of Genghis Khan, was being made by the RKO Company. Costumes were bad and dialogue worse, but none of that mattered, since the filmed starred John Wayne – a sort of Mongolian Maverick. The crew was based in St George, 150 miles from Yucca Flat, where, a year earlier, two particularly nasty atomic bombs had been tested. They were called Dirty Harry and Dirty Simon – 'dirty' being atomic lingo for a bomb that produces an extraordinary amount of radiation. Las Vegas casino operators have always been thankful for the fact that the wind at the Nevada Test Site blows dependably toward Utah, or, put bluntly, that fallout drops on Mormons, not gamblers. Much of the fallout from Harry and Simon came to earth in Snow Canyon, where *The Conqueror* was filmed. Add a lot of horses to kick up the dust and you get the picture. To compound the damage, director Dick Powell took 60 tonnes of the distinctively pink Utah soil with him for purposes of continuity when he transferred filming to the RKO studio in Hollywood.

Ninety-one of the 220 people who worked on the film at the Utah location developed some form of cancer. Forty-six died prematurely. Cancer killed, among others, Powell, Wayne, Susan Hayward and Agnes Moorehead. 'With these numbers, this case could qualify as an epidemic,' University of Utah radiological health director Dr Robert Pendleton has commented.[1] To claim that the Bomb struck down a slice of the Hollywood community might be reckless, since back then almost every actor smoked. But it does make you think.

At first, testing atom bombs in the Pacific seemed adequate, and certainly convenient. But it soon became clear that the Marshall Islands could not accommodate American nuclear ambitions. Driven by the need to reduce the lead times between tests and to cut costs, the idea of a continental site grew popular. Its necessity became more urgent after the Soviet explosion of Joe I in 1949 and the consequent intensification of the Cold War.

The AEC wanted to locate the site in North Carolina, near Cape Hatteras. The prevailing wind there blew out to sea, which meant that fallout would travel toward Bermuda and Western Europe, rather than poisoning Americans. Unfortunately, the US government did not own Cape Hatteras, but it did own suitable land in Nevada.

On 18 December 1950, Truman approved the establishment of a facility in southern Nevada, not far from Las Vegas. Around 350 square miles of the Las Vegas–Tonopah Bombing and Gunnery Range was set aside as a permanent nuclear weapons test site. The government, and most residents of the other forty-nine states, have always considered Nevada a fitting place to do unpleasant things. The bleak, hostile, seemingly endless desert seems suitable for no other purpose than dumping loathsome waste, or blowing up bombs. There are few other places in the United States where a 50-kiloton bomb has little noticeable effect on the landscape. Nevada is proof that man's bomb is big, but God's earth is bigger.

An official announcement, released on 11 January 1951, offered reassurance to those living close by:

> Health and safety authorities have determined that no danger from or as a result of AEC test activities may be expected outside the limits of the Las Vegas Bombing and Gunnery Range. All necessary precautions, including radiological surveys and patrolling of the surrounding territory, will be undertaken to insure that safety conditions are maintained.[2]

The first device was exploded on 27 January 1951. A short time later Governor Charles Russell voiced a common sentiment: 'It's exciting to think that the submarginal land of the proving ground is furthering science and helping national defense. We had long ago written off that terrain as wasteland, and today it's blooming with atoms.'[3] The first devices were tested on Frenchman's Flat, but, after windows were blown out in Las Vegas, the tests were moved further north to Yucca Valley.

Testing brought new meaning to the term 'boomtown'. By 1967 the site had expanded to about 1,350 square miles. By the mid-1980s, approximately nine per cent of the workforce in the southern part of the state was dependent directly or indirectly on the testing programme. At that time, 240 federal employees were involved, 7,100 personnel in private contracting companies and 11,300 support workers, making the NTS the state's second largest employer. The payroll totalled $301 million. At its peak, testing injected $1 billion annually into the Nevada economy.[4]

The workforce was almost exclusively male, which might have meant a lot of sexually frustrated bombers. Fortunately for the men, Nevada was the only state in the Union where prostitution was legal. In 1942, President Roosevelt ordered the suppression of prostitution near military bases, but that order was lifted in 1948. In dusty towns around the test site, brothels bloomed like desert flowers after a storm. Off-duty soldiers filed out of the Test Site's main gate and made for the Chicken Ranch in Pahrump, the Shamrock brothel in Lathrop Wells, or any of the other establishments along Nevada State Highway 375. In their quest to feel the earth move, test site employees injected millions into the Nevada economy.

Testing was not just a matter of making sure that new weapons worked. It was also about building public confidence. In a Cold War devoid of battlefield success, tests were ersatz victories, providing reassurance that the nation's security was properly managed. This was one great advantage of the Nevada site over those in the Pacific. Nevada was conveniently visible; journalists and politicians were invited to observe the tests and were treated lavishly while at the site. From specially built bleachers they watched America flex her atomic muscles.

The tests were also designed to impress the enemy. 'In our conflict with the powerful communistic countries which strive for world domination', Teller commented in 1958, 'it may be too much to hope for uninterrupted peace. If we abandon [weapons testing], we shall enable the Red bloc to take one country after another.' In the early 1950s Strauss argued that 'the weapons which we test are essential . . . they have been and may well continue to be a deterrent to devastating war'.[6]

Analysis was not confined to the bombs themselves. A series of experiments were conducted in the early 1950s to assess the physical and psychological effects of atomic explosion on soldiers, so that techniques for conducting warfare on a nuclear battlefield could be developed. Around 90,000 soldiers participated in these exercises, which were practice for the 'massive retaliation' strategy by which NATO planned to counter the Warsaw Pact's superiority in conventional forces.

Mock installations were constructed and military hardware was placed in harm's way so that its susceptibility to nuclear explosion could be measured. Instant forests were planted with hundreds of recently-cut pine trees so that the arid desert would resemble more closely the Western European terrain over which the atomic soldiers might advance. After the exercises, Private Bill Bires of the 231st Engineer Combat Battalion and his comrades would haul away the blasted equipment and tidy up the site, sometimes within hours of the detonation. On one occasion, a group of VIPs observed an explosion from nearby bleachers. They were equipped with a radiation monitor and were carefully checked before leaving the site. 'This amused us because no one had ever checked us with Geiger Counters before and we worked at the Ground Zero areas every day,' Bires recalled. 'The Platoon leaders and other key individuals had film badges, but none of the rest of us did.'[7]

After the first test, Operation Buster-Jangle, researchers concluded that the psychological effects of nuclear explosions on trained soldiers were no cause for concern. Eighty-three per cent of the troops said they would volunteer to participate in a similar exercise in the future, 78 per cent expressed confidence in the safety of the exercises and 62 per cent claimed they would have no difficulty being sent into actual combat involving nuclear weapons.[8] But then behaviour specialists from Johns Hopkins University judged the test insufficiently realistic. In response, the Pentagon approved a second series and pressured the AEC to relax safety standards in order to simulate battlefield conditions more closely. Under the new guidelines, soldiers were positioned just 2,000 yards from the blast and the maximum allowable radiation dose was raised to 6 rems, in comparison to the AEC standard of 3.9 rems. The AEC accepted the changes on the grounds that military training has to be dangerous in order to be realistic. Since the government was interested to study the penetrative powers of radioactivity, some soldiers were ordered to swallow tiny radiation monitors. These were attached to a long string, allowing them to be pulled out of the stomach immediately after the test.

Brigadier General H. P. Storke subsequently boasted that 'for the first time in known history, troops successfully attacked directly toward ground zero immediately following the atomic explosion'. But the government's quest for verisimilitude eventually grew reckless. The Hood test in June 1957 was the largest above ground blast to take place at the Nevada site, with a payload of 74 kilotons. One of the guinea pigs was Robert Carter, a seventeen-year-old Air Force recruit:

> The explosion went off, and I remember feeling the confusion that just blew me, it just blew me 40 feet into the mountainside and all those men with me. I felt elbows, I felt my head hit the ground. I felt dirt in my ears, my nose, it went down my throat. I had a bloody nose. I felt all those terrible things that you don't want to go through in your whole life. I remember the ground so hot that I couldn't stand on it, and I was just burning alive. I felt like I was being cooked. After the shot my coveralls were cracked and burned, there was so much heat.[9]

The soldiers were encouraged by appeals to their masculinity, not to mention their patriotism. 'You can remember,' Storke told his troops, 'with a sense of pleasure and accomplishment, that you were a real pioneer in experimentation of the most vital importance to the security of the United States.'[10] Some men undoubtedly bought the bull, but others felt manipulated.

The Americans were not alone in treating human beings like laboratory rats. The Soviets, on the understanding that NATO would use nuclear weapons on German battlefields, staged exercises similar to Buster-Jangle in the Turkestan Military District beginning in 1951, with the important exception that the nuclear explosion was simulated. A few years later, however, real bombs were used. An exercise in September 1954 involved 44,000 troops, each of whom had to sign a promise to remain quiet about the incident for twenty-five years. 'The troops . . . which took part . . . went without fear into the region of the atomic explosion, even to ground zero, overcame the zones of radiation and carried out the missions that had been set for the units and formations,' the official report commented.[11] Some years later, soldiers started getting sick.

When, in response to the Bravo shot, Kurchatov warned that thermo-nuclear war would destroy civilization, the Soviet military decided to challenge his doomsday scenario. According to Major General Valentin Larionov, troops were marched into the contaminated zone within a half hour of the blast.

> Marshal Bulganin, who was in charge of the exercise, said that the results showed none of the troops . . . had been exposed to high enough levels of radiation to warrant fear of this weapon. And so an atomic war was not as frightening as the imperialists would have us believe.[12]

American tests had similar purpose, as evidenced by commentary from a propaganda film:

> Shot day. Camp Desert Rock. H minus five hours. Like all too many people both in and out of the military, before these men got their assignment for this operation they had many misconceptions about the bomb and its effects. Some of them thought they would never again be able to have families. Some of them expected to glow for hours after the bomb went off. Many of them were afraid. They had never taken the time or invested the effort to learn the facts about what to do in case of atomic warfare. . . . In the minds of many of the men there was doubt and fear before. Now there is confidence, confidence that comes only with experience. Just treat it with respect rather than fear. Use a little common sense. And observe a few basic precautions. . . . We made it. And so can anyone else who goes through this kind of operation.

Russell Dann recalls reading an Army pamphlet which assured soldiers that 'the radiation from an atomic weapon, when burst in the air, is all gone in a minute and a half. After that time, no significant radiation exists on the ground.'[13] This was sufficient to make him feel confident about the tests, since the government obviously wouldn't lie. Two decades later he was sterile, had no teeth, no hair, was deaf in one ear and a quadriplegic. Then came the cancers.

Common sense was not enough to protect James Yeatts, who took part in Operation Tumbler-Snapper. 'We had no protective clothing or equipment, not even a gas mask,' he recalls.

When the bomb was detonated, we had our backs to the blast, kneeling with our hands over our eyes and our eyes closed. The flash was so bright we could see the bones in our hands. Then we turned to see the fireball form. The shock wave hit us and knocked me backward. The dust was so thick that we could not see anything. After the dust settled we marched toward Ground Zero until the radiation got too hot.

Within two months, Yeatts started suffering from 'rectal abscesses, headaches, nausea and severe back pains' that persisted into the 1960s. By the tenth anniversary of the test, all his teeth were gone. 'They became so loose, I could pull them with no pain.' Then he developed respiratory problems. By 1980 he was terribly weak and emaciated, his weight having fallen to 103 pounds. 'I can only walk a few steps. I am now losing control of my bowels and urine.'[14] A son, born in 1969, suffered from a multitude of birth defects which doctors judged radiation-related:

the sutures in his head were grown together, a severe heart problem, an imperforate anus, he had only one kidney and an obstruction in the urinary tract. He had to have a colostomy at one day old. At three months old he had a 'Pots procedure' operation on his heart. He had a ureterostomy at six months, which will be permanent. A pull through was done on his rectum at 2 years old. At the age of 5 he had open heart surgery.

'It is not enough for the Government to use me for a guinea pig,' Yeatts complained, 'but to cause something to children years later is more than I can take.'[15] While many men feel that they were treated like guinea pigs, the metaphor is perhaps inappropriate. Sheila Gray, who has studied similar tests involving British servicemen, argues that 'The men were not proper guinea pigs because they were not tested afterwards. They were sacrificial lambs.'[16]

British servicemen sent to Christmas Island for nuclear tests entertained themselves by watching *The Incredible Shrinking Man* and *The Amazing Colossal Woman*, both of which deal with the theme of radiation-created mutants. Whether their commanding officers had a wicked sense of humour, or simply lacked an appreciation of irony, is not clear. In total, 22,000 British, 14,000 Australian and 500 New Zealand soldiers took part in British atomic tests. Radiation risks were barely mentioned. 'There were many talks and lectures in the camp theatre . . . all designed to reassure,' Jim Haggas, who took part in the tests, recalls. 'We were told about the island and the climate, the sailing, the swimming and the fishing, but little or nothing about the tests, the fall-out, the precautions, the possible risks and hazards.'[17] He feels, in retrospect, that the need to underline Britain's membership in the nuclear club took precedence over the desire to protect men involved in the tests. Senior officers took a view more suited to actual war, namely that the sacrifice of soldiers is warranted if national survival is at stake.

Monte Bello Island, one of the British test sites off the northwestern coast of Australia, is today considered so dangerous that visits are limited to one hour. Yet at the time few precautions were taken. 'When the bomb went off I was standing on the beach in my shorts and sandals – there was no protective gear,' Tom Duggan, a British serviceman, recalled. 'Later I swam in lagoons there and ate fish from the sea.'[18] Though the presence of radioactivity was not denied, no one seems to have suggested that it was dangerous. 'They told us you could just wash it off,' Bill Paterson, an Australian veteran, recalls.[19] The need to maintain secrecy also inspired a reluctance to tell ordinary servicemen about the hazards they were facing. Answers came many years later in the form of radiation-related diseases.

In 1956 servicemen at the Maralinga test site were deliberately exposed to radiation. In 2001, after years of denial, the British government was forced to admit that twenty-four soldiers were marched into contaminated areas shortly after a blast. But officials rejected claims that the men were guinea pigs, claiming that the tests were not designed to assess the effect of radiation on humans. 'The object was to discover what types of clothing would give the best protection against radioactive contamination in conditions of warfare,' an Australian Central Command memo read.[20] Judged by the number of radiation-related illnesses which subsequently developed among the men involved, the protective clothing quite clearly did not protect.

Given its vast expanse of sparsely populated land, Australia seemed perfectly suited to testing. Yet this apparent suitability led to a devil-may-care attitude. British complacence was compounded by the lack of vigilance shown by the Australian government. Prime Minister Robert Menzies saw bombs and thought dollars. Since he didn't much like Australia, he felt no qualms about blowing it up.* In this atmosphere of indifference, little attempt was made to limit harmful effects. Security was lax, with the boundaries of the range not properly patrolled. Since the tests were conducted hundreds of miles from population centres, little consideration was given to the appropriate weather conditions in which to conduct them and because fallout was expected to dissipate over land populated by Aborigines, concern was low. Warning signs were printed in English, which many Aborigines could not read.

---

* Returning from a trip to England in 1941, he wrote in his diary that 'a sick feeling of repugnance grows in me as I near Australia'. (Geraldine Brooks, *Foreign Correspondent*, p.11.)

First to raise concerns was the biochemist Hedley Marston, who had originally been asked to measure radioactive iodine in local animals after the Maralinga tests. Never one to follow orders, the pugnacious Marston extended his survey as far as Adelaide, where he found radioactive particles in the air and in the thyroids of sheep and cattle on surrounding farms. Meanwhile, the government was officially claiming that no humans or animals were exposed to radiation. When Marston decided to blow the whistle, he ran up against a carefully orchestrated conspiracy of silence in which many scientists colluded. He published his findings in a specialist journal but was astonished to find that only one tiny rural paper subsequently picked up the story. Full details of his findings were not circulated until 1985, when a royal commission finally investigated the tests. It is nevertheless possible that Marston's revelations influenced the British decision to cease all testing in Australia after October 1957. They went to Nevada instead.

The Americans also tested protective clothing, but they used pigs instead of human beings. Since the pigs were expendable, they were exposed to the full fire and fury of the bomb. Army-style uniforms, authentic right down to the zippers, buttons and drawstrings, were specially tailored for 111 White Chester pigs in an operation inevitably dubbed the 'Charge of the Swine Brigade'. Let loose in close proximity to two successive nuclear blasts, the poor animals did not fare well. Though seventy-two were killed instantly, the Army was delighted with the tests. In another project, a small herd of Holstein and Jersey dairy cows were allowed to graze on the test site to see how radionuclides might be transported through the food chain. But, since there is no pasture in the area, feed had to be brought in from outside, thus calling into question the legitimacy of the test. The Department of Energy nevertheless announced that no detrimental effects were detected – a nice piece of PR for the bomb.

The American government was fully aware that the welcome accorded the tests would last only as long as Nevada residents felt safe. A plethora of promotional material provided a constant stream of reassurance. Several thousand copies of a little green booklet entitled *Atomic Tests in Nevada*, distributed in March 1957, emphasized the importance and safety of the tests:

> You people who live near Nevada Test Site are in a very real sense active participants in the Nation's atomic test program. You have been close observers of tests which have contributed greatly to building the defenses of our country and of the free world. . . . Every test detonation in Nevada is carefully evaluated as to your safety before it is included in a schedule.

Readers were assured that after six years of open-air nuclear tests, 'all such findings have confirmed that Nevada test fallout has not caused illness or injured the health of anyone living near the test site'.[21] But residents were advised that the risk could be minimized still further through a number of simple precautions. People should stay indoors for a few hours until fallout had passed. 'If you were outdoors . . . you might be advised to bathe, wash your hair, dust your clothes, brush your shoes, etc.' 'Fallout', the pamphlet admitted, 'can be inconvenient, but your best action is not be worried about [it].'[22]

In the casino capital, the American government gambled with gamma rays. It banked on the fact that radiation-related illnesses have a long gestation period and are difficult to diagnose. Downplaying the risks of fallout was motivated by two aims. Firstly, removing the radiation threat made the bomb less horrible. Preposterous as that might seem now, it was logical at the time. There was no escaping the fact that the bomb was a hugely powerful destructive force. But, with a bit of effort, one could protect oneself from the explosion – or so it was suggested. Radiation, however, was a different sort of threat. It could not be seen, smelt or immediately felt. Victims were often ignorant of the fact that they had been exposed. The sinister uncertainty of radiation made the weapon more frightening and unpalatable. For this reason, fallout had to be downplayed, because the government could not afford a populace crippled by fear.

Secondly, testing itself was seen as essential to survival in the Cold War. In 1955 Strauss argued that abandoning the tests would 'imperil our liberty, even our existence'. Two years later, the new AEC chairman Willard Libby gave Americans a simple choice: 'the terrible risk of abandoning the defense effort which is so essential under present conditions to the survival of the Free World against the small controlled risk from weapons testing'. The standard AEC chorus went: 'fallout is much less dangerous than falling behind the Russians'. The tests were sometimes presented as a solution to their own dilemma: one official claimed that they helped to 'speed the development of weapons with greatly reduced radioactive fallout, that is to say, so-called clean weapons'.[23]

The striking feature of this public relations package was the consistent denial that any serious damage was being done to people or animals in the path of the fallout. 'The American people can be assured that the rigorous safeguards which govern the tests are designed to prevent injury to the people of any community or city,' Strauss claimed in 1955.

> Rigid precautions are taken to hold the fallout from Nevada test shots to an absolute minimum. Suitable weather conditions are selected. . . . Radioactive fallout from the Nevada tests also is minimized by the manner in which the shots are fired. Most of the Nevada explosions occur well above the surface of the earth, with the result that only small amounts of earth are drawn up into the cloud.

Strauss emphasized that 'the Commission's medical and biological experts do not believe that this small amount of additional exposure [from testing] is any basis for serious concern'.[24] Much higher exposure, he argued, occurred from medical X-rays, background radiation, or cosmic rays.

While most Americans fully supported the tests, a conspicuous minority argued that they threatened the health of the planet. In 1955, Herman Muller, an expert in the field of gene mutation, warned that the effect of radioactive fallout on human gonads would cause long-term genetic damage. Echoing the claim, fellow geneticist A. H. Sturtevant argued that 'There is no possible escape from the conclusion that the bombs already exploded will ultimately result in the production of numerous defective individuals – if the human race itself survives for many generations.' In 1957 the chemist and social activist Linus Pauling estimated that 10,000 people had died or were dying from leukaemia caused by radioactive fallout. Zoologist Curt Stern stoked fears further by stating that 'everyone in the world harbors in his body small amounts of radioactivity from H-bomb tests: "hot" strontium in bones and teeth, "hot" iodine in thyroid glands'.[25] Contrary to AEC advice, critics of the tests insisted that there was no such thing as a safe level of exposure. In one of the more imaginative public protest campaigns, the Greater St Louis Citizens' Committee for Nuclear Information called upon mothers around the US to send in 50,000 baby teeth so that levels of radioactive contamination could be assessed.

Similar warnings emanated from the Soviet Union. Early in 1957, Kurchatov asked Sakharov to write a denunciation of American claims that they had developed a 'clean' bomb. The article was originally designed for propaganda, but Sakharov took a humanitarian line. He calculated that a one-megaton 'clean' bomb would release enough radioactive carbon to cause 6,600 deaths over 8,000 years. Most scientists did not dispute these findings; they simply found the casualties too negligible to be worthy of concern. Sakharov disagreed:

> The remote effect of radiocarbon does not reduce the moral responsibility for future lives. Only an extreme deficiency of imagination can allow one to ignore visible suffering. The conscience of the contemporary scientist cannot distinguish the suffering of his contemporaries and that of posterity.

Sakharov insisted that, while the effect of one bomb might be negligible, the US and USSR were not content to test just one bomb. The only solution seemed to be an agreement to ban atmospheric testing. Such a ban, he claimed, 'will directly save the lives of hundreds of thousands of people, and it also promises even greater indirect benefits, reducing international tensions and the risk of nuclear war, the fundamental danger of our times'.[26] Kurchatov encouraged Sakharov toward further work on this theme, making sure that subsequent articles received wide international distribution. Khrushchev backed the campaign, but Russian tests continued.

In the United States, officials stubbornly ignored mounting evidence of danger and questioned the loyalty of the Bomb's critics. 'It became unpatriotic and perhaps unscientific to suggest that atomic weapons testing might cause deaths throughout the world,' Dr Karl Morgan of the Oak Ridge Health Physics Lab recalled. He felt that mercenary scientists too willingly danced to the government's tune. As late as 1979, Walter Weyzen, acting Director of the DOE's Division of Human Health and Assessments, argued that 'in spite of the extensive publicity on the association of adverse health effects and weapons testing, there are no scientific data to support this'.[27] Much more honest was a 1955 AEC report which declared that 'the degree of risk must be balanced against the great importance of the test program to the security of the nation'.[28]

Over time, AEC officials painted themselves into a corner. In order to sell the test programme, they had to argue that it was safe. Such a claim, however, meant they could not urge citizens to protect themselves, because to do so would contradict the message that they were safe. Thus, the AEC in effect encouraged people to become victims.

On one occasion, no amount of spin could disguise the fact that a serious mishap had occurred. In the spring of 1953, three tests resulted in dangerously high levels of radioactive fallout around St George. Since the exposure exceeded AEC limits, the townspeople were advised to stay indoors and roadblocks were set up to control the flow of people into the area. The most obvious effect was evident among sheep being taken to lambing sheds in Cedar City. Out of a flock of 11,710 animals, 1,420 ewes and 2,970 new lambs died within weeks. When the shepherds attempted to sue the government for compensation, their case was denied on the grounds that no direct connection to the tests could be proven.

The largest bomb ever exploded within the United States was detonated in 1971 on the island of Amchitka. Environmentalists (a new word back then) protested that the island was a staging post for over 100 species of migratory birds and home to walruses, sea otters and sea lions. Ignoring their objections, James Schlesinger, then chairman of the AEC, insisted there was 'virtually zero likelihood of any damage', even though his own geologists had reported an unstable substrata. Protesters tried to disrupt the tests by taking boats close to Amchitka, an action which eventually inspired the founding of Greenpeace. A gag order imposed by Richard Nixon prevented crucial evidence from reaching the attention of Supreme Court justices, who gave their approval on 6 November 1971. Just five hours after the ruling, the big bomb exploded.

An estimated 1,000 sea otters were killed instantly, their skulls crushed by the shock wave. Other marine mammals were found with eyes blown out or lungs ruptured. Thousands of birds perished, their spines snapped or their legs pushed through their bodies from the force of the blast. Of greater long-term concern was the fact the blast ruptured the earth's crust, sucking the White Alice creek into a new underground aquifer, where henceforth it became a conduit for radioactive elements. A few months later, samples taken from the blood and urine of Aleuts living nearby revealed dangerously high levels of tritium and cesium-137. Measurements taken in 1996 showed continued leakage into the Bering Sea. An unusual incidence of cancers has become apparent among the Aleuts and those who worked at the site. In response to allegations of incompetence, Dr Paul Seligman of the DOE's Office of Health Studies employed a well worn excuse: 'the priorities at the time were weapons production and the defense of the nation'.[29]

As is the nature of radiation, damage caused during the heyday of atmospheric testing only became apparent many years later. In early 1963, Dr Harold Knapp, an AEC scientist, warned that original estimates of harm might be wrong by a factor of 100 or 1,000. He was particularly concerned about young children who drank milk from cows that grazed downwind from the NTS. Around the same time, Dr Edward Weiss of the US Public Health Service discovered unusual leukaemia clusters in southwestern Utah which seemed linked to NTS operations. Four years later, Weiss released further data showing that the incidence of thyroiditis had doubled and thyroid cancer had quadrupled during the years 1948–1962. Further research by the Center for Disease Control and the National Cancer Institute backed up these findings, though both bodies were reluctant to pronounce on the cause. The AEC continued its policy of denial, maintaining that clusters found by Weiss were chance occurrences.

'You can't help but feel uneasy when you look up and see one of those clouds,' a Nevada farmer commented in the late 1950s. 'You don't know what the hell it is all about – and as for the AEC – I wouldn't believe them on a stack of Bibles.'[30] The alleged victims, who dubbed themselves downwinders, grew more persistent over time. 'My father and I were both morticians,' Elmer Pickett, a lifelong resident of St George, recalled. 'When these cancer cases started coming in I had to go into my books to study how to do the embalming, cancers were so rare. In '56 and '57 all of a sudden they were coming in all the time. By 1960 it was a regular flood.'[31] Illness led to revelation and thence to group consciousness.

A teenager in the 1950s, Darlene Phillips worked during the summer at Bryce Canyon. She was fascinated by the tests.

Everybody at the dorm . . . would get up early, before dawn, and get on the catwalk which faced west. It would be kind of chilly, and we would count down with it because we knew what time it was to go off. Then you would see the whole sky light up as if the sun were coming up backwards, and even the shadows of the trees would be wrong, casting their shadows in the other direction. And I should have known then that the world was upside down, that it was wrong, but I didn't.

Some years later, Phillips suffered from anaemia and immune system problems. She lost some of her hair. As she battled with her own health, two family members died in quick succession. Five years earlier, they had been prospecting in Nevada, downwind from the NTS, when a bomb exploded. Some soldiers eventually came by and advised them to wash their car and take a shower as soon as possible, but provided no other details about the danger they had encountered.[32]

'We accepted all this,' one downwinder reflects. 'It was our government and we accepted it.'

We didn't connect it to people's cancer at first. It takes a while. . . . The people of St George, after the 1953 blast, some of the people got a little nervous . . . People had to have cars washed down . . . The AEC guys came by to soothe all the ruffled feathers. . . . And yet so many people died from that. You'd have to be blind, deaf, and dumb not to see it. And it's pretty horrendous. . . . That big old Army president we had. I'd like to dig him up and hit him in the head.[33]

A sense of betrayal gradually developed. The people of southern Utah felt that their inherent trust in the government had rendered them the perfect target for fallout – they would serve their country by being saps. They inevitably wondered what the government might have done with its bombs if instead the wind had blown toward California.

The United States is a big country and St George a small place. The cries of the downwinders were lost in a desert of ignorance and apathy. The testing programme coincided with a time when public trust in the government was high. Not until the post-Watergate period did assurances about safety begin to be widely questioned. When, in 1955, E. C. Leutzinger, a state legislator, introduced a resolution to prevent further testing in Nevada, he was universally derided. The *Review-Journal* commented: 'More power to the AEC and its atomic detonations. We in Clark County who are closest to the shots, aren't even flickering an eyelid.' Leutzinger's bill, which had few supporters, died a slow death by committee. When a constituent wrote to Nevada Senator George Malone objecting to the testing, he replied that 'this country must not discontinue testing until other nations agree to do likewise. . . . I am confident that every precaution is being taken to insure that these tests do not endanger the lives of our people or the health of future generations and the work of our own Atomic Energy Commission will be the best guidepost.'[34]

For most people in Nevada, the atomic blast had the same pleasant sound as the chink-chink of a cash register. The programme not only brought government money and jobs, it also proved a boon to the tourist industry. Each atomic blast attracted a flood of tourists keen to feel the rumble, see the flash and gawp at the mushroom cloud. The visitors gave their spare cash to the casinos, thus pouring more money into the state's coffers. Enterprising hotel operators took to organizing package tours to coincide with tests. The Sands sponsored the Miss Atomic Bomb pageant, in which contestants wore a flatteringly shaped cutout of a mushroom cloud pinned to their swimsuits. (One inevitably wonders if they answered 'world peace' when asked about their hopes for the future.) House rules in some casinos provided a second chance if dice or the roulette wheel were disturbed by an atomic tremor. The Flamingo Hotel beauty salon offered an exclusive 'atomic hairdo', which, through extensive back-combing, resembled a mushroom cloud. The style was popular at parties organized to coincide with test shots, where hosts served specially designed and quite lethal 'atomic cocktails'. Guests danced the 'Atomic Bomb Bounce' to the smashing beat of the Atom Bombers, a group describing themselves as the 'Detonators of Devastating Rhythm'. Those who preferred laughter to dancing enjoyed Jackson Kay, the 'Original Atomic Comic'.

The Las Vegas tourist board supplied handy blast calendars to aid the planning of trips, and sponsored courtesy buses (with pre-packed picnic boxes) to the best vantage points. In 1955, the Sunday travel section of the *New York Times* advised readers on accommodation for those who wanted to witness a bomb blast. The author promised that the pastime was entirely safe – 'virtually no danger from radioactive fallout'. The epony-mous 'Atomic View Motel' boasted a vantage point that did not require the guest to leave the poolside in order to view the blast.

Las Vegas merchants timed sales to coincide with tests. Prices were vaporized, blasted, detonated, smashed or nuked. One store offered five-dollar gift certificates to the first ten customers to enter after a blast. Local government even got in on the act. Clark County incorporated the mush-room cloud into its seal, a motif also used on the phonebook. Local magnates occasionally berated the AEC for failing to take account of the tourist industry when scheduling tests. Long pauses were anathema, as was any talk of a test ban treaty. But the greatest scorn was reserved for doom-merchants who spread talk of harmful effects. Even after the infamous Dirty Harry shot, the *Review-Journal* commented: 'We like the AEC. We welcome them to Nevada for the tests because we, as patriotic Americans, believe we are contributing something in our small way, to the protection of the land we love.'[35]

Howard Hughes did not agree, though he only started protesting against the tests after they went underground. In 1967, he began a prolonged battle to get the tests stopped, claiming they were bad for his hotel business. He lobbied the AEC, threatened to withdraw his hotels from Las Vegas and contributed funds to candidates opposed to testing. Direct appeals to Lyndon Johnson urged the President to see the issue through the eyes of a Nevadan. 'Nevada . . . should no longer be treated like a barren wasteland,' Hughes argued.[36] When the government failed to respond, Hughes sent his trusted assistant, Robert Maheu, to Washington with envelopes full of cash with which to bribe the President. Maheu, rather wisely, decided that it was not a very good idea and never made the offer.

Hughes was typical neither of America, nor indeed of Nevada. One of the most striking features of the massive NTS is the tiny protests which occurred at its gates. Test site workers referred to the protesters as freaks, which, in the true meaning of the word, is what they were. The aggressive testing programme was possible in large part because of the overwhelming support of the American people. One poll taken in 1962 (after a brief moratorium on testing) found that 66 per cent favoured a resumption, even though a similar proportion accepted that fallout carried long-term danger.[37] Americans bought the argument that weapons were essential to protect their home from Communism. If weapons were needed, so too were tests. Granted, unease about the harmful effects gradually grew, but the AEC was fortunate in having to defend a programme that killed very slowly.

It was not a good time to be a snake, a scorpion, a lizard or a rabbit in southern Nevada. Animals that had adapted so well to the harsh desert environment suddenly encountered a new, man-made challenge. At one time, the biggest threat to their lives was a hawk or well-armed rancher. Now they faced the very real possibility of being vaporized. Yet wildlife did not go unheeded on the Test Site. Along the roads that traverse the complex today, occasional signs read 'Caution: Tortoise Crossing'. It's not clear if these are a recent addition; one suspects they're not. The irony of the signs probably never occurred to those who exploded the bombs. It's difficult to sense subtlety in an environment of explosion.

Along those same roads, the deer and the antelope graze as they always have. One is tempted to look for an extra antler or a second tail, but there are no obvious signs of mutation. They seem totally oblivious to the weirdness of their home. The authorities are now trying to 'erase the fingerprint' by removing the unsightly portakabins and equipment dumps which clutter the site. Again, there's that absence of irony. A few ugly structures can be removed, but nothing can be done about areas that will remain dangerously radioactive for thousands of years. And the craters, like footprints of a giant elephant, are permanent.

CHAPTER 14

To the Brink

On 30 October 1961, the Soviets tested a 50-megaton bomb – the biggest ever exploded – over Novaya Zemlya island in the Arctic. A cameraman in an observer aircraft watched in awe:

> our aircraft emerged from between two cloud layers and down below in the gap a huge bright orange ball was emerging. The ball was powerful and arrogant like Jupiter. Slowly and silently it crept upwards. . . . Having broken through the thick layer of clouds it kept growing. It seemed to suck the whole earth into it. The spectacle was fantastic, unreal, supernatural.[1]

The flash could be seen 1,000 kilometres away, despite heavy cloud cover. The mushroom cloud rose to sixty-four kilometres, and the atmospheric disturbance orbited the earth three times.

An observer recalled 'a remote, indistinct and heavy blow, as if the earth has been killed'. Those who later visited ground zero witnessed an eerie scene:

> The ground surface of the island has been *levelled*, swept and licked so that it looks like a skating rink. The same goes for rocks. The snow has melted and their sides and edges are shiny. There is not a trace of unevenness in the ground. . . . Everything in this area has been swept clean, scoured, melted and blown away.[2]

In clear air, the bomb would theoretically have been capable of inflicting third degree burns to a person standing 100 kilometres distant. As it was, an observer over 250 kilometres away felt the thermal pulse. Again in theory, such a weapon could cause complete destruction of all structures within a radius of twenty-five kilometres, and severe damage to most construction within thirty-five kilometres. In fact, due to atmospheric focusing, damage was apparent far beyond the theoretical range. In villages hundreds of kilometres away wooden houses were completely destroyed and roofs were blown from stone structures.

The bomb, built at Arzamas-16, was 8 metres long, 2 metres in diameter and weighed more than 20 tons. A specially constructed railway line extended into the factory so that the device could be assembled on a flatcar and subsequently camouflaged to look like a freight car. Since it was too large to fit through the bomb bay of the Tu-95 bomber, sections of the plane's fuselage were cut away and the bomb simply suspended beneath the superstructure. The parachute used to slow its descent was so huge that construction of it caused temporary shortages in the Russian hosiery industry.*

The bomb's yield (which might actually have been 57 megatons, but why quibble?) was ten times the combined total of all the explosives used during the Second World War. That seems impressive, but in fact the device had been intentionally muted. The bomb itself was supposed to be a three-stage device (fission-fusion-fission) designed to yield 100 megatons, but in the tertiary stage uranium was replaced with lead.

But why? What is the purpose of a 100-megaton bomb or, for that matter, one half that size? The Soviets were not very clear on this question. Gavriil Kudryavtsev, the director of the test site, claimed that the weapon was essential because 'In those days the strike accuracy of our missiles was insufficient. The only way to compensate for this was to increase the power of the warhead.'[3] But, in truth, it was far too large to transport by missile. And, with a payload this heavy, the Tu-95 was incapable of intercontinental bombing. Nor was it applicable to Europe. A 100-megaton weapon would be sufficient to erase small countries like Belgium, Holland and Denmark. But, if the bomb had been dropped on England, the fallout would have caused widespread fatalities in Warsaw Pact countries. If it had been dropped on West Germany, Soviet citizens would have received a lethal radioactive dose. In other words, the bomb had no military utility. Leo Feoktisov, a designer at Chelyabinsk-70, remains contemptuous of the device: 'It was not some super-discovery, but merely an increase in weight and size. Did that make sense? Building up yields in this simple fashion looked to us both trivial and useless. In those days, we were obsessed with a very different idea - miniaturization.'[4]

The bomb's nickname, 'Tsar Bomba', is an insider's joke – an ironic reference to the Russian tendency to make massive artefacts of no actual utility.† In truth, it was not a weapon but a political gesture designed to frighten the Americans and to underline Soviet disgust with arms control and test ban negotiations. Like a boy in a pissing contest, the Soviets had dramatically demonstrated that they had greater power.

---

* Or so it is claimed. This might be a big exaggeration designed to go with a big bomb. It is nevertheless beyond dispute that the parachute was very large.

† At the Kremlin one can find the world's largest bell (Tsar Kolokol) and the largest cannon (Tsar Pushka), both of which are equally impressive and equally useless.

'Tsar Bomba' has to be analysed against the backdrop of superpower relations in the decade before its detonation. On 10 May 1955 the Soviet Union proposed to the UN Disarmament Commission a measure to cease weapons tests. But negotiations quickly stalled when complex verification issues were raised. Over subsequent years, the UN applied moral pressure on the nuclear nations to agree upon a ban. Progress was hindered by their tendency to play political games by attaching additional arms control measures to test ban proposals. Verification consistently proved the most significant obstacle to agreement.

On 17 October 1956, Premier Bulganin rejected the need for an international verification system. 'Would not the best guarantee against the violation of such an agreement', he wrote to Eisenhower, 'be the mere fact that secret testing of nuclear weapons is impossible and that consequently a government undertaking the solemn obligation to stop making tests could not violate it without exposing itself to the entire world as the violator of an international agreement?'[5]

Alarmed by talk of a ban, Teller argued that the Russians would be able to evade existing monitoring mechanisms. He told Eisenhower that the Russians would use a test ban as an opportunity to surge ahead in the arms race. On the strength of Teller's argument, Eisenhower insisted on real measures of control, 'not simply a mirage'.[6] The Soviet Union then proposed more comprehensive measures that included an international supervisory commission and a network of monitoring posts. Khrushchev followed this up by announcing in March 1958 that the USSR would discontinue testing and called upon the US to reciprocate. Feeling manipulated, Eisenhower declined, a decision that made him appear uncooperative. When the Western Powers proposed a system of monitoring much more intrusive than the Soviet Union was prepared to contemplate, Khrushchev accused them of deliberately wrecking the negotiations and, not long after, resumed tests.

The Soviet resumption of testing, intended as an expression of anger, lasted only until 3 November 1958. Contrary to expectation, the nuclear powers conducted no more tests for the next three years. Eisenhower insisted that the 'voluntary moratorium' was in no way binding, but would remain in force until further notice. Khrushchev muttered something similar. Meanwhile, various proposals were put forward, more as gamesmanship than as genuine attempts to reach agreement.

The Paris conference of 1960 seemed a real opportunity for progress. Eisenhower had high hopes: 'It would be a ray of light in a world that is bound to be weary of the tensions brought about by mutual suspicion, distrust and arms races.'[7] Then, on 1 May, Khrushchev reported that an American U-2 spy plane had been shot down over the Soviet Union. Eisenhower at first denied engaging in missions of this type, but was then forced into an embarrassing admission after the Russians produced the pilot and the plane. Khrushchev, spitting fury, walked out of the conference on the first day, dashing all hopes for a test ban or arms control.

Progress was hindered further by the 1960 presidential election which hung on the issue of the 'missile gap' – a crisis invented by worriers at RAND and exploited by the Democrats. Earlier, on 12 November 1957, the National Intelligence Estimate had forecast that the Soviets would have 500 operational ICBMs by the end of 1962, while the US would have only around sixty-five. Other estimates put the Soviet figure closer to 1,000. On the strength of this evidence, Eisenhower was lambasted for allowing the Soviets to open up a dangerous lead in missiles. A delighted Air Force used the data to jack up its budget requests. In fact the crisis was bogus, as Herbert York, then an adviser at the Pentagon and White House, discovered:

> When I . . . got to Washington . . . I had access essentially to everything about the Soviet Union that related to technology and military preparedness and so forth, I saw what other people didn't see. . . . I came to the view very soon that . . . the Soviet threat had been greatly exaggerated and it was still being greatly exaggerated. And it looked like it was going to continue to be greatly exaggerated.[8]

Not until well after the election did new methods of counting reveal that the Soviets would have only 150 missiles by 1962. Later, the estimate fell to fifty. Then, in the autumn of 1961, after a comprehensive analysis of satellite reconnaissance was completed, the USSR was discovered to have only four operational SS-6 missiles, with another twenty SS-7 and SS-8 sites under construction. A desperate Tommy Power, who had depended on the higher figures to justify his funding requests for SAC, subsequently argued that some monastery towers, grain silos and a Crimean War memorial were in fact missile sites, disguised by the devious Russians.

Though John Kennedy won the election, the missile issue proved an albatross around his neck. In order to preserve his credibility, he had to maintain a hard line toward the Soviets. With remarkable prescience, Soviet intelligence predicted that Kennedy's victory would mean 'a speeding-up of the arms race and, therefore, a further straining of the international situation with all the consequences that result from this'.[9] As if to confirm this prediction, Kennedy launched the disastrous Bay of Pigs operation, an ill-conceived plan to liberate Cuba, just ten weeks after taking office. In the aftermath of that debacle, Khrushchev took the opportunity to move on West Berlin, on the assumption that Kennedy would be unable to respond properly. The Soviets began disrupting NATO's communication and supply network into West Berlin. Like a deadly game of chess, each

Soviet move was met with an equally determined NATO response. On 27 October, Soviet and American tanks faced off at close range, with gunners poised to open fire. In the midst of the crisis Robert McNamara, Kennedy's defence secretary, consulted a senior NATO commander about the likely scenario:

> I asked . . . what further moves we should expect and how we should respond. He said the Soviets would probably do *a* and we *b*; they *c* and we *d*; they *e* and we *f*; and then they would be forced to *g*. And when I said, 'What do we do then?' he replied, 'We should use nuclear weapons.' When I asked how he expected the Soviets to respond, he said, 'With nuclear weapons.'[10]

Reason, however, prevailed. The superpowers decided not to test their respective knowledge of the alphabet. We should remind ourselves that, at the time of the Berlin Crisis, the Soviets had not 1,000 ICBMs, not 500, but just four. If there was ever a time to launch a devastating first strike, this was it. But the US did not attack, perhaps because a RAND counter-force study, sent to the Cabinet the previous September, had acknow-ledged that an American first strike, no matter how successful, could not prevent some Soviet bombs from getting through, with the result that two million Americans might die. That was enough to make a nuclear con-frontation over Berlin unthinkable and appeasement logical. The US had to live with the Soviet construction of a wall isolating West Berlin. As Kennedy candidly admitted to his aides, 'It's not a very nice solution, but a wall is a hell of a lot better than a war.'[11]

Crisis was averted, but tension did not ease. That tension poisoned any attempts to reach agreement on a test ban, though the voluntary moratorium continued. But then the French threw a spanner into the works. With peculiarly Gallic logic, they argued that their proposed test, scheduled for 13 February 1960, would not break the moratorium since they would not, technically, be 'resuming' testing, having never tested before. France exploded its bomb on schedule, and three more tests followed over the next fourteen months. Failing to appreciate the beauty of the French argument, the Soviets announced on 15 May 1961 that they would resume testing if the French refused to desist. Even though the French did not immediately proceed with plans for a fifth test, the Soviets resumed testing on 31 August. The US followed suit a fortnight later.

The door which had been slightly ajar when Kennedy was elected was now slammed shut, locked and bolted. Instead of talking, the superpowers were trading insults. Then came Tsar Bomba, essentially a large exclamation mark at the end of a string of expletives.

Khrushchev wanted to 'show the imperialists what we can do'.[12] On 10 July 1961, he met Sakharov and told him of his desire for a very big bomb. Exact specifications were not discussed, but Sakharov certainly understood that his leader wanted something much bigger than anything so far tested. The challenge lay not just in size, but also in the rapidity of development; Khrushchev wanted the bomb to form part of a test series scheduled to begin in early September.* Sakharov and his team designed and built the bomb in just sixteen weeks.

Tsar Bomba was a gesture of defiance and yet another demonstration of Soviet technological might. Since the aim was to impress, secrecy was discarded. Khrushchev took delight in throwing out hints about what was to come, and detailed information about the power of the device was released well before the test. He clearly enjoyed the opportunity to strut:

> I want to say that our tests of new nuclear weapons are . . . coming along very well. . . . We have said that we have a 100-megaton bomb. This is true. But we are not going to explode it, because even if we did so at the most remote site, we might knock out all our windows. We are therefore going to hold off for the time being and not set the bomb off. . . . But may God grant, as they used to say, that we are never called upon to explode these bombs over anybody's territory. This is the greatest wish of our lives!
>
> In strengthening the defense of the Soviet Union we are acting not only in our own interests but in the interests of all peaceloving peoples, of all mankind. When the enemies of peace threaten us with force they must be and will be countered with force, and more impressive force, too. Anyone who is still unable to understand this today will certainly understand it tomorrow.[13]

When Sakharov, who took part in the construction, was asked why the bomb was needed, he offered a wry smile and simply repeated, in briefer form, Khrushchev's message: 'Let this device hang over the heads of the capitalists, like a sword of Damocles.'[14]

Khrushchev was keen not only to impress those outside the Soviet Union, but also those within; the test was timed to coincide with the final sessions of the Twenty-Second Party Congress. Had the bomb resulted in a lower than promised yield or, worse, not exploded at all, the consequences for Sakharov's team would have been catastrophic. 'If we don't make this thing', he remarked, 'we'll be sent to railroad construction.'[15] One suspects that the punishment would have been far worse.

Tsar Bomba was the last device on which Sakharov was fully involved, both intellectually and emotionally. At the meeting on 10 July, he had urged Khrushchev not to resume testing, on the grounds that a resumption would 'seriously jeopardize the test ban negotiations, the cause of

---

* In fact the first test in the series took place on 30 August.

disarmament, and world peace'. Khrushchev responded by publicly rebuking Sakharov for 'poking his nose where it doesn't belong'. The assembled scientists were told:

> Leave politics to us – we're the specialists. You make your bombs and test them, and we won't interfere; we'll help you. But remember, we have to conduct our policies from a position of strength. We don't advertise it, but that's how it is! There can't be any other policy. Our opponents don't understand any other language.

Khrushchev ended: 'I'd be a jellyfish and not Chairman of the Council of Ministers if I listened to people like Sakharov!'[16]

Despite his misgivings, Sakharov wanted Tsar Bomba to succeed, but for reasons decidedly different than Khrushchev's. For him, the weapon provided an opportunity to demonstrate how ridiculous and dangerous the arms race had become. Like Bohr, Sakharov hoped that eventually a bomb would be created which was big enough to bring leaders to their senses, forcing them to recognize the futility of conflict.*

After the test, Khrushchev encouraged rumours that the bomb was to be incorporated into the Soviet nuclear arsenal. On 16 January 1963, he explicitly stated that the Soviet Union had a 100-megaton weapon ready for use. But, in truth, this seems just another example of nuclear tub-thumping. Feoktisov insists that the '100 megaton giant – the pride of Arzamas-16 – was made only once – for the test'.[17] That would make sense, since its purpose was to impress and no advantage could be gained from repetition. Washington feigned indifference, but it is hard to ignore a blast that big. Kennedy assured the American people that it was not necessary 'to explode a 50-megaton nuclear device to confirm that we have many times more nuclear power than any nation on earth'. He added: 'in terms of military strength, the US would not trade places with any nation on earth'.[18]

In truth, the US response was less rational than Kennedy's speech suggested. 'It became obvious that . . . there was no containing [the Russians],' Herbert York recalled. 'They were shooting not just this big bomb, but lots and lots of them and we essentially did the same thing. We went and, you know, we got bombs from wherever we could find 'em and took 'em to Nevada and shot them just in order to respond to these Russian tests. It was a crazy period.'[19]

★   ★   ★

---

* Sakharov, both an idealist and a pragmatist, also hoped for peaceful applications for the weapon, speculating that an explosive force of this magnitude might be used to prevent earthquakes or to deflect asteroids or comets from a collision course with the Earth.

In October 1962 the craziness very nearly got out of hand. On the 14th, a U-2 overflight of Cuba discovered that the Soviets were installing ballistic missiles on the island. 'The purpose of these bases can be none other than to provide a nuclear strike capability against the Western Hemisphere,' Kennedy told the American people eight days later. He explained that the medium range missiles could hit cities as far away as Washington DC, while the intermediate missiles could hit targets 'as far north as Hudson Bay, Canada, and as far south as Lima, Peru'.

Kennedy referred to statements made by the Soviets just five weeks earlier that 'the armaments and military equipment sent to Cuba are designed exclusively for defensive purposes'. He went on to explain how the advent of nuclear weapons had changed the definition of hostile action. 'Nuclear weapons are so destructive and ballistic missiles are so swift, that any substantially increased possibility of their use or any sudden change in their deployment may well be regarded as a definite threat to peace.' Such a 'deliberately provocative' challenge had to be met 'if our courage and our commitments are ever to be trusted again by either friend or foe'.[20]

What, one wonders, was Khrushchev thinking? The missiles in Cuba seem to have been a quick-fix solution to a severe strategic imbalance. A year earlier the US had publicly acknowledged that the missile gap was a sham; in fact, in all areas of nuclear weaponry the US outpaced her rival. According to some estimates, the US had a nine-to-one advantage in deliverable nuclear weapons.* This imbalance jeopardized Khrushchev's leadership. In his memoirs, he claimed that he installed the missiles to protect Cuba and 'to deter America from starting a war', an explanation which, though accurate, was not the whole story.[21] The move was designed to offset the overwhelming American nuclear superiority with a gesture potent in both force and symbolism. The missiles gave the Soviets an assurance that, whatever happened, they would be able to destroy some American cities.

Nevertheless, since the missiles were not sufficient to achieve an effective first strike, their use would have led to a massive and lethal American retaliation. But using the weapons was not really an issue. Khrushchev probably assumed that Kennedy would complain loudly about them, but he would not push his insistence on removal to the point of war, because that would mean the certain destruction of some American cities. The USSR would be allowed to keep the missiles intact, thus providing a quick and easy answer to the strategic imbalance – deterrence on the cheap. This explanation accords with Khrushchev's attempt to restrain military

---

* In the autumn of 1961, the Soviet Union had 44 ICBMs and 155 heavy bombers, while the US had 156 ICBMs, 144 missiles in Polaris submarines and 1,300 heavy bombers.

spending, against the pressure of Kremlin hawks. The Cuba gamble might have been an inexpensive way to satisfy hawks (who demanded an answer to American superiority) while still remaining within spending goals. Or, the missiles might have had a very specific strategic purpose, namely to knock out SAC command facilities, which could not otherwise be reached by weapons based in the USSR. This, too, might have been designed to silence Kremlin hawks.

Khrushchev's big mistake was in misjudging Kennedy. He seems to have been genuinely mystified when Kennedy demanded the removal of the missiles and seemed prepared to go to war. Khrushchev could not understand why the US assumed the right to place missiles in Turkey and Western Europe but would not allow the Soviets to place missiles in Cuba. 'How then does the admission of our equal military capabilities tally with such unequal relations between our great states?' he asked Kennedy at the height of the crisis. 'This cannot be made to tally in any way.'[22] The Americans were not, however, in a mood to understand Soviet feelings of inferiority or injustice; the only thing that mattered to them was that nuclear weapons were being deployed just ninety miles from Key West.

The two tides were playing poker with thermonuclear cards. Kennedy would not allow the missiles to remain, but wanted to remove them without going to war. Khrushchev thought he could bully the young, inexperienced president. LeMay interpreted Kennedy's cautious approach as evidence of cowardice and sought to inject some mettle into the administration. He advised that the only way to remove the missiles was to destroy them. As he saw it, Cuba provided the perfect opportunity to demonstrate the supremacy of his forces, and perhaps to win the Cold War in one stroke. 'The Russian bear has always been eager to stick his paw in Latin American waters,' he argued. 'Now we've got him in a trap, let's take his leg off right up to his testicles. On second thoughts, let's take his testicles off too.'[23]

In the interest of understanding, we should perhaps spare a thought for poor Curtis LeMay. He had devoted the better part of his career to the creation of an invincible nuclear force capable of destroying the enemy with one stroke. Yet the moment the Soviets developed the capacity to deliver even one nuclear weapon to the United States, they achieved a form of deterrence fatal to LeMay's plans. Throughout the 1950s, he had argued that 'we could have won a war against Russia. It would have cost us essentially the accident rate of the flying time, because their defences were pretty weak.'[24] But by the time of the Cuban Missile Crisis, his plan for killing a nation was nearing the end of its shelf life. He understood, more than anyone, that Cuba offered the last opportunity to use his beloved bombers for the purpose they were intended.

It required considerable courage for Kennedy to resist the advice of his generals, who argued that every minute's delay in launching an air strike would reduce its effectiveness. Robert Kennedy recalled:

> When the President questioned what the response of the Russians might be, General LeMay assured him that there would be no reaction. President Kennedy was sceptical. . . . 'They, no more than we, can let these things go by without doing something. They can't, after all their statements, permit us to take out their missiles, kill a lot of Russians and then do nothing. If they don't take action in Cuba, they certainly will in Berlin.'[25]

Kennedy instead imposed a blockade on Cuba, increased surveillance of the island, and reinforced the US base at Guantanamo, while demanding that the Soviets withdraw their missiles. He understood that Khrushchev did not want war, but had to find a way to allow the Soviets to retreat gracefully. 'We don't want to push him to precipitous action,' Kennedy told his aides. 'I don't want to put him into a corner from which he cannot escape.'[26] Meanwhile, he prepared the American people for all-out war.

'No one can foresee precisely what course it will take or what costs or casualties will be incurred,'[27] he warned of the coming conflict. That statement was truer then Kennedy perhaps realized. While he was trying to restrain his generals, they were doing everything they could to undermine him. On the 24th, the SAC commander General Tommy Power (who, in a lunacy contest, might actually have beaten LeMay) sent a message to his units designed to prepare them for the coming fight. The message was broadcast uncoded – Power wanted the Soviets to hear it. Two days later SAC decided to launch a test missile from Vandenburg Air Force Base toward Kwajalein Island in the Pacific, oblivious to the possibility that, in the crisis, the test might be misinterpreted by the Soviets. Meanwhile, a U-2 spy plane 'accidentally' strayed over Siberia, causing Khrushchev to warn that, in the present circumstances, such a plane could be easily misinterpreted for a bomber, with fateful consequences. At the height of the crisis, SAC bombers deliberately flew past their turnaround points toward Soviet airspace, a move Russian radar operators might understandably have interpreted as a signal that war had begun.

Armageddon stood in wait of a single presidential order or a single impatient act by a sailor or airman. The latter was more likely. Power had the authority 'to order retaliatory attack . . . if time or circumstances would not permit a decision by the President' – an American version of the headless chicken scenario.[28] In other words, if a junior officer in some remote radar base had mistakenly drawn the conclusion that Soviet missiles had been launched, Power might have retaliated without bothering to check with the President. In Cuba, Soviet field commanders were given similar authority to launch their medium range missiles if they found themselves under threat of attack. The war could therefore have started without Kennedy or Khrushchev deciding to fight. On 28 October, a US radar station picked up evidence of a Soviet missile launched from Cuba heading for Tampa. Only after considerable panic was it discovered that the 'missile' was in fact a computer test tape. At Volk Field in Wisconsin, nuclear-armed F-106s from the Air Defense Command were scrambled on 25 October after a base in Minnesota reported an imminent attack. A guard at the base thought he saw someone climbing the sector fence. The intruder turned out to be a bear – a real one, not the metaphoric Russian kind.

Many people in America and around the world had expected just such a showdown ever since the explosion of Joe I. Those who had built shelters felt smug; those who hadn't felt foolish. Some people read civil defence literature for the first time; others gathered essential keepsakes. Grocery shelves were emptied of canned goods. Local government officials dug disaster guidelines from dusty cabinets and struggled to make sense of what they were supposed to do. Sexual inhibitions fell away at the same time that contraception seemed ridiculously optimistic. (Nine months later a mini baby boom was apparent.) Schoolchildren worried that Halloween might be cancelled.*

The world waited. At the missile sites, work continued at frenetic pace, suggesting that the Soviets were hurrying to render the weapons operational. The entire crisis was distilled into a single tense moment in the waters off Cuba on 24 October. Soviet ships were challenged by the American blockade. Guns were aimed and torpedoes primed. And then the Soviets turned away. On 27 October, Khrushchev sent an anguished telegram to Kennedy: 'We are both engaged in a tug of war, pulling on either end of a rope and therefore tying a knot that, once tied, neither of us will ever be able to undo. If war should break out, it would not be in our power to stop it – war ends when it has rolled through cities and villages, everywhere sowing death and destruction.'[29] A second message was less conciliatory, so Kennedy ignored it and replied that he was 'very much interested in reducing tensions'.[30] Meanwhile, behind the scenes a deal was struck. The Soviets agreed to remove their missiles from Cuba on the understanding that the Americans would eventually remove some missiles from Turkey and would promise not to invade Cuba.

For eleven days a catastrophic war had been a very real possibility. We now know that the Soviets had more missiles in Cuba than the CIA had estimated at the time, and that they were ready for launch, thus calling

---

* In late October 1962, I was a seven-year-old looking forward to Halloween. But, then, even though the missile crisis had passed, my mother forbade me from going out trick-or-treating, as she was certain that nuclear war would break out while I was walking the streets in my skeleton costume.

into question LeMay's confidence that the sites could be destroyed at minimal cost to the United States. As for Power, he had all his planes in the air, circling over the Mediterranean and Northern Canada, ready to attack the minute the Soviets made one false move. At the appropriate signal, the US was ready to deliver nearly 3,000 weapons, with a total payload of 7,000 megatons. Such an attack would have killed at least 100 million people and would probably have ushered in a catastrophic nuclear winter in the Northern Hemisphere. (That possibility had not yet been imagined by scientists or Pentagon planners.) One mistake, one tiny miscalculation, one minuscule misreading of signals and the world might have been destroyed. Khrushchev expressed satisfaction that 'reason will triumph, that war will not be unleashed, and peace and the security of the peoples will be insured'.[31] But no amount of rhetoric could hide the fact that he had picked a stupid fight and lost.

When the crisis receded, LeMay felt not relief but regret. To his dying day, he maintained that an air strike would have removed both the missiles and the Communists from Cuba. 'In my mind there wasn't a chance we would have gone to war with Russia because we had overwhelming strategic capability and the Russians knew it.'[32] And, even if war had resulted, he felt certain that it could have been won and that the communist menace could have been eradicated. 'We lost the war as a result of the Cuban missile crisis,' LeMay afterwards insisted.[33]

Kennedy saw things differently. Chastened by the crisis, he sought ways to create a less dangerous world. On 10 June 1963, during a speech at American University, he talked about peace.

> What kind of peace do we seek? Not a Pax Americana enforced on the world by American weapons of war. Not the peace of the grave or the security of the slave. I am talking about genuine peace, the kind of peace that makes life on earth worth living, the kind that enables men and nations to grow and to hope and to build a better life for their children – not merely peace for Americans but peace for all men and women – not merely peace in our time but peace for all time.

Kennedy argued that peace was essential because war was unthinkable. In a tone reminiscent of Oppenheimer and Bohr, he stated that

> Total war makes no sense in an age when great powers can maintain large and relatively invulnerable nuclear forces and refuse to surrender without resort to those forces. . . . It makes no sense in an age when the deadly poisons produced by a nuclear exchange would be carried by wind and

water and soil and seed to the far corners of the globe and to generations yet unborn.

Kennedy still believed that 'the expenditure of billions of dollars every year on weapons acquired for the purpose of making sure we never need to use them is essential to keeping the peace'. He had not abandoned deterrence. But, in contrast to the dominant policy of the previous eighteen years, he now claimed that the bombs were 'not the only, much less the most efficient, means of assuring peace'.

The President implored the American people to assume a more accommodating attitude toward the Soviets. He asked them to look beyond the Soviet government to the Russian people, who deserved praise for 'their many achievements – in science and space, in economic and industrial growth, in culture and in acts of courage'. These were fine words, but the speech was not mere rhetoric. Kennedy introduced concrete proposals designed to ease tension and avert the chance of a future confrontation, including talks then in progress in Geneva which had the long-term aim of 'general and complete disarmament'.

The most significant aspect of the speech was Kennedy's call for a renewed effort to outlaw nuclear tests. This, he claimed, 'would check the spiralling arms race . . . increase our security . . . [and] decrease the prospects of war'. He announced that agreement had been reached to hold three-power meetings on a test ban in Moscow. In order to signal his sincerity, he pledged that the United States would not be the first to resume tests in the atmosphere.

New efforts toward a comprehensive ban quickly foundered on the same obstacles that had dogged previous attempts. But then Khrushchev, on 2 July 1963, proposed a ban on tests in the atmosphere, in outer space, and under water. This could be easily policed with existing methods of verification. The logjam was broken and agreement followed quickly. A formal treaty was ratified in Moscow on 5 August 1963 by US Secretary of State Dean Rusk, Soviet Foreign Minister Andrei Gromyko and British Foreign Minister Alec Douglas-Home.

Explaining the treaty to the American people, Kennedy claimed that 'For the first time, an agreement has been reached on bringing the forces of nuclear destruction under international control.' That was an exaggeration since, a few paragraphs later, he admitted that the treaty would not 'mean an end to the threat of nuclear war. It will not reduce nuclear stockpiles; it will not halt the production of nuclear weapons; it will not restrict their use in time of war.' In truth, it merely drove testing underground, where it was much more difficult to monitor. Kennedy admitted that the importance of the treaty was mainly symbolic – indicative of a cooling of tensions. 'It can symbolize the end of one era and the beginning of another . . . an historic mark in man's age-old pursuit of peace.'[34]

Sakharov saw the treaty for what it was, namely an agreement to stop polluting the atmosphere with radioactive substances. It was, he later argued, 'of historic significance. It has saved the lives of hundreds of thousands, possibly millions of people who would have perished had testing continued.'[35] Though the ban had widespread support, the military-industrial complex made known its disdain. Scientists and soldiers argued that the government had been led astray by agitators spreading nasty rumours about fallout. John Foster, director at Livermore, maintained that the fallout question 'has no bearing on the major issue' and Norris Bradbury, his counterpart at Los Alamos, regretted that 'fallout from atmospheric testing has been so played up rather recently'. Never one to mince his words, Teller argued that 'these two questions, the test ban and the fallout, are linked only by propaganda'.*[36]

On news of the treaty the editors of the *Bulletin of the Atomic Scientists* moved the hands of the Doomsday Clock back ten minutes, to twelve minutes to midnight. The treaty was, they felt, 'the first tangible confirmation . . . that a new cohesive force has entered the interplay of forces shaping the fate of mankind'.[37]

But, then, on 16 October 1964, China (which had refused to sign the Limited Test Ban Treaty) tested its first nuclear device at the Lop Nor test site. Mao had long been publicly contemptuous of nuclear weapons, but had secretly coveted them, in part because they had become a prerequisite of great power status. China and the Soviet Union at first co-operated in nuclear research, but this ended in 1960 as a result of the widening breach between them. Since that first test, China has conducted around forty-five tests, or about one a year. The last atmospheric test was conducted on 16 October 1980. Eventually, China developed the whole range of atomic hardware, including thermonuclear weapons, tactical devices, missiles, bombers, and submarines.

The propaganda film produced after the first Chinese test is an interesting blend of old icons with new. Young Chinese maidens in flowing gowns dance a stylized ballet with rifles slung over their shoulders. Technicians polish shiny stainless steel tubes. Soldiers fit radiation masks to horses. Cut to a vast control panel with hundreds of blue, red and yellow lights. Then, a bomb explodes, crowds cheer and the atomic-age cavalry charge forward into the nuclear battlefield, soldiers shooting from the saddle. God knows what it was supposed to mean or what the cheering crowds thought they were celebrating.

---

* Teller once told the journalist Christopher Hitchens that one of the greatest obstacles to progress in the nuclear age was 'the propagation of unreasoning and unverified fears concerning the danger of radiation'. Teller went on to suggest that 'a little radiation can be good for you'. (*The Nation*, 19 September 1994.)

★   ★   ★

Arms control treaties are never inspired solely by a noble consideration of what is right. They are instead self-interest wrapped in virtue. The Test Ban was a response to the growing unease with atmospheric testing. The nuclear powers understood that, if further expansion of their arsenals was desired, tests would have to be conducted in a way that did not alarm the public. The Test Ban achieved this, while also conveying an impression of rapprochement. In actual fact, testing increased after the treaty and arsenals continued to expand.

But, in truth, testing was not as important in the wider scheme of armaments policy as it had been in the decade immediately after the Second World War. After 1955, the most important developments in nuclear weaponry occurred not in the nature of atomic devices, but in the way they travelled to their targets. One of the more profound developments was the submarine launched ballistic missiles (SLBMs) which had the advantage of being much less vulnerable to first strike than ground based missiles. The American Polaris submarine carried sixteen SLBMs, with a range of 1,500 miles, and an accuracy to within two miles. Vice Admiral 'Jumping' Joe Williams, a nuclear submarine captain, accepted that Polaris was cynically brutal:

> The Polaris system to begin with was really a city killer. It was an extremely survivable assured destruction capability that the Soviets knew they could not destroy and knew that if they conducted a first strike, that system would some day be available to retaliate. It might take some time to get the message to them from a destroyed national headquarters, but at some day the missile warheads would come raining in and they would pay the price. I don't think that there would have been any hesitation on the part of any commanding officer to launch. Did we think about what was back home? Sure we did, but you didn't let that control your actions. Time to think about that after you'd done your duty.[38]

SLBMs were eventually combined with a new generation of missiles known as Multiple Re-entry Vehicles, or MRVs, which contained a number of warheads able to spread destruction over a wider area. In 1962, the standard Polaris SLBM had a single 800-kiloton warhead. Two years later, the missiles were upgraded to comprise three 200-kiloton MRV warheads. This technically meant less explosive power, but increased the number of targets that could be hit.

At the Kremlin, the Cuban crisis contributed to a strategic policy shift. With deterrence on the cheap discredited, the Soviets sought to build a more powerful and credible arsenal based on their own soil. 'Our lack of nuclear armaments and the weakness of the Soviet Union came as a shock to the Soviet leadership,' Nikolai Detinov, formerly of the Soviet Defence Ministry, recalled. 'It was like a cold shower for the government, who realized that these weaknesses had to be overcome.' Larionov recalled 'a syndrome to catch up and overtake, to try and show everyone that we weren't far behind the Americans, that we too had nuclear weapons. There were those who said that we can only prevent a nuclear war if we oppose world imperialism with a force of similar strength.'[39]

This meant a new generation of missiles, in particular the SS-9 and SS–11 ICBMs. Meanwhile, the ability of Polaris to approach very close to targets in the USSR while remaining undetected frightened the Soviets, who feared that it would allow the US to develop a first-strike capability. They responded by building the 'Yankee' submarine missile system, effectively launching an arms race within an arms race. While alarmists in the United States interpreted these moves as a Soviet attempt to achieve strategic dominance, they were in truth merely an attempt to achieve the parity that had eluded them in the late 1950s.

The American SIOP devised for 1962, an expanded version of earlier plans, envisaged a pre-emptive first strike involving 3,423 weapons totalling 7,847 megatons. This would result in the immediate death of 285 million Russians and Chinese. Planners did not bother to estimate the collateral damage in Eastern Europe, nor the effects of fallout in the rest of the world. The most notable feature of the plan was its inflexibility: fine-tuning it to suit the nuances of a particular conflict was something the military refused to contemplate. There was only one plan. China was included because it was part of an assumed Sino-Soviet bloc. Some weapons were even targeted on poor little Albania, even though it wanted nothing to do with the Soviet Union and had no real beef with the United States. In other words, the plan called for killing Communists simply because they were Communists.

The missile crews understood their job perfectly. They were chosen for their single-mindedness; those inclined to discretion were discarded. 'It would be done before we had time to stop and think about what we were doing,' Tom Denchy, a member of a Titan missile crew, said of his assigned role in the future war. 'It doesn't take all that long and it was just automatic. There was no question in our mind that this was the thing to do.' His colleague Ray Hersey was certain that 'If we had ever received a launch message over the PAS system, I . . . would have had absolutely no doubt that my life expectancy was measured in probably less than a half an hour and the only question was, would we be able to launch this missile before the incoming hit us.'[40] Deterrence depended on men like Hersey and Denchy.

Before 1962, the US could have 'won' a nuclear war, at a cost of perhaps two million American dead. But that was an intolerable price to pay. In other words, both Berlin and Cuba had demonstrated that the ability of both sides to inflict immense destruction proved an effective impediment to nuclear war. Yet the analysts at RAND found this too constraining. They argued that, since the prospect of the US implementing its SIOP carried too high a price, the communists were allowed to get away with expansionist actions around the world. Vietnam was only the latest example of how nuclear weapons were ineffective at countering conventional aggression. Kennedy and McNamara shared the frustration RAND analysts had been articulating for some time. Indeed, if RAND had been able to design a president they would have come up with someone pretty close to Kennedy. His idea of 'flexible response' seemed the perfect solution to the straitjacket imposed by Eisenhower's New Look. Kaufman, Kahn and their friends at RAND welcomed the opportunity to incorporate their counterforce ideas into Kennedy's more flexible strategy.

McNamara began by attacking the inflexibility of SIOP, pointing out that it might not always be necessary to kill millions of Chinese and Albanians. Against enormous resistance, he forced the military to adopt a less rigid plan. After this victory, he quickly moved on to a reconsideration of the 'massive retaliation' strategy of the Eisenhower era. On 5 May 1962, in Athens, he delivered his 'No Cities' speech to a gathering of NATO foreign and defence ministers. Kaufman, who delighted at the opportunity to turn his ideas into governmental policy, essentially wrote the speech. NATO ministers were told that

> the US has come to the conclusion that to the extent feasible, military strategy in general nuclear war should be approached in much the same way that more conventional military operations have been regarded in the past. That is to say, our principal military objectives, in the event of nuclear war stemming from a major attack on the Alliance, should be the destruction of the enemy's military forces while attempting to preserve the fabric as well as the integrity of allied society. Specifically, our studies indicate that a strategy which targets nuclear forces only against cities or a mixture of civil and military targets has serious limitations for the purpose of deterrence and for the conduct of general nuclear war.[41]

The Soviets saw 'No Cities' as a massive confidence trick. 'It was simply an attempt to make nuclear war morally acceptable,' Larionov thought. 'It was an attempt to deceive oneself.'[42]

As it turned out, counterforce was discredited before the ink dried on McNamara's speech. Though Kaufman was supposed to be a genius, a simpleton could have devised the answer to his plan. If the US concentrated on military targets, the Soviets had only to increase the number of targets. Counterforce was a blueprint for unlimited proliferation.

Furthermore, the events of 1962 had revealed a great gulf between theory and reality. Cuba and Berlin had graphically demonstrated that, for all its apparent logic, counterforce could never really be deployed. The cost in lives was simply too high. Many years later McNamara reflected on a realization reached because of Cuba:

> I will surprise you by stating that I believe parity existed . . . at the time of the Cuban missile crisis. The United States then had approximately five thousand strategic warheads, compared to the Soviet's three hundred. Despite an advantage of seventeen to one in our favor, President Kennedy and I were deterred from even considering a nuclear attack on the USSR by the knowledge that, although such a strike would destroy the Soviet Union, tens of their weapons would survive to be launched against the United States. These would kill millions of Americans. No responsible political leader would expose his nation to such a catastrophe.[43]

McNamara came to realize that the idea of limited nuclear war was obscene because, no matter how strict the limits, millions would die. Furthermore, the Soviet deployment of submarine-launched missiles made counterforce increasingly difficult. With the idea discredited, McNamara transformed the notion of mutually assured destruction into a strategy, which was called, appropriately, MAD. 'It's not mad!' he still insists. 'Mutual assured destruction is the foundation of deterrence. Today it's a derogative term, but . . . those who denigrate it, don't understand deterrence. If you want a stable nuclear world . . . it requires . . . an understanding that if either side initiates the use of nuclear weapons, the other side will respond with sufficient power to inflict unacceptable damage.'[44] In the bizarre logic of nuclear confrontation, MAD seemed sensible and counterforce seemed madness.

'Assured destruction is the very essence of the whole deterrence concept,' McNamara argued in a speech on 18 September 1967. 'We must possess an actual assured-destruction capability, and that capability also must be credible. The point is that a potential aggressor must believe that our assured-destruction capability is in fact actual, and that our will to use it in retaliation to an attack is in fact unwavering.' Henceforward, force levels were calculated on the basis of ensuring that 'unacceptable damage' could be inflicted upon the USSR. To McNamara, this meant half of the Soviet industrial potential destroyed and 25 per cent of the population killed. In reality, this could be achieved with just 400 megatons of weaponry. But, as McNamara explained:

> When calculating the force required, we must be conservative in all our estimates of both a potential aggressor's capabilities and his intentions.

Security depends upon assuming a worst plausible case, and having the ability to cope with it. In that eventuality we must be able to absorb the total weight of nuclear attack on our country . . . and still be capable of damaging the aggressor to the point that his society would be simply no longer viable in twentieth-century terms. That is what deterrence of nuclear aggression means. It means the certainty of suicide to the aggressor, not merely to his military forces, but to his society as a whole.

The US needed thousands of nuclear weapons, the ability to destroy its enemy many times over, not for aggressive purposes, but in order to prevent the enemy from contemplating an aggressive first strike. The US did not want a first-strike capability, but neither would it allow the Soviets to achieve one. 'We will never permit our own assured-destruction capability to drop to a point at which a Soviet first-strike capability is even remotely feasible.'[45] The strategy left little room for arms reduction, since any reduction, unless duplicated by the adversary, increased susceptibility to a first strike and reduced the capacity to deliver a second strike. Mutual distrust was a necessary component of mutually assured destruction.

At the time, the differences between the two sides were irreconcilable; they seemed not to inhabit the same planet. Yet both behaved in a remarkably similar fashion. They had the same fears and reacted to those fears in the same way. 'We felt that they were trying to take over the . . . world and actually we were . . . their largest stumbling blocks in that effort,' Denchy recalled. Mikhail Mokrinski, a Soviet bomber pilot, used virtually the same language: 'The Americans were aggressors who wanted to conquer the whole world and we had to protect the world.'[46]

After the Cuban Missile Crisis, tensions between the superpowers cooled. Khrushchev's idea of peaceful coexistence was realized. But détente was built upon military security, not political agreement. While the world felt safer, safety was based upon an inexorable expansion of nuclear arsenals. By 1969 the superpowers were, between them, spending more than $50 million a day on nuclear armaments. The two sides felt secure because each had the ability to destroy the world many times over. MAD might not have been madness, but neither was it very sane.

CHAPTER 15

How We Learned to Stop Worrying and Love the Bomb

Shortly after the Trinity test, William Wyre, who lived near Alamogordo, spotted soldiers with little black boxes outside his home. 'I went out there and asked them what they were doing and they said they were looking for radioactivity. Well, we had no idea what radioactivity was back then. I told them we didn't even have the radio on.' Some time later Wyre's beard turned white and his black cat turned into a tabby. But neither he nor his wife Helen was particularly worried. 'People weren't afraid of the government back then,' she recalled. 'It was a time of innocence. People were trusting. . . . It was a happy time to live.'[1]

The bomb destroyed this innocence, but not immediately. While scientists and philosophers (and scientists masquerading as philosophers) agonized about this new, terrible power, most Americans celebrated the Bomb, which seemed proof of their country's greatness. For them, the mushroom cloud symbolized not doom, but progress. The word 'atomic' suggested modernity, power and technological might. Most people believed Truman when he promised that mastery of the atom would lead to the 'happiest world the sun has ever shone upon'.[2]

At least one baby – Atomic Victory Trotter – was named in celebration of the bomb, as were dozens of racehorses: Cosmic Bomb, Atom Buster, Sir Atom, etc.[3] As Americans travelled the interstate highways in the 1950s and 1960s, they stayed at the Atomic Motel, ate submarine sandwiches at the Atomic Café, and sipped potent Atomic Cocktails at the Atomic Saloon. In 1946, General Mills offered an Atomic Bomb Ring for fifteen cents and a Kix cereal boxtop. The company was inundated with 750,000 orders. Jewellery of a different sort was sold on New York's Fifth Avenue:

BURSTING FURY – Atomic Inspired Pin and Earring. New fields to conquer with Atomic jewellery. The pearled bomb bursts into a fury of dazzling colors in mock rhinestones, emeralds, rubies and sapphires. . . . As daring to wear as it was to drop the first atom bomb. Complete set $24.75.[4]

The 1947 Manhattan telephone directory listed forty-five companies using the word 'atomic' in their names, including the Atomic Undergarment Company – makers, one presumes, of nuclear knickers.[5] When an AEC facility was built in southern Idaho, the small town that sprouted nearby called itself Atomic City. In Richland, Washington, the high school close to Hanford chose the name 'bombers' for their mascot. Johnson High School of Savannah, Georgia, called themselves the Atom Smashers, in recognition of the nearby weapons plant. Children watched 'Atom Ant' cartoons and Boy Scouts competed for an atomic energy merit badge. In a 1946 radio show, Bob Hope joked that Valentine's Day messages should read: 'Will you be my little geranium, until we are both blown up by uranium?'[6]

The Bomb became an immediate Hollywood star. In 1946, MGM produced *The Beginning or the End*, a docu-drama about the Manhattan Project. The film was originally supposed to provide sober warning. The Oak Ridge chemist Edward Tomkins wrote to his former high school student, the actress Donna Reed, suggesting that Hollywood should 'tell the people of the world some inherent facts about the bomb'. Before long, however, national interest and the pursuit of profit proved the enemy of honesty. Groves, who was given final script approval (plus $10,000 in consultancy fees), made sure the film did not cause alarm. While it did not hide the weapon's destructive power, it cast the scientists as American heroes and asserted that Hiroshima saved lives. In one scene, Matt Cochran, a physicist, sacrifices his life in order to prevent a nuclear accident. Before he dies, he writes a last letter to his pregnant wife:

> Atomic energy is the hand [God] has extended to lift us from the ruins of war and lighten the burdens of peace. . . . We have found a path so filled with promise that when we walk down it we will know that everything that came before the discovery of atomic energy was the dark ages.

'If our sin as scientists was to make and use the atomic bomb', Szilard remarked after the film's release, 'then our punishment was to watch *The Beginning or the End*.'[7]

Producers of action films welcomed the dramatic potency nuclear power provided. One of the first was *The Atomic City* (1952), in which the son of a brilliant physicist is kidnapped by an evil Communist eager to secure nuclear secrets. The message is clear: Americans could be trusted with the Bomb, Communists could not. The credibility of the stories was enhanced by the real-life exploits of Fuchs and the Rosenbergs. That propaganda should masquerade as entertainment was nothing new, but this mixture was doubly potent when applied to the Bomb, which combined mystery and suspense with enormous power. Destruction of apocalyptic proportions had suddenly become a matter of fact, not mere science fiction.

Songwriters took to the atomic theme with great enthusiasm, capital-izing on the temper of the times by weaving political messages into their work. During the Korean War, Jackie Doll and His Pickled Peppers sang:

> There'll be fire, dust and metal, flying all around,
> And the radioactivity will burn them to the ground
> If there's any Commies left they'll be all on the run
> If General MacArthur drops the atomic bomb.[8]

Lowell Blanchard and the Valley Trio managed to combine Bomb and Jesus in a single melody:

> Everybody's worried 'bout the 'tomic bomb
> But nobody's worried 'bout the day my Lord will come.
> When hell hit! Great God Almighty! Like an atom bomb,
> When He comes, when He comes . . .[9]

Exploring the same theme, Hawkshaw Hawkins insisted that

> The Lord held out his mighty hand
> So that others in the world might understand
> That wars could never be and this world it must be free
> When they found the mighty, mighty Atomic Power.[10]

On the flip side of Bill Haley's 1954 hit single 'Rock Around the Clock' was a song called 'Thirteen Women', a post-apocalypse nuclear fantasy in which a bomb devastates a town leaving just one male and thirteen female survivors. What results is the ultimate male utopia – the women attend to the man in every conceivable way. Striking a chord for equality, Ann-Margret reversed the roles in her 'Thirteen Men'.*

As a sexual metaphor, the Bomb was particularly well-endowed. There was nothing little about Little Boy. The new missiles were long, hard and sleek, in marked contrast to the stubby bombs of the pre-atomic age. In Cold War films, tankers copulate with bombers (in *Dr Strangelove* to the tune of 'Try a Little Tenderness'). The bikini bathing suit appeared just four days after the first test on Bikini Island, the designer explaining that he gave it that name 'because of its explosive, dangerous potential'.[11] Just

---

* While musicians and comedians made extensive use of the idea that sexual inhibition would evaporate after the Bomb dropped, 'experts' felt genuine worry. An article in the *Journal of Social Hygiene* in 1951 warned that counsellors and clergy should be prepared for an explosion of sexual hunger after a nuclear attack. Shelters, the article advised, should be stocked with adequate supplies of penicillin to combat a VD epidemic.

a month after Hiroshima, *Life* featured a full page spread of Linda Christians, a bathing beauty who MGM press agents dubbed the 'anatomic bomb'.[12] Capitalizing upon the metaphor, songwriters offered tunes with twenty-megaton sexual energy. Amos Milburn's 'Atomic Baby' could 'do more damage than five atomic bombs'. With tongue firmly in cheek, Sheldon Allman sang:

> Radioactive mama, hold me tight
> Radioactive mama treat me right
> Radioactive mama we'll reach critical mass tonight
> Well when we get together clear away the crowd
> There won't be nothing left except a mushroom shaped cloud
> . . .
> Well since I kissed you baby, that evening in the park,
> I lost my hair and eyebrows and my teeth shine in the dark.[13]

Even Doris Day, that paragon of propriety, got in on the act. In a little known Broadway musical, an 'attractive hick' gives her a 'radioactive tic', making her heart beat like a Geiger counter. Rather fortunately, the musical had a short half-life.

The welcome given to the bomb was due in part to widespread ignorance about radioactivity. In the inter-war period, radiation (and radium in particular) had been touted as a great panacea. Physicians and patent medicine peddlers celebrated the therapeutic effects of the magical rays. Radium salves, facial creams, inhalants and injections were sold freely over the counter. A drink called Radithor was briefly marketed in the 1930s. Most people were familiar with X-rays, which were thought to be entirely harmless. Coin-operated fluoroscopes could be found next to pinball machines in amusement arcades. The Foot-O-Scope, which enabled precise fitting of shoes, made its first appearance in Chicago in the 1920s. Eventually shoe stores nationwide bought 10,000 such machines, which remained in operation until the early 1950s. Children delighted in seeing their toes wiggle inside their shoes.

Though scientists were more knowledgeable than the public about radiation, their level of ignorance is still astonishing by today's standards. When technicians were sent to the Trinity site immediately after the blast, the radiation-exposure limit was set at five roentgens per individual, a level now considered highly dangerous. In 1946, visitors were briefly allowed into the Trinity site to collect Trinitite, and a motel in Socorro sold it as souvenirs. A bank in Santa Fe gave samples to new customers, and one woman was known to have made a necklace out of it. In late September 1945, more than 1,000 US servicemen were sent to Hiroshima and Nagasaki to help reconstruction, remaining on site until late autumn. So confident were the authorities about the safety of the area that they did not provide the soldiers with protective clothing or dosimeter badges, nor did they instruct them in basic precautionary measures. Water was taken from local reservoirs.

Behind the scenes, highly secret experiments were being conducted to study the effects of radiation on human beings. Between 1945 and 1947, thirty-one patients at hospitals in New York, Oak Ridge, San Francisco and Chicago were injected with bomb grade plutonium, without their full knowledge. When the details of the experiments were finally released, the son of one of the women injected remarked bitterly: 'I was over there fighting the Germans who were conducting these horrific medical experiments. At the same time, my own country was conducting them on my mother.'[14] The similarity with Nazi Germany goes further. Inmates at prisons in Washington and Oregon had their testicles exposed to X-rays in order to determine the amount of radiation necessary to cause sterility. The exact same experiment was performed in German concentration camps. In 1950, one AEC physician admitted that the experiments had 'a little of the Buchenwald touch'.[15]

Until the early 1950s the official Army line was that no radioactive fallout had resulted from the Trinity blast, in spite of evidence to the contrary. Hereford cattle, grazing on the Chupadera Mesa thirty miles from ground zero, lost hair on their backs soon after the blast. The hair grew back, but without colour. The Los Alamos Health Division bought four of the radiated cows which became instant celebrities; dubbed 'atomic calves' or 'rada cows' they toured the region like circus freaks.[16] Plans were put forward to establish an atomic bomb museum, with the radiated cows a key exhibit. Eventually, the government bought up all the affected cattle and kept them under close observation. When no other abnormal symptoms developed and they reproduced normally, they became propaganda for the Bomb – evidence that fallout was nothing to fear. Needless to say, the AEC did not publicize the fact that some years later many of the cows developed skin cancers.

Since the public needed to be sold on the virtues of a nuclear arsenal, the gory details from Hiroshima and Nagasaki were suppressed. War correspondent Wilfred Burchett got to Hiroshima on 9 September 1945 and found thousands of people dying of a mysterious disease not yet identified. After reporting this fact in the *Daily Express*, he was bullied by occupation officials who took his camera and notebooks, while accusing him of falling prey to 'Jap propaganda'.[17] When the physicist Harry Daghlian was hospitalized on 21 August 1945 after a criticality experiment at Los Alamos went awry, the government blocked all reporting of his condition, since it would otherwise confirm the suffering of the Hiroshima victims. Within five hours of his death on 14 September,

Daghlian's mother received a life insurance cheque for $10,000, courtesy of the US government.

Radiation, if spoken about at all, continued to be presented as a great panacea. A feature in *Collier's* in May 1947 predicted a 'golden age of atomic medicine'. Accompanying the article was a montage of a smiling man emerging from a mushroom cloud leaving his wheelchair behind. Chancellor Robert Hutchins of the University of Chicago predicted that 'The atomic city will have a central diagnostic laboratory but only a small hospital, if any at all, for most human ailments will be cured as rapidly as they are diagnosed.' Lewis Strauss admitted that radiation could cause mutations, 'but we should remember that these changes can be produced also by any number of agents from sunlight down to the garden crocus'. 'I thought some of the stuff . . . was pretty silly,' Herbert York recalled of the AEC-inspired propaganda effort. 'They began to talk about radiation exposure in terms of sunshine units. One of the dumbest phrases to come down the pike in a long time. You know, designed to somehow put a happy face on it.'[18]

Groves told a Congressional hearing that death from radiation was 'very pleasant'.[19] He maintained that those suffering from mild exposure, such as employees at Los Alamos who received an accidental dose, needed only a short vacation and they would be right as rain. In 1955, *US News and World Report* published an article clearly designed to downplay fears inspired by Hiroshima. It pointed out that only 100 survivors out of 190,000 had contracted leukaemia and that no genetic damage was apparent in children born after the bombing. 'The Atomic Age is here,' the magazine concluded, 'let's not be afraid of it.'[20]

One civil defence pamphlet, still in use as late as 1972, attempted to explain fallout in terms the public would understand. The pamphlet told how alpha, beta, and gamma rays, produced in the explosion, could penetrate the skin and cause illness. But these same rays, the pamphlet explained, had enormous potential for good. They would provide clean energy, medicines and cures for otherwise fatal illnesses. The invisible rays were personified as bathing beauties with little banners across their chests identifying them as alpha, beta, or gamma.[21] The massive PR effort apparently worked: a Gallup poll in 1948 found 61 per cent of college-educated Americans thought atomic energy would do more good than harm.[22]

While the government gave radiation a happy face, science fiction writers like Isaac Asimov, Theodore Sturgeon and Chandler Davis suggested otherwise, writing of cataclysmic war and horrible mutation. Because of Hiroshima, these topics were now placed in a contemporary setting, rather than as some far off fantasy. Radiation and mutation also provided a rich source of inspiration for filmmakers. In *The Atomic Kid* (1952), Mickey Rooney accidentally suffers a massive dose of radiation which causes his eyes to spin and his skin to glow. These qualities somehow render him valuable to the enemy – enter stage right some shifty characters with appalling Russian accents. Rooney is eventually saved by the group principally to blame for his condition, namely the military. His rescuers manage to find a cure – the film ends with the kid atomic no longer. The radiation theme was again visited in *The Amazing Colossal Man* in which an officer exposed to harmful rays begins to grow at the rate of eight feet per day. Again, however, the military comes to the rescue, this time destroying the giant, but not before he destroys Las Vegas. An inevitable sequel followed with *The Amazing Colossal Woman*.

Radiation has the opposite effect in *The Incredible Shrinking Man*, in which the protagonist receives a harmful dose when a radioactive cloud engulfs his boat (an incident perhaps intentionally reminiscent of the *Lucky Dragon*). Shortly afterwards he begins to shrink, an effect which offered enormous creative opportunity for set designers. Beneath the action plot about a man who finds his world more threatening by the day, there runs a metaphoric message about humanity growing increasingly impotent against the threat of nuclear power. A similarly serious message is conveyed in *The Day the Earth Caught Fire* (1961) which starts with the earth being knocked off its axis by atomic testing. The Russians and Americans are forced to cooperate in order to correct the problem. Though the ambiguous ending leaves it unclear whether their effort is successful, there is no escaping the underlying message about the need for international cooperation.

Film audiences in the 1950s feasted on an endless diet of mutation. *Godzilla*, a film about a giant reptile which terrorizes Japan, appeared around the same time as the Bravo shot. The lizard's ability to spit nuclear fire was an allegorical representation of the threat of nuclear war. In *Them!*, the western United States is terrorized by colonies of giant ants. While most viewers saw a run-of-the-mill science fiction movie, the film was in truth a serious statement about the dangers of testing. In the same genre, but less earnest, was *The Night of the Lepus*, in which the world is threatened by giant bunnies.

While mutant films were intended as entertainment, they inevitably raised awareness of the Bomb, if in distorted form. They reinforced an image of science out of control, of man losing the ability to shape his world, and of impending doom. Within the space of a decade, the naïveté displayed by William Wyre in 1945 had disappeared. It was difficult to maintain innocence in a world so explosive. Nuclear weapons allowed, for the first time, the word 'apocalypse' to be used literally. When, in the mid-1950s, an eight-year-old boy was asked by a *Time* magazine reporter what he wanted to be when he grew up, he replied: 'Alive!'

But, though fear of the Bomb was undoubtedly present, few were actually consumed by fear. Ordinary people had an extraordinary capacity to ignore its perils. 'I am only one of many people who take life as it comes,' one respondent told a Cornell University survey. 'If I have to live in a country where there are earthquakes, surely there would be no point in my going to bed every night in fear of an earthquake.' Another person assumed a fatalistic attitude to his own frailty: 'Why should my heart be heavy over something I can't possibly control?' Einstein complained that the American public, 'having been warned of the horrible nature of atomic warfare, has done nothing about it and to a large extent has dismissed the warning from its consciousness'.[23] What is remarkable is not the complacency, but rather that some found it surprising. A society cannot exist in constant fear. To worry about the bomb made life impossible, therefore the solution was not to worry. Only a select few could translate their fear into a determined campaign of protest.

The Russian bomb should perhaps have destroyed this complacency, but it did not do so. In February 1950, one poll found that 68 per cent of respondents thought that the Soviet Union would use an atomic weapon against the United States. But distrust of the Russians merely increased trust in nuclear weapons. Though polls consistently revealed that fear of war outpaced other concerns (such as the economy), they did not show an attendant abhorrence of the Bomb. In fact, it seems the American public wanted more and bigger bombs, which promised security in a threatening world. In 1950, one poll found 73 per cent in favour of a bomb 'which might be a thousand times more powerful than the atom bomb'. When asked specifically about the H-bomb a short time later, 69 per cent approved of the idea. The Bravo incident had little effect on this support, with 71 per cent supporting continued improvement of the hydrogen bomb through testing in the South Pacific. Similar support was apparent whenever, throughout the 1950s, polls asked whether the testing programme should be continued.[24]

Out in the middle of the Nevada Test Site there lies a weird collection of atomic artefacts. Prototype shelters sit battered and torn. A mock bridge sprouts from the desert, its huge I-beams twisted like a beer can. The area reminds one of the macabre bodies at Pompeii which still rigidly evoke a power that passed long ago. Amidst the rubble, there sits a bank vault. Back in the 1950s, American financial institutions wanted to find out how to protect their money in the event of nuclear war. They asked the nice chaps at the AEC to conduct an experiment. A vault was placed in the desert and encased in a cocoon of six-inch-thick reinforced concrete. Mock valuables were placed inside, the door was closed and a bomb exploded nearby. Today the vault lies intact, but the concrete and rebar are peeled away like the skin of a banana, indicating the direction of the blast. As a metaphor for the priorities of the nuclear age, it's perfect.

Like the fake money in that vault, American society had to be protected. The threat in question, however, was not actual war but rather fear of war. 'An adequate civil defence program', argued Paul Nitze in 1957, 'is of utmost importance because the freedom of the United States government to take strong actions in the cold war . . . will depend in increasing measure upon firm public morale.'[25] In order to maintain public support for the Bomb, the government encouraged citizens to believe that they could survive a nuclear attack. 'If there is an ultimate weapon', Val Peterson of the Federal Civil Defense Administration warned, 'it may well be mass panic – not the A-bomb.' As one expert attested, civil defence programmes were an emotional inoculation. FCDA pamphlets like 'Atomic Survival', 'Survival City' and 'Survival Under Atomic Attack' were designed not only to instruct, but also to maintain morale.[26] 'At first I thought civil defense made sense,' York reflected.

> But what . . . I discovered is it wasn't civil defense per se. They wanted civil defense in order to make sure that the American people would not be too frightened. . . . I remember talking with Nelson Rockefeller about it. He said, what we need to do is stiffen the backbone of the American people, that's why we need civil defense. Not to save lives, but to make people believe that they can survive a nuclear war. So they won't be so soft on Communism or so concerned about war. I said that's a dumb idea for having civil defense. It's not merely dumb, it's wrong.[27]

York's criticism went unheeded. Like the elaborate exercises in the Nevada desert, American civil defence was a carefully stage-managed performance designed to pull the wool over the people's eyes.

Formed in January 1951, the FCDA became the Bomb's PR agency. Katherine Graham Howard, one of its more prominent spokespersons, felt that her role was to 'prepare people to *live through* an atomic attack, not to die in one'.[28] New York ad agencies competed for the lucrative civil defence portfolio. Leading magazines like *Newsweek, US News and World Report, Collier's* and *Ladies' Home Journal* willingly provided space for 'informative' articles. Television networks, eager to demonstrate their patriotism, gave free airtime to FCDA broadcasts. The networks also aired live broadcasts of weapons tests; with H-bomb explosions attracting audiences in excess of 100 million. Cooperation was so close that it became virtually impossible to distinguish FCDA propaganda from independent reporting.

In the spirit of wartime, Hollywood joined the crusade. George Burns, Gracie Allen, Groucho Marx, Arthur Godfrey and Bing Crosby all volunteered their services to the FCDA. But the real star was undoubtedly the cartoon character Bert the Turtle.

> There was a turtle by the name of Bert.
> And Bert the Turtle was very alert.
> When danger threatened him he never got hurt.
> He knew just what to do.
> He'd duck and cover, duck and cover, duck and cover.
> He did what we all must learn to do.
> You and You and You and You
> Duck and cover, duck and cover, duck and cover.[29]

Young Americans were encouraged to imitate Bert by going into the 'duck and cover' position when the air raid warning sounded. By assuming the foetal position with hands interlocked behind the head, the individual could increase the chance of survival. Public service broadcasts sought to instil reflexive reactions to nuclear attack:

> Without warning you are startled by an intense flash of light. You have seconds before the shock wave will hit you, before the debris starts flying. Hit the dirt! Get behind the nearest and best shelter – a ditch, a depression of any kind – but get down![30]

In schools, duck and cover drills were taught alongside lessons about crossing the road and not talking to strangers. Schoolchildren were taught to assume the position underneath their desks; baby boomers grew up believing that a wooden desk would protect them from a 10-megaton blast.

The 1946 Strategic Bombing Survey put paid to comfortable assumptions that American cities might cope better than Hiroshima and Nagasaki. 'The . . . overwhelming bulk of the buildings in American cities could not stand up against an atomic bomb bursting a mile or a mile and a half from them,' the report maintained. The warning was intentionally pessimistic, designed to spur Americans to action. 'The almost unprotected, completely surprised cities of Japan suffered maximum losses from atomic bomb attack. If we recognize in advance the possible danger and act to forestall it, we shall at worst suffer minimum casualties and disruption.' In other words, 'despite its awesome power, [the atomic bomb] has limits of which wise planning will take prompt advantage'. The report drew attention to the fact that the few hundred people in Nagasaki who had gone to a shelter had survived, despite close proximity to ground zero. 'Without question, shelters can protect those who get to them against anything but a direct hit. Adequate warning will assure that a maximum number get to shelters.'[31]

Though vigilance was essential, awareness could not be allowed to turn into despair. This meant that the government had to toe a fine line between providing enough information about nuclear war and too much. Horror had to be emphasized, but so too did heroic scenarios of people surviving. The obsessive secrecy that governed all nuclear policy was designed as much to keep Americans ignorant of the Bomb's true nature, as it was to keep the Soviets in the dark. Thus, fallout was seldom discussed, ostensibly for reasons of security, but in truth so as to encourage the assumption that survival was possible.

The FCDA wanted to graft a military ethos onto domestic civilian routine, thus strengthening both the family and the nation. But Eisenhower stopped short of appointing a soldier to head the body, fearing that it would imply that society needed to be militarized in order to meet the Soviet threat. 'We can't be an armed camp,' he argued in 1953. 'We are not going to transfer ourselves into militarists. We are not going to be in uniform, going around yelling "Heil" anything.'[32] Toward this end, a centralized system was rejected, on the grounds that 'if too much of our national effort is expended for military and civil defense purposes, the very liberties we are trying to make secure will themselves be endangered'.[33] In other words, to protect freedom, actual protection was diluted. The American people retained the right to be apathetic, even if apathy endangered their lives.

At the Nevada Test Site, so-called 'Doom Towns' were constructed, with great attention to detail, in order to study civil defence. Typical houses were stocked with contemporary furniture, appliances, etc. On the coffee table were the latest magazines and popular foodstuffs stocked the refrigerator. The homes were populated with mannequins dressed in chain store fashions and cars were parked nearby. A bomb was then detonated. A film of one such test told viewers how to interpret the rubble:

> Remember this dining room group? . . . Injury, perhaps death in a tangle of debris – the result of being unprepared. House number one nearest ground zero – almost complete destruction, a mass of rubble and debris. Yet, in the lean-to shelter you discover indications that a human being might have survived the blast with simple protection.[34]

Some reporters, allowed to inspect the Doom Towns soon after the blast, could not resist lurid detail:

> People played by dummies lay dead and dying in basements, living rooms, kitchens, bedrooms. . . . A mannequin mother died horribly in her one-story house of precast concrete slabs. Portions of her plaster and paint body were found in three different areas. A mannequin tot . . . was blown out of bed

and showered with needle-sharp glass fragments. . . . A simulated mother was blown to bits in the act of feeding her infant baby food.[35]

The tone was not meant to promote pessimism, but rather an awakening. Americans were encouraged to conclude that these 'people' had only themselves to blame for not taking greater precautions. Houses by themselves would not provide protection. The residents of Doom Town were dummies. Clever people would survive.

The nuclear bomb would be defeated by the nuclear family. Since it was impossible for the government to protect everyone, responsibility was shifted to the family, in the process reinforcing cherished social patterns. 'The new stronghold of national security is our homes,' Howard proclaimed. Government publications outlined each family member's responsibilities. Father would supply the technological know-how and brute strength to build a shelter or reinforce the home. Mother was uniquely qualified to look after matters of health, food and hygiene. The children would perform the myriad small tasks necessary to survival, in the process learning valuable lessons about social responsibility. Underlying the message was the assumption that American society was inherently stronger because it was family-based – not communal or communistic.

The outward and visible sign of a stable family was a clean, well-maintained home. It followed, therefore, that the cleaner the home the better the chances of survival. In keeping with this theme, fallout was turned into an ordinary domestic challenge. It was simply dust and could be eradicated by wiping surfaces in the usual manner. The vacuum cleaner became an essential weapon in the Cold War. Fallout on the body could be washed away. Good housekeeping would defeat the Bomb.

These messages were driven home in *Panic in the Year Zero*, in which a typical middle-class family learns to cope with the traumatic aftermath of a nuclear attack. No practical advice was provided; the film instead concentrated on moral lessons about the personal qualities needed to survive. The family's initial difficulties are clearly due to lack of preparation and their inability to act as a team. In the end, however, they survive because they are a family, and are strengthened by what they have endured. And, no surprise, the father emerges as the wise, strong leader – the commander of the family unit. In other words, the qualities essential for coping in a nuclear war were, by coincidence, the very same qualities that made for a stable, morally righteous society. Clean-living, honest, upright, patriotic families would have the best chance of survival. Even if civil defence procedures were never actually needed, learning them would strengthen the American way of life.*

---

* One civil defence group placed the Bible top of the list of the most important things to take into a shelter.

In 1959, attention focused on the Powners – a typical nuclear family of husband, wife and three children – who went into a shelter in the basement of the Princeton psychology building where they were closely observed for two weeks. The results delighted psychologists and civil defence officials alike. The family emerged with 'a very positive attitude toward shelter life'. Only the middle child suffered from occasional low moods, while the three-year-old was kept contented with mild tranquillizers. As for the adults, they had whiskey to dull the sharp edges of confinement, not to mention an unexpurgated copy of *Lady Chatterley's Lover*. 'It really wasn't as bad as I thought,' Mr Powner confessed, presumably in reference to the shelter, not the book. 'Shelters are practical and I think everyone should build one in his own home.'[36]

The organizers of Project Hideaway (as it was called) were especially delighted by its effect on family relations. Mr Powner admitted that he had enjoyed spending more time with his children, and felt that his family had become closer. The children, forced to spend all hours together in a confined space, found ways to get along. In other words, the shelter was doubly advantageous: it protected the family *and* enhanced family values. The exercise also drove home a crucial message: chances of survival were linked to family stability. So pleased were the organizers with their experiment that they recommended that families might occasionally go into their shelter (*sans* bombs) just to spend time together. The overnight stay would offer undiluted togetherness punctuated by the 'excitement of camping out'.[37]

In 1959 *Life* magazine featured Melvin and Maria Mininson who spent their honeymoon in a backyard shelter. The stunt, organized by the Miami firm Bomb Shelters, Inc., attracted over 100 applicants. In exchange for spending two weeks in a 6 feet by 14 feet shelter where the temperature often exceeded 90° Fahrenheit, the Mininsons were given a real honeymoon in Mexico. Photos showed the couple collecting the items they intended to take into the shelter and then kissing as they entered. A fortnight later they emerged, bleary eyed, but satisfied that both their marriage and the idea of survival had been consummated.

Howard maintained that civil defence would allow families 'to keep their homes, not to lose them, to protect and preserve their families, not to scatter and dissolve them'.[38] But that was simply ad-speak. The family-centred approach relied on Soviet cooperation: the enemy would have to attack in the evening or at weekends, when parents and children were more likely to be together. A really cooperative enemy would time missiles to coincide with when the meal was done, the dishes tidied away* and the

---

* An untidy kitchen could be lethal in a nuclear attack. With dishes lying around, people could get killed by flying saucers.

family gathered around the television watching *Leave it to Beaver*. Civil
defence advice carefully avoided the more plausible scenario that an attack
might come when dad was at work, mom at home and the kids scattered
in different schools. In such a situation family stability would be irrelevant. The family would not even be able to use the shelter it had built for
itself. More realistic was the advice given by National School Studios,
which launched a scheme to provide identity badges for schoolchildren.
'Should it be necessary to evacuate the children during school hours it is
also necessary to identify them,' its memo to parents proclaimed much
more ominously than was probably intended.[39]

The family model on which civil defence advice was predicated was, in
truth, no longer typical. In 1950s America roles were more confused,
especially if mother, out of necessity or desire, worked outside the home.
The great irony of the Cold War is that officials tried consciously to reverse
the trend toward women's liberation stimulated by the two world wars.
This did not mean that women declined in importance, rather that their
importance was stressed in more traditional terms. 'They are the ones that
will do the cooking and they will do the mothering of the children and
the husbands,' Dr Stafford Warren of UCLA argued. Mothering 'satisfies
the woman and gets her mind on the immediate problem – the things she
can do and do well'.[40] Women were important because they were women,
not because they could do men's jobs. Howard maintained that civil defence
was the 'prudent extension of existing protective services' already
performed by women.[41] If, as the literature suggested, the home was the
first domino in the Cold War, mother was supremely important. After a
nuclear attack, society's recovery would have to start from the ground up
– from the home. 'Women were never so important as in the year 1951,
the sixth year of the Atomic Age,' Dorothy Houghton, of the General
Federation of Women's Clubs, argued. 'We bear greater responsibility than
ever before for the preservation of life.'[42]

It followed that the more skilled the housewife the more secure the
family and nation:

> In Grandma's day, her well-stocked pantry safeguarded the family against
> such emergencies as floods, blizzards, hurricanes and other devastations that
> rendered outside food sources inaccessible. Superbomb hazards of today
> furnish similar reasons for householders to maintain a 'Grandma's Pantry'
> with a 7-day stock of food supplies. . . .Grandma's Pantry, in homes of the
> Atomic Age, may save many thousands of lives.[43]

Preparing tasty dishes in the shelter would maintain morale. Betty
Crocker, the much-loved icon of General Mills, advised the FCDA on
post-Apocalypse cuisine, while one civil defence pamphlet suggested 'how

to . . . make do with bricks and rubble and grates that you might find so that you [can] cook'.[44] Cleanliness was also important since the tidy home was less susceptible to fire and less likely to harbour disease and infection. Howard told women that 'The highest military authorities in our country stressed . . . that good housekeeping is one of the best protections against fire in an atomic blast.'[45] An AAUW book on civil defence tested women on their civil defence awareness as it applied to their homes. Those who scored in the lowest group were told: 'you deserve what you get'.[46] In other words, nuclear annihilation was just reward for slovenliness.

In *House in the Middle* the FCDA spotlighted three typical houses in a row. The house on the left had been allowed to deteriorate structurally – Dad's fault. The one on the right was a mess inside – Mom's fault. The middle house was a model of cleanliness and good order. After the big bad wolf fired his nuclear weapons, the family in the middle managed to survive, while the other two were crushed by the weight of their own indolence. 'Remember, civil defense housekeeping saved the house in the middle,'[47] the film reminded those who still didn't get it.

Logic suggests that it would have made more sense to prepare people for the inevitable chaos of loved ones becoming separated and for the need to act communally by helping strangers. But this presumes that civil defence was designed to protect people, which it was not. Real protection required a realistic conception of the apocalypse. This was something the government did not want to encourage. Instead, blithe assumptions were piled together into a flimsy house of cards. The possibility that the family might be separated was addressed by provision of a 'welfare inquiry' card which would supposedly trigger an official search for the missing family member. This assumed that the bureaucracy to process these cards would survive. A 'safety notification card' would enable a person separated from his family to notify relatives of his whereabouts. The cards did not require postage, but did require a postal service and houses with mailboxes. Come rain, come snow, come nuclear annihilation, the mail would get through.

Experience from the Second World War had shown that civil defence was easier to provide to groups than to separate families. But such an approach did not harmonize with American individualism. It would not do to fight communism by adopting a communal approach. Thus, even though public shelters made strategic sense, the political reality favoured a home-centred approach. Self-help not only relieved the government of a huge financial burden, it also reinforced core values. If the people came to expect atomic welfare, they might, it was feared, soon demand social welfare. Behind the homilies about self-help lay a stark message: blanket protection was beyond the capacity of the political authority. This was apparent from the relatively meagre budget allocated the FCDA. From 1951–8 it survived on a total of $450 million, while the Department of Defense spent around $20 billion annually.

The FCDA accepted that government would need to provide 'temporary substitute arrangements' to ensure 'that no one goes without at least the minimum of food, clothing, shelter and other services necessary to maintain life'. But the emphasis was on temporary; relief schemes would be limited to about two weeks, after which the individual was supposed to fend for himself. One FCDA manual stressed: 'Individuals and families decrease the welfare load by taking steps for their own survival, maintenance and other welfare needs.'[48]

Occasionally, dissenting voices were heard. Congressman Chet Holifield thought the government relied too heavily on examples of the plucky British surviving the Blitz – 'the tin hats and sand buckets of the last war would seem rather pathetic in the awful glare of an atomic blast'. Others worried about the time limits placed on government assistance. 'When those ten days are up', one official remarked, 'there may still be 5,000 children with no parents, families with no homes, savings gone, and jobs gone. The organization for handling that kind of job is a stupendous one.'[49]

In keeping with the self-help ethic, Americans were encouraged to build their own shelters. These embodied everything good about America. The individual took control of his own fate. The family unit was preserved. Building the shelter echoed myths of the pioneer who, with his bare hands, carved his homestead out of the wilderness. Attempting to capitalize on the crisis, a Chicago Savings and Loan firm in 1959 offered a special financing scheme for building shelters. Potential borrowers were reminded that the shelter could double as a wine cellar, hobby room or a suitably soundproof place for children to practise the violin.

In truth, the homemade shelter was an example of government compromise. The first civil defence studies, published in 1950, envisaged a system of public and private shelters costing $3.1 billion, to be funded by federal and state taxes. Officials accepted that this would not protect everyone – to do so would cost perhaps one hundred times as much. 'If we try to construct shelters for all the people', James Wadsworth of the FCDA argued, 'the economy would not stand for it, the materials would not be there, the manpower would not be there, and the taxpayers would not stand for it.' Opposition arose not simply on budgetary grounds but also because of residual hostility to New Deal style public works programmes. Missouri Republican Murray Short warned that a comprehensive shelter programme could lead to a 'lot of vicious boondoggling and waste'.[50] But even the limited programme proved unpalatable; Congress refused to release the $3.1 billion requested.

The Truman government looked briefly at the idea of evacuation but concluded that a public transport system capable of allowing a mass exodus from cities simply did not exist. In any case, the idea was politically hazardous since it suggested that the bombs could not be survived, that panicked flight was the only option and that cities would be surrendered even before the bombs fell. But the big bombs of the 1950s, and particularly the problem of fallout, caused Eisenhower to look again at evacuation. A new plan involved moving 62 million people from designated target areas to reception centres fifteen to twenty miles outside cities. Evacuees were supposed to depart the moment the siren sounded and were not to detour to pick up family or friends. They were to arrange their own travel, which, in the American context, naturally meant private cars. Rural residents would help state and local officials with the care of their 'guests'. Planners anticipated that the stay would be short, with people returning to their homes within days or, at most, a week.

The best efforts of the Ad Council were required to paper over the flaws in this plan. If workers (mainly men) all jumped into their cars and headed out of town at the sound of the siren, how would their families get away? Where would the evacuees sleep, especially if the attack came in winter? How would city dwellers return to their homes within a week if those homes no longer existed? Remarking on the difficulty of selling the scheme, one senior official pointed out that 'no more serious challenge in the field of mass public education has ever confronted us'.[51]

Responding to the challenge, the FCDA staged 'Operation Alert', a series of mock air raid drills held around the country between 1954 and 1961. Pamphlets were sent to homes explaining the practice procedures and notices were posted everywhere to ensure maximum participation. 'PRAY FOR PEACE – PREPARE FOR SURVIVAL' the billboards pronounced. These drills, while touted as a huge success, in truth highlighted the impracticality of evacuation. Just as the government could not hope to provide shelters for every citizen, so too it could not hope to train every citizen to escape. Granted, some impressive demonstrations were staged, like when 37,000 schoolchildren were evacuated from Mobile, Alabama in 1955, but these were simply vast exercises in participatory theatre, carefully stage-managed by an army of FCDA directors.

One high profile exercise occurred in 1955 when 15,000 federal employees, including the President, were evacuated from Washington to an encampment in rural Virginia. 'President Eisenhower leads the way in a test evacuation of the entire executive branch,' a newsreel subsequently proclaimed. 'The chief executive heads for a secret retreat. The first time the government has abandoned the capital since it was burned in the war of 1812.'[52] From the reception centre, Eisenhower sent soothing words: 'We're here to determine whether or not the government is prepared in time of emergency to continue the functions of government so there shall be no interruption in business that must be carried on.' He concluded by urging the American people to pray 'that this kind of disaster never comes to the United States'.[53] In private, Eisenhower called the exercises futile.

Though the media generally played along with the government on matters of civil defence, scepticism occasionally surfaced. *Newsweek* reported that, in a mock evacuation of the Rockefeller Center, thousands of workers had ignored the sirens, including some civil defence officials. More damaging were the doubts about the feasibility of the scheme. Planners in Milwaukee calculated that roads would become so choked with traffic that it would take over seven hours to evacuate all 870,000 residents of the city.

The FCDA's response had an air of desperation. Peterson suggested that residents of Chicago and New York were already experts at evacuation since they practised it every day on their commute. When asked about the thousands of citizens who would not make it to the reception centres before the bomb dropped, AEC chairman Willard Libby stated that they 'could merely dig a hole and crawl in it and stay there for a few hours'.[54] Peterson suggested that highways could be equipped with buried concrete pipes into which evacuees unable to reach the centres could crawl.

No amount of preparation could overcome simple apathy. On 22 July 1957, at 4.30 a.m., a fire-alarm operator in Schenectady, New York accidentally set off the city's air raid siren. Out of a population of over 100,000, only one man heeded the warning, packing his pregnant wife into his car and driving several hours into the countryside, before turning back when his car radio reported no news of an attack. Mayor Samuel Stratton subsequently confessed that he simply sat up in bed and then pulled up the covers and went back to sleep. Though some residents jammed police phone lines (precisely what they were not supposed to do) most reacted like Stratton. The county civil defence director subsequently claimed that the population obviously knew how to tell a false alarm from a real one, but, in truth, the incident revealed that most people wanted nothing to do with civil defence.[55]

A few people expressed their disapproval through active dissent. Mary Sharmat objected vehemently to Operation Alert, refusing to take part in the 1959 exercise. 'I felt that nuclear air-raid drills taught fear and hate towards an enemy', she later explained, 'and I could not . . . [obey] a bad law.' A responsible housewife, she prepared a roast beef for her family before starting her career as a protester. 'If I were to be in prison for awhile, they would have plenty of roast beef for sandwiches.' She realized the importance of appearing respectable and therefore took her small son with her to reinforce this image. 'For the occasion, I wore a black and white checkered cotton suit with matching red accessories. Jimmy wore a new blue linen outfit that looked adorable. When arrested, we would appear our very best. Newspapers could never identify us as "beat-niks".'

At first, civil defence authorities could not fathom why anyone would refuse to comply. The police, feeling decidedly uncomfortable, could not bring themselves to arrest Sharmat, thus denying her the publicity she wanted. But before long she discovered that other women had done the same thing elsewhere in the city. They decided to organize.

> We had a strong weapon in the hand of any woman; the telephone. We felt that if we devoted an hour a day on the telephone for the next year, together our efforts would be able to locate eight, maybe ten, mothers who would agree to refuse to take shelter together in a group.

By the following year's exercise, the group had expanded to over 500 people, much to the chagrin of the New York police. On the eve of the protest, the police chief phoned Sharmat, 'shaking with tension. He said that the police did not wish to arrest any ladies. He begged us to stay home. He was sincerely concerned about the children. He asked if there would be any resistance to arrest as the police found it most embarrassing to "manhandle" a woman.' As it turned out, the protest had grown too big. Sharmat wanted mass arrests, but the police and civil defence authorities refused to comply. Only twenty-eight random arrests were made, mostly of women who appeared 'disreputable' – i.e. dressed in trousers and sneakers. By the following year, protests had spread across the country. The police, annoyed at having to arrest respectable women, pleaded with Civil Defence authorities to cancel future exercises. Operation Alert was cancelled after 1961 (but not, according to the authorities, because of the protests).[56]

Opposition of a different sort was organized by SANE, the National Committee for a Sane Nuclear Policy. It was formed in 1957 when a disparate group of high profile peace activists reached critical mass. Norman Cousins of the *Saturday Review* and Clarence Pickett of the American Friends Service Committee were selected as co-chairmen. SANE followed a course rather similar to that of CND, though its demonstrations were rather more modest affairs. Given the reputation of Cousins and Pickett, the group could not easily be ignored, but its effect on public perceptions of the arms race was minuscule. Opposition to the bomb was seldom manifested in an active desire to get rid of it.

The greatest mistake of the anti-nuclear campaigners was perhaps their stubborn reliance upon fear as a mechanism for arousing opposition. In an article in *Collier's* in January 1946, the chemist Harold Urey declared: 'I write this to frighten you. I'm a frightened man, myself. All the scientists I know are frightened – frightened for their lives – and frightened for *your* life.'[57] From the scientists' revolt of 1946, through CND and SANE, to the campaigns of recent years, one notes a consistent tendency to deploy grim images of ubiquitous death. Appropriate though these images might be, ordinary people do not want to live in fear. Instead of arousing action, the images encourage apathy. 'Scaring the daylights out of everyone so no one can think, inducing hysteria and unreasoning fear,' Lilienthal complained in 1947, 'is not going to get us anywhere . . . Fear is an unreliable ally; it can never be depended on to produce good.'[58]

The BBC took a similar view. In 1966, it produced *The War Game*, a feature-length documentary about the aftermath of a nuclear attack on Britain. The attack results as the logical consequence of the massive retaliation strategy: the US threatens to use atomic weapons in Vietnam, the USSR threatens to occupy Berlin, NATO and the Warsaw Pact face off in Eastern Europe, and the bombs start to fall. The film, which uses mock interviews and newsreels, shows people being asphyxiated in fallout shelters, a child ripped from its mother's arms by the nuclear wind, police using shotguns to put the injured out of their misery. The film won an Academy award in 1967 and the *Observer* thought it 'may be the most important film ever made'. But the BBC declined to screen it on the grounds that it was 'too horrifying'.[59] It would not be shown for another twenty years.

With evacuation impossible and public shelters too costly, concerned citizens were left to look after themselves. Government pronouncements made a virtue of necessity, arguing that 'The national fallout shelter policy is based *firmly* on the philosophy of the obligation of each property-owner to provide protection on his own premises.' In truth, private shelters harmonized with public desire: people did not want to flee their homes, nor did they want to huddle with strangers. One FCDA official praised a citizen's request for blueprints:

> Your typically 'American' attitude of accepting the responsibility for thinking about the protection of your own family . . . and not asking for financial assistance from the government to do your job for you is most encouraging. I am sure that most of our citizens will act and think just as you are doing. This attitude makes our democratic way of life in the US worth fighting for.[60]

But, as with evacuation schemes, government shelter policy revealed deep ignorance. Officials failed to realize that only 62 per cent of American homes were owner occupied and only half had access to a basement. No consideration was given to the large number of families who lived in apartments. The shelter issue had great potential to divide the haves from the have-nots. The *New York Times* reported that some residents were trying to construct shelters secretly so that neighbours wouldn't invade when the bombs started falling. The Catholic magazine *America* advised that it was ethically permissible to shoot anyone who tried to break into one's shelter.[61] In a letter to Kennedy, Arthur Schlesinger warned that private shelters undermined 'the sense of community cooperation which will be indispensable in the case of attack. It is an invitation to barbarism.'[62]

Practical advice was often inappropriate to the payload of weapons available. 'Operation Doorstep' (1953) and 'Operation Cue' (1955) at the Nevada Test Site were supposed to offer lessons useful to private shelter builders, but the government failed to mention that the bombs used in those exercises were about the size of Little Boy, or one hundred times less powerful than the Soviet weapons actually targeted on America. The test houses were painted white to reflect the heat of the explosion, and contained no electrical wiring, gas pipes or oil furnaces, so as to reduce the risk of fire. With tongue in cheek, *Time* concluded that the test had demonstrated that 'shelters will protect some people who happen to live in wooden houses at the proper distance from an explosion that does not set the houses on fire or spray them with radioactivity'.[63] Nor was it mentioned that when the blast hit, everything inside the house – perfume bottles, knick-knacks, the toaster, the dog – turned into a lethal missile. As the men in SAC used to say, 'if the bomb doesn't kill you the flying toilet seats will'.[64]

One NTS exercise involved lining up various cars to test their resilience to nuclear explosion. The results delighted the FCDA, which suddenly saw millions of mobile bomb shelters. A pamphlet called *Four Wheels to Survival* was quickly rushed into print. 'Shelter is an unexpected bonus you get from your car,' it announced. 'More importantly, the car provides a small movable house. You can get away in it – then live, eat, and sleep in it.'[65] Rather more bizarre was a handbook produced in 1962 which showed a family escaping to sea in a cabin cruiser. John Kenneth Galbraith jokingly remarked to Kennedy that it was 'a design for saving Republicans and sacrificing Democrats . . . I am not at all attracted by a pamphlet which seeks to save the better elements of the population, but in the main writes off those who voted for you.'[66]

All the hard work by the FCDA could easily be undone by Hollywood, which persisted in exploiting the Bomb's potential for horror. In 1959, the film version of Nevil Shute's *On the Beach*, starring Gregory Peck, Ava Gardner and Fred Astaire, focused attention on the sinister ubiquity of fallout. The film, like the book, had a massive worldwide impact. Alarmed by its effect, the *New York Daily News* complained that it pandered to 'Western defeatists and/or traitors who yelp for scrapping the H-bomb'.[67] Eisenhower's civil defence director Leo Hoegh considered it 'very harmful because it produced a feeling of utter hopelessness, thus undermining . . . efforts to encourage preparedness'.[68]

★ ★ ★

Cold War rhetoric clouded debate over the best way to protect the people. The 'communal' approach adopted by the Soviets was continually lambasted, without any objective assessment of what the USSR was actually doing about civil defence. Katherine Howard attacked the Soviet's 'evil regimentation':

> We know of at least one nation's home defense program that is heavily manned by men and women who have no choice as to whether or not they wish to participate. . . . Their duties are thrust upon them . . . by the same iron-fisted bureaucracy that regulates every other activity in their daily lives.[69]

Behind Howard's criticism there lurked a basic truth: the Soviet civil defence system was more comprehensive than the American and provided better protection. This was in part because the Soviets perceived no ideological objection to communal shelters. But the main explanation for the difference was because greater effort was devoted to the problem in the USSR. While the Americans talked endlessly about the issue, the Soviets took action. At the height of the Cold War, some 70,000 government officials administered a complex system of shelters, evacuation planning and leadership dispersal. Placement and construction of defence industry facilities took consideration of the need to protect them in the event of nuclear war. In practice, this meant a highly dispersed armaments industry.

Keen to make neglect seem virtuous, American officials argued that their limited programme underlined the nation's peaceful intent. In contrast, it was argued that the Soviets had instituted a more comprehensive civil defence system because they were preparing for attack. One American study in the 1970s claimed that the Soviets could, by protecting the population, keep their losses to under 10 million, in other words, less than half what they suffered in the Second World War. The effort, so the argument went, was designed to make a nuclear war tolerable and therefore winnable, or, at the very least, to diminish the deterrent power of the American arsenal. Many Americans found it difficult to accept that Soviet civil defence might have the same motivation as in the US, namely the desire to preserve society and save lives.

The Soviets spent 1 per cent of their military budget on civil defence; the Americans 0.1 per cent. In neither country, therefore, was protection of the population a significant concern relative to the procurement of arms. Both believed that offence provided the best defence. The Soviets also encountered the same problem of selling preparedness to a sceptical public. Maria Stepanova, a Soviet civil defence instructor, recalled: 'When people began to realize how dangerous these weapons were, they used to joke that if a nuclear bomb was dropped nearby all there'd be left to do was to cover yourself with a white bedsheet and crawl to the cemetery. If you could make it to the cemetery, that is.'[70]

Howard was right; in their approach to civil defence the Americans steered clear of regimentation. But the great problem with a voluntary programme is that it required volunteers. In 1951, the University of Michigan found that only 64 per cent of those polled gave an accurate response when asked what the term 'civil defence' actually meant. The same survey revealed that 68 per cent believed that American armed forces could protect cities from nuclear attack. Three years later the researchers found that only 17 per cent were aware of local civil defence programmes and only two per cent had participated actively. In 1952, the FCDA discovered that only 20 per cent of the population had taken any steps, no matter how minor, to prepare for attack. Though the vast majority preferred shelters to evacuation, only a tiny number were willing to build them. In September 1951 the *New York Times* reported that a recently established firm devoted to private shelter construction had closed due to lack of business. Figures for actual construction vary widely but all confirm that enthusiasm was minimal. One 1960 survey counted just 1,565 private shelters in the thirty-five states surveyed, or one for every 100,000 individuals.[71] Despite this apathy, a consistent majority of urban dwellers sincerely believed that the Soviets wanted to destroy their city. In other words, though Americans expected war, they were not prepared to do anything about it.

The civil defence agencies made repeated attempts to rouse the people out of their apathy. Perhaps the most bizarre was an LP produced by the Office of Civil Defense entitled *Complacent Americans*. The businessman narrator, in a manner reminiscent of George Bailey in *It's a Wonderful Life*, reflects on his past life after being killed in a nuclear explosion:

> I, the complacent American, thinking that no one would ever attack an American city. And I told my friends that nuclear war would never happen. . . . but it did. I always thought I was a good American – patriotic and civic minded. But I was wrong. I failed myself and my country.

The complacent American watches people safely waiting out the attack in fallout shelters and reflects that he preferred to go bowling instead of attending the preparedness meetings. He recalls that he has tickets to a baseball game, but 'I know now that there will be no tomorrow night because Death does not attend a baseball game'. Unlike George Bailey, the complacent American does not get a second chance. 'Shall I pray? My God, I guess it is too late for even prayers now.' Side Two presents a more sober talk by a Civil Defense official on how people can avoid a similar fate. It concludes: 'Follow all these rules and you WILL survive!'[72]

'Civil defence is a farce,' *Harper's* argued in 1955, 'and a farce only slightly relieved by the fact that very few people ever thought it otherwise.'[73] Judged by the standard of providing protection, the programme was a massive failure. But the beauty of the voluntary system was that it gave the impression that something was being done, while leaving it to individual citizens to decide for themselves if action was appropriate. 'We do not feel that the Federal Government should impose requirements on the personal affairs of any family,' one FCDA publication assured. 'There is one thing that the Federal Government should not be asked to do – and that is to make a decision *for you*.'[74] The entire programme had more to do with protecting values than protecting people.

One consistent theme emerged from opinion polls: the public thought civil defence futile. Gone were the innocence and naïveté of 1945. Most people understood what the Bomb could do. Though they did not object to the Bomb, they did revolt against the lies told on its behalf. They questioned how assurances about the survivability of nuclear war could possibly accord with hydrogen bombs hundreds of times more powerful than Fat Man. Government pronouncements about fallout seemed equally hollow. Nor did it look good that well dressed, respectable housewives were taking their young children out into the streets to protest against Operation Alert. But while this growing scepticism toward the government's message alarmed bureaucrats, it was never converted into a solid opposition to the Bomb. Most people still felt that protection lay in more bombs. In the end, the American government reacted quite cleverly to latent protest. It simply stopped talking about the bomb, stopped telling people they could survive and stopped encouraging them to take steps to protect themselves. The talking stopped, and so too did the unease.

Some time after 1963, Bert the Turtle retired and took up quiet residence in the film archives. Air raid siren tests stopped screeching every Monday at noon.* Schoolchildren neither ducked nor covered. Backyard shelters were neglected and in some cases dismantled (no easy task, given that they were built to withstand a nuclear blast). Anti-nuclear groups imploded – reduced to tiny collections of diehards arguing with each other over arcane policy. In early 1964 the Student Peace Union decided to disband when only twenty-five delegates showed up to its national conference. America had, it seems, learned to stop worrying and love the bomb.

The threat of nuclear war did not disappear. But the peaceful resolution of the Cuban Missile Crisis seemed to suggest that the superpowers

---

* When I was growing up I thought that if the Soviets were really clever they would attack on a Monday at noon.

would act rationally in a crisis and stop short of destroying the world. Though missile arsenals continued to grow, so too did a spirit of détente. Meanwhile, the ban on atmospheric testing buried the annoying problem of fallout. Other matters distracted attention from bombs, including the war in Vietnam, civil rights, sex, drugs and rock and roll.

Cuba brought the superpowers to their senses. Out of that crisis came the Limited Test Ban treaty, followed by other agreements which reinforced a sense of restraint. The Hotline Agreement allowed the American President and the Soviet Premier to communicate more effectively in the event of a crisis.* The 1967 Outer Space Treaty deemed that weapons could not be placed in orbit around the earth or on the moon. In the same year, the treaty of Tlatelolco established that Latin America was to be a nuclear free zone, though Argentina refused to ratify. The 1971 Sea Bed Treaty prohibited the placing or testing of nuclear weapons on the ocean floor.† Even though arsenals continued to expand, the world seemed slightly safer.

Then came the Nuclear Non-Proliferation Treaty, ratified on 5 March 1970. The agreement did not reduce the number of nuclear weapons, nor did it curb the arms race. It simply prohibited proliferation to previously non-nuclear countries. The nuclear powers agreed not to help non-nuclear states acquire atomic weapons and the non-nuclear states agreed not to start their own weapons programmes. In other words, those who had would continue to have, while those who lacked would continue to lack. The treaty was signed by 111 countries, but not by France, Israel, South Africa, China, Cuba, Pakistan, India, Brazil or Argentina. In reality, the treaty is simply an agreement by over 100 countries not to do what they never had any intention of doing. It does not prevent the export of nuclear technology for energy generation – a significant flaw since an atom bomb proceeds logically from a nuclear power plant. But, despite these flaws, the NPT remains important symbolically as a standard of acceptable behaviour against which the aspirations of megalomaniacs can be measured.

Behind the symbolic agreements, the Cold War still raged and mutual distrust still governed superpower relations. MAD still seemed sensible. Richard Nixon once boasted that 'I can go into my office and pick up the telephone and in twenty-five minutes seventy million people will be dead'.[75] If he was guilty of anything, it was of underestimating the numbers he could kill. While the threat of war seemed to recede in the 1960s, its potential consequences grew more frightening – for those who bothered

---

* The hotline was used during the Six Day War in 1967. Johnson reputedly told Kosygin 'If you want war, you'll get war.' The chat wasn't exactly friendly, but the hotline served its purpose of keeping communication open and immediate, and, in so doing, served to reduce tension.

† France and China refused to ratify it.

to pay attention. Public apathy did not enable nuclear proliferation, but it did make it easier.

Nobel peace prize winner Philip Noel-Baker found it depressing that nations could agree on the inconsequential while leaving important issues in dispute. 'While disarming Antarctica', he remarked, 'we got 7,000 weapons in Europe; we should have disarmed Europe and put those weapons in Antarctica.' The NATO plan, first formulated in the 1950s, still called for the first use of nuclear weapons in response to a Soviet conventional attack. NATO would hit large cities like Prague and Warsaw and use smaller tactical weapons on the battlefield. The Russians, it was hoped, would then realize that more significant destruction of their homeland would follow and they would withdraw. All this was based on a very shaky assumption that at some point good sense would prevail. 'During my six years on the NATO Military Committee', Lord Louis Mountbatten recalled, 'I never missed an opportunity of saying, loud and clear, that the actual use of tactical nuclear weapons could only end in escalation to total global nuclear destruction, and for that reason no one in their senses would contemplate their use.'[76]

In *The Essence of Security* (1968), the former US Defense Secretary Robert McNamara confessed that the nuclear superiority which the US enjoyed over the Soviet Union 'is both greater than we had originally planned and more than we require'. So how did this happen? McNamara explained that, in the quest for deterrence, caution ruled: 'a strategic planner . . . must prepare for the worst plausible case and not be content to hope and prepare for the most probable'. In other words, proliferation was fuelled by ignorance; since each side was unaware of the other's capabilities, both had to assume the worst. 'If we had had more accurate information about planned Soviet strategic forces, we simply would not have needed to build as large a nuclear arsenal as we have today.' Yet, in expanding their arsenal to protect themselves, the US encouraged their enemy to do the same. 'Clearly the Soviet buildup is in part a reaction to our own buildup since the beginning of the 1960s,' McNamara admitted. 'Soviet strategic planners undoubtedly reasoned that, if our buildup were to continue at its accelerated pace, we might conceivably reach in time a credible first-strike capability against the Soviet Union.'[77]

In 1969, the new National Security Advisor Henry Kissinger told Congress that the US had no plans to expand its nuclear arsenal, quite simply because there was no need. Kissinger still believed in MAD.

With no advantage to be gained by striking first and no disadvantage to be suffered by striking second, there will be no motive for surprise or pre-emptive attack. Mutual invulnerability means mutual deterrence. It is the most stable position from the point of view of preventing all-out war.[78]

Stability was, however, difficult to maintain since both superpowers continually expanded their arsenals and improved their delivery systems, thus disturbing the equilibrium. The US and the USSR were like greyhounds chasing a mechanical rabbit called security which they could never possibly catch. In the past, better weapons, or more of them, equalled better protection. Now, that equation no longer applied. Measures taken to ensure a second-strike capability were inevitably interpreted by the enemy as an attempt to establish a first-strike capability. Every defensive measure seemed aggressive to the other side.

As time passed, technology provided better protection against a first strike. In the early days of missiles it took hours to prepare a weapon for firing, which gave advantage to the aggressor. With the evolution of automatic firing systems, it grew easier to respond quickly to an attack and thus to guard against a successful first strike. These systems were combined with sophisticated detection and tracking apparatus, allowing missiles to be launched before attacking missiles arrived. But these improvements also increased the risk of accidental war. Automated responses and quick retaliation capabilities shortened the time which might be devoted to contemplation or negotiation – leaders might have to act instinctively instead of carefully deliberating. In the book *Fail-Safe* (1962), the dramatic impact of the story is increased because of the time it takes for accidentally launched American weapons to reach Soviet territory, time which is used for frantic negotiation between the two leaders. By the 1970s this window for negotiation was slammed shut by technological improvements supposedly designed to improve security.

In Peter George's *Two Hours to Doom* (published in the US as *Red Alert*), a demented SAC commander launches a nuclear attack on the Soviet Union. Apocalypse threatens because the Soviet Union employs an automated response system – machines can decide to go to war even if human beings desire otherwise. But disaster is averted when the bomber crashes before the weapons are released. The same story was given a more catastrophic ending by Stanley Kubrick who, in *Dr Strangelove* (1964), turned nuclear war into the blackest of black comedies. The cast of characters grimly parodies the dark forces then controlling American nuclear strategy. Generals Jack Ripper (Sterling Hayden) and Buck Turgidson (George C. Scott) seem only slightly exaggerated versions of Curtis LeMay, while the titular Dr Strangelove (Peter Sellers) is a composite of Kissinger, Teller and von Braun, with a bit of Kahn thrown in for good measure. As a comment on the absurdity of nuclear rivalry, the film is a masterpiece, but it was simply too clever to affect popular perceptions of the Bomb. Viewers who praised it as a brilliant film still implicitly supported (by their apathy) the tenets of MAD which Kubrick sought to undermine.

★ ★ ★

The nuclear arms race was based on the idea that each power would be able to attack at will; that bombers and missiles would always get through. Defence against attack did not seem possible. But, then, in the 1960s, the Soviet Union began exploring the possibility of an anti-ballistic missile system, much to the chagrin of the United States. 'We can hit a fly in space,' Khrushchev boasted, not altogether accurately.[79] The Soviets claimed that the idea was entirely innocent. 'We thought of it as an umbrella,' Nikolai Detinov, formerly of the Soviet Defence Ministry, recalled. 'Would an umbrella harm anybody? If it rains, you open it up. That was how we saw the ABM system. It was an umbrella to protect our population against a possible missile strike.'[80] The Americans, on the other hand, suspected that the Soviets were trying to increase their chances of surviving a nuclear strike and, by so doing, working toward a first-strike capability. MAD was suddenly undermined because destruction was neither assured nor mutual.

The issue caused strident disagreement within the Johnson administration. As Kaufmann advised McNamara, defensive weapons were about five times more expensive than the missiles they countered. In other words, any ABM system could easily be overwhelmed by deploying more ICBMs. In truth, ABM was 90 per cent bluff. The Americans developed penetration aids like chaff and decoy missiles, designed to fool the Soviet defences. Though the Joint Chiefs unanimously favoured development, McNamara stood firm, dismissing ABM as a dangerous waste of money which would escalate the arms race.

Multiple Re-Entry Vehicles (MRV), the newest generation of ICBMs, answered the ABM threat by breaking into separate warheads which would scatter in different directions. No ABM system could deal with so many targets. MRV therefore rendered ABM pointless. MRV's chief weakness was, however, its inaccuracy; once the missile split into separate warheads, targeting became erratic. But then came MIRV, or Multiple Independently targeted Re-entry Vehicles. As the name implies, each warhead is equipped with its own guidance system to carry it to a precise target along a predetermined path. An even more effective response came with MARV, or Manoeuvrable Re-entry Vehicle. Instead of the warheads following a predetermined path, they would have the capability to change course if necessary to avoid ABM defences. In other words, the warhead would independently 'decide' the best course to a target.

The attacker, in other words, retained the advantage. In the weird world of MAD this was not such a bad thing. Having come to this realization, both the Soviet Union and the United States by 1972 felt comfortable signing the ABM treaty, thus abandoning what could not in fact be achieved. But, though MRV had been developed to counter ABM, the abandonment of ABM did not slow deployment of the new systems. The failure to limit MRVs meant that, over the next decade, the US and USSR would add 12,000 nuclear warheads to their arsenals.

Because the Americans were initially better at making smaller weapons, they needed less powerful rockets than the Soviets. But, after the introduction of MRV and MIRV, the more powerful Soviet rockets allowed them to mount a larger number of warheads on each missile than the Americans could manage. Yet despite this potential Soviet advantage, Nixon pushed forward with MIRV, rejecting the notion that a negotiated ban might be advantageous. In fact, the new development eventually allowed the Soviets to move ahead in the number of ICBM warheads, while maintaining near parity with the Americans in the number of actual missiles. 'I would say in retrospect that I wish I had thought through the implications of a MIRVed world more thoughtfully in 1969 and 1970 than I did,' Kissinger later admitted.[81]

In 1968, the Board of the *Bulletin of the Atomic Scientists* met to consider what seemed a worsening world situation. China and France had both gone nuclear. Wars were raging in the Middle East, in Vietnam and on the Indian subcontinent. World military spending was steadily increasing at the same time that money devoted to development was shrinking. Nuclear weapons were becoming more accurate, more powerful, and, worst of all, more numerous. The Board decided that the Doomsday Clock should reflect the heightening tension. The hands were moved from twelve to seven minutes to midnight.

For the next few years the hands moved backwards and forwards, reflecting the state of nuclear diplomacy. Then, having skirted the issue for years, the superpowers began to discuss ways to limit proliferation. The Strategic Arms Limitation Talks (SALT) of the early 1970s were, as the name implied, an attempt to reduce the pace of the arms race which otherwise threatened bankruptcy. Both sides approached the talks with self-protective cynicism. As had been the case during the test ban negotiations, the Soviets were reluctant to agree to anything that would involve extensive inspections and monitoring. The negotiations nevertheless provided the opportunity for the Americans to learn something about their adversaries. 'The Soviets really had it in their . . . gut, in the marrow of their bone . . . this inherent right of a nation to defend itself,' Helmut Sonnenfeldt, an American SALT adviser, discovered. Since the Americans had always assumed that Soviet weapons were designed for attack, that was a salutary lesson.[82]

The caution that McNamara described nevertheless still governed behaviour. For this reason, neither side wanted a settlement that might leave it measurably weaker. In fact, both sought an agreement that cemented existing advantages. In other words, SALT was nothing more than an attempt to define an equilibrium with which both sides could feel comfortable. The only benefit was that it perhaps limited arms expenditure. The world was not a safer place, since each side retained the ability to destroy the other many times over.

SALT, like the previous nuclear agreements, was important mainly as a symbol. The fact that the superpowers could agree on something, however inconsequential, seemed grounds for hope. In 1972, on the strength of the SALT and ABM treaties, the Doomsday Clock was moved back to twelve minutes to midnight.

Buried within the endless detail of the 1946 Strategic Bombing Survey there lies an interesting fact about the effect of the atomic bomb on Hiroshima and Nagasaki:

> There is reason to believe that if the effects of blast and fire had been entirely absent from the bombing, the number of deaths among people within a radius of one-half mile from ground zero would have been almost as great as the actual figures and the deaths among those within 1 mile would have been only slightly less. The principal difference would have been in the time of the deaths. Instead of being killed outright as were most of these victims, they would have survived for a few days or even 3 or 4 weeks, only to die eventually of radiation disease.[83]

Within this statement lay the seeds of an idea that would germinate thirty years later. The Bomb was, first and foremost, a weapon for killing people. In the process of its very efficient murder, it also caused immense destruction which, in certain circumstances, was inconvenient. Was there perhaps a better way? Might it be possible to make a bomb that killed, but did not destroy?

In the nuclear age, each superpower possessed the capacity to destroy his enemy virtually completely, but each was prevented from using that power by the knowledge that equal destruction would be returned. This, according to Kissinger, is 'the greatest paradox of the nuclear age. Power has never been greater; it has also never been less useful.'[84] Frustration with nuclear impotence inspired talk of the neutron bomb, first formally mooted by the Americans in 1977. The aim was to develop a small nuclear weapon which did not cause great destruction outside the immediate area of detonation, but was sufficiently 'dirty' to emit radiation capable of wiping out an enemy force. The idea seemed particularly relevant to the problem of an attacking Soviet Army in Central Europe. In such a situation, conventional nuclear weapons might destroy the enemy, but would also destroy that which was being protected, namely Germany.

The idea of a bomb which killed people but left buildings intact was too distasteful for most people. It seemed the ultimate manifestation of the capitalist ethic – buildings had a higher value than people. Critics also argued that a nuclear weapon is still a nuclear weapon no matter how small – deployment of the neutron bomb would lead inevitably to full-scale nuclear confrontation. Reacting to the protest, President Jimmy Carter told his aides that he 'did not wish the world to think of him as an ogre'. On 26 March 1978 he confessed that 'he had a queasy feeling about the whole thing; that his Administration would be stamped forever as the Administration which introduced bombs that kill people but leave buildings intact; and that he would like to find a graceful way out'.[85] An escape was found a short time later, but it was hardly graceful.

Just before he became President in 1976, Carter questioned the American approach to non-proliferation:

> by enjoining sovereign nations to forgo nuclear weapons, we are asking for a form of self-denial that we have not been able to accept ourselves. I believe we have little right to ask others to deny themselves such weapons for the indefinite future unless we demonstrate meaningful progress towards the goal of control, then reduction and ultimately, elimination of nuclear arsenals . . . It is time, in the SALT talks, that we complete the stage of agreeing on ceilings and get down to the centerpiece of SALT – the actual negotiation of reductions in strategic forces and measures effectively halting the race in strategic weapons technology. The world is waiting, but not necessarily for long. The longer effective arms reduction is postponed, the more likely it is that other nations will be encouraged to develop their own nuclear capability.[86]

Despite this promising indication of a desire to disarm, the Carter presidency brought research on the neutron bomb, deployment of Cruise missiles in Europe, the commissioning of the first Trident submarine and a doubling of the number of warheads targeted at the Soviet Union. Yet despite this massive escalation of the arms race, most people around the world remained apathetic about nuclear weapons.

A US Congress study in 1978 revealed that the American nuclear arsenal was far bigger than it needed to be. At that time, Congress estimated that the US could still count on having 4,900 thermonuclear warheads after a Russian surprise attack. If the Americans were given warning of that attack, around 7,500 warheads would survive and be ready for retaliation. This would give the US the capacity to destroy 90 per cent of Soviet military targets, 80 per cent of industrial targets, all government installations and 90 million people. By any standard of measurement, that is a credible second strike. In contrast, an American first strike was thought to be able to destroy all but 400 Soviet nuclear warheads.

'We have gone on piling weapon upon weapon, missile upon missile, new levels of destructiveness upon old ones,' a tired George Kennan, the architect of containment, remarked in 1981. 'We have done this helplessly, almost involuntarily, like the victims of some sort of hypnotism, like men in a dream, like lemmings headed for the sea.'[87] When Secretary of Defense Dick Cheney conducted a review of the SIOP in 1991, he concluded that it 'was not a nuclear war plan . . . it seemed like a jumble of processed data. . . . Every time the Pentagon bought a new nuclear weapons system to match the Soviet's . . . Omaha had simply found targets for the added warheads and rearranged the SIOP math formulas.' As the number of weapons increased, the definition of a military target widened, eventually including shoe factories. One analyst confessed that deterrence was defined as 'going after what the adversary values. If he values his grandma, we have to target grandmas.'[88]

In contrast to Kennan, Nitze argued that the American arsenal was not big enough. His Committee on the Present Danger (CPD) was formed to focus attention on the threat posed by Soviet nuclear expansion. 'By its continuing strategic nuclear buildup', the CPD warned, 'the Soviet Union demonstrates that it does not subscribe to American notions of nuclear sufficiency and mutually assured deterrence. Soviet nuclear offensive and defensive weapons are designed to enable the USSR to fight, survive and win an all-out nuclear war.'[89] The CPD argued that SALT inhibited the US from responding adequately to the Soviet threat.

In 1980, Carter ran for re-election against the CPD's man, Ronald Reagan, who based his campaign on the contention that America had gone soft. Reagan won by a landslide.

The world began to worry again.

CHAPTER 16

Mid-Life Crisis

In the early 1980s, protesters at the Greenham Common Women's Peace Camp expressed their displeasure with the deployment of Cruise missiles by hanging soiled sanitary napkins and tampons on the perimeter fence of the American missile base. In the annals of peace protest, the tactic is surely the most bizarre. But then bizarre behaviour was the norm in the 1980s.

The camp was started in 1981, shortly after the announcement of the planned deployment of Cruise. Protesters vowed they would not leave Greenham Common until the missiles were removed, a promise that worried well-healed local residents. But, before long, the dynamics of the group became more important than the weapons they protested against. The women envisaged a communal society free of social or gender division but were disappointed to find that their male comrades wanted to lead. They also feared that the presence of men would inevitably lead to violent confrontations with police. So, in an extraordinarily assertive move, the women ordered the men to leave, in the process turning their camp into a demonstration not just against missiles but also against patriarchy. As they explained, they needed 'space to find our own ways of working . . . to find our strengths, how to assert ourselves'.[1] Their style of protest emphasized their gender: they knitted a web around the base, hung nappies on the fence and used photos of their children to punctuate their hatred of nuclear weapons. These tactics were devised with genuine sincerity but left the group vulnerable to misogynist ridicule. In addition, lesbians in the camp provided a rich source of inspiration for right-wing journalists intent on smear. Lurid press coverage encouraged ever more provocative behaviour from some women who, though averse to physical aggression, did not disclaim the psychological kind. Overt displays of lesbian affection were designed to unnerve male soldiers guarding the base. Before long, discussion of the bizarre behaviour on Greenham Common hardly mentioned Cruise, much to the annoyance of mainstream CND.

Seven time zones away from Greenham Common, just outside the entrance to the Nevada Test Site, another group of protesters gathered in the early 1980s. The dusty patch of land on which they congregated belonged to the Bureau of Land Management, for the simple reason that no one else wanted it. When the protesters arrived the government did not object since it was keen to keep the 'movement' contained and out of harm's way. The land, naturally enough, was dubbed Peace Camp, but no one quite knows by whom. It has to be said that the protesters were a bit late – to be accurate, about thirty years late. In the 1950s, when tests were frequent and fallout nasty, protesters were few. In the 1980s, the tests were hidden underground but the protests were much more visible, an indication of just how much Ronald Reagan had disturbed the nuclear equilibrium.

The government's welcome extended no further than providing a plot of land; it did not want the dissidents to feel comfortable, otherwise they might be inclined to stay. Neither water nor shelter were available, other than that which the protesters brought themselves. The heat and harsh landscape tested commitment. No one came simply for fun.

Peace protesters did not always protest peacefully. There were occasional assaults on the base, though that is perhaps too grand a description for a few individuals attacking the fence with cheap wirecutters bought from TruValue in nearby Tonopah. Some agitators lay down in front of trucks waiting to enter the camp, but they got up when the trucks started to move. Others chained themselves to the cattle guard on the road – clever officials responded by removing the guard. Two holding pens were built by the side of the road to detain those who misbehaved. One pen was for males, the other for females – mixing genders in such a super-charged atmosphere seemed unwise. In a land of uncompromising heat, a spell in the pens qualified as cruel and unusual punishment. The offenders were probably delighted when they were formally arrested and bussed to Beatty, where they could spend the night in air-conditioned cells.

The size of the crowds depended to a large extent on the state of Cold War tensions, particularly the actions of the Reagan administration. Crowds were naturally larger when tests were scheduled. As an attempt to focus attention on the dangers of nuclear war or on American weapons policy, the protests were not very successful. The Test Site went about its business, oblivious to the flea on its tail.

The protesters – in Nevada or Greenham Common – were the sharp end of public unease. Thanks to Reagan, the world was again worried about the Bomb. After twenty years of fragile calm, nuclear confrontation suddenly seemed possible. In 1983, the Italian weekly *Panorama* despaired that a 'second Cold War has begun', and comparisons were made to Cuba in 1962 and Berlin in 1948. The American Sovietologist Sweryn Bialer felt sure that 'a test is coming between the superpowers. The Soviets are frustrated, angry. They have to reassert their manhood, to regain their influence in the international arena.'[2]

To add to the people's misery the astronomer Carl Sagan and the biologist Paul Ehrlich, in a highly publicized study, concluded that, if less than half the nuclear arsenals of the US and USSR were detonated, the resultant cloud of dust and smoke would block out the sun's rays for over a year, causing a 'nuclear winter' in which millions would die from freezing and starvation.

On 1 January 1984, *Time* magazine named Reagan and Yuri Andropov, the Soviet premier, Men of the Year – not for what they had achieved, but to draw attention to the crisis they embodied. 'There is grave danger', the editors felt, 'if not of war tomorrow, then of a long period of angry immobility in superpower relations; of an escalating arms race bringing into US and Soviet arsenals weapons ever more expensive and difficult to control; of rising tension that might make every world trouble spot a potential flash point for the clash both sides fear.'[3]

But how did we get here? What happened to détente? What happened to nuclear apathy?

In fact, the crisis predated Reagan's presidency. The 1970s had been a period of genuinely improving relations between the superpowers, but underneath the surface tensions simmered. New risks began to accumulate: India went nuclear, the Soviet Union embarked upon a difficult war in Afghanistan, nationalist wars proliferated and the spectre of terrorism heightened fears everywhere.

In February 1970, Nixon, in his State of the World address, articulated the abiding frustration of the nuclear age: 'Should a President, in the event of nuclear attack, be left with the single option of ordering the mass destruction of enemy civilians in the face of the certainty that it would be followed by the mass slaughter of Americans?'[4] Responding to his cue, a new group of eggheads at the Pentagon and RAND struggled to find ways to fight a limited nuclear war, in the process traversing the same ground covered by Brodie, Kaufman and McNamara a generation before. A harbinger of the new zeitgeist came in the autumn of 1973 when a National Security Defense Memorandum proclaimed that the US needed 'a more flexible nuclear posture' which would 'not preclude . . . use of nuclear weapons in response to conventional aggression'.[5] In contrast to the 1960s, Western European nations, frightened by the steady expansion of Soviet nuclear forces, now enthusiastically supported counterforce. Confirming the strategic shift, Carter signed Presidential Directive 59 on 25 July 1980, formally acknowledging a move away from MAD.

Fighting a limited war was one thing, winning it another. Carter's detractors doubted that the US had the capacity to implement an effective counterforce strategy. In 1976, Nitze raised the spectre of Soviet nuclear blackmail in *Foreign Affairs*, arguing that the Soviet ICBM advantage would enable them to eliminate most American missiles with a devastating first strike. American retaliation would then be limited to less dependable SLBMs and bombers. Central to Nitze's argument was the idea that a 'shelter gap' had developed. 'As the Soviet civil defense program becomes more effective', he wrote, 'it tends to destabilize the deterrent relationship' because the US can 'no longer hold . . . the Soviet population as a hostage to deter a Soviet attack'. He claimed that, given the ubiquity of Soviet shelters, an American strike might kill only three per cent of their population, an acceptable loss. But, since hitting Soviet cities would inevitably cause the Soviets to respond in kind, any US president would suffer a 'paralysis of will' and give in to Russian nuclear blackmail.[6] Nitze warned that the proposed SALT II treaty would prevent the US from responding effectively to this threat. The Nitze argument was shouted from every corner by his friends in the Committee on the Present Danger.

Reagan's election in November 1980 reflected widely held fears that the US, under Carter, had grown dangerously weak. His campaign team (thirty-two members belonged to the CPD) cleverly exaggerated the perils facing the US in order to create a demand for their man. But Reagan's aggressive response to those perils made the world more dangerous. Partly in response to Reagan, the Doomsday Clock was moved to four minutes to midnight in 1981 – suggesting that the situation was more hazardous than at any time since the development of the hydrogen bomb.

That assessment was given credence when members of the Reagan administration openly spoke of their belief in biblical prophecies of Armageddon. 'Every day I think that time is running out,' Defense Secretary Caspar Weinberger confessed. Interior Secretary James Watt remarked that he did 'not know how many future generations we can count on before the Lord returns'. A significant number of Americans seemed to agree. A 1984 poll found that 39 per cent believed that the Bible contained references to atomic destruction while 25 per cent thought they were among the chosen to be saved from nuclear holocaust.[7]

Those less certain of salvation devoted their energy to the nuclear freeze movement which called upon both superpowers to institute an immediate halt to the production, testing and deployment of atomic weapons. A Gallup poll in May 1981 showed 72 per cent support for a freeze, an issue prominent at all levels in the 1982 elections. Nevertheless, while support for a freeze was high, so too was backing for defence spending increases and other policies designed to 'get tough' with the Soviets. Though fear had risen, so too had trust in Reagan. Many people were therefore inclined to agree when he called the freeze idea 'a very dangerous fraud' perpetrated by those 'who want the weakening of America'. A freeze, he insisted, would 'prevent the essential and long-overdue modernization of US and allied defenses and would leave our aging forces increasingly vulnerable'.[8]

By the time Reagan became president, the SALT talks had been going on for nearly a decade, while arsenals steadily expanded. Though SALT II, signed in June 1979, was hailed as a major achievement, in truth it merely limited the pace of expansion. Each side was allowed to add another 4,000 warheads to their armouries by 1985, while tactical weapons were completely ignored. The development of new weapons systems was effectively sanctioned, with each superpower allowed to deploy one new system in the lifetime of the treaty, set at five years.

In June 1982, the Strategic Arms Reduction Talks (START) commenced, the aim being to reduce the number of ICBMs. But Reagan's commitment to reduction was called into question by his insistence on the need to beef up the American arsenal. The White House carefully cultivated an image of American military weakness and Soviet duplicity. 'You often hear that the United States and the Soviet Union are in an arms race,' Reagan told the American people on 23 November 1982. 'The truth is that while the Soviet Union has raced, we have not. . . . Today, in virtually every measure of military power the Soviet Union enjoys a decided advantage.'[9] With smoke and mirrors, the administration convinced Congress and the American people of the urgent need for massive increases in military spending.

One of Reagan's pet projects was the MX missile system, an idea dating back to Nixon. Designed as a response to the first-strike threat of Soviet MIRV missiles, it combined the merits of the traditional hardened silo with the unpredictability of a mobile launcher. The proposed project involved 200 missiles, 4,600 missile shelters and 10,000 miles of roads deployed in an area bigger than Wales. Each missile would be installed on a loop consisting of twenty-three different silos from which it could be launched. The missile would periodically (and randomly) travel to a new silo, thus making its precise location difficult to detect. To confuse things further, decoy missiles would travel other routes. In order to achieve a first strike, the Soviets would have to score 4,600 direct hits – destroying each of the silos in the network. The $50 billion price tag had previously been the biggest obstacle to implementation. On 23 November, however, Reagan offered Americans a scaled down version, insisting that 'MX is the right missile at the right time'.[10]

Reagan's warnings about the Soviet military build-up were not complete fabrications. The massive superiority which America had enjoyed in the 1960s had evolved into a situation of rough parity. By 1985, the US still had a lead in strategic warheads of 11,188 to the Soviets' 9,907. With intermediate range and tactical weapons included, the Americans had 20,924 warheads against the Soviets' 19,774. Unable to tolerate equality, Reagan maintained that 'the United States . . . is still well behind the Soviet Union in literally every kind of offensive weapon'. His aide, Jeanne Kirkpatrick, warned about 'the growing vulnerability of the United States. For the first time in American history an adversary has the ability to destroy our country . . . The Soviet advantage in nuclear missiles is real and still growing. Our capacity for deterrence is minimal and still declining.'[11]

Reagan reiterated an argument first proposed by the CPD, namely that the Soviets were developing a first-strike capability.

> Everything that has been said, and everything in their manuals indicates that, unlike us, the Soviet Union believes that a nuclear war is possible. And they believe it's winnable, which means that they believe that if you could achieve enough superiority, then your opponent wouldn't have retaliatory strike capability.[12]

The President pointed in particular to the Soviet advantage in ICBMs. Though the number of missiles on each side was roughly equal, the much more powerful Soviet rockets allowed them to place as many as ten warheads on a single missile. Reagan repeated the warning first raised by Nitze in 1976, arguing that the Soviets' superiority in ICBMs would allow them to blackmail the US. The logic was shaky but the argument was delivered with sufficient gravitas to convince most Americans.

The Soviet premier Leonid Brezhnev dismissed as 'absurd and utterly unfounded' the notion that his country sought a first-strike capability. He argued, with some logic, that the Soviet quest for parity was simply a natural desire for security. In June 1982, he assured the UN General Assembly that the USSR would 'not . . . be the first to use nuclear weapons'. His Defence Minister, Dmitri Ustinov, confirmed that 'Only extraordinary circumstances – a direct nuclear aggression against the Soviet state or its allies – can compel us to resort to a retaliatory nuclear strike as a last means of self-defence.'[13]

In one area, the Soviets had an indisputable lead. Beginning in 1976, they deployed the RSD-10 missile, more commonly known by the Western designation SS-20. Up to 1983, the SS-20 provided the USSR with an advantage over NATO in Intermediate Range Ballistic Missiles. The first version packed a 650-kiloton warhead, but was later modified to carry three 150-kiloton MIRV warheads. The fact that they were carried on mobile missile launchers rendered them virtually invulnerable. By 1979, 120 SS-20s had been deployed, 50 on the Chinese border and the rest targeted at Europe.

NATO answered with Cruise, one of the most controversial developments of the Reagan era. Deployed in Europe in 1983, Cruise and Pershing II restored the NATO advantage in intermediate range missiles. The original plan called for 108 Pershing II and 112 Cruise missiles to be sited in West Germany, with a further 352 Cruise missiles divided between Great Britain (160), Italy (96), the Netherlands (48) and Belgium (48). Like SS-20, Cruise was launched from mobile units – aircraft, ships or large lorries. But they had the added advantage of a new guidance system which made them difficult to track and frighteningly accurate. Hitherto, missiles followed ballistic trajectories; in other words, after the initial thrust, they arrived at their target by free fall. This meant that they could be put off course by meteorological conditions. Cruise provided its own guidance, by way of satellite tracking systems and onboard computers containing pre-programmed maps of the terrain over which they would travel. In effect, the missile took itself to its target by the best possible route. Since they travel on an unpredictable, erratic path, they are extremely difficult to detect and destroy. The 200-kiloton warhead is capable of accuracy to within thirty metres.

The real purpose of Cruise was never adequately explained – some called it 'a solution in search of a problem'. Its accuracy suggested a first-strike weapon suitable to counterforce, yet it was too slow for that purpose, requiring two hours to travel from Britain to the Warsaw Pact countries. If it was meant to be a second-strike weapon, there were existing systems that could perform that function better. It was developed not because it was needed, but because computer technology and guidance systems had progressed to such an extent to allow a missile to guide itself. Oppenheimer, it will be recalled, once said that scientific developments are motivated not by what is necessary but by what is possible. The phenomenon is not peculiarly American. Andrew Cockburn, an expert on the Soviet military, argues that the USSR also developed weapons when they became scientifically possible – 'only afterward [was] the threat discovered that the weapon [was] supposed to meet'.[14] Lord Zuckerman, who saw this same phenomenon unfold in Great Britain, once remarked that 'the decisions which we make today in the fields of science and technology determine the tactics, then the strategy, and finally the politics of tomorrow'.[15]

While the 1980s saw the people of Europe in vehement protest against deployment of Cruise and Pershing II, their governments welcomed the weapons. European politicians saw the missiles as an effective answer to SS-20, but also as a solution to the age-old conundrum of American commitment to Europe. Governments in Bonn, London and Rome had worried about how the US might respond to a Soviet attack on Western Europe with intermediate range missiles. Since such an attack would not endanger the American people, would the US strike back? Though the

Americans claimed they would respond by deploying ICBMs launched from the United States, that promise seemed thin, since such a response would inevitably cause the Soviets to retaliate against American cities. On 16 October 1981, Reagan admitted that a nuclear war confined to Europe was entirely conceivable. 'I could see where you could have the exchange of weapons against troops in the field without it bringing either one of the major powers to pushing the button,' he confessed. While this was, in truth, simply an honest summary of NATO strategy, it frightened Europeans.[16] Cruise answered these fears by placing a significant proportion of American strategic forces in Europe, thus tying the US irrevocably to a European war.

In 1940 Warner Brothers released *Murder in the Air*, the central premise of which was a new weapon called the Inertia Projector. This device was capable of firing high-energy rays which would disable the electrical systems of enemy planes from a great distance, sending them crashing to the earth. In the film a Navy admiral boasts that the device not only makes the United States invincible in war, but, in so doing, promises to become the 'greatest force for world peace ever discovered'.[17] The star of the film was Ronald Reagan.

Forty-three years later, on 23 March 1983, President Reagan called upon the American people to support a package of defence proposals costing $1.6 trillion. This was, he argued, 'part of a careful, long-term plan to make America strong again after too many years of neglect'. In order to convince the American people of its necessity, Reagan encouraged them to believe that 'the Soviets . . . have enough accurate and powerful nuclear weapons to destroy virtually all of our missiles on the ground'. He insisted that the Soviet military build-up was intended for offensive purposes, not simply to deter.

The Reagan speech is remembered not for his warnings about nuclear inferiority but for the first mention of what came to be known as Star Wars (since few people recalled the Inertia Projector, they preferred references to a more recent film*). His 'strategic defence initiative' (SDI) was designed to refute the assumption that the missile would always get through. 'I've become more and more deeply convinced that the human spirit must be capable of rising above dealing with other nations and human beings by threatening their existence.' This was basically ABM

---

* Reagan must also have seen Alfred Hitchcock's *Torn Curtain*, an espionage film which centres on attempts to protect the secret of an anti-missile system. At one point, an American agent, played by Paul Newman, says 'We will produce a defensive weapon that will make all nuclear weapons obsolete, and thereby abolish the terror of nuclear warfare.' (Fitzgerald, p.23.)

Mark II, made more plausible thanks to Captain Kirk and Luke Skywalker. Reagan called upon Americans to 'turn to the very strengths in technology that spawned our great industrial base and that have given us the quality of life we enjoy today' – a clever tactic which countered an imagined weakness with an assumed strength. The Soviets (so the argument went) could not possibly compete with American technological prowess. The nuclear game would be changed to suit American skills. 'I call upon the scientific community in our country, those who gave us nuclear weapons, to turn their great talents now to the cause of mankind and world peace, to give us the means of rendering these nuclear weapons impotent and obsolete.' He might as well have said, 'May the Force be with you.'*

Reagan admitted that the project might take decades to complete and would cost vast amounts of money. 'But isn't it worth every investment necessary to free the world from the threat of nuclear war? We know it is.' He was also aware that the Soviets might interpret SDI as part of an American attempt to obtain a first-strike capability. 'If paired with offensive systems', he admitted on 23 March 1983, 'it can be viewed as fostering an aggressive policy.'[18] But he refused to allow that interpretation to deter him, since the world could rest confident in 'a simple premise: The United States does not start fights. We will never be an aggressor. . . . Our only purpose – one all people share – is to search for ways to reduce the danger of nuclear war.'[19] In other words, while the US needed Star Wars in order to feel safe, the Soviets apparently only needed trust. The new Premier Mikhail Gorbachev addressed this double standard in November 1985:

> They say: 'Believe us . . .' I then said: 'Mr President, I call on you to believe us. We have said we will not be the first to use nuclear weapons and we would not attack the United States. Why then do you, while preserving the defence capability on Earth and underwater, intend to start the arms race also in space? You don't believe us? This shows you don't. Why should we believe you more than you believe us?

Reagan replied with a rather dubious reference to the past: 'When the United States was the only country in the world possessing these awesome nuclear weapons, we did not blackmail others with threats to use them. . . . Doesn't our record alone refute the charge that we seek superiority, that we represent a threat to peace?' The administration's argument was weakened when Weinberger welcomed SDI on the grounds that, 'if we can get a system . . . which we know can render their weapons impotent, we

---

* Richard Perle, one of the hard men of the Reagan administration, candidly admitted that SDI was 'the product of millions of American teenagers putting quarters into video machines'. (Powaski, p.34.)

would be back in a situation [where] . . . we were the only nation with the nuclear weapon'.[20]

To bolster his case, Reagan then made the bizarre suggestion that the US might actually share the technology, allowing both superpowers to shelter under the same umbrella. This proposal began to unravel when subjected to simple logic. Was the world really supposed to believe that Reagan would share cutting edge research with the regime he called the 'Evil Empire'? At the time, the US was reluctant to share its discoveries with its closest ally, Great Britain, and had only recently refused to license the sale of personal computers to the USSR. Yet this preposterous suggestion was repeated so many times, and with such apparent sincerity, that one can only conclude Reagan must have believed in it wholeheartedly.

If SDI had a precise origin, it was seventeen years earlier when Reagan, then running for governor of California, met Teller. The two fell in love instantly. Teller's fantasies appealed to Reagan's limitless imagination and can-do spirit. Soon after the election, Reagan toured the Livermore lab, and learned about Teller's idea of an anti-missile defence system. 'He clearly comprehended the technology,' Teller concluded, probably too charitably. After Reagan became President, Teller enjoyed virtually unrestricted access to the White House. He convinced Reagan that Livermore could build an X-ray laser – powered by an atom bomb – which would give the US 'assured survival' in a nuclear war.

Reagan desperately wanted to believe in his country's limitless potential. This led him to filter out the more sober assessments of scientists like Bethe, who called SDI 'dangerous fantasy'. He elaborated: 'It is difficult to imagine a system more likely to induce catastrophe than one that requires critical decisions by the second, is itself untested and fragile and yet is threatening to the other side's retaliatory capacity.'[21] In Congress, Senator (and former astronaut) John Glenn complained:

> I can't see this. The President far oversold this. . . . If he wants to appear to be Buck Rogers out there, defending the country, that is fine. I appreciate that. But I just cannot see us going through all this business of deployment, doing decision-making and all of that business when the basic system has not even been invented.[22]

Despite strident objections, Congress approved funding, in part because rejecting it would weaken the administration's position in future arms negotiations with the Soviets. As a result, billions were spent on a chimera.*

---

* Some companies made a fortune pursuing a fantasy. In 1983 and 1984, 87 per cent of the SDI budget went to just ten companies, and 77 per cent went to the states or districts represented by members of the Congressional armed services committees. (Wills, p.427.)

Teller completely misrepresented what Livermore could do. Many years later, George Keyworth, Reagan's scientific adviser, admitted that 'the whole argument for . . . SDI . . . was a pack of lies, unadulterated lies'.[23] Yet Teller, like the Teflon president who sponsored him, escaped censure.

Star Wars ignored a basic fact of the nuclear age, namely that offence is so much easier and cheaper than defence. An example from the pre-atomic age illustrates the inevitable futility of any attempt to defend against nuclear missiles. On 28 August 1944, the British had their most successful day against V-weapons. Of 101 launched, 97 were shot down before reaching London. This was, by any standard, a remarkable achievement. Yet, had those weapons been equipped with nuclear warheads, no one would celebrate the success. Granted, defences had improved dramatically since 1944, but not nearly as dramatically as the missiles themselves. Moreover, any defensive system could easily be overwhelmed by increasing the number of missiles with which it had to deal. Since the cost of each missile was less than the defensive weapon designed to destroy it, Star Wars promised bankruptcy before it promised protection.

Star Wars aside, Reagan's military programme was not a radical departure from the Nixon/Carter era. But the massive expansion of arsenals that occurred in the 1970s had taken place against a background of détente. Nixon and Brezhnev regularly spoke to each other and professed commitment to peaceful coexistence. What made Reagan different – and a great deal more frightening – was his apparent determination to alienate his adversary. 'The only morality they recognize is that which will further their cause,' he argued. 'They reserve unto themselves the right to commit any crime, to lie, to cheat.' The Soviets were 'the focus of evil in the modern world . . . we are enjoined by Scripture and the Lord Jesus to oppose [them] with all our might'. Soviet Marxism, Reagan claimed, would 'wind up on the ash heap of history', a somewhat unfortunate choice of imagery.[24] Reagan's aggressive language, when combined with his military build-up, seemed to suggest that he was determined to destroy the Soviet Union.

Reagan's approach undermined many of the assumptions upon which the stability of the previous seventeen years had been based. Deterrence had been built upon MAD, which Reagan thought was 'the craziest thing I ever heard of'. It reminded him of 'two westerners standing in a saloon aiming their guns at each other's head – permanently'.[25] His team seemed actively to plan for confrontation and sought ways to win a nuclear war. In 1980, his running mate George Bush described how a nuclear contest might be won: '[if] you have survivability of command and control, survivability of industrial potential, protection of a percentage of your citizens, and you have a capability that inflicts more damage on the opposition than it can inflict on you. That's the way you can have a winner.' In what came to be known as the 'Weinberger Doctrine', the Defense Secretary argued that 'should deterrence fail and strategic nuclear war with the USSR occur, the United States must prevail and be able to force the Soviet Union to seek earliest termination of hostilities on terms favorable to the United States'.[26] His plans called for a nuclear force capable of 'decapitating' the Soviet leadership and a strategy which would allow the US to control the climb up the 'escalation ladder'.[27] Critics worried that planning along these lines made confrontation more likely.

Diplomacy gave way to invective. Andropov complained that Reagan's idea of dialogue in reality meant 'obscenities alternating with hysterical preaching'.[28] Lord Carrington, the former British Foreign Secretary, derided what he called 'megaphone diplomacy'. The deterioration of super-power relations inspired another adjustment of the Doomsday Clock one minute forward in 1984, the editors arguing that 'the blunt simplicities of force threaten to displace any other form of discourse between the super-powers'.[29] The former Defense Secretary James Schlesinger, no cuddly pacifist, agreed: 'Our weakened ability to communicate with the Soviets adds modestly, though measurably, to the risk of a clash of arms.'[30]

Not surprisingly, arms control talks abruptly stalled. 'Everything is finished,' Soviet negotiator Yuli Kvitsinsky commented after walking out of talks with Nitze. Shortly afterwards, the USSR broke off the INF* nego-tiations in Geneva, accusing the US of wanting to 'launch a decapitating nuclear first strike'.[31] They subsequently announced that they would increase the number of SS-20s targeted at Western Europe, expand the number of submarines patrolling American coasts and deploy more tactical nuclear weapons in Eastern Europe. 'By trying to lessen our security', Kvitsinsky remarked, 'the United States has lessened its own security.'[32] When the Kremlin refused to set a date for the resumption of START, not to mention the long-running talks on reducing conventional forces in Europe, it meant that, for the first time in fourteen years, the two super-powers were not talking to each other. Arms control and détente seemed distant memories. Reagan, however, stubbornly insisted that his 'modern-ization' of the military would eventually force the Soviets to negotiate. 'Unless we demonstrate the will to rebuild our strength and restore the military balance, the Soviets, since they are so far ahead, have little incen-tive to negotiate with us.'[33] George Kennan saw things differently: 'Never in my thirty-five years of public service, have I ever been more afraid of nuclear war.'[34]

---

* The Intermediate Range Nuclear Forces (INF) talks began in November 1981. As they dealt with intermediate forces, they were separate from the START talks, which began the following June.

Superpower tension was only one source of nuclear angst. Elsewhere, the chickens released by Eisenhower in the 1950s came home to roost. His 'Atoms for Peace' programme had encouraged poor nations to build nuclear power plants. Those plants produced surplus plutonium which was coveted by aspiring bomb-makers. When India joined the nuclear club, she did so with plutonium that came from a nuclear power plant which the Canadians, encouraged by the Americans, had helped build.* Ironically, Canada was one of the most enthusiastic supporters of the non-proliferation treaty. India's nuclear capability encouraged her bitter enemy Pakistan to go down the same road; Prime Minister Zulfiqar Ali Bhutto promised 'Pakistan will have nuclear weapons, even if our people have to eat grass'.[35] When asked about the proliferation problem during the 1980 presidential campaign, Reagan replied: 'I just don't think it's any of our business.'[36]

South Africa also took advantage of Eisenhower's largesse. The withdrawal of Portugal from her colonies created tensions which made the Johannesburg government nervous. Alarm bells rang when Cuba sent 50,000 troops to Angola. The prospect of Soviet-sponsored intervention in the region worried white South Africans, already paranoid because of the growing strength of anti-apartheid forces. In this context, the possibility of attaining a nuclear capacity that could be used either to hold the Soviets at bay or to bargain with the Americans seemed enormously attractive. The amiable French provided help with building a reactor and the Israelis offered guidance in building a bomb, in exchange for South African uranium. The nuclear club now had eight members; calculations of atomic equilibrium were thrown into chaos. Israel's nuclear capability, which was supposedly to protect her from her enemies in the Middle East, made those enemies covetous of the same sort of power.

The world grew genuinely afraid. Fear was reflected in, and exacerbated by, television. In the United States, some 100 million viewers tuned in to *The Day After*, a drama about a nuclear attack on the US, seen through the eyes of a few Kansas residents. After ABC persuaded the producers to tone down the more graphic scenes, in order to make it acceptable for prime time viewing, what resulted was a thermonuclear version of *The Waltons*. While the film deals reasonably well with the immediate horror of atomic attack, it treads lightly over the aftermath – the disease and starvation of nuclear winter. It nevertheless had a profound effect upon the American people, provoking the Secretary of State George Schultz to appear on national television immediately after the screening to offer

---

* The Americans supplied the deuterium for the reactor.

assurances that the Reagan administration was doing everything it could to prevent nuclear holocaust.

Much more harrowing was *Threads*, screened in Britain. At the beginning, Ruth Beckett (Karen Meagher) and Jimmy Kemp (Reece Dinsdale) are two ordinary young people in love. But then the Bomb falls. Jimmy disappears after the blast, while Ruth is left to cope. At one point, on the verge of starvation, she finds a dead sheep and eats it, despite realizing it is probably radiated. The sheep's bloody coat then provides warmth in the nuclear winter. Human kindness takes the form of a man who gives Ruth dead rats to eat. Her baby, conceived two months before the attack, is born in a world rendered medieval. With hospitals gone, Ruth gives birth alone, cutting the umbilical cord with her teeth. Her daughter grows up quickly in a world without order or joy. At times the characters stare blankly toward the audience, as if pleading to be released from their nightmare.

Toward the end, the film jumps forward ten years, when recovery of a sort has begun. Steam engines are widely used. But the new generation is completely illiterate, and many suffer from horrible deformities. Those who had struggled to survive over the previous decade now die of radiation-related illnesses. Ruth falls victim to leukaemia, leaving her daughter to cope as best she can with no real means of support. The film ends with her daughter, just thirteen, giving birth to a horribly mutated stillborn child. *Threads* is about death, but also about survival. And that is the sting in its tail, for the struggle to survive is usually the stuff of heroic tales. In this case, the will to live is a curse and ultimately futile. The post-apocalyptic world is populated by people who loot and murder for food, yet the moral code to condemn their actions has itself been vaporized. The title refers to the fragile threads that hold society together and become so easily unravelled. Or, as the film proclaims, 'the connections that make society strong also make it vulnerable'.[37]

Filmmakers and novelists proved much better at imagining the aftermath of nuclear attack than did the analysts at RAND or the FCDA. In fiction, the chaos caused by the Bomb is not limited to buildings destroyed or lives lost, but instead extends deep into the fabric of society. In Russell Hoban's *Riddley Walker*, society regresses to the Iron Age – with education a casualty of the nuclear holocaust, language itself is left shattered and distorted. The message is clear: thermonuclear weapons smash civilization with the same ruthless efficiency as they destroy buildings. A survivor in James Herbert's *Domain* discovers that 'everything, anything, they could find was for the taking: food, clothing, shelter, bodies, and lives – all were included. There was no control anymore, just survival.' In Herbert's story, the earth is inherited by huge rats. 'It seemed that the mutant vermin were in a conspiracy with the powers who had ordered the all-out destruction of mankind: what those lunatic powers could not kill off, the rats were happy to clear up.'[38] No one at RAND ever thought about rats.

Unease about the bomb was sufficiently prevalent to produce a niche market for anti-nuclear rock music. In the 1980s, Sting released 'Walking in Your Footsteps' and 'Russians', U2 offered 'Seconds' and 'Bullet the Blue Sky', while INXS shouted out 'Guns in the Sky'. The video accompanying Frankie Goes to Hollywood's 'Two Tribes' showed Reagan and Andropov in a boxing match – a rather pathetic attempt at a sophisticated political message. As was the case with the anti-war songs of the 1960s, the medium obscured the message. Most listeners enjoyed the songs without paying much attention to the subject matter. How many Bob Dylan fans, for instance, realize that his 'A Hard Rain's A-Gonna Fall' is about nuclear destruction? The same could be said about the most successful Bomb film of the 1980s, *War Games* (1983), in which a young computer geek very nearly triggers Armageddon. While the film had some important things to say about the bizarre logic of deterrence, most viewers saw a light-hearted action story.

The American government reacted to public fear in the same way that it had in the 1950s, namely with pious exhortations about civil defence. But the 1980s generation was much more aware of the dangers of radiation, and much more inclined to doubt glib assurances about the chances of survival. Given this level of awareness, it seems bizarre that civil defence literature produced in the 1980s was no more sophisticated than in the days of Bert the Turtle. In 1981, Thomas Jones, deputy Under-Secretary of Defense, advised that, in the event of a nuclear attack, citizens should 'Dig a hole, cover it with a couple of doors and then throw three feet of dirt on top. . . . It's the dirt that does it. . . . If there are enough shovels to go around, everybody's going to make it.'[39] References were made to the fact that nuclear attacks upon Hiroshima and Nagasaki had been closely followed by a Japanese economic miracle, as if to suggest that atomic war could benefit a nation.

Perhaps the most wacky suggestion came from the Lawrence Livermore lab. It proposed that people might protect themselves from the worst effects of nuclear attack by making for the nearest body of water. In order to maximize protection, they should wear numerous layers of clothes and remain about four feet below the surface for as long as possible, while minimizing the time spent at the surface gasping for air. The report, for which Livermore received $176,000 in consultancy fees from the federal government, admitted that the workers in question would have to be good swimmers, but also advised that they should 'tether themselves to a flotation device with a 10 foot line'.[40] It was in this climate of unreality that *The*

Atomic Café was released. The film, a compendium of nuclear newsreels from thirty years before, poked fun at the previous generation's naïve assumptions about nuclear weapons and war. But, with a new generation of advisers suggesting that people could swim to safety, laughter proved painfully hollow.

In the nuclear arena, Great Britain has always behaved like the boy who shows up at a party in flared trousers, only to discover that everyone else has returned to straight legs. This tendency to miss the beat was especially apparent in the approach to civil defence. The matter was virtually ignored until 1972, when quite suddenly the Home Office embarked upon a concerted effort to prepare the country for war. Discussions with the emergency services and local government representatives led to a four-year strategy outlined in *Home Defence 1972-1976*. Local authorities were given responsibility for devising civil emergency plans for their area. By the end of the prescribed period, little of substance had been achieved. Then, in 1977, the Home Office commissioned the scientist James Cotterill to conduct a review of shelter policy. His committee took nearly three years to produce a deeply pessimistic report which concluded that providing shelters for the civilian population would cost £70 billion, or four times the annual defence budget. Beyond the matter of cost, the committee drew attention to the huge practical problems associated with stockpiling food and water.

On 7 August 1980, the Conservative Home Secretary William Whitelaw announced that, under the new Home Defence Review, the government would increase spending on civil defence from £13.7 million to £45 million, a significant increase but far short of Cotterill's ambitious programme. Instead of shelters, the British got hollow assurances from Whitelaw that 'Most houses in this country offer a reasonable degree of protection against radioactive fallout from nuclear explosions and protection can be substantially improved by a series of quite simple do-it-yourself measures.'[41]

The most obvious and controversial manifestation of this new policy was the pamphlet *Protect and Survive*, published in 1980 and distributed to every household. Citizens were advised to construct a fall-out room within the home:

> You will need to block up windows in the room, and any other openings, and to make the outside walls thicker, and also to thicken the floor above you, to provide the strongest possible protection against the penetration of radiation. Thick, dense materials are the best, and bricks, concrete or building blocks, timber, boxes of earth, sand, books and furniture might all be used.

While you're at it, you should paint all the windows in the house white, to reflect away the heat flash. An inner refuge should be constructed within the fall-out room by using doors to make a lean-to and piling books, sand, or bags of clothing around it. Sufficient provisions like food, water, and toilet paper should be stored to last for fourteen days. This recommendation was not based on any scientific assessment of the dispersal rate of fallout, but rather because it equalled, well, two weeks. 'If a death occurs while you are confined to the fall-out room place the body in another room and cover it as securely as possible. Attach an identification.'[42]

Critics argued that the government should put its effort into preventing nuclear war, not in preparing for it, since protection against the bomb was futile. The pamphlet had a curious effect upon the nation's mentality, given that it forced people to start thinking about a threat which most had preferred to ignore. The best rebuttal came from Raymond Briggs whose book *When the Wind Blows* (subsequently made into a film) tells of an ordinary family struggling earnestly to follow government advice after the bombs have fallen. As in *Threads*, the value of survival is rendered dubious by the horrors of the post-apocalypse.

The response to *Protect and Survive* reflected the divisive politics of Thatcherite Britain. Most Conservatives supported civil defence as a natural corollary to a strong military. Labour's response was much more complicated. The party had long been embroiled in a row over nuclear weapons which, at various stages, threatened to tear it apart. Some supported Britain's nuclear deterrent, others bitterly opposed it. The latter group was divided between hardline advocates of unilateral disarmament and those who wanted a nuclear-free Britain but realized that to campaign for it would be political suicide. Civil defence exacerbated this bitter wrangle. Some Labour local authorities initiated the 'Nuclear Free Zone' movement under which they vowed to ban nuclear facilities from their areas and refused to cooperate with civil defence plans.

In 1982, public discontent led to the cancellation of Operation Hard Rock, a large-scale civil defence exercise. But, despite this U-turn, the government stubbornly insisted that its broad plans would remain in force. In response to widespread non-compliance in Labour-controlled areas, the government passed the Civil Defence Regulations Act in 1983, legally compelling local authorities to participate in exercises. But, in 1988, a Home Office investigation into the level of preparedness revealed a widespread refusal to implement the new legislation. This failure was not always an expression of political opposition, since civil defence cost money which councils did not have.

Reagan's combativeness, reinforced by his political soulmate Margaret Thatcher, breathed life into CND, virtually moribund since the 1960s. Internal strife and factionalism had weakened the group from within, while the peaceful resolution of the Cuban Missile Crisis had undermined its purpose. Activists found it deeply frustrating that ordinary people had learned to live with the bomb. By the early seventies, the left's focus had shifted toward the counter-culture and Vietnam. 'We were concerned with *real* issues,' the journalist Peter Fuller recalled. He and his comrades 'regarded CND with faint contempt, as something passé and irrelevant, a bit like a cross between the Fabians and the League Against Cruel Sports'.[43] In 1970, CND had fewer than thirty active groups, a full-time staff of only four and a virtually non-existent regional organization. The only big thing about it was its debt. When the press paid attention, it was only to heap scorn.

Some progress was made in the 1970s, but it was noticeable only to those intimately familiar with the dark days of decline. The group gained some credibility by linking itself to the ecology movement, particularly the opposition to nuclear power. Spirits were raised when, in 1972, the Labour Party agreed *in principle* to unilateral disarmament. CND activists, always more interested in principle than politics, were delighted at the way the party had invited an albatross to sit on its neck.

The imminent arrival of Cruise and Trident caused CND to rise phoenix-like. Attendance at meetings increased, as did sales of publications. A new spirit was evident among a new generation of protesters. Permanent camps were set up at Greenham Common and at Faslane in Scotland. On 26 October 1980, 70,000 people marched to Trafalgar Square for a rally to protest against Cruise and Trident – an event which evoked the spirit of the Aldermaston marches.

A year later, over 300,000 Germans marched in Bonn against deployment of Pershing II and Cruise. Protests drew a crowd of 150,000 in London, and a similar number in Brussels and Rome. At the INF negotiations, Nitze was genuinely worried that European governments would be persuaded by the protests to cancel their commitment to Cruise and, as a result, destroy his bargaining position. Discontent was also palpable behind the Iron Curtain. The Soviets were taken aback by the resistance to deployment of SS-20s in Poland and Romania.

Within Britain, the resurgence of CND meant that many of the arguments of the late 1950s were replayed. The relationship with the Labour Party continued to be problematic, with CND not trusting Labour to implement unilateral disarmament and Labour activists resenting the way CND threatened to derail the party. Class issues endangered the alliance – to most workers, CND seemed a collection of middle-class, muesli-eating mothers in handmade jumpers who breastfed baby outside a missile base while Daddy worked for the capitalists in the city. For many on the left, nuclear disarmament was a dangerous distraction which jeopardized Labour's return to power. The same old factionalism continued, as did the tendency of members to 'do their own thing' – as evidenced at Greenham Common.

The historian E. P. Thompson wanted to move away from the nationalist egotism which had long characterized CND. His brainchild, European Nuclear Disarmament (END) sought to 'place Europe . . . at the centre of the story'[44] and to emphasize that SS-20 missiles were as great a threat as Cruise. The anti-Cruise protests sweeping Europe could, he hoped, be turned into a unified movement. But within Britain, the idea fell on stony ground, due in part to the left's traditional enmity toward Europe. An even bigger problem was that leftists had already decided that the US was the evil element in the nuclear equation. The idea that the USSR might also be at fault required a broad-mindedness which most did not possess.

In 1982 the Labour Party conference voted two to one in favour of unilateralism. The majority of the shadow cabinet, on the other hand, feared that the policy would be an electoral disaster. They were right. While the 1983 election manifesto was not strictly speaking unilateralist, it did commit the party to getting rid of Britain's weapons while seeking a bilateral agreement with the Soviet Union to eliminate an equivalent number. The senior Labour MP Gerald Kaufman called it 'the longest suicide note in history'.[45] The accuracy of that description was revealed to Denis Healey on the first day of the campaign when Yorkshire miners, who were militant on industrial issues, made clear their disdain for unilateral disarmament.

With CND resurgent, the hostile press began to pay attention again. Journalists took sinister delight in reporting about activists who thought that the way to get rid of Cruise was to knit a long scarf around the missile base and hang tampons on the fence. Though the press was undoubtedly unfair, the antics of the Greenham women seemed weird even to lifelong supporters of CND. Feminists objected to the heavily maternalist message. The problem reached a climax when the women flatly refused any mixed-sex actions at the base. CND, respecting the women's wishes, was therefore unable to organize a significant protest to mark the actual deployment of Cruise at Greenham Common, the first arrival of the missiles on European soil. CND very nearly split over the issue.

Some lessons had been learned. In contrast to the 1960s, CND now had the sense to cut their cloth to suit the political wind. Unilateralism was not abandoned, but, at the same time, the respectable face of the movement – represented by Monsignor Bruce Kent and Joan Ruddock – voiced limited demands like 'no Cruise', 'no Trident' and 'cut the defence budget' which seemed plausible. Particularly effective were arguments which expressed the cost of weapons in terms of the number of schools or hospitals that might be built instead. The most impressive action by the anti-nuclear movement, however, was undoubtedly the tracking of Cruise missile convoys. Proponents of the weapons system had long argued its greatest strength was that it was virtually invulnerable because it could 'melt' into the countryside. But a few protesters, armed only with enthusiasm, managed to follow deployment exercises around the countryside, accompanied all the time by the media.

In the end, all this had little effect. The fate of nuclear weapons would be decided by high-level dialogue in Geneva, Vienna and Reykjavik, not by activists camping out at Faslane or Greenham Common. And it is difficult to escape the conclusion that the enthusiasm for CND had more to do with fear than with principled opposition to nuclear weapons. As was the case in the 1960s, when fear abated, so too did the movement.

In the mid-1980s, a high ranking American official is reputed to have remarked 'Well, any day you don't execute the SIOP is a good one.'[46] The remark encapsulates the precarious atmosphere of those times.

In late 1983 Reagan the warmonger morphed into Reagan the peacemaker. This strange transformation still confounds analysts. What seems clear is that, though he was an old man, he was not set in his ways. A number of events increased his fear of nuclear war and that fear was eventually translated into a sincere desire for rapprochement. The first event was the shooting down of a Korean airliner in September 1983 – Soviet pilots had mistaken it for a hostile aircraft. The episode forced Reagan to consider the dire consequences that might result if 'a Soviet military man with his finger close to a nuclear button [made] an even more tragic mistake'.[47] The second monumental event was the screening of *The Day After* which, by all accounts, left Reagan severely depressed and determined to 'do all we can . . . to see that there is never a nuclear war'.[48] The populist president seems to have been affected by the film precisely because it was a story about ordinary Americans. Then came a NATO exercise of November 1983 called Able Archer which the Soviets briefly interpreted as an actual preparation for a nuclear strike. Had the Soviets stuck strictly to their 'launch-on-attack' policy, they might have released their nuclear weapons.* Reagan later admitted that he was genuinely surprised to discover that the Soviets thought the US capable of an unprovoked attack. The combination of these events, not to mention a desire to be remembered as a peacemaker, convinced Reagan of the need to negotiate. 'The stakes were too high for us not to try to find a common ground where we could meet and reduce the risk of Armageddon.'[49]

The new Soviet premier, Gorbachev, seemed to Reagan actually human. The two got on famously; out of their camaraderie came a cooling of tensions. But more important than personal relations were the grim facts

---

* The policy calls for missiles to be launched on the first indication that an attack is imminent, in order to prevent them being destroyed by incoming missiles.

of economic reality. The expansion of her nuclear arsenal had virtually bankrupted the USSR. The Soviets had to admit that they could not run at the pace Reagan set, particularly not with a new arms race starting in outer space. On 3 October 1985, Gorbachev told the deputies of the National Assembly:

> Our chief task is to make the economy more effective and dynamic . . . it is not difficult to understand that the most important conditions for the attainment of these goals is not only a peace we can count on but also a quiet, normal international situation. These priorities also determine our foreign policy.[50]

At a series of high level summit meetings, the path toward genuine arms reduction was charted. But it was by no means a smooth path. At Geneva, in the autumn of 1985, Gorbachev's willingness to agree to massive reductions snagged on his insistence that SDI be abandoned. Reagan refused to smother his precious child. In Reykjavik the following October, the two leaders went so far as to propose the complete elimination of nuclear weapons within ten years, but Reagan again refused to yield on Star Wars. 'I've said again and again the SDI wasn't a bargaining chip,' he told Gorbachev. 'I've told you, if we find out the SDI is practical and feasible, we'll make that information known to you and everyone else so that nuclear weapons can be made obsolete.'[51] He stubbornly insisted that SDI would make the world a safer place. 'I could no more negotiate on SDI than I could barter with your future,' Reagan told the American people.[52]

Though the talks achieved nothing substantial,* the world sensed that a corner had been turned. Reagan encouraged this interpretation: 'Believe me, the significance of that meeting at Reykjavik is not that we didn't sign agreements; the significance is that we got as close as we did.'[53] This feeling was confirmed in December 1987 when the INF treaty paved the way for the elimination of SS-20, Pershing and Cruise, the first actual reduction of arsenals in the lifetime of the Bomb. The weapons which had caused so much anguish when they were deployed were suddenly removed with comparatively little fanfare. Critics inevitably pondered the point of it all. 'The building and deployment of hundreds of new missiles in Europe must have cost a huge amount of money,' Alexander Bovin remarked in the *Moscow News* on 8 March 1987. 'And if we agree to destroy these missiles: Why then were they built? Why were they deployed? It is not only me who

---

* Reagan aides were apparently delighted at the failure of an agreement which would have proved impossible to implement. James Schlesinger, the former Defense Secretary, remarked: 'We must accept the astonishing irony: it was the impasse over SDI that saved us from the embarrassment of entering into completed agreements from which subsequently we would have had to withdraw.' (Wills, p.464.)

is asking these questions. It would be very good to have competent answers.'[54]

Gorbachev, unlike his predecessors, saw security as 'a political task' which could only be achieved 'through political means'. He recognized that, even though the accumulation of arms over the previous fifteen years had been for purely defensive purposes, it had not been perceived as such by the West and had not therefore been successful. Security, he discovered, 'can only be mutual'.[55] However simple that realization might seem, it had managed to elude leaders on both sides during the Cold War. Bombs begat bombs. During the period 1963–80 the superpowers had enjoyed improved political relations but at the same time had expanded their nuclear arsenals and had continued to fight proxy wars around the world. Thus, despite political détente, tensions remained high. Gorbachev recognized that real progress could not occur until political détente was accompanied by military détente. But recognition was not enough. Though he managed to allay some distrust which the West (and particularly the US) felt toward the USSR, real progress would not come until 1989 when the Soviet edifice began to crumble. Americans found it easy to like an emasculated enemy.

In 1987, a hugely significant event occurred at a White House party. In attendance was Gorbachev – the presence of a Soviet premier would have been unthinkable just three years earlier. Another guest was Edward Teller, the embodiment of Reagan's nuclear fantasies. When the two were introduced, Gorbachev refused to shake Teller's hand. Teller claims he was 'shocked and hurt'.[56] Progress is sometimes painful.

In acknowledgement of the INF treaty, the Doomsday Clock was moved back three minutes, to six minutes to midnight. Meanwhile, in late 1989, F. W. de Klerk announced that South Africa was abandoning its nuclear weapons programme. Sceptics argued that this was simply an attempt to ensure that the bombs would be kept out of the hands of any future black government, but most people cared not to speculate on the reasons for these blessings. A short time later, with the collapse of Communist regimes in Eastern Europe and the end of the Cold War, the Doomsday Clock was moved again, this time to ten minutes to midnight.

The old soldiers of the Cold War remain convinced of their importance in saving the world. They believe that they kept the Communists at bay long enough for the USSR to destroy itself. Lt. General Edmundson looks back fondly at a career well spent:

> I believed it at the time, and I still believe that SAC was the major force that kept the Russians from stepping off the deep end until they spent themselves into oblivion. . . . I think that SAC and the capability that we built into SAC, and having a man like General LeMay around at the time to run

it, is what enabled us to reach a point where the Berlin Wall would come tumbling down and people would be saving blocks of it to take home for souvenirs.[57]

The women of Greenham Common see things differently. They vowed to stay at their camp until the Cruise missiles were removed. When the missiles were removed they congratulated themselves on their achievement, rather like the lunatic who thinks the sun rises because he wakes up in the morning.

The women stayed until 2000, though no one quite knows why.

CHAPTER 17

Fallout

In Chaparral, Nevada, the end of the Cold War was not cause for celebration. The town, which supplied prostitutes for workers at the Test Site, went into steep decline when the NTS officially ceased operation in 1998. Like the mining towns of Nevada's past, Chaparral seemed destined to become a ghost town. But, as its website boasts, 'Chaparral refused to wither and die'. Kitty Storm, owner of the Pigeon Ranch, was elected mayor on a promise to revive the town and its main industry. She launched the High Desert Film Festival (no prizes for guessing what type of films) to attract a new crop of visitors. At the height of the Cold War, the town's slogan was 'Chaparral. You'll come for the whores. You'll stay for the whores.' But the Army didn't stay. 'We'll leave the red light on for you,' the town now promises.

Or so it seems. Chaparral is in fact the invention of an imaginative filmmaker. *The Independent*, directed by Stephen Kessler, takes a wry look at military downsizing and the 'peace dividend'. Like all good comedy, it's painfully close to the truth. Across Nevada, the departure of the Bomb was widely mourned. Nowhere was this more the case than in the dusty towns bordering the Test Site, where cold warriors once sought warmth.

In 1991, in acknowledgement of the decision by the Soviet Union and the United States to sign the Strategic Arms Reduction Treaty (START), the Doomsday Clock was moved to seventeen minutes to midnight. It was a hugely symbolic adjustment, the first time the minute hand had been out of the last quadrant and, as such, reflective of the euphoria which greeted the end of the Cold War. Close on the heels of this agreement came negotiations on a Comprehensive Test Ban Treaty which was ratified in 1996.[*]

The tests stopped, but the dying didn't.[†] In 1998, the US government commissioned a study by the Institute for Energy and Environmental

---

[*] Up to the time tests halted, the US had conducted 1,030 tests, the Soviet Union 715, France 210, Britain 45 and China 45.
[†] The French, ignoring the move away from testing, had resumed in 1995.

Research into the health problems caused by nuclear fallout. The IEER's report, released in early 2002, stunned the government, since casualty rates far exceeded anything yet released. The report estimated that fallout could cause cancer in 80,000 Americans, leading to perhaps 15,000 deaths. Particularly worrying was the fact that the areas affected were not confined to the usual domicile of the downwinders, but included sixteen states, from Washington and California in the West to Vermont and New Hampshire in the East. 'Any person living in the contiguous United States since 1951 has been exposed to radioactive fallout,' the study concluded; 'and all organs and tissues of the body have received some radiation exposure.'[2]

Lisa Ledwidge, an IEER biologist, found it ironic that the government had warned suppliers of photographic film so that they could protect their stock from exposure, but did not warn milk producers. Dr Arjun Makhijani, the IEER president, claimed that 'farm children . . . who drank goat's milk in the 1950s in high fallout areas were as severely exposed as the worst exposed children after . . . Chernobyl'. The IEER study had concentrated mainly on thyroid cancer because its connection to fallout is clearest. Other cancers probably resulted, but irrefutable blame would be difficult to prove.[3] 'I consider the whole idea of subjecting people to a toxic influence without their consent is an outrage whether it's done for weapons testing or nuclear power,' Dr John Gofman, a one-time member of the Manhattan Project, has remarked. 'You have no right to do that to people . . . I don't consider the Department of Energy a credible agency. I don't see how you could . . . for the lies . . . they told.'[4]

Out in Australia, one hears a similar story. The atomic soldiers have been the most organized in campaigning for compensation, but organization has not brought much success. Of 358 claims filed with the Military Compensation and Rehabilitation Service by October 2002, just nine have succeeded. Ric Johnstone has to have 'a half a pound of meat cut out' of his body every six months to keep the cancer at bay. Like many other claimants, he suspects that the delays in paying compensation are motivated by the government's cynical assumption that, with each passing year, the number of cases will inevitably decline as victims die off. If so, it's a successful strategy: the membership of the Australian Nuclear Veterans Association peaked at over 2,000, but by 2002 was down to 600. 'The fucking government has killed me and now they won't even give my wife anything,' Johnstone complains.[5]

In December 2001 Shirley Denson claimed that her late husband Eric, an RAF pilot, had been forced to fly his plane several times through a mushroom cloud after a test on Christmas Island in 1958. He subsequently developed a range of illnesses which caused severe depression, leading to his suicide in 1976. After a long struggle, Shirley managed to win a war widow's pension from the British government in 1998, but then decided to take the case further. She now alleges that the British government 'knowingly and maliciously' exposed her husband to deadly radiation. Scotland Yard launched a criminal investigation, which immediately brought a denial of guilt by the Ministry of Defence. 'The allegations that servicemen were used as guinea pigs are not true,' a spokeswoman said. 'We've been looking at it for many years . . . but don't believe there are major problems. The standards at the time were complied with but standards now are very different.'[6] That's not exactly true. Ian Greenhalgh, the solicitor for another victim, Tom Duggan, uncovered a report indicating that officials were fully aware of the dangers to soldiers on Christmas Island, but ignored their own findings. On the strength of this evidence, Duggan successfully won compensation in December, 2001.[7]

The worst poisoning has received the least attention. Out in Russia, the nuclear cities remain highly polluted places, due to careless practices in the 1950s. The natural deactivation of the Techa river system will take hundreds of years to complete. On its banks is Muslyumovo, the most radioactive village on earth. Here, gene-mutations are fifteen times more likely than in the rest of the Russian Federation. Actual figures for radiation-related illnesses have probably been grossly underestimated, since, during the Cold War, the Soviet government feared that publicity about cancer clusters would pinpoint the secret locations of nuclear facilities. One doctor claims that he and his colleagues were told to falsify death certificates by entering 'something else, either a stroke, or a severe heart attack, or even chronic heart disease . . . to put down cancer as a cause of death was just not allowed'.

Since the mid-1950s, the river has been off limits, but the fence bordering it is now a rusted tangle of metal and residents ignore advice to stay away. Fish in the river were found to have levels of radiation twenty times higher than normal. When local children fishing on the banks were told of these findings they seemed oblivious. 'We eat these fish,' they replied. 'It's like they say, "you can't infect the infected".' The average life span for a Muslyumovo woman is 47 and for a man 45 (the national averages are 72 and 69, respectively). 'We're all sick,' one woman confesses. 'It's some kind of dying generation.' The residents have resigned themselves to an early death – 'You can't escape your fate', one man remarks. They don't want to leave because their roots are in the area and, in any case, who has the money to move? In 1997 the province administration finally agreed that resettlement was warranted, but, since the decision occurred at the height of the Russian economic crisis, it has not been implemented. Meanwhile the village slowly dies. According to a local osteopath, the birth of children without hands, legs or feet (or indeed any limbs) is by no means unusual. That said, according to one resident, 'There aren't many births, the women don't want to have children. Who needs more cripples?'[8]

Radiation has killed with the same slow cruelty out in the Pacific, where cancers started appearing around ten years after the first tests. Tumours and leukaemia were particularly prevalent among those who had been children when the ill-fated Bravo test took place. Of twenty-one Rongepalese under the age of 12 at the time, nineteen developed thyroid tumours. Under pressure, Congress granted a total of $750,000 in compensation to the islanders in 1964. A further $25,000 was paid to every victim of thyroid cancer in 1977, in addition to $1,000 to every islander resident at the time of the blast.[9]

The number of victims was greatly reduced by the American policy of resettlement, but that merely replaced a tragedy with an injustice. 'Bikini is like a relative to us,' Lore Kessibuki remarked. 'Like a father or a mother or a sister or a brother, perhaps most like a child conceived from our own flesh and blood. And then, to us, that child was gone, buried and dead.'[10] The islanders were first moved to Rongerik, which unfortunately lacked the resources to allow them to feed themselves. In 1947, the journalist Harold Ickes found natives 'actually and literally starving to death'. They were then moved to Kili, a lush island full of coconut plantations 400 miles south of Bikini. To the Americans, this seemed a perfect solution, but the Bikini people are fishermen, not farmers. The rough seas around Kili made fishing difficult and hindered the approach of supply ships. Before long, the islanders were starving again. 'Even through all of these hardships . . . we still held high hopes that the Americans would help us,' one islander recalled. What they wanted most was to return to Bikini. 'America, America, America–where are you?'[11]

In 1967 the US government concluded that 'the exposures of radiation that would result from the repatriation of the Bikini people do not offer a significant threat to their health and safety.'[12] The first natives returned in 1969 and the rest were supposed to follow by 1973. But, then, new tests revealed 'higher levels of radioactivity than originally thought', particularly in coconuts, pandanus and local crabs, all part of the native diet. The great homecoming was postponed. In 1978 the first group of returnees were told to leave immediately – tests had revealed that the island would remain uninhabitable for a least a century. 'We kept believing in our proverb that 'everything was in God's hands' and that one day God would help us return to our homelands,' one islander remarked. 'When I think of the years and years that it will take to clean Bikini until the poison is totally eradicated and therefore safe for our children, I get extremely depressed,' Kilon Bauno complains. 'I will die long before this occurs.'[13]

In June 1975 Congress awarded $3 million to the displaced islanders and, when it became apparent that they would not be able to return to their home, an additional $12 million was granted three years later. The Marshall Islands Nuclear Claims Tribunal was established in 1988 to assess personal injury claims throughout the archipelago. The scale of compensation ranges from $12,500 for a benign tumour to $125,000 for leukaemia. By the end of 1997, $63,127,000 had been awarded to or on behalf of 1,549 people.[14] On 5 March 2001, in a separate claim brought by the people of Bikini, the US government agreed to pay damages of nearly $565 million as a final settlement of all claims. In the meantime, cleanup efforts continue. These involve replacing the topsoil to a depth of 15 inches and replanting most of the coconut and pandanus trees.

In 1946, E. B. White wrote of the terrible irony of using the world's most terrible weapon to destroy a virgin paradise. 'Bikini Lagoon, although we have never seen it, begins to seem like the one place in all the world we cannot spare. . . . It seems unspeakably precious, like a lovely child stricken with a fatal disease.'[15] The bombs destroyed not just an island, but also a way of life. 'We have incorporated many American customs and practices into our own,' Mayor Tomaki Juda admits, with considerable regret:

> the money that they give us, and that we use daily, is the American dollar. We buy American goods, in fact, most of the products sold in our stores come from America. Rice, tea, coffee, flour, sugar, Spam, cola, corned beef, automobiles, VCRs and televisions. Our children grow-up watching American movies. This causes our children, increasingly, to adopt the American value system and their customs as depicted on film.[16]

In 1996 the people of Bikini, in an effort to boost their economy, opened the famous atoll to the outside world as a diving, sportfishing and tourist destination. The area has been rated one of the ten best scuba diving spots in the world by a host of dive magazines. The chief attractions are the ships sunk during Operation Crossroads, declared radiologically safe by the Lawrence Livermore Laboratory. Divers can explore the USS *Saratoga*, the only aircraft carrier available for diving, and the *Nagato*, the ship on which Admiral Yamamoto directed the Pearl Harbor attack. As for the atoll itself, the IAEA has declared, 'There is no radiological risk in visiting,' though it does warn that 'eating locally grown produce, such as fruit, could add significant radioactivity to the body'. While this prevents long-term habitation, it is supposedly not a threat to tourists.[17]

Exploding bombs in paradise still appeals. The French, who find test ban treaties inconvenient to their nuclear ambitions, can't bring themselves to test bombs on their own soil. That privilege has instead been reserved for Algeria, or for French possessions in the South Pacific. In 1995 President Jacques Chirac decided to resume nuclear testing in Moruroa Atoll, much to the disgust of natives nearby. 'We don't want to be French guinea pigs anymore!' Oscar Temaru, the mayor of Papeete in

Tahiti, complained. 'Where is the democracy? Where is the humanity?' Moruroa, which lies 1,000 kilometres from Tahiti, is where the French conducted more than 150 tests thirty years earlier. To this day, they refuse any independent measurement of radiation levels, though they insist that the water is untainted and fish are safe to eat. Natives dispute these claims, citing evidence of sickness among those who worked in the atoll, or who have eaten fish from there.

The tests provoked a much-publicized protest by Greenpeace, which sent its ship *Rainbow Warrior II* to the region. (The first *Rainbow Warrior* had been blown up by the French ten years earlier.) Upon sailing into the test area, the ship was promptly attacked. 'The commandos came on with ladders, completely covered except their eyes,' Pamela Ward, a Greenpeace activist, recalled. 'They were all armed. Everything happened so fast. You can't help but think of every bad "Rambo" movie you've ever seen.'[18] The outcry was fierce, but also brief – probably exactly what the French had expected.

Meanwhile, out in Nevada, some of the predictions made by the AEC during the bad days of testing have proved faulty. It now seems that plutonium (half-life: 250,000 years) from the Test Site has leached into the water table of southern Nevada, something which was not supposed to happen. But no one quite predicted Nevada's massive population explosion and the havoc this would cause to the water supply. At the same time that the population has expanded, so too has the gambling industry. Gamblers stay in hotels where they use lots of water. But what seems a disaster is apparently nothing of the sort, at least according to Pat Mulroy, general manager of the Las Vegas Valley Water District. 'The plutonium doesn't concern me', she confessed, 'because the flow pattern is not toward Las Vegas.'[19] Water heads for the lowest point, which in this case is, perhaps appropriately, Death Valley. For the moment, at least, Nevada remains safe for gamblers.

Health risks exist even where no bombs were exploded. Since the 1950s British Nuclear Fuel's Sellafield facility has pumped around 500 pounds of plutonium and other radioactive isotopes into the Irish Sea. Suspicious cancer clusters in the area have been blamed on this discharge, and lobsters caught in the area are unsuitable for consumption. Dangerous radiation sometimes spreads by unexpected means. In the late 1990s, a garden in nearby Seascale was discovered to be so highly contaminated that BNFL was forced to remove the top soil. It transpired that hundreds of pigeons which had been roosting on the Sellafield site were fed by villagers three miles away and left behind radioactive droppings. The Ministry of Agriculture subsequently issued a formal warning to the public about the dangers of eating pigeons. One has to wonder how many British diets were disrupted.

The cost of nuclear weapons goes far beyond the money needed to build them. Richard Rhodes recalled a conversation with a senior Washington official charged with overseeing the long-delayed cleanup of the nuclear arms industry:

> Americans worry about nuclear power primarily these days, because they think the waste is a problem. It's not the waste from our nuclear power reactors. That's all sitting in swimming pools at the reactors, nice and confined. It's the enormous waste all over the country from building bombs, where the military was always able to tell itself, 'We'll worry about that later. There's a war on.' And it's even worse in Russia. They estimate officially, by their government estimates, that 40 per cent of the Soviet land mass is seriously polluted with radioactive and other military wastes.

'It was as if we nuked ourselves,' he concluded.[20]

According to Dr Eli Rips, if one removes all the spaces separating words in the Bible and then subjects this long series of letters to computerized 'skip sequence' searching, the decoded message that emerges tells of a nuclear holocaust which will occur in the year 2006. The author Michael Drosnin claims that this code predicted the World Wars, the assassination of Kennedy and the death of Princess Diana. As for the predictions of a nuclear holocaust, Drosnin takes a safe road. 'The Bible code', he claims, 'is not a promise of divine salvation. It is not a threat of inevitable doom. It is just information. Its message is that we can save ourselves.' In other words, if the Bomb explodes in 2006, it proves the code is right, but if it doesn't, it shows we have taken heed – which also proves the code is right. Perhaps, in a former career, Drosnin might have written horoscopes.

Since the Bomb provides a handy metaphor for the apocalypse, it has often been incorporated into the millenarian visions of modern-day mystics. The Church Universal and Triumphant bought 12,000 acres in Montana and set the faithful to work building nuclear bunkers in anticipation of a holocaust predicted by its leader, Elizabeth Claire Prophet. Another sect, the True Way, led by Hon-Ming Chen, spread the news that God would arrive at Chen's home in the Dallas suburb of Garland, Texas, by flying saucer on 31 March 1998. His arrival would spark the 'Great Tribulation', a series of disasters culminating in the nuclear destruction of the world in late 1999. A chosen few (in other words, Chen's followers) would escape with God in his flying saucer to another galaxy. When the appointed date arrived, God failed to visit Garland, though Chen claimed that strong winds and unusual cloud patterns over the suburb indicated his presence. When the following year failed to bring nuclear holocaust, Chen's sect quietly faded away.[21]

Cult leaders frequently offer followers protection from nuclear devastation. L. Ron Hubbard, founder of the controversial Church of Scientology, boasted exclusive access to a detox method which neutralizes radiation. Robert Earl Burton, the charismatic leader of the Fellowship of Friends, told his followers that Apollo, his headquarters in the foothills of the Sierra Nevada in California, would, because of its spirituality, be protected from a nuclear holocaust which would occur in 2006. Burton's potent message attracted a large following of well-educated and wealthy faithful, but his nuclear shield could not apparently deflect scandal. His cult died out after revelations that he brainwashed his faithful into 'absolute submission', in order to feed his 'voracious appetite for sexual perversion'.[22]

While some sects warn of nuclear holocaust, others try to bring it about. In the mid-1990s Russian investigators uncovered evidence that the Japanese doomsday cult, Aum Shinrikyo, tried to buy nuclear warheads, or, at the very least, nuclear knowledge. The leader, Shoko Asahara, built his sanctuary at Kamikuishiki, on the lower slopes of Mount Fuji, a multipurpose compound combining holy place, headquarters, lab, death factory and bunker. For most of 1994, Aum disciples busily prepared for a nuclear calamity which was supposed to occur after Pluto entered Sagittarius on 18 January 1995. Asahara claimed that an earthquake in the Kobe region would precede an American nuclear attack upon Japan. His followers were encouraged to believe that his Cosmo-Cleaner would protect them from radiation. Granted, no one wins prizes for predicting earthquakes in Japan, but the fact that a devastating quake hit Kobe on 17 January 1995 caused some people to take notice. But then the US failed to fulfil its end of the prediction. Asahara subsequently turned to another method of attracting attention, namely the sarin gas attack on the Tokyo subway later that year.[23] The subsequent trial brought revelations of involvement in extortion, drug running, mob connections, etc. Though Japanese authorities thought the cult had been eradicated, police raids in May 1999 uncovered a partially constructed nuclear bunker and Geiger counters.[24]

In Tom Clancy's *The Sum of All Fears*, an Arab terrorist group brings the world to the brink of nuclear disaster after it finds a nuclear weapon which an Israeli bomber 'lost' twenty years earlier. The terrorists recruit a disgruntled East German scientist who takes the plutonium core from the bomb and builds a thermonuclear device. Each element of the plot has sufficient plausibility to make the book frighteningly credible.

In the wake of the September 11th attacks, there has been much speculation about the vulnerability of major cities to nuclear terrorism. A bomb can be made with less than seven kilograms of plutonium, an amount about the size of a can of Coke. Every day, around 1.25 million people enter the US, while 1.36 billion kilos of cargo arrive by sea and another 4.66 million kilos by air. Less than five per cent of the cargo arriving is physically inspected. Shielding of enriched uranium and plutonium can make them virtually impossible to detect with radiation monitors – a physical search is the only foolproof method.[25] A recent study suggested that a 12.5-kiloton device exploded in the port area of New York would kill around 65,000 people immediately. Over the long term, another 200,000 radiation-related deaths could be expected.[26]

In 1964, the US conducted a top-secret study to see how easy it would be for an amateur to build a bomb. Dave Dobson and Bob Selden, both of whom had physics Ph.D.s but no experience in weapons work, were given the task of designing a bomb on the basis of information readily available in any good library. Early in the experiment, they decided to go for the tough challenge of building an implosion bomb, rather than a gun device. Two and a half years later, they came up with a design. 'We produced a short document that described precisely . . . what we proposed to build and what materials were involved,' Selden later explained. 'The whole works, so that this thing could have been made by Joe's Machine Shop downtown.'[27] Experts analysed the design and decided that, on paper, Selden and Dobson had produced a bomb as powerful as Fat Man.

As Clancy has suggested, the problem is even easier today, given improvements in machinery and computers. The difficulty lies in securing the radioactive core. Unfortunately, the world supply of surplus plutonium continues to grow, in part because of the decommissioning of nuclear weapons since 1992. Keeping track of the plutonium has become increasingly difficult. The problem is complicated by Russia's belief that plutonium and enriched uranium should be used in the generation of electricity. 'We have spent too much money making this material just to mix it with radioactive waste and bury it,' the Russian Minister of Atomic Energy, Viktor Mikhailov, remarked in 1995.[28] Nor has the US been conspicuously successful at solving its own disposal problem.

In late 1992, thieves broke into the apartment occupied by the grandson of the Russian physicist Igor Tamm. Items of obvious value – electronic equipment, expensive clothes and antique silver – were ignored. Instead, they took letters signed by Einstein, Heisenberg and Born, an autographed photo of Sakharov and the gold Lomonosov medal given by the Academy of Sciences. In other words, these were knowledgeable burglars with a pre-set plan of what to steal. They probably wanted Tamm's Nobel Prize medal but could not find it. Police subsequently surmised that the thieves were probably scientists who had fallen on hard times. Sergei Leskov, a science reporter for *Izvestia*, thinks that the Tamm burglary is indicative of the precarious state of the Russian nuclear industry. He contends that about

80 per cent of scientists who work within the Academy of Sciences system are discontented with their life and would like to leave the country.[29]

In late 1996, Vladimir Nechai, director of Chelyabinsk-70, shot himself. In his suicide note, he wrote that he could no longer stand to watch his life's work disintegrate, nor could he face devoted workers who had not been paid for five months. After attending the funeral, Grigory Yavlinsky, leader of the liberal Yabloko party, wrote: 'I could not look at these people without compassion. Here was the pride of Russian science; here were the physicists of world stature, dressed in their threadbare jackets and faded shirts with frayed cuffs.' He wondered if Moscow, and indeed the world, understood 'how dangerous it is to drive people who hold the nuclear arsenal in their hands to this state'.[30] According to estimates by the US Department of Energy, nuclear facilities within the former Soviet Union hold enough weapons-grade materials to make 40,000 bombs.[31]

Russia's nuclear cities have always been very bleak places: fortress towns shut off from the outside world. Conditions were at best basic and safety standards low. But since 1992, the situation has actually deteriorated, due primarily to the near bankruptcy of the Russian government. The sociologist Valentin Tikhonov, after interviewing 500 residents of these cities, found most employees desperate to escape. Highly skilled workers receive wages of less than $50 per month. When he interviewed them, most had not received pay rises for years, and more than 60 per cent admitted that they have been forced to take second jobs. 'I am simply fed up with this life,' one commented. 'In a word, it's a dog's life,' another remarked. Many feed themselves by growing potatoes on private patches. In September 1998, around 47,000 nuclear industry workers joined protests over the fact that $400 million in wages remained unpaid.[32] The director of Krasnoyarsk-26 subsequently warned that 'the social tension in the shops and factories has reached the critical level, and its consequences are unpredictable'.[33] These desperate workers have valuable expertise highly coveted by anyone eager to make a bomb. One in seven surveyed confessed a desire to work abroad. Of those, 46 per cent said they would work in the military field and six per cent claimed they would work anywhere at all, regardless of the nature of the regime. 'I would like to go abroad with pleasure,' one worker remarked. 'Sometimes I don't have enough money even to buy cigarettes, so I am in the depths of despair.'

Some efforts have been taken to retool the nuclear cities. The German firm BASF has established a facility in Krasnoyarsk-45 and Intel has penetrated Arzamas-16. But still-tight security arrangements impede effective commerce. The cities need to become more 'normal', while still protecting the secrets that lie within. Some employment opportunities exist in dismantling of arms, disposal of fissile materials and other nuclear-related enterprises. These can be profit-making, but they need seed-corn financing, which has not been forthcoming. The Russian Ministry of Atomic Energy (Minatom) estimates that 35,000 workers, or half the workforce, will have to be laid off by 2005.

Recognizing the risk, the US government established the Nuclear Cities Initiative in March 1997, designed to create new jobs in three of the hardest hit areas. But, by the end of 1999, the initiative had created only 100 jobs, an embarrassment to its organizers. The Republican-led Congress then slashed the budget from its original $12.5 million per year to $7.5 million, a figure experts claim is insufficient even to maintain operations in one of the nuclear cities.[34]

The Kurchatov Institute revealed in 1992 that two of its scientists had been approached by the Tajura Nuclear Center in Libya and offered jobs at $2,000 per month. Russian authorities still maintain tight control over their workers, and restrict travel to countries considered untrustworthy. But strict regimentation is detrimental to the free economy Russia is keen to create. 'While internal security practices may have so far prevented mass migrations, the potential risk seems likely to grow along with the growing desperation of the population,'[35] Jon Wolfstahl, of the Carnegie Endowment for International Peace, warns.

Yuri Smirnov (no relation to the nuclear physicist) was arrested in 1992 for stealing 1,538 grams of highly enriched bomb-grade uranium from the laboratory where he worked. Feeling contrite, he later explained that he had been driven to desperation because of the Russian economic crisis. At his lab, procedures allowed for an 'irretrievable loss' of around three per cent. Through careful handling of the material, he was able to siphon off small amounts which no one noticed was missing. While not very precise about his intentions, he thought perhaps he would collect about 1,200 grams and then sell it for $500. 'That was my salary for two years,' he explained. 'I needed a new refrigerator, and a new gas stove. The old fridge had already been there for 40 years, and a 30-year-old gas stove that had never been changed. And my apartment needed to be renovated. That's all. I didn't need to make a big profit.' The most frightening aspect of Smirnov's story is how easy it was to steal the uranium. He simply walked out of the laboratory doors every once in a while with a small vial containing 60 grams of uranium-235 in his shirt pocket. It had not occurred to officials that better security was needed, since workers had always been entirely trustworthy. In the end, Smirnov was arrested before he could figure out how to sell the material. His arrest was entirely accidental; he was picked up when some friends were hauled in for a minor crime.

In September 1998, a US team visiting the Kurchatov Institute in Moscow was shown a building containing 100 kilos of highly enriched uranium. The facility was unguarded because the Institute could not afford to pay a guard. Elsewhere, MVD sentries have left their posts to forage for food or because they lacked winter uniforms to keep them warm on patrol. Surveillance equipment was shut down because electricity bills had not been paid. In the midst of the 1998 crisis, General Igor Volynkin assured the press that the MVD was fully capable of protecting Russia's nuclear weapons, though he did acknowledge that salary payments were three months in arrears. Some officers had received vegetables in lieu of wages. Keen to help, the Defence Minister Igor Sergeyev encouraged officers to look for 'additional sources of sustenance' – soldiers would be allowed time off to forage for mushrooms and berries.[36]

In May 1998 General Alexander Lebed revealed to Congressman Curt Weldon that the Russians had long possessed a 'suitcase bomb'. While not, strictly speaking, the size of a suitcase, the device was sufficiently portable to be carried by two people and had a yield of one kiloton. Because it was not a strategic weapon, it had never been covered by arms agreements and was therefore extremely difficult to trace. During Weldon's visit to Moscow, Lebed claimed that he could account for only 48 of the 132 devices originally made. 'We don't know what the status of the other devices were, we just could not locate them,' he explained. Lebed's claims were subsequently verified by Alexei Yablokov, former scientific adviser to Boris Yeltsin. Though both Yablokov and Lebed were merely drawing attention to a potential problem, they were accused of treason for talking openly about it. Meanwhile, rebels in Chechnya boasted that they had two of the devices, a claim echoed by a group of radical Palestinians. In December 1998, Russian Defence Minister Igor Sergeyev maintained that the weapons were all accounted for and would be destroyed by the year 2000. Weldon had no reason to doubt Sergeyev, but he was still not confident that the Russians knew the whereabouts of each bomb. Russia watchers surmise that, rather than weapons actually being missing, the problem might simply have arisen because of chaotic and sometimes overlapping governmental accounting – not the sort of reassurance likely to reassure.[37]

In October 2001, the Russian Defence Ministry revealed that on two occasions terrorist groups had tried to break into nuclear storage sites, but were repulsed. According to the IAEA, between 1993 and 2002 there were 175 cases of nuclear trafficking, 18 of which involved enriched uranium or plutonium.[38] It is known that al-Qaeda agents have tried to buy uranium from South Africa and have pursued links with nuclear scientists in Pakistan. In November 2001, *Time* speculated that al-Qaeda might have purchased twenty of the Russian suitcase bombs for $30 million plus two tonnes of opium.[39]

It must be borne in mind that, in the aftermath of the September 11th attacks, stories of nuclear smuggling sell newspapers. There seems no limit to the public's hunger for frightening news and the willingness of journalists to feed that hunger. So far, sting operations have netted plenty of criminals willing to smuggle fissile materials, but little evidence of actual transactions. This means that the buyers have either escaped detection, or that they simply do not exist, or perhaps that security – especially in Russia – is tighter than is commonly assumed. In fact, some analysts fear that high profile sting operations might encourage copycat crimes, thus creating a problem where one did not previously exist. In April 1995, the FBI claimed that 'no definitive proof of international organized crime involvement in trafficking in actual weapons-grade materials has been noted to date'.[40] Mark Hibbs, a journalist who has studied the problem in considerable depth, has yet to find a 'single case of bomb grade material from the Russian inventory or any other inventory getting into the hands of a party, a group of terrorists, a rogue state, [or] a country which wants to make a nuclear bomb'. He suggests that the entire 'problem' might in fact be a convenient stick with which to hit the Russians.[41]

In 1990, the Soviet government officially acknowledged the existence of Arzamas-16. Five years later, at the formal request of residents, Yeltsin agreed to change the name back to Sarov. It remains a tightly controlled area, with entrance and exit carefully monitored by armed guards. Many residents prefer it that way. 'If a referendum were held today to take [the fences] down, I'd predict it would be defeated unanimously,' says Yevgeny Avrorin of the All-Russia Scientific Research Institute for Theoretical Physics. He says the fences are useful for keeping out the criminals and thugs who plague Russian society. Inside the closed cities, life seems safe. 'Nobody is afraid to go outside after dark.'[42] Pilgrimages to the shrines of St Serafim have resumed and the town has begun to exploit the marketability of its water, which is supposed to have healing powers – though one suspects that now it is more likely to kill. The end of the Cold War inspired the establishment of a sister-city relationship with Los Alamos, which includes scientific exchanges, cultural missions and a pen pal arrangement between high school students. In May 1995, on the occasion of a visit by a Los Alamos civic delegation, the local Sarov paper remarked: 'The idea of sister-city relationships is one of "people-to-people", of citizen diplomacy from "heart-to-heart". Only in this way will the ice left from the Cold War be melted.'[43]

While Russian facilities have withered, some American ones have thrived. The US still spends roughly $35 billion per year on its nuclear arsenal, so there's plenty of money to keep wizards at work. But the labs have had to adapt; an increasing amount of effort is devoted to 'peace' projects rather than simply the manufacture of new weapons. Livermore, for instance, has devised a range of monitors to enforce the Comprehensive Test Ban Treaty. It has also developed, in partnership with the Russians, technologies for dismantling weapons. But the big money is currently in instruments for the detection of weapons of mass destruction held by rogue states or terrorist groups.

There's a good road into Los Alamos – bombs need good roads. The town is something of an anomaly. New Mexico is predominantly Hispanic or Native American, working class and poor. Los Alamos is mainly white or Oriental, middle class and comfortable. The first golf course in the state was built there. In the local Starbucks conversations are about particles, mesons, neutrinos and things counted in billions. In the mid-1990s, in an attempt to come to terms with a brave new world, the lab adopted the motto 'Los Alamos, a customer focused, unified laboratory'. But no one quite knew what that meant. No one quite knew what to do next. 'The lab has no right to rely on its history to maintain itself,' one particularly perceptive scientist contends.[44] Out in the Tech Areas, which stretch into the mountains, the synthetic juxtaposes uneasily with rugged nature. The office of the Human Genome Project is just twenty minutes away from Bandolier National Monument with its prehistoric cave dwellings. The future is wrapped in the past.

With remarkable talent for euphemism, the Nevada Test Site now calls itself 'AN ENVIRONMENTAL RESEARCH PARK'. Its purpose has shifted from testing to dumping. There were always hints of this. When a plane carrying nuclear weapons crashed in Greenland, the contaminated soil was scooped up and taken to Nevada. Low-level waste from around the country ends up in Nevada for the simple reason that most states do not permit its disposal. Habit will turn to policy if the construction of a massive radioactive waste dump at Yucca Mountain goes ahead. In 1996, construction of a device assembly facility (DAF) was completed. Decommissioned weapons, many of them the result of the 'peace dividend', were to be taken to the DAF to be disarmed. In case of accident, the roof is designed to fall in on itself, thus sealing the offensive radiation. The government originally hoped that peace could be profitable – Nevada could make money dismantling Soviet bombs. Unfortunately, the old Soviet republics are short on cash, so their bombs, or at least the cores, grow more dangerous with each passing year.[45]

In July 2002, work began on a $12.3 million Test Site Museum, to be housed on the campus of the University of Nevada, Las Vegas. Visitors will be issued a 'security pass' on entry, similar to the dosimeter badges once worn by employees at the NTS. A virtual tour will be offered and films of explosions will be shown. Supporters of the project have come from both sides of the nuclear debate, since both expect the exhibits to bolster their cause. Funding has come from a combination of state and federal grants, in addition to private donations. A proposal to raise funds through the sale of special commemorative licence plates, which featured a mushroom cloud and the words 'Nevada Test Site', were, however, cancelled on the grounds that 'the design had created controversy and was insensitive to the times'.[46]

Some people despise the Bomb, while others are drawn irresistibly to it. A website calling itself the Bureau of Atomic Tourism offers a virtual tour of important nuclear sites, including Alamogordo, Los Alamos, Tinian, Hiroshima and Bikini. For those who prefer the real thing, a number of missile silos have been turned into museums, convenient places to take a break along the road to the Grand Canyon or Disneyland. Once a month, visitors can enjoy a full day tour of the Nevada Test Site. 'You are going to see a lot of cool stuff,' the guide promises as the bus enters the complex.[47] Among the attractions are the pens where 1,200 pigs did their national service. Near St Andrews, in Scotland, a former nuclear bunker is run as a museum. Visitors can witness a simulated attack in the war room, wander through the dormitories, and wonder what it would have been like to be among the chosen. The truly strange have held weddings in the bunker chapel. A similar bunker near Bonn was put up for sale in November 1998 because the facility no longer seemed necessary. In previous lives, the bunker served as a facility to assemble V-2 rockets and, before that, a train tunnel. It now seems destined to become a mushroom farm. In the reading room one finds a large poster of a Caribbean sunset, intended perhaps to remind occupants of a world so recently destroyed.[48]

Nuclear weapons continue to provide enormous inspiration for film-makers. The villain is more villainous and the hero more heroic if the destruction of the world is at stake. On perhaps a dozen occasions James Bond has saved the world from nuclear destruction. In the film *Armageddon*, nuclear weapons are used to protect the earth from destruction by aster-oids. The film follows closely a line of thinking popular at Livermore, namely that nuclear weapons, or a Star Wars defence system, might be the only means by which to protect the earth from cosmic collision. The Nestlé Corporation capitalized on the film's popularity by marketing a 'Nuclear Chocolate' candy bar, much to the disgust of peace activists who called it 'an outrageous effort . . . to desensitize our children to the danger of nuclear weapons'.[49]

On 11 June 2002, Butterfields, a San Francisco auction house, held a sale of military memorabilia which included some items from the *Enola Gay* mission. The master clock on the plane and navigator Theodore Van Kirk's Bible went for $37,000, and a valise, radio headset and other items for $46,000. But the most controversial items were two small plugs – one red, one green – which, when removed, armed Little Boy. These had been retained as keepsakes by crewmember Lieutenant Morris Jeppson after the mission. The thumb-sized plugs were bought for $167,500 but the US government stepped in with a Federal Court injunction blocking the sale on the grounds that the plugs are government property and part of a bomb design which remains classified. On 15 June US District Court Judge Susan Illston rejected the government's case, mainly on the grounds that the government had done nothing to take possession of the plugs when they were displayed during an earlier exhibition at the Smithsonian to mark the fiftieth anniversary of the atomic bombings of Japan.[50]

That exhibition revealed the pitfalls of remembering the Bomb. The curator's original plan was attacked by the Navy because it cast the Americans in a bad light. Under enormous pressure from the military establishment and from Congress, the museum eventually re-designed the exhibit, which in turn provoked a hostile reaction from liberal historians. The latter were then labelled 'revisionist' — a synonym for disloyalty – by those on the political right. 'All revisionist speculation should be elimi-nated,' the Air Force Association demanded in one of its many press releases, inevitably raising speculation as to the military's preferred method of eliminating those who did not think in the correct manner. In an incred-ibly lame attempt at apology, the Smithsonian's secretary, I. Michael Heynman, remarked: 'In this important anniversary year, veterans and their families were expecting, and rightly so, that the nation would honor and commemorate their valor and sacrifice. They were not looking for analysis, and, frankly, we did not give enough thought to the intense feel-ings such an analysis would evoke.'[51] The episode began as a very public debate over the morality of the bombing. It developed into a much wider disagreement over America's conception of herself. Americans like to believe they were a force for good in the twentieth century, yet that concep-tion is confused by the fact that they are the only ones ever to have used the Bomb. Confusion causes unease.*

On 25 January 1995, a Russian radar crew spotted a fast moving object over the Barents Sea which it could not identify. Such an event has always caused alarm for the very simple reason that a missile launched from an American submarine in the area could reach the Russian mainland in just ten minutes, thus providing little time to identify the true nature of the threat. To the radar crew's surprise, the object suddenly separated into several sections, rather like a MIRV missile would. They relayed the infor-mation and a specified routine commenced, which included notifying Russian strategic forces. But then, eight minutes after the alarm was first

---

* That said, only a minority suffer from confusion. Periodic polls have shown remarkably consistent support for the bombings, with about two-thirds still believing them justified.

sounded, the mysterious object fell into the sea. It was actually a Norwegian rocket designed to study the Northern Lights. The Norwegians had informed the Russians of the launch weeks before, but this information had not been passed to the radar crew.

The press, eager for a good story, claimed that the world had tottered on the brink of nuclear war. Bruce Blair, of the Center for Defense Information, agrees with this assessment, arguing that the likelihood of errors will grow because the Russian economic crisis has meant that 'early warning and command systems have fallen on hard times, and they are deteriorating in physical respects'. Retired Russian general Vladimir Belous concurs that 'the prospect of a mistake has become particularly dangerous. A fateful accident could plunge the world into the chaos of a thermo-nuclear catastrophe.'[52] But, Ashton Carter, Assistant Secretary of Defense in the Clinton administration, disagrees. 'I think fundamentally Russia knows that we're not going to attack them with nuclear weapons, that no crisis of the kind that could develop in the Cold War, like the Cuban Missile Crisis, is likely to develop between the United States and Russia in today's circumstances.' General Vladimir Dvorkin, formerly of the Strategic Rocket Forces and more recently a top adviser to the Russian Minister of Defence, agrees with Carter. He argues that Russia would never launch a massive retaliatory strike 'based on one rocket or missile or even . . . two or three missiles . . . No, that is all in the land of fantasy.'[53]

Or is it? On 20 March 1993, two submarines – one Russian, one American – collided. Though this did not trigger an international crisis, tensions were ratcheted. The American vessel, the USS *Grayling*, was a nuclear powered attack sub whose purpose it was to tail the Russian Delta-class submarine, which usually carries 16 SLBMs. Damage was surprisingly light but embarrassment huge. The *Grayling* was following a practice established in the 1980s designed to enable, in the event of war, a sizable naval attack on the Soviet Union's Arctic bases, in order to relieve pressure on NATO forces in Central Europe. But why had the tactic survived, if tensions between the two countries had supposedly eased? Yeltsin asked this very question. An embarrassed President Clinton called the incident 'regrettable' and confessed: 'I don't want it ever to happen again.' Yet, a short time later, an anonymous Defense Department official, when asked if the Navy had any plans to change its Arctic strategy, replied, 'It's something that we've never historically addressed.'[54]

Enemies are enemies no longer, but trust has not flourished. By 1996, euphoria had given way to concern among those on the board of the *Bulletin of the Atomic Scientists*. They noted with disappointment that START II had not been implemented, nor were agreements on chemical and biological weapons ratified. The international arms trade had not, as hoped, gone into decline. The peace dividend proved a chimera. 'In the past four years, it has become clear that opportunities have been missed, open doors closed.'[55]

Old habits die hard. One of the greatest obstacles in the way of arms reduction is the resilience of assumptions formed in the bad old days of the Cold War. In May 1994 the US and Russia formally agreed not to target missiles at each other, but the target sets in the computers have not been changed. In other words, programming the missiles to hit Moscow or Washington would take only a matter of minutes. The number of missiles needed is still calculated by counting the number of targets in an enemy's territory, even if that enemy is no longer an enemy. The US and the USSR once claimed that they each needed 10,000 warheads to maintain a credible deterrent. In the late 1990s, the number had been reduced to 2,500 and has since fallen to around 1,000. Yet the precise basis for calculating these requirements remains mysterious – and probably deeply flawed.

The US still has a SIOP that dictates how the weapons would actually be used in the event of war. The SIOP remains top secret, so much so that even senior Senators who should be in the loop are denied access. Senator Bob Kerrey, the ranking member of the Senate Intelligence Committee, discovered as much when he asked for information about targeting plans in 2000. When Kerrey sought help from Blair, the latter explained, quite succinctly, that the US needed 2,500 weapons, because there were 2,260 vital Russian targets. But when Kerrey then asked for official explanation as to the rationale behind these targets, the Defense Department and SAC simply stonewalled. 'The assumptions that guide the calculations of how many weapons you need on target haven't been subject to any systematic policy oversight for decades,' Janne Nolan, a nuclear defence analyst, argues. She recalled how, when Secretary of Defense Dick Cheney ordered a targeting review in 1991, 'he was shocked by the idiotic redundancy that had been built into these plans'. For instance, the Pushkino radar facility, an unremarkable above-ground site, was targeted with sixty-nine weapons, for no apparent reason.[56] After an interview with the Defense Secretary William Cohen in 1997, the journalist Stephen Rosenfeld concluded that no significant policy shift had occurred with the end of the Cold War. 'For now we are, and for many years will be, ready to fight Russia or China or a rogue or terrorist in the instant massive Cold War way.'[57]

There are signs that Russia, at least, has come to terms with the new world order. Vladimir Dvorkin, head of a Russian think tank, argues that 'The model of nuclear deterrence that existed during the Cold War must be radically changed since it is senseless to deter the United States from an attack, nuclear or conventional.' Some Russians are even suggesting that bilateral negotiations with the US are no longer logical and that Russia should instead pursue her own disarmament schedule based upon the force she can afford to maintain. A unilateral programme of arms reduction might leave Russia with a force similar in size and purpose to that of France.[58]

First came the United States, then the USSR, then Britain and France. Though four nuclear powers was more unstable than two, the all-important bi-polarity in the distribution of weapons meant that deterrence was quite easy to calculate. But then a few non-aligned nations – China, South Africa, Israel, India – joined the nuclear club and things got a bit confusing. In 1998, Pakistan revealed that it had carried out five nuclear tests. A short government statement announced that 'these tests had become imperative keeping in view Indian nuclear tests and threats to Pakistan's security'.[59]

North Korea has nuclear aspirations, as did Iraq before the 2003 war. At various times, Libya, Iran, South Korea, Argentina, Brazil and Taiwan have also indicated a desire to develop nuclear weapons. The neat mathematics of a world in which atomic weapons were once possessed by two mutually antagonistic power blocs has been replaced by a much more chaotic distribution. The burning question is whether deterrence will continue to work as the list of nuclear nations grows. If some nuclear powers do not possess enough weapons to destroy an adversary completely can MAD still apply? In other words, is a small arsenal more dangerous than a large one? And does the abiding truth of the Cold War, namely that leaders will act rationally when faced with nuclear destruction, apply in the case of someone like Osama bin Laden?

In 1996 the Doomsday Clock was moved to nine minutes to midnight, partly in response to the nuclear status of India and Pakistan, but also 'to dramatize the failure of world diplomacy in the nuclear sphere; the increased danger that the non-proliferation regime might ultimately collapse; and the fact that deep reductions in the numbers of nuclear weapons, which seemed possible at the start of the decade, have not been realized'.[60] The situation is critical yet little attention is being paid to it. Concern about nuclear weapons decreased significantly when the Cold War ended, yet the weapons still exist and the danger of their being used has perhaps increased. In 1996, a member of the Clinton administration confessed that 'on the worry list, arms control comes in somewhere between the strength of the Mexican peso and the fight against drugs'.[61] The *Bulletin*, which during the Cold War provided a forum for discussing the dangers of nuclear confrontation, has seen its circulation drop from 21,000 to just 7,000 in recent years.[62] Tourists who visit nuclear sites see them as relics of the past. Anti-nuclear groups like CND have virtually disappeared.

On 4 December 1996, General Lee Butler, former commander of SAC, took the extraordinary step of publicly advocating the complete abolition of nuclear weapons. In a speech at the National Press Club, he described how he had lost faith in deterrence. He was, he claimed,

> deeply troubled by what I see as the burden of building and maintaining nuclear arsenals; the increasingly tangled web of policy and strategy as the number of weapons and delivery systems multiply; the staggering costs; the relentless pressure of advancing technology; the grotesquely destructive war plans; the daily operational risks; and the constant prospect of a crisis that would hold the fate of entire societies at risk.

Times had changed, Butler warned, therefore the perpetuation of Cold War strategic policies was highly dangerous. He expressed alarm at the 'renewed assertions of the utility of nuclear weapons, especially as regards response to chemical or biological attack', but in particular expressed 'grave doubt that the present highly discriminatory regime of nuclear and non-nuclear states can long endure [without] a credible commitment by the nuclear powers to eliminate their arsenals'. He was horrified at the 'prospect of a world seething with enmities, armed to the teeth with nuclear weapons, and hostage to maniacal leaders strongly disposed toward their use'. Butler followed this speech by issuing a joint statement with General Andrew Goodpaster calling upon nations to reduce their nuclear arsenals 'as rapidly as world conditions permit'. On the following day, generals and admirals from seventeen countries signed a joint statement affirming their deep conviction that arsenals should be taken off their present state of alert, and that 'long-term international nuclear policy must be based on the declared principle of continuous, complete and irrevocable elimination of nuclear weapons'.[63]

The Butler/Goodpaster initiative inspired a brief flurry of debate and then faded into the nuclear background. Critics argued that nuclear weapons could not be uninvented and that getting rid of them merely exposed righteous powers to blackmail by unscrupulous ones. Rather predictably, Teller rose to the defence of deterrence and condemned talk of eliminating nuclear weapons as hopelessly naïve. His argument gained credence in the aftermath of the September 11th terrorist attacks when any notion of reducing American military power was widely ridiculed. To many Americans, the actual use of the Bomb seems more justifiable than at any time since 1945.

George W. Bush has a different idea of how to deal with the problems Butler outlined. On 1 May 2001 the President told the American people of his desire to embark upon a Star Wars defence system. Some listeners must have thought they had entered a time warp. But a distinct difference existed between Bush's proposals and those of Reagan twenty years earlier.

Reagan had proposed SDI as an answer to the threats of the Cold War, while Bush argued that such a system was needed precisely because the Cold War was over. The safe certainties of that period had disappeared. Back then, Bush maintained, 'Few other nations had nuclear weapons and most of those who did were responsible allies, such as Britain and France. We worried about the proliferation of nuclear weapons to other countries, but it was mostly a distant threat, not yet a reality.' In contrast, there were now more nuclear powers, more countries with chemical and biological weapons and more nations with the missile capacity to deliver weapons of mass destruction. Bush argued, with considerable logic, that security could no longer be based upon MAD – 'the grim premise that we can destroy those who seek to destroy us'. He therefore wanted to 're-think the unthinkable, and to find new ways to keep the peace'. Deterrence was insufficient on its own, because it was based on enemies acting predictably, something which could no longer be assumed. Since the terrorist has no return address, mutually assured destruction provides no protection.

Standing in Bush's way was the ABM Treaty, which he wanted to scrap. 'This treaty does not recognize the present, or point us to the future,' he argued. 'It enshrines the past. No treaty that prevents us from addressing today's threats, that prohibits us from pursuing promising technology to defend ourselves, our friends and our allies is in our interests or in the interests of world peace.' Bush recognized that a missile shield would alarm the Russians and throw calculations of deterrence into chaos. But, like Reagan before him, he made light of these fears, even going so far as to suggest that Russia and America might work together in mutual defence.[64] He also advocated opting out of the CTBT, a proposal that caused a frisson of excitement in the nuclear ghost towns of Nevada.

Bush admitted that 'efforts to reduce the threat to our country from weapons of mass destruction [might] be less than fully successful'. This was especially true at a time when enemies were more likely to smuggle weapons into the country rather than deliver them by missile. This implied only one response, namely civil defence. 'Prudence dictates that the United States be fully prepared to deal effectively with the consequences of such a weapon being used here on our soil.'[65] After the speech, Americans began looking in basements again. For the first time in years, construction firms have reported new contracts to build nuclear shelters. Bert the Turtle dusted off his shell and started planning a comeback tour.

The Oregon Institute of Science and Medicine (OISM), a group a great deal more bizarre than its name suggests, has worked tirelessly to persuade Americans to dig up their garden again. According to a spokesperson, 'if one prepares for the worst, the worst is less likely to happen. Effective American civil defense preparations would reduce the probability of nuclear blackmail and war.' This view has been endorsed by Teller, who wrote the foreword to *Nuclear War Survival Skills*, a massive self-help book published by OISM. The manual argues that much of the pessimism about what a nuclear attack would be like is based on myth.[66] A similar message is put forth by the ARK II Fallout Shelter Site, a website devoted to all aspects of nuclear survival. ARK II has set up a registry which, in the event of nuclear catastrophe, will help survivors get in touch via the internet – an idea about as plausible as 1950s assumptions that American survivors might find each other through the US Postal Service.

In a 1995 episode of *The Simpsons*, Sideshow Bob threatens to detonate a ten-megaton missile (which he steals from an Air Force hangar) unless all television is eliminated. 'In a world without television . . . the survivors will envy the dead,' Krusty remarks. The episode is an extended parody of nuclear madness, homage to an age gladly gone. The world (or at least television) is saved when Sideshow Bob fails to notice that the missile carries the notice: 'Best before November 1959'.[67]

As with so many *Simpsons* episodes, this one was painfully close to the truth. Bombs do indeed have a limited shelf life. 'These weapons were designed to last about twenty years,' one Los Alamos scientist remarks. 'We have no idea how they will behave after fifty years.' Time erodes. 'Hydrogen embrittles metal. Neutrons disrupt all kinds of materials. And each type of weapon is going to get old in its own way.'[68] What if we threw a war and nothing exploded?

The experts insist that the only sure way to tell if a bomb will explode is to explode one. But testing has been banned. The alternative is to break down every process in the bomb and submit it to computerized simulation. 'Analyzing the aging is a stochastic problem,' an expert claims. 'It is technically much harder than designing the bombs in the first place. To do the job well with the computers we have now is like trying to cut down a sequoia with a nail file.'[69] The experts complain, but get on with their work. Nowadays, it's all that keeps them busy.

Scientists and technicians who once built thousands of bombs now devote their energy to breaking them down. Dismantling, a highly complicated task, is not a job for a coward. First, the warhead's cover is removed and the non-nuclear components separated. Then, the fissile material and high explosives are removed, a process carried out in an explosion proof cell, to prevent the dispersal of fissile materials in the event of an accidental detonation. The technicians then have to deal with the weapon's carcass, which can consist of up to 6,000 separate parts. Since the weapons were designed to be difficult to dismantle (as a foil against theft and sabotage), taking them apart is complicated. A better method is to dip the carcass in liquid hydrogen to make it brittle, and then drop a 300-pound weight on it. This conveniently smashes the mechanism into thousands of indistinguishable pieces, thus preserving secrecy. As part of the various arms control agreements, precise procedures for verifying the process have been developed. The death of each bomb is closely watched.

While precise schedules for decommissioning weapons have been agreed under the various treaties, Russian disarmament has assumed its own inevitability. Submarines and bombers have reached the end of their useful life and are not being replaced. As for the missiles, one Russian expert claims, 'Everything ends . . . a moment comes when everything starts to collapse or fall apart. Each piece of equipment has a moment when the construction simply gets old . . . the silo, the container, the body of the missile . . . are corroded, fungus eats through the metal, things start to grow on it – God knows what.' Another commentator summed up the inevitable fate for Russian strategic forces: 'they are running out of steam, out of money and out of time'.[70]

The really hard problem, however, is what to do with the fissile material. It is perhaps fitting that substances so hard to make have also proved so difficult to destroy. All the plutonium from all the dismantled weapons is still stored in bomb-ready form. Processes designed to render it harmless are hugely expensive. A cheaper option is to do what one usually does with anything unwanted: bury it. The preferred method is to encase the material in concrete, place it in steel drums, and place those drums in tunnels dug deep into the earth (in Nevada, of course). But the guarantee that comes with that process expires after 10,000 years. That will perhaps provide time for some clever scientist to think of a better idea. Or perhaps the world will be destroyed and it won't really matter.

In 1998, the Brookings Institute conducted an audit of the American nuclear weapons programme. According to their estimates, the weapons, testing, delivery devices, defence programmes, dismantling and waste management cost a total of $5.8 trillion.[71] So was it a worthwhile investment? The Bomb's advocates, most prominent among them Teller, argue that it has ensured peace between the superpowers since 1945. Nuclear weapons, he argues, brought about 'an unprecedented situation in history: that low-cost military power should become available and nonetheless not be used for conquest, or for the imposition of our wishes in general, but rather for the sole purpose of deterrence, stability and peace on a global scale'.[72] Granted, the fact that nearly sixty years have passed without a major war between the superpowers is significant. It is especially so since man has not grown peaceful, as indicated by the hundreds of 'small' conflicts during that period.

The atomic bomb altered the meaning and value ascribed to peace.

Wars still exist, but they must not become nuclear. Honour and prestige do not figure as prominently in international relations as they once did, for the very simple reason that honour is pointless if defending it means thermonuclear war. Not long after the Cuban Missile Crisis, Kennedy remarked: 'Above all, while defending our own vital interests, nuclear powers must avert those confrontations which bring an adversary to a choice of either a humiliating defeat or a nuclear war.'[73] In another era, that would have been called appeasement. During the Cold War, the nuclear powers regularly appeased, though they never called it that. Cuba was an act of appeasement, as was Berlin. The Bomb forced the superpowers to settle huge issues of disagreement – huge, certainly, in comparison to the tiny problems that sparked the slaughter of the First World War. To recall what Bohr and Oppenheimer once hoped, the Bomb has indeed been big enough to force statesmen to act sensibly.

Some believers in deterrence have taken their faith to the point of fanaticism. In the 1960s, the French general Pierre Marie Gallois argued that there should be no restrictions on membership to the nuclear club, since each nuclear power will deter all the others. The idea was taken up by the American political scientist Kenneth Waltz who has, in effect, argued that the non-proliferation treaty causes more harm than good. Citing the case of India and Pakistan, John Mearsheimer feels that 'nuclear weapons are a superb deterrent for states that feel threatened by rival powers'. He feels that the US will have to learn to live with proliferation. 'We should try to manage and contain this process, but we cannot stop it.'[74]

Opponents of the bomb often base their argument on an idealized vision of what human beings might become. Yet they have never provided the magic formula for ridding the world of aggression. Proponents, on the other hand, are pessimists: they accept man's flaws and believe that the Bomb is the first effective impediment to our inclination to destroy each other. It is difficult to reject that argument, based as it is on an undeniable notion of human nature. Would the crisis of 2002 have sent India and Pakistan into bloody war, if not for the fact that both had nuclear weapons?

But if the Bomb has been, as Bohr and Oppenheimer once hoped, big enough to destroy war itself – or at least major war – was it necessary to have so many? Probably not. Mutually assured destruction could easily have been achieved with a tiny fraction of the weapons actually deployed. But the very bigness of the Bomb has ensured an obsession with bigness. It's only defence is itself, thus the quest for absolute safety inspired a quest for absolute power. Both superpowers wanted merely to protect themselves, yet the process of protection was itself threatening, inspiring a tit for every tat.

Despite all its extravagance, mutually assured destruction was balanced.

That balance is now gone. The Cold War is over. Gone, it seems, are the justifications for deterrence. If the weapon was indeed only ever designed to keep the peace, where is the logic for keeping these weapons, especially if (except perhaps in the case of Pakistan and India) there is no animosity between those who possess them? Without an enemy to deter, the Bomb becomes simply an aggressive weapon. Yet against whom can it conceivably be used, and under what circumstances? And, as Butler asked, is it possible to discourage proliferation if the current nuclear powers insist on retaining their weapons? It should come as no surprise that some nations are jealous about the exclusive membership of the nuclear club.

On the other hand, fission cannot be collectively forgotten. The potential to make a nuclear weapon will not disappear. And, however amoral, expensive and seemingly bankrupt the policy, deterrence remains the most effective defence against nuclear weapons yet conceived. Gorbachev's vision of a nuclear-free world might on the surface have seemed entrancing, but it would have played into the hands of the nuclear outlaws. It might also have meant a return to the international politics of the pre-1945 period. Zbigniew Brzezinski perhaps rightly called Gorbachev's ideas 'a plan for making the world safe for conventional warfare'.[75]

The Bomb is a weapon which reflects the flawed nature of human beings – their distrust of each other, their craving for power and their obsession with things big. It was developed by scientists whose quest for discovery caused them to ignore the implications of their work. It was seized upon by politicians and soldiers who confused power with security and lacked the imagination to understand that the atom bomb was something new. It has, because of its bigness, perhaps forced men to act more rationally in the application of force. But it is just a bomb – a power, not a personality. The extent to which it seems to have a character lies merely in the fact that it acts like a mirror, reflecting our own inadequacies. Some time ago, Victor Weisskopf remarked how science had unlocked so many of the secrets of the world. But, he insisted, 'The important parts of the human experience cannot be reasonably evaluated within the scientific system. There cannot be an all encompassing definition of good and evil, of compassion, of rapture, of tragedy or humor, of hate, love, or faith, of dignity and humiliation, or of concepts like the quality of life and happiness.'[76] Because science has not provided an answer to those mysteries, a final verdict on the Bomb remains impossible.

Notes

A Note on the Sources

Secondary sources are listed below by author name and, if necessary, date of publication to distinguish between multiple publications by the same author. Fuller citations are available in the bibliography. Many of the primary sources used in the book have been taken from the internet. Referencing these is problematic, since website addresses change frequently. Rather than providing a detailed web address which might prove out of date soon after publication of this book, I have simply noted that the source in question is taken from the internet. Readers wanting to locate the complete document can use a search engine to find it. References pertaining to online journals, like *Physics Today* and *Bulletin of the Atomic Scientists*, lack page numbers as these are not always available in online editions.

Preface
1 Boyer (1998), p. 89.

Chapter One: *Killing is Easy*
1 Vivian Verne, 'Kensington Gardens', in Reilly, p. 120.
2 Rhodes (1986), p. 779.
3 Ibid., p. 742–3.
4 Giulio Douhet, *The Command of the Air*, pp. 8–10.
5 *Hansard*, 10 November 1932.
6 'Atomic Bomb: Decision' (Internet).
7 Rhodes (1986), p. 44.
8 Wells, pp. 23–4.
9 Rhodes (1986), p. 172.
10 Ibid., p. 140.
11 Wells, p. 13.

Chapter Two: *Neutrons and Nations*
1 Rhodes (1986), p. 137.
2 Holloway, *Stalin*, p. 26.
3 Titus, p. 2.
4 Rhodes (1986), pp. 92–3.

5 Jungk, p. 3.
6 Holloway, *Stalin*, p. 36.
7 Rhodes (1986), p. 113.
8 Szasz, p. 9.
9 Goodchild, p. 20.
10 Jungk, p. 49.
11 Rhodes (1986), p. 152.
12 Jungk, p. 17.
13 Rigden, p. 12.
14 Holloway, *Stalin*, p. 37.
15 *Los Angeles Times*, 27 April 2002.
16 Jungk, pp. 50–1.
17 Rhodes (1986), p. 186.
18 Jungk, p. 37.
19 Ibid., pp. 62–3.
20 Ibid., p. 68.
21 Weale, p. 43.
22 Meitner and Frisch, p. 240.
23 Rhodes (1986), p. 264.
24 Jungk, p. 52.
25 Rhodes (1986), pp. 266–8, p. 274.
26 Ibid., p. 275.
27 Weart and Szilard, pp. 54–5.
28 Rhodes (1986), p. 293.
29 Ibid., p. 296.
30 Landau, n.p.

31 Leo Szilard, Memo: 21 September 1942, in 'The Oppenheimer Years', *Los Alamos Science*, p. 8.
32 Rhodes (1986), p. 308.
33 Jungk, p. 91.
34 Rhodes (1986), p. 305.
35 Williams and Cantelon, pp. 12–13.
36 Jungk, pp. 86–7.
37 Rhodes (1986), p. 314.
38 Roosevelt to Einstein, 19 October 1939, in *Atomic Archive* (Internet).
39 Teller, *Memoirs*, p. 148.
40 Rhodes (1986), p. 317.
41 Teller, *Memoirs*, p. 149.
42 Rhodes (1986), p. 323.
43 Frisch-Peierls Memorandum, February 1940 (Internet).
44 Frisch, p. 126.
45 Rhodes (1986), p. 330, p. 334.
46 Ibid., p. 367.
47 Cassidy, n.p.
48 Jungk, p. 92.
49 Rhodes (1986), p. 339.
50 Ibid., pp. 331.
51 Jungk, pp. 111–12.
52 Williams and Cantelon, pp. 19–23.
53 Rhodes (1986), p. 372.
54 Stimson, p. 98.
55 Baker, p. 43.
56 Rhodes (1986), p. 384.
57 Jungk, pp. 104–5.
58 Bohr to Heisenberg, n.d., Bohr Institute (Internet).
59 Bohr, draft of letter to Heisenberg, n.d., Bohr Institute.
60 Bohr, random notes, n.d., Bohr Institute.
61 Cassidy, n.p.
62 Ibid.
63 Goodchild, p. 47.
64 Jungk, p. 127.
65 Speer, pp. 301–4.
66 Goodchild, p. 74.
67 Rose, p. 1.
68 Holloway, *Stalin*, p. 90.
69 American Institute of Physics, 'Farm Hall Transcripts' (Internet).
70 Rhodes (1986), p. 406.
71 Jungk, p. 114.
72 Oak Ridge Heritage and Preservation Association website (Internet).

Chapter Three: *Born in Manhattan*

1 Rhodes (1986), pp. 524–5.
2 Ibid., p. 406.
3 Groves, p. 4.
4 Ibid., p. *xvi*.
5 Ibid., p. 19.
6 Rhodes (1986), p. 431.
7 Goodchild, p. 63.
8 Groves, p. 40.
9 Goodchild, p. 60.
10 Groves, p. *v*.
11 Goodchild, pp. 56–7.
12 Groves, p. 31.
13 Ibid., p. 49.
14 Rhodes (1986), p. 449.
15 Thorpe and Shapin, p. 564.
16 Groves, p. 63.
17 Jungk, p. 147.
18 Teller, 'The Laboratory of the Atomic Age', p. 190.
19 Thorpe and Shapin, p. 573.
20 Ibid., p. 553.
21 Chevalier, p. 11.
22 Thorpe and Shapin, p. 575.
23 Ibid., p. 577.
24 Goodchild, p. 117.
25 Ibid., p. 32, p. 73.
26 Rhodes (1986), pp. 448–9.
27 Jungk, p. 129.
28 Brazier to Duffield, 18 October 1943, Los Alamos Museum

exhibit.

29 Feynman, p. 108.

30 Memo of the Los Alamos Project: n.d., in 'The Oppenheimer Years', *Los Alamos Science*, p. 10.

31 Williams and Cantelon, p. 31.

32 Oppenheimer to R. G. Sproul, 18 September 1943, in 'The Oppenheimer Years', p. 10.

33 Rhodes (1986), p. 408.

34 Weale, p. 96.

35 Thorpe and Shapin, p. 545.

36 Feynman, pp. 107–8.

37 Rhodes (1986), p. 452.

38 Thorpe and Shapin, p. 547.

39 Szasz, p. 22.

40 Ibid., p. 15, p. 18.

41 Rhodes (1986), p. 468.

42 Goodchild, p. 120.

43 Groves, p. *vi*.

44 Szasz, p. 22.

45 Rhodes (1986), p. 566.

46 Goodchild, p. 79.

47 'Reflections', *Atomic Archive* (Internet).

48 Groves, p. 140.

49 Jungk, p. 120.

50 Williams and Cantelon, p. 31.

51 Rhodes (1986), p. 432.

52 'ORNL: the First 50 Years', in *Oak Ridge National Laboratory Review* (1992) (Internet).

53 Weale, p. 86.

54 Szasz, p. 14.

55 Rhodes (1986), p. 442.

56 Groves, p. 54.

57 Michele Gerber, 'Legend and Legacy: Fifty Years of Defense Production at the Hanford Site' (Internet).

58 'The Boom and Bust Cycle: A 50-Year Overview of the Economic Impacts of Hanford Site Operations on the Tri-Cities, Washington' (Internet).

59 Groves, p. 92.

60 Rhodes (1986), p. 500.

61 Groves, pp. 230–1.

62 Ibid., p. 239.

63 Bernstein, p. 139.

64 Truman, p. 87.

Chapter Four: *It's a Boy!*

1 Szasz, p. 65.

2 Titus, p. 13.

3 Leslie Groves, Diary, 2 July 1945 (Internet).

4 AEC, *In the Matter of J. Robert Oppenheimer* (Internet).

5 Norris Bradbury, Memo: 9 July 1945, in 'The Oppenheimer Years', *Los Alamos Science*, p. 22.

6 Goodchild, p. 152.

7 Ibid., p. 153.

8 Ibid., p. 155.

9 *Albuquerque Journal*, 16 July 1995.

10 Szasz, p. 77.

11 Rhodes (1986), p. 668.

12 Goodchild, pp. 161–2.

13 Rhodes (1986), p. 672.

14 *J. Robert Oppenheimer and the Atomic Bomb: The Day After Trinity*, Big Little Picture Company (1997) (Video).

15 Goodchild, p. 162.

16 Enrico Fermi, Trinity Test, Eyewitness Accounts (Internet).

17 Groves to Stimson, 18 July 1945, Truman Library (Internet).

18 Cyril Smith, Trinity Test, Eyewitness Accounts (Internet).

19 *New York Times*, 16 July 1970.

20 Szasz, pp. 90–1.

21 *Albuquerque Journal*, 28 October 1999.

22 Szasz, p. 84.
23 *Albuquerque Journal*, 28 October 1999.
24 Szasz, pp. 85–6.
25 Groves to Stimson, 18 July 1945, *Atomic Archive* (Internet).
26 Groves, p. 298.
27 Groves to Stimson, 18 July 1945.
28 Szasz, p. 145.

Chapter Five: *Decisions*
1 Roosevelt broadcast, 1 September 1939 (Internet).
2 DeGroot, p. 178.
3 Rhodes (1986), p. 342.
4 WGBH Educational Foundation, *The Race for the Superbomb*, 1999 (Internet).
5 Jungk, p. 178.
6 Landau, n.p.
7 Groves, p. 184.
8 Jungk, p. 172, p. 202.
9 Bohr, 'Open Letter to the United Nations', 9 June 1950 (Internet).
10 Jungk, p. 174.
11 Rhodes (1986), p. 530.
12 Williams and Cantelon, p. 45.
13 Sherwin, p. 110.
14 Rhodes (1986), p. 509.
15 Ibid., p. 638.
16 Stimson to Truman, 25 April 1945, Truman Library (Internet).
17 Truman, p. 87.
18 Groves, p. 264.
19 Jungk, p. 182.
20 Bernstein, pp. 143–6.
21 Jungk, p. 182.
22 Minutes of the Interim Committee, 31 May 1945, Truman Library.
23 Jungk, p. 186.
24 Scientific Panel of the Interim Committee, 16 June 1945, Truman Library.
25 Walter Brown Diary, 22, 24 July 1945 (Internet).
26 Stimson Diary, 14 May 1945 (Internet).
27 Stimson Diary, 15 May 1945.
28 'The Franck Report' (Internet).
29 Minutes of the Interim Committee, 21 June 1945, Truman Library.
30 Szilard petition, 17 July 1945 (Internet).
31 Teller (1962), p. 13.
32 Teller to Szilard, 4 July 1945, *Atomic Archive* (Internet).
33 Groves to Lord Cherwell, 4 July 1945 (Internet).
34 Rhodes (1986), p. 590.
35 Ibid., p. 584.
36 Sherwin, p. 145.
37 Rhodes (1986), p. 627.
38 Summary of Target Committee Meetings on 10 and 11 May 1945 (Internet).
39 Stimson Diary, 24 July 1945.
40 Rhodes (1986), p. 650.
41 McCloy Diary, 29 May 1945 (Internet).
42 Stimson to Truman, 2 July 1945 (Internet).
43 Bissell Memo, 7 July 1945 (Internet).
44 Magic Intercepts, 13 July 1945 (Internet).
45 Bissell Memo.
46 Groves, p. 293.
47 Truman to Bess Truman, 18 July 1945 (Internet).
48 Truman Diary, 18 July 1945, Truman Library.
49 Stimson Diary, 22 July 1945.
50 McCloy Diary, 23/24 July 1945.

51 Churchill, pp. 669–70.

52 Truman Diary, 24 July 1945.

53 Stimson, pp. 105–7.

54 Alperovitz, p. 407.

55 Giovannitti and Freed, p. 319.

56 Khrushchev, p. 81.

Chapter Six: *Genshi Bakudan*

1 Walter Brown Diary, 24 July, 3 August 1945 (Internet).

2 Weale, pp. 131.

3 Rhodes (1986), p. 701.

4 Ibid., p. 704.

5 Ibid., p. 707.

6 Weale, pp. 137–41.

7 Sankichi Tōge, 'August Sixth', in Lifton, pp. 441–2.

8 'Voices of A-bomb Survivors' (Internet).

9 Goodchild, p. 166.

10 Rhodes (1986), p. 717.

11 'The Spirit of Hiroshima' (Internet).

12 Manhattan Engineer District, 'The Atomic Bombings of Hiroshima and Nagasaki' (Internet).

13 Groves, pp. 321–2.

14 Groves/Oppenheimer telephone transcript, 6 August 1945 (Internet).

15 Goodchild, p. 167.

16 Rhodes (1986), p. 736.

17 Ibid., p. 717, p. 722.

18 Hersey, pp. 38–9.

19 'Voices of A-bomb Survivors'.

20 Ibid.

21 Rhodes (1986), p. 721.

22 Hersey, p. 48.

23 'Children of Hiroshima' (Internet).

24 Hersey, p. 66, p. 75.

25 Groves, p. 324.

26 Cox, p. 21.

27 'The Atomic Bombings of Hiroshima and Nagasaki', Avalon Project (Internet).

28 Rhodes (1986), p. 457.

29 Morita, pp. 1–3.

30 'The Atomic Bombings of Hiroshima and Nagasaki', Avalon Project.

31 Jungk, p. 211.

32 Ibid., p. 213.

33 'The Spirit of Hiroshima'.

34 Cox, p. 21.

35 Hersey, p. 82.

36 'The Spirit of Hiroshima'.

37 Alvarez, p. 8.

38 White House Press Release on Hiroshima, *Atomic Archive* (Internet).

39 'ORNL: the First 50 Years' (Internet).

40 Groves, pp. 333–5.

41 'Farm Hall Transcripts', *Atomic Archive*.

42 Cable, Senator Richard B. Russell to President Truman, 7 August 1945, Truman Library.

43 Truman to Russell, 9 August 1945, Truman Library.

44 *New York Times*, 10 August 1945.

45 White House Press Release on Hiroshima, *Atomic Archive*.

46 Leaflet, 6 August 1945, Truman Library.

47 Rhodes (1986), p. 738.

48 Goodchild, p. 168.

49 Official Bombing Order (General Thomas Handy to General Carl Spaatz), 25 July 1945 (Internet). *See also* Goldberg.

50 Groves, p. 344.

51 War Department Press Release, 9 September 1945 (Internet).

52 Rhodes (1986), p. 740.
53 War Department Press Release, 9 September 1945.
54 'A-bomb dropped as it could not be taken back', *Asahi Shimbun* (Internet).
55 Groves, p. 344.
56 War Department Press Release, 9 September 1945.
57 Raisuke Shirabe, 'My Experience of the Nagasaki Atomic Bombing' (Internet).
58 Cox, p. 25.
59 Shirabe.
60 Manhattan Engineer District, 'The Atomic Bombings of Hiroshima and Nagasaki' (Internet).
61 Ibid.
62 Rhodes (1986), pp. 742–3.
63 Goldberg, n.p.
64 Rhodes (1986), p. 742.
65 Butow, pp. 1–3.
66 Office of Naval Intelligence, Interrogation of Sakomizu Hisatsume, Chief Cabinet Secretary, June 1946, Truman Library.
67 Boyer (1998), p. 10.
68 Lifton and Mitchell, p. 37.
69 Samuel McCrea Cavert to Harry Truman, 9 August 1945, Truman Library.
70 Truman to Cavert, 11 August 1945, Truman Library.
71 *Atomic Café*, Jayne Loader, 1982 (Video).
72 White House Press Release, 6 August 1945.
73 *US News and World Report*, 15 August 1960, p. 71.
74 Goodchild, p. 169.
75 *Santa Fe New Mexican*, 8 August 1945.
76 Goodchild, p. 169.
77 Szasz, p. 3.
78 'Song of Hiroshima', words and music by Koki Kinoshita, English version by Ewan MacColl (Internet).

Chapter Seven: *Nuclear Giants and Ethical Infants*
1 Feynman, p. 136.
2 Lifton, p. 59.
3 Rhodes (1986), p. 732.
4 'The Spirit of Hiroshima' (Internet).
5 Kunkel, p. 370.
6 *The New Yorker*, 31 August 1946.
7 *New York Times*, 30 August 1946.
8 Smith, pp. 80–1.
9 Alperovitz, p. 445.
10 Shapin (2000), n.p.
11 *US News and World Report*, 15 August 1960, pp. 68–71.
12 Manhattan Engineer District, 'The Atomic Bombings of Hiroshima and Nagasaki' (Internet).
13 Morita, pp. 1–2.
14 Szasz, p. 150.
15 United States Strategic Bombing Survey, 'Japan's Struggle to End the War', 1 July 1946, Truman Library (Internet).
16 Shapin (2000), n.p.
17 Holloway (1994), p. 132, p. 164.
18 Baker, p. 61.
19 Blackett, pp. 137–40.
20 Shapin (2000), n.p.
21 Transcript of Truman interview, c. 1955, Truman Library.
22 Truman to Kupcinet, 5 August 1963, Truman Library.
23 *Chicago Tribune*, 11 August 1945.
24 Goodchild, pp. 170–3.

25 Ibid., p. 170.
26 Rhodes (1986), p. 761.
27 Goodchild, p. 174.
28 Shapin (2000), n.p.
29 Rhodes (1986), p. 779.
30 Jungk, p. 236.
31 Einstein statement, 22 January 1947 (Internet).
32 Rhodes (1986), p. 762.
33 Wells, p. 54, p. 73.
34 Ibid., p. 91, p. 131.
35 Jungk, p. 182.
36 Minutes of the Interim Committee, 31 May 1945, Truman Library.
37 Groves, p. 409.
38 White House press release, 6 August 1945, Truman Library.
39 Graybar, n.p.
40 Stimson to Truman, 11 September 1945, Truman Library.
41 Clinton Anderson to Truman, 25 September 1945, Truman Library.
42 Herken, pp. 35–9.
43 Stimson Diary, 4 September 1945.
44 Herken, p. 48.
45 Holloway, p. 157.
46 'Fulton Speech', *Atomic Archive* (Internet).
47 *The Story of the Atom Bomb: Trinity and Beyond* (Video).
48 'Interviews with Bikini Elders', Bikini Website (Internet).
49 Jack Neidenthal, 'A Short History of Bikini Atoll', Bikini Website.
50 Titus, p. 37.
51 *Atomic Café* (Video).
52 Titus, p. 38.
53 *Trinity and Beyond*, Peter Kuran (director), 1995.
54 *Newsweek*, 1 July 1946.
55 Jungk, p. 246.
56 Graybar, n.p.
57 *Chicago Tribune*, 3 July 1946.
58 *Saturday Review*, 10 August 1946.
59 *Newsweek*, 8 July 1946, p. 19.
60 Report by the Joint Chiefs of Staff Evaluation Board, 30 July 1946, Truman Library.
61 Ibid.
62 Titus, p. 41.
63 Ibid., pp. 41–2.
64 US Strategic Bombing Survey, 30 June 1947 (Internet).
65 Goodchild, p. 179.
66 Herken, p. 160.
67 Ibid., p. 161.
68 Ibid., *frontispiece*.
69 Goodchild, p. 180.
70 Baruch Plan, *Atomic Archive*.
71 *Washington Post*, 2 July 1946.
72 Graybar, n.p.
73 Titus, p. 45.
74 Jungk, p. 253.
75 *Los Angeles Times*, 27 April 2002.
76 *Los Angeles Times*, 3 March 2002.
77 Boyer, p. 16.
78 Shapin (2000), n.p.

Chapter Eight: *On a Russian Scale*

1 Holloway, *Cold War International History Project Bulletin* (Fall, 1994), pp. 8–9.
2 Leskov, n.p.
3 Zhukov, pp. 674–5.
4 Fuchs statement, 27 January 1950 (Internet).
5 Leskov, n.p.
6 Albright and Kunstel, n.p.
7 *The Race for the Superbomb* (Internet).
8 Sagdeev, n.p.
9 Leskov, n.p.
10 Sagdeev, n.p.
11 Beria to Stalin, 28 November 1945, *CWIHPB*, Issue 4, pp. 50–1.

12 Holloway, *Stalin*, p. 10, p. 19.
13 Khariton and Smirnov, n.p.
14 Holloway, *Stalin*, p. 79.
15 Ibid., p. 101.
16 Kurchatov to Beria, 29 September 1944, *CWIHPB*, Issue 4, p. 5.
17 Montefiore, p. 443.
18 Werth, p. 925.
19 Hennessy, pp. 15–16.
20 Holloway, *Stalin*, p. 171.
21 Ibid., p. 171.
22 Ibid., p. 260.
23 Minutes of the Interim Committee, 1 June 1945, Truman Library (Internet).
24 Clinton Anderson to Truman, 25 September 1945, Truman Library.
25 Herken, p. 99.
26 Holloway, *Stalin*, p. 132.
27 Ibid., p. 305.
28 Rothstein, n.p.
29 Khariton and Smirnov, n.p.
30 Kurchatov notes of 25 January 1946 meeting, *CWIHPB*, vol. 4.
31 Holloway, *Stalin*, p. 149.
32 Holloway, 'Soviet physics', n.p.
33 Ibid.
34 Stone, n.p.
35 *The Race for the Superbomb.*
36 Kurchatov notes of 25 January 1946 meeting, *CWIHPB*, vol. 4, p. 5.
37 Khariton and Smirnov, n.p.
38 Holloway, 'Soviet physics', n.p.
39 Sakharov, p. 164.
40 *The Race for the Superbomb.*
41 Stone, n.p.
42 Holloway, 'Soviet physics', n.p.
43 Khariton and Smirnov, n.p.
44 *The Race for the Superbomb.*
45 Khariton and Smirnov, n.p.
46 Ibid.
47 Holloway, *Stalin*, p. 187.

48 Ibid., p. 200.
49 Ibid., p. 216.
50 *The Race for the Superbomb.*
51 Montefiore, p. 531.
52 Holloway, *Stalin*, p. 216.
53 York, p. 33.
54 Ibid., pp. 34–5.
55 Williams and Cantelon, pp. 116–17.
56 Hennessy, pp. 34–5.
57 Khariton and Smirnov, n.p.
58 'Loose Nukes', PBS *Frontline* (Internet).
59 Sagdeev, n.p.

Chapter Nine: *Embracing Armageddon*

1 *Albuquerque Journal*, July 1995.
2 *Winnipeg Free Press*, 16 April 1999.
3 Kaplan, p. 27.
4 Kegley and Wittkopf, p. 22.
5 Herken, p. 218.
6 Rosenberg, D. (1981–2), p. 68.
7 *The Race for the Superbomb* (Internet).
8 Ibid.
9 Ibid.
10 Kaplan, p. 143.
11 Herken, p. 271.
12 *The Race for the Superbomb.*
13 Holloway, *Stalin*, p. 229.
14 Ibid.
15 *The Race for the Superbomb.*
16 Ibid.
17 Montefiore, p. 533.
18 'Soviet Intentions and Capabilities', 20 February 1950, Truman Library (Internet).
19 Joint Intelligence Committee, Report on the Implications of Soviet Possession of Atomic Weapons, February 1950 (Internet).
20 National Security Council, 'NSC-68: United States Objectives and

Programs for National Security'
14 April 1950 (Internet).
21 Hennessy, p. 28, p. 30, p. 35.
22 Jungk, p. 231.
23 Herken, p. 112.
24 Jungk, p. 242.
25 *Business Week*, 12 January 1957.
26 Jungk, pp. 254–5.
27 Bohr, 'Open Letter to the United Nations', 9 June 1950 (Internet).
28 Williams and Cantelon, pp. 79–92.
29 Holloway, *Stalin*, p. 229.
30 'The Boom and Bust Cycle: A 50-Year Overview of the Economic Impacts of Hanford Site Operations on the Tri-Cities, Washington' (Internet).
31 Gerber, 'Legend and Legacy: Fifty Years of Defense Production at the Hanford Site' (Internet).

Chapter Ten: *To Little Boy, A Big Brother*
1 Rhodes (1986), p. 417.
2 Interim Committee Log, 25 September 1945, Truman Library (Internet).
3 *The Race for the Superbomb* (Internet).
4 Rhodes (1986), p. 757.
5 Teller (1983), p. 192.
6 Jungk, p. 273.
7 *The Race for the Superbomb.*
8 Jungk, p. 273.
9 Goodchild, p. 199.
10 *The Race for the Superbomb.*
11 Beria to Stalin, 28 November 1945, *CWIHPB*, Issue 4, pp. 50–1.
12 Khariton, et al., n.p.
13 Goncharov, 'Beginnings', p. 50.
14 Sakharov, p. 94, p. 96.
15 *The Race for the Superbomb.*

16 Holloway, *Stalin*, p. 299.
17 'GAC Report, 30 October 1949', *Atomic Archive* (Internet).
18 Boyer (1998), p. 52.
19 Rhodes (1986), p. 770.
20 York, p. 60.
21 Williams and Cantelon, p. 129.
22 Rhodes (1995), p. 407.
23 Williams and Cantelon, p. 131.
24 *The Race for the Superbomb.*
25 Bethe Letter, *Scientific American*, April 1950.
26 Jungk, p. 287.
27 Bethe Petition, *Bulletin of the Atomic Scientists*, May/June 1950.
28 Jungk, pp. 288–9.
29 Schweber, p. 166.
30 *The Race for the Superbomb.*
31 Khariton, et al., n.p.
32 *The Race for the Superbomb.*
33 Jastrow, p. 27.
34 Bethe, 'Memorandum on the History of the Thermonuclear Program', 28 May 1952 (Internet).
35 Schweber, p. 166.
36 Rhodes (1986), p. 773.
37 AEC, *In the Matter of J. Robert Oppenheimer* (Internet).
38 Jungk, p. 295.
39 Bethe (1982), p. 51.
40 Teller (1964), p. 54.
41 'The E. O. Lawrence Tradition of Excellence', Livermore website (Internet).
42 Ibid.
43 Ibid.
44 *Trinity and Beyond*, Peter Kuran (director), 1995.
45 Rhodes (1995), p. 511.
46 Libby, p. 303.
47 *The Race for the Superbomb.*
48 Ibid.

49 Goncharov, 'The Race', p. 57.
50 Smirnov and Zubok, p. 14.
51 *The Race for the Superbomb.*
52 Khariton and Smirnov, n.p.
53 Holloway, *Stalin*, p. 307.
54 Rhodes (1986), p. 778.
55 Smirnov and Zubok, p. 15.
56 *The Race for the Superbomb.*
57 Hirsch and Matthews, n.p.
58 Bethe (1990), n.p.
59 Cox, p. 43.
60 *The Race for the Superbomb.*
61 Khariton, et al., n.p.

Chapter Eleven: *The New Look*
 1 Teller (2001), p. 466.
 2 Personal recollection.
 3 Eisenhower Inaugural Address,
    1953 (Internet).
 4 Williams and Cantelon, p. 113.
 5 Jungk, p. 336.
 6 Oppenheimer, p. 525.
 7 Kaplan, p. 48.
 8 Hastings, pp. 213–18.
 9 Roy Acuff, 'Advice to Joe',
    Columbia Music, 1951.
10 Holloway, *Stalin*, p. 282 .
11 Boyer (1998), p. 35.
12 *The Race for the Superbomb*
    (Internet).
13 Herken, pp. 334–6.
14 Hastings, p. 394.
15 Rhodes (1995), p. 446.
16 Boyer (1998), pp. 38–9.
17 Billings-Yun, p. 78.
18 Gurtov, pp. 57–8.
19 Kaplan, pp. 180–1.
20 Ibid., p. 176.
21 McNamara, pp. 21–2.
22 Gurtov, pp. 57–8.
23 *The Race for the Superbomb.*
24 Rosenberg, D. (1981–2), p. 25.

25 McNamara, pp. 22–3.
26 Ibid., p. 33.
27 Kaplan, pp. 190–1.
28 Williams and Cantelon, pp.
    104–11.
29 Titus, p. 32.
30 Ibid., p. 31.
31 *The Race for the Superbomb.*
32 Khariton, et al., n.p.
33 *The Race for the Superbomb.*
34 Sakharov, pp. 193–5.
35 *The Race for the Superbomb.*
36 Ibid.
37 Sakharov, pp. 193–5.
38 *The Race for the Superbomb.*
39 Cox, p. 40.
40 Defense Nuclear Agency, Castle
    Series, 1984, 1 April 1982
    (Internet).
41 Titus, p. 49.
42 Defense Nuclear Agency, Castle
    Series, 1984, 1 April 1982.
43 *The Race for the Superbomb.*
44 Titus, p. 47.
45 Strauss Statement on the Bravo
    Incident, 31 March 1954, and
    Japanese government response
    (Internet).
46 Kurchatov, Report on the Danger
    of Atomic War, n.d. (1954)
    (Internet).
47 Jungk, p. 312.
48 *The Race for the Superbomb.*
49 *The Most Contaminated Spot on the
    Planet*, Log In Productions, 1994.
50 Teller testimony, *In the Matter of J.
    Robert Oppenheimer* (Internet).
51 AEC, *In the Matter of J. Robert
    Oppenheimer*, 29 June 1954
    (Internet).
52 Hirsch and Matthews, n.p.
53 *The Race for the Superbomb.*
54 Bundy, p. 270.

55 Titus, p. 77.

56 Boyer (1998), pp. 88–94.

57 Stone, n.p.

58 *The Race for the Superbomb.*

59 Smirnov and Zubok, p. 14.

60 Ibid., pp. 14–15.

61 Ibid., p. 15.

62 Holloway, *Stalin*, pp. 338–9.

63 Ibid., p. 343.

64 Smirnov and Zubok, p. 14, pp. 15–16.

65 Ibid., pp. 17–18.

66 Kaplan, p. 212.

67 Kahn, p. 20.

68 Ibid., pp. 45–6, p. 646.

69 Newman, p. 67.

70 Rhodes (1995), p. 566.

71 Kaplan, p. 246.

72 Cox, p. 228.

73 Gary Stephens, 'Three Hours from Armageddon' (Internet).

74 *The Race for the Superbomb.*

75 Heuser, pp. 68–9.

76 *The Guardian*, 9 October 1975.

77 *The Race for the Superbomb.*

78 Lees-Milne, p. 68.

79 Russell-Einstein Manifesto, 9 July 1955 (Internet).

80 Cox, p. 27.

81 Bundy, p. 254.

82 *The Race for the Superbomb.*

83 Ibid.

84 Tom Lehrer, 'We Will All Go Together When We Go', 1959, Rhino Records.

85 Teller (1962), p. *viii.*

86 Smirnov and Zubok, p. 16.

87 Foot, pp. 74–5.

88 Eisenhower Farewell Address, 1961 (Internet).

89 Ibid.

90 Shapin (2002), n.p.

91 Herken, p. 215.

92 Holloway, *Stalin*, p. 247.

93 CNN, *The Cold War*, Episode 12: 'MAD', 1998 (Internet).

94 Holloway (1984), p. 151.

95 *The Race for the Superbomb.*

96 Kaplan, p. 135.

97 *New York Times*, 16 May 2000; *Nature*, 4 May 2000.

Chapter Twelve: *Symbols, not Weapons*

1 Cox, p. 181.

2 Heuser, p. 95.

3 Hennessy, p. 47, p. 49.

4 Ibid., p. 48.

5 Gowing, p. 483.

6 *Hansard*, 23 October, 1952.

7 Sophie Jerram, 'Living Without the Bomb', The Physics Room (Internet).

8 Arnold, p. 41.

9 Boyle, pp. 123–4.

10 Hennessy, p. 44.

11 Ibid., pp. 54–5, p. 58.

12 Ibid., pp. 57–9.

13 Moore, n.p.

14 Hennessy, p. 46.

15 My thanks to Elizabeth Trueland for this recollection.

16 Hennessy, p. 122.

17 Ibid., p. 133, p. 181.

18 Ibid., p. 192.

19 Ibid., p. 62.

20 Ibid., pp. 64–5, p. 44.

21 Ibid., p. 62, pp. 64–6.

22 Cox, p. 175.

23 Hansard, 31 January 1963.

24 Craig, pp. 245–6.

25 Healey, p. 302.

26 Hennessy, pp. 73–4.

27 Taylor, p. 289.

28 *Manchester Guardian*, 4 October 1957.

29 Hinton, p. 160.
30 Ibid.
31 *Manchester Guardian*, 5 April 1958
32 Priestley, pp. 554–6.
33 Hinton, p. 157, p. 159.
34 *Manchester Guardian*, 5 April 1958.
35 Foot, p. 72.
36 Taylor, p. 291.
37 Delmas, p. 240.
38 Ibid.
39 Vanke, p. 121.
40 Barbier, p. 103.
41 Vanke, p. 120.
42 Ibid., p. 121.
43 Barbier, p. 103.
44 McNamara, 'No Cities Speech', 1962, *Atomic Archive* (Internet).
45 *The Times*, 1 April 1987.
46 Cox, p. 176.

Chapter Thirteen: *Testing Times*
 1 *People*, 10 November 1980, p. 44.
 2 US Atomic Energy Commission notice (Internet).
 3 Titus, p. 97.
 4 Ibid., p. 68.
 5 'The Situation in Nevada', *World Sex Guide*; Chicken Ranch Website (Internet).
 6 Titus, p. 76.
 7 'The Atomic Duty of Private Bill Bires' (Internet).
 8 Titus, p. 61.
 9 Gallagher, p. 57.
10 Titus, p. 63.
11 Holloway, *Stalin*, pp. 326–7.
12 *The Race for the Superbomb* (Internet).
13 Rosenberg, H., p. 17.
14 Wasserman and Solomon, *Killing Our Own*, n.p. (Internet).
15 Ibid.
16 *Sunday Herald*, 8 April 2001.
17 Haggas, p. 18.
18 *Sunday Herald*, 30 December 2001.
19 *The Age*, 9 October 2002.
20 *Daily Telegraph*, 14 May 2001.
21 AEC, *Atomic Tests in Nevada*, March 1957, p. 2, p. 4, p. 15.
22 Titus, p. 82.
23 Ibid., p. 74, p. 76, p. 85.
24 Ibid., pp. 80–4.
25 Jungk, p. 311.
26 Sakharov and Zubok, p. 16.
27 Titus, p. 85.
28 Walker, J. S., p. 20.
29 *In These Times*, 8 August 1999.
30 Walker, p. 23.
31 *Life*, June 1980, p. 36.
32 Gallagher, p. 274.
33 Wasserman and Solomon, n.p.
34 Titus, pp. 96–8.
35 Ibid., p. 96.
36 Bartlett and Steele, p. 344.
37 Titus, p. 87.

Chapter Fourteen: *To the Brink*
 1 Adamski and Smirnov, p. 19.
 2 Ibid.
 3 Ibid.
 4 'The Tsar Bomba' (Internet).
 5 FAS, 'Limited Test Ban Treaty' (Internet).
 6 Ibid.
 7 Ambrose, pp. 569–70.
 8 *The Race for the Superbomb* (Internet).
 9 Gromyko to Khrushchev, 3 August 1960, *CWIHPB* (Fall, 1994), p. 66.
10 McNamara, p. 8.
11 Hitchcock, p. 220.

12 'The Tsar Bomba'.
13 Adamski and Smirnov, n.p.
14 Ibid.
15 Ibid.
16 Sakharov, pp. 216–17.
17 'The Tsar Bomba'.
18 *Financial Times*, 13 October 2001.
19 CNN, 'The Cold War', Episode 12, 'MAD'.
20 'Address to the American People about the Cuban Missile Crisis', *Atomic Archive* (Internet).
21 Khrushchev, pp. 494–5.
22 Holloway (1984), p. 89.
23 Rhodes (1995), p. 574.
24 Ibid., p. 565.
25 Ibid., p. 575.
26 Blum, p. 87.
27 Kennedy, 'Address to American People' (Internet).
28 Rhodes (1995), p. 571.
29 McNamara, p. 10.
30 Blum, p. 88.
31 Williams and Cantelon, p. 250.
32 Rhodes (1995), p. 574.
33 *The Race for the Superbomb*.
34 John Kennedy, 'Address to the American People on the Nuclear Test Ban', 26 July 1963, *Atomic Archive*.
35 Sakharov website (Internet).
36 Titus, p. 102.
37 'Minutes to Midnight: The history of the Doomsday Clock' (Internet).
38 CNN, *The Cold War*.
39 Ibid.
40 Ibid.
41 McNamara, 'No Cities Speech', 5 May 1962, *Atomic Archive*.
42 *The Cold War*, CNN.
43 McNamara, pp. 44–5.
44 *The Cold War*, CNN.
45 McNamara, 'Mutual Deterrence Speech', 18 September 1967, *Atomic Archive*.
46 *The Cold War*, CNN.

Chapter Fifteen: *How We Learned to Stop Worrying and Love the Bomb*
1 *Albuquerque Journal*, 28 October 1999.
2 Boyer (1998), p. 28.
3 Graybar, n.p.
4 Boyer (1994), pp. 10–11.
5 Ibid., p. 10.
6 Ibid., p. 21.
7 Lifton and Mitchell, pp. 73–4, pp. 362–8.
8 Jackie Doll and His Pickled Peppers, 'When They Drop the Atom Bomb', 1951.
9 Lowell Blanchard, 'Jesus Hits Like an Atom Bomb', 1946.
10 Hawkshaw Hawkins, 'When They Found the Atomic Power', 1947, King Records.
11 *The Race for the Superbomb* (Internet).
12 Boyer (1994), p. 85.
13 Sheldon Allman, 'Radioactive Mama', 1960, Hi-Fidelity Records, Inc.
14 *Newsweek*, 27 December 1993.
15 Boyer (1994), p. *xi*.
16 Szasz, p. 132.
17 Boyer (1998), p. 169.
18 *The Race for the Superbomb*.
19 Jungk, p. 228.
20 Boyer (1998), p. 242.
21 *The Race for the Superbomb*.
22 Boyer (1998), p. 31, p. 69.
23 Jungk, p. 247, p. 249.
24 Titus, p. 87.
25 Kaplan, p. 138.
26 McEnamey, p. 38.

27 *The Race for the Superbomb*.
28 McEnamey, p. 3.
29 Jayne Loader, *Atomic Café*, 1982 (Video).
30 *The Race for the Superbomb*.
31 'The Effects of Atomic bombs on Hiroshima and Nagasaki', *US Strategic Bombing Survey*, 30 June 1946 (Internet).
32 McEnamey, p. 20.
33 Ibid., p. 21.
34 The Race for the Superbomb.
35 Titus, p. 96.
36 McEnamey, p. 68.
37 Ibid., p. 80.
38 Ibid., p. 78.
39 NSS memo to schools and civil defence authorities, March 1955 (Internet).
40 Stafford Warren, 'The Woman's Role in Atomic Warfare', Washington Conference of the National Woman's Advisory Committee, 1956 (Internet).
41 McEnamey, p. 109.
42 Ibid., p. 106.
43 AEC Press Release, n.d. (Internet).
44 May, p. 105.
45 McEnamey, p. 110.
46 Ibid., p. 113.
47 Federal Defense Administration, *The House in the Middle*, 1954.
48 McEnamey, pp. 26–7.
49 Ibid., p. 28, p. 42.
50 Ibid., p. 46.
51 Ibid., p. 49.
52 *The Race for the Superbomb*.
53 McEnamey, p. 50.
54 Ibid., p. 51.
55 *Harper's Magazine*, November 1957.
56 Mary Sharmat, statement regarding her Civil Defence protest (Internet).
57 Boyer (1998), p. 171.
58 Ibid., p. 172.
59 Schwartz, p. 354.
60 McEnamey, p. 53, p. 59.
61 McHugh, p. 36.
62 Kaplan, p. 312.
63 *Time*, 6 July 1953.
64 As quoted by a former SAC pilot.
65 McEnamey, p. 55.
66 Kaplan, p. 311.
67 *New York Times*, 17 January 1960.
68 Boyer (1998), p. 110.
69 McEnamey, p. 61.
70 CNN, 'The Cold War'.
71 McEnamey, p. 65.
72 *Complacent Americans*, CONELRAD (Internet).
73 *Harper's Magazine*, October 1955, p. 24.
74 McEnamey, p. 86.
75 Cox, p. 99.
76 Ibid., pp. 124–5, p. 134.
77 Ibid., pp. 96–7.
78 Ibid., p. 71.
79 Bethe (1991), p. 134.
80 *The Cold War*, CNN.
81 McNamara, p. 66.
82 The Cold War, CNN.
83 SBS, 'The Effects of Atomic Bombs on Hiroshima and Nagasaki' (Internet).
84 Cox, p. 101.
85 Brzezinski, pp. 302–5.
86 Cox, p. 185.
87 Boyer (1998), p. 107.
88 Nolan, p. 30, pp. 44–5.
89 McNamara, p. 48.

Chapter Sixteen: *Mid-Life Crisis*

1 Hinton, p. 192.

2 *Time*, 1 January 1984.
3 Ibid.
4 Williams and Cantelon, p. 227.
5 Kaplan, p. 370.
6 Nitze, p. 33.
7 Boyer (1998), pp. 151–4.
8 Powaski, p. 20.
9 *New York Times*, 23 November 1982.
10 Ibid.
11 McNamara, p. 40.
12 Ibid., pp. 47–8.
13 Ibid., pp. 27, 50.
14 Haslam, p. *xi*.
15 Cox, p. 150.
16 Haslam, p. 200.
17 Fitzgerald, p. 23.
18 McNamara, p. 98.
19 Ronald Reagan, 'Address to the Nation on Defense and National Security', 23 March 1983, *Atomic Archive* (Internet).
20 McNamara, p. 99, pp. 102–3.
21 Fitzgerald, p. 249.
22 Pressler, p. 136.
23 Shapin (2001), n.p.
24 *Time*, 1 January 1984.
25 Fischer, p. 104.
26 McNamara, p. 20, p. 137.
27 *New York Times*, 30 May 1982.
28 *Time*, 1 January 1984.
29 'Minutes to Midnight: The history of the Doomsday Clock' (Internet).
30 *Time*, 1 January 1984.
31 Ibid.
32 Powaski, p. 27.
33 *New York Times*, 23 November 1982.
34 Powaski, p. 18.
35 Foot, p. 60.
36 Powaski, p. 29.
37 BBC Television, *Threads*, 1984.

38 Herbert, pp. 346–7, p. 455.
39 Scheer, p. 20, p. 21.
40 *Los Angeles Times*, 22 October 1984.
41 Cox, p. 229.
42 *Protect and Survive*.
43 *Time Out*, November 1980.
44 Hinton, p. 184.
45 Healey, p. 500.
46 *The Race for the Superbomb* (Internet).
47 Powaski, p. 39.
48 Ibid., p. 18.
49 Reagan, p. 14.
50 Haslam, p. 157.
51 Reagan, p. 677.
52 Powaski, p. 60.
53 Ibid.
54 Haslam, p. *ix*.
55 Ibid., p. 162.
56 Teller (2001), p. 534.
57 *The Race for the Superbomb*.

Chapter Seventeen: *Fallout*

1 Chapparal website (Internet).
2 *Financial Times*, 1 March 2002.
3 *CNN.com*, 1 March 2002 (Internet).
4 Gallagher, p. 302.
5 *The Age*, 9 October 2002.
6 *The Age*, 30 December 2001.
7 *Sunday Herald*, 30 December 2001.
8 *The Most Contaminated Spot on the Planet*, Log In Productions, 1994.
9 Alexander, pp. 30ff.
10 'Interviews with Bikini Elders' (Internet).
11 Ibid.
12 Jack Neidenthal, 'A Short History of Bikini Atoll', Bikini Website.
13 'Interviews with Bikini Elders'.

14 Report from the Marshall Islands Nuclear Claims Tribunal, 1997 (Internet).

15 Boyer (1994), p. *xviii*.

16 'Interviews with Bikini Elders'.

17 Bikini website.

18 Ron Gluckman, 'No Boom Boom Here' (Internet).

19 Thomson, p. 360.

20 *The Race for the Superbomb.*

21 *Los Angeles Times*, 4 November 1996.

22 Ibid.

23 *The New Yorker*, 1 April 1996.

24 *US News and World Report*, 31 May 1999.

25 Powaski, p. 244.

26 Helfand, n.p.

27 *The Guardian*, 24 June 2003.

28 National Defence University, *Strategic Assessment 1995* (Internet).

29 Khariton and Smirnov, n.p.

30 *New York Times*, 15 November 1996.

31 Stone, n.p.

32 *Washington Post*, 27 November 1998; *Moscow Times*, 8 September 1998.

33 Wolfstahl, pp. 15–17; von Hippel, pp. 21–3.

34 Ibid.

35 Wolfstahl, p. 16.

36 Bunn, n.p.

37 Ibid.

38 IAEA press release, 1 November 2001 (Internet).

39 *Time*, 12 November 2001.

40 Powaski, p. 242.

41 Frontline, 'Loose Nukes' (Internet).

42 Stone, n.p.

43 *Los Alamos Science* (1996), p. 45.

44 Bailey, p. 183.

45 Thomson, p. 284.

46 *Las Vegas Sun*, 5 July 2002.

47 Personal recollection.

48 *The Independent*, 24 November 1998.

49 'Grandmothers for Peace International Declares National Boycott of all Nestle Products', July 1998 (Internet).

50 *Los Angeles Times*, 13 June 2002; *Las Vegas Review-Journal*, 15 June 2002.

51 Boyer (1998), p. 267.

52 Powaski, p. 197.

53 'Russian Roulette', PBS *Frontline* (Internet).

54 Bowermaster, n.p.

55 Bulletin of the Atomic Scientists website.

56 Lortie, pp. 22–9; Nolan, p. 30.

57 Nolan, p. 61.

58 Powaski, pp. 202–3.

59 Pakistani government statement on nuclear tests, *Atomic Archive*.

60 Bulletin of the Atomic Scientists website.

61 *Los Angeles Times*, 18 December 1996.

62 Shapin (2001), n.p.

63 General Lee Butler, speech to National Press Club, 4 December 1996; Butler, joint statement with General Andrew Goodpaster, 4 December 1996; Statement on Nuclear Weapons by International Generals and Admirals, 5 December 1996 (Internet).

64 George W. Bush, 'Address to the American People about Ballistic Missile Defense', 1 May 2001, *Atomic Archive*.

65 White House Statement on Domestic Preparedness Against Weapons of Mass Destruction, 8 May 2001, *Atomic Archive*.

66 See OISM website and *Nuclear War Survival Skills* (Internet).

67 Fox Television, *The Simpsons*: 'Sideshow Bob's Last Gleaming'.

68 Bailey, pp. 180–1.

69 Ibid., p. 181.

70 Powaski, pp. 201–3,

71 Blair, p. *xxii*.

72 Teller (1993), p. 33.

73 Blum, p. 82.

74 *New York Times*, 17 May 1998.

75 McNamara, p. 87.

76 *Los Angeles Times*, 27 April 2002.

Select Bibliography

Unless indicated otherwise the place of publication is London.

Adamski, Viktor and Yuri Smirnov. 'Moscow's biggest bomb: The 50-megaton test of October 1961', *Cold War International History Project Bulletin* (Fall, 1994)

Albright, Joseph and Marcia Kunstel. 'The youngest spy', *Bulletin of the Atomic Scientists* (Jan./Feb. 1998)

Alexander, Ronni. *Putting the Earth First: Alternatives to Nuclear Security in Pacific Island States*. Honolulu, 1994

Alperovitz, Gar. *The Decision to Use the Atomic Bomb*. New York, 1995

Alvarez, Luis. *Alvarez*. New York, 1987

Ambrose, Stephen. *Eisenhower: The President*. 1984

Arnold, Lorna. *Britain and the H-Bomb*. 2001

Bailey, Janet. *The Good Servant: Making Peace with the Bomb at Los Alamos*. New York, 1995

Baker, Paul, ed. *The Atomic Bomb: the Great Decision*. New York, 1968

Barbier, Collette. 'The French decision to develop a military nuclear programme in the 1950s', *Diplomacy and Statecraft* (March 1993)

Bartlett, Donald and James Steele. *Empire: the Life, Legend and Madness of Howard Hughes*. New York, 1979

Bernstein, Barton. 'The Atomic Bombings reconsidered', *Foreign Affairs* (Jan./Feb. 1995)

Bethe, Hans. 'Comments on the History of the H-Bomb', *Los Alamos Science* (Fall, 1982)

—— *The Road from Los Alamos*. New York, 1991

—— 'Sakharov's H-Bomb', *Bulletin of the Atomic Scientists* (Oct. 1990)

Beukel, Erik. *American Perceptions of the Soviet Union as a Nuclear Adversary*. 1989

Billings-Yun, Melanie. *Decision Against War: Eisenhower and Dien Bien Phu*. 1954

Blackett, P. M. S. *Fear, War and the Bomb*. New York, 1949

Blum, John Morton. *Years of Discord*. New York, 1991

Bodanis, David. $E=mc^2$: *A Biography of the World's Most Famous Equation*. 2000

Bowermaster, Jon. 'The last front of the Cold War', *The Atlantic Online* (Nov. 1993)

Boyer, Paul. *By the Bomb's Early Light*. Chapel Hill, NC, 1994

—— *Fallout*. Columbus, OH, 1998

Boyle, Peter, ed. *The Churchill-Eisenhower Correspondence, 1953-1955*. Chapel Hill, NC, 1990

Brooks, Geraldine. *Foreign Correspondent*. New York, 1998

Brzezinski, Zbigniew. *Power and Principle*. New York, 1983

Bundy, McGeorge. *Danger and Survival*. 1990

Bunn, Matthew. 'Loose nukes fears: anecdotes of the current crisis', *Global Beat* (5 Dec. 1998)

Burdick, Eugene and Harvey Wheeler. *Fail-Safe*. New York, 1962

Butow, Robert. *Japan's Decision to Surrender*. Stanford, 1954

Cassidy, David. 'A historical perspective on *Copenhagen*', *Physics Today* (July 2000)

Chevalier, Haakon. *Oppenheimer: The Story of a Friendship*. New York, 1965

Churchill, Winston. *Triumph and Tragedy*. Boston, 1953

Clancy, Tom. *The Sum of all Fears*. 1993

Craig, F. W. S. *British General Election Manifestos, 1918-1966*. 1970

Cox, John. *Overkill*. 1971

DeGroot, Gerard. *Liberal Crusader*. 1993

Delmas, Jean. 'Military Power in France', in E. diNolfo, ed. *Power in Europe II: Great Britain, France, Germany and the origins of the EEC 1952–72*. Berlin, 1992.

Douhet, Giulio. *The Command of the Air*. New York, 1942

Ferrell, Robert, ed. *Harry S. Truman and the Bomb*. Worland, WY, 1996

Feynman, Richard. *Surely You're Joking Mr Feynman!*. New York, 1985

Fischer, Beth. *Reversal: Foreign Policy and the End of the Cold War*. 1997

Fitzgerald, Frances. *Way Out There in the Blue*. New York, 2000

Foot, Michael. *Dr Strangelove, I Presume*. 1999

Frayn, Michael. *Copenhagen*. 1998

Frisch, Otto. *What Little I Remember*. Cambridge, 1976

Gallagher, Carole. *American Ground Zero*. New York, 1994

Giovannitti, Len and Fred Freed. *The Decision to Drop the Bomb*. 1965

Goldberg, Stanley. 'What did Truman know, and when did he know it?', *Bulletin of the Atomic Scientists* (May/June 1998)

Goncharov, German. 'Beginnings of the Soviet H-Bomb program', *Physics Today* (Nov. 1996)

—— 'The race accelerates', *Physics Today* (Nov. 1996)

Goodchild, Peter. *Oppenheimer: Shatterer of Worlds*. New York, 1985

Gowing, Margaret. *Independence and Deterrence*. 1974

Graybar, Lloyd J. 'America faces the atomic age: 1946', *Air Chronicles* (1984)

Grossman, Andrew. *Neither Dead Nor Red*. New York, 2001

Groves, Leslie. *Now It Can Be Told*. New York, 1962

Gurtov, Melvin. *The First Vietnam Crisis*. New York, 1967

Haggas, Jim. *Christmas Island: The Wrong Place at the Wrong Time*. 1997

Hahn, Otto. *My Life*. New York, 1970

Haslam, Jonathan. *The Soviet Union and the Politics of Nuclear Weapons in Europe, 1969-87*. Ithaca, NY, 1990

Hastings, Max. *The Korean War*. 1987

Healey, Denis. *The Time of My Life*. 1989

Helfand, Ira, et al. 'Nuclear terrorism', *BMJ* (9 Feb. 2002)

Hennessy, Peter. *The Secret State*. 2002

Herbert, James. *Domain*. 1984

Herken, Gregg. *The Winning Weapon*. Princeton, 1981

Hersey, John. *Hiroshima*. New York, 1966

Heuser, Beatrice. *The Bomb*. 2000

Hinton, James. *Protests and Visions*. 1989

Hirsch, Daniel and William Matthews. 'The H-bomb: who really gave away the secret?', *Bulletin of the Atomic Scientists* (Jan./Feb. 1990)

Hitchcock, William. *The Struggle for Europe*. 2003

Hoban, Russell. *Riddley Walker*. Bloomington, IN, 1988

Holloway, David. 'How the bomb saved Soviet physics', *The Bulletin of the Atomic Scientists*, (1994)

—— 'Soviet Nuclear History', *Cold War International History Project Bulletin* (Fall, 1994)

—— *The Soviet Union and the Arms Race*. New Haven, 1984

—— *Stalin and the Bomb*. New Haven, 1994

Irving, David. *The Virus House*. 1968

Jastrow, Robert. 'Why Strategic Superiority Matters', *Commentary* (March 1983)

Jungk, Robert. *Brighter than a Thousand Suns*. New York, 1958

Kahn, Herman. *On Thermonuclear War*. Princeton, 1960

Kaplan, Fred. *The Wizards of Armageddon*. Stanford, 1983

Kegley, Charles and Eugene Wittkopf. *The Nuclear Reader*. New York, 1985

Khariton, Yuli and Yuri Smirnov. 'The Khariton version', *Bulletin of the Atomic Scientists* (May 1993)

Khariton, Yuli, et al. 'The way it was', *Bulletin of the Atomic Scientists* (Nov./Dec. 1996)

Khrushchev, Nikita. *Khrushchev Remembers*. New York, 1970

Kunkel, Thomas. *Genius in Disguise: Harold Ross of The New Yorker*. New York, 1995

Landau, Susan. *The Road Less Travelled* (Internet)

Lees-Milne, James. *A Mingled Measure: Diaries 1954-1972*. 1994

Leffler, Melvin. *A Preponderance of Power: National Security, the Truman*

    Administration, and the Cold War. 1992

Leskov, Sergei. 'Dividing the glory of the fathers', *Bulletin of the Atomic Scientists* (May 1993)

Libby, Leona Marshall. *The Uranium People*. New York, 1979

Lifton, Robert. *Death in Life: Survivors of Hiroshima*. New York, 1967

Lifton, Robert and Greg Mitchell. *Hiroshima in America*. New York, 1995

Lortie, Bret. 'A do-it-yourself SIOP', *Bulletin of the Atomic Scientists* (July/Aug. 2001)

Los Alamos National Laboratory, 'The Oppenheimer Years', *Los Alamos* (Winter/Spring, 1983)

Luongo, Kenneth and Matthew Bunn. 'Preempting a Russian nuclear meltdown', *Global Beat* (5 Dec. 1998)

May, Elaine Tyler. *Homeward Bound*. New York, 1988

McCrea, Frances and Gerald Markle. *Minutes to Midnight*. Newbury Park, CA, 1989

McEnamey, Laura. *Civil Defense Begins at Home*. Princeton, 2000

McHugh, L. C. 'Ethics at the Shelter Doorway', *America* (30 Sept. 1961)

McNamara, Robert. *Blundering into Disaster*. New York, 1986

Meitner, Lise and Otto Frisch. 'Disintegration of uranium by neutrons: a new type of nuclear reaction', *Nature* (11 Feb. 1939)

Mendl, Wolf. *Deterrence and Persuasion*. 1970

Montefiore, Simon Sebag. *Stalin: The Court of the Red Tsar*. 2003

Moore, Richard. 'Where her majesty's weapons were', *Bulletin of the Atomic Scientists* (Jan./Feb. 2001)

Morita, Akio. *Made in Japan*. New York, 1986

Newman, James. 'On Thermonuclear War', *Scientific American* (March 1961)

Nitze, Paul. 'Assuring strategic stability in an era of detente', *Foreign Affairs* (Jan. 1976)

Nolan, Janne. *An Elusive Consensus*, Washington, 1999

Oppenheimer, J. Robert. 'Atomic weapons and American policy', *Foreign Affairs* (July 1953)

Powaski, Ronald. *Return to Armageddon*. Oxford, 2000

Pressler, Larry. *Star Wars: The Strategic Defense Initiative Debates in Congress*. New York, 1986

Priestley, J. B. 'Britain and the nuclear bombs', *New Statesman* (2 Nov. 1957)

Protect and Survive. 1980

Reagan, Ronald. *An American Life*. 1990

Reilly, Catherine, ed. *Scars Upon My Heart: Women's Poetry and Verse of the First World War*. 1981

Rhodes, Richard. *Dark Sun: The Making of the Hydrogen Bomb*. New York, 1995

—— The Making of the Atomic Bomb. Harmondsworth, 1986

Rigden, John. 'Isidor Isaac Rabi: walking the path of God', Physics World (Nov. 1999)

Rose, Paul Lawrence. Heisenberg and the Nazi Atomic Project. Berkeley, 1998

Rosenberg, David. 'American atomic strategy and the hydrogen bomb decision', Journal of American History (1979)

—— 'A smoking radiated ruin at the end of two hours', International Security (Winter, 1981–2)

Rosenberg, Howard. Atomic Soldiers. Boston, 1980

Roshwald, Mordecai. Level 7. New York, 1959

Rothstein, Linda. 'Kapitsa on Beria', Bulletin of the Atomic Scientists (May 1993)

Sagdeev, Roald. 'Russian scientists save American secrets', Bulletin of the Atomic Scientists (May 1993)

Sakharov, Andrei. Memoirs. New York, 1990

Scheer, Robert. With Enough Shovels: Reagan, Bush & Nuclear War. New York, 1982

Schoenberger, Walter Smith. Decision of Destiny. Columbus, OH, 1969

Schwartz, Richard. Cold War Culture. New York, 1998

Schwartz, Stephen, ed. Atomic Audit. Washington, 1998

Schweber, S. S. In the Shadow of the Bomb. Princeton, 2000

Shapin, Steven. 'Don't let that crybaby in here again', London Review of Books (7 Sept. 2000)

—— 'Guests in the President's House', London Review of Books (18 Oct. 2001)

—— 'Megaton Man', London Review of Books, (25 April 2002)

Sherwin, Martin. A World Destroyed. New York, 1977

Shute, Nevil. On the Beach. Thirsk, 2000

Smirnov, Yuri and Vladislav Zubok. 'Nuclear Weapons after Stalin's Death: Moscow Enters the H-Bomb Age', CWIHPB (Fall, 1994)

Smith, Alice Kimball. A Peril and a Hope: The Scientists' Movement in America: 1945-7. Chicago, 1965

Speer, Albert. Inside the Third Reich. New York, 1970

Stimson, Henry. 'The decision to use the Atomic Bomb', Harper's Magazine (Feb. 1947)

Stone, Richard. 'Russia: nuclear strongholds in peril', Science (8 Jan. 1999)

Sudoplatov, Pavel. Special Tasks: The Memoirs of an Unwanted Witness – A Soviet Spymaster. Boston, 1994

Szasz, Ferenc. The Day the Sun Rose Twice. Albuquerque, 1984

Taylor, A. J. P. A Personal History. 1983

Teller, Edward. 'The Laboratory of the Atomic Age', Los Alamos Science (1993)

—— *The Legacy of Hiroshima*. 1962

—— *Memoirs*. Cambridge, MA, 2001

—— 'Seven hours of reminiscences', *Los Alamos Science* (Winter/Spring 1983)

Thomson, David. *In Nevada*. 1999

Thorpe, Charles and Steven Shapin. 'Who was J. Robert Oppenheimer?', *Social Studies and Science* (Aug. 2000)

Titus, A. Constandina. *Bombs in the Backyard*. Reno, 1986

Truman, Harry S. *Years of Decision*. New York, 1955

Vanke, Jeffrey. 'De Gaulle's atomic defence policy in 1963', *Cold War History* (Jan. 2001)

von Hippel, Frank. 'Help the nuclear cities, help ourselves', *Bulletin of the Atomic Scientists* (Nov./Dec. 2000)

Walker, J. Samuel. *Permissable Dose*. Berkeley, 2000

Walker, Mark. *Nazi Science*. New York, 1995

Wasserman, Harvey and Norman Solomon. *Killing Our Own*. New York, 1982

Weale, Adrian, ed. *Eye-Witness Hiroshima*. New York, 1995

Weart, Spencer R. and Gerturde Szilard, *Leo Szilard: His Version of the Facts*. Boston, 1979

Wells, H. G. *The World Set Free*. 1976

Werth, Alexander. *Russia at War, 1941-1945*. 1964

Williams, Robert and Philip Cantelon, ed. *The American Atom*. Philadelphia, 1984

Wills, Garry. *Reagan's America*. New York, 1988

Wolfstahl, Jon. 'Surveying the nuclear cities', *Bulletin of the Atomic Scientists* (July/Aug. 2001)

Wyden, Peter. *Day One: Before Hiroshima and After*. New York, 1984

York, Herbert. *The Advisors: Oppenheimer, Teller and the Superbomb*. San Francisco, 1976

Zhukov, Georgii Konstantinovich. *The Memoirs of Marshal Zhukov*. New York, 1971

Index